CW00766266

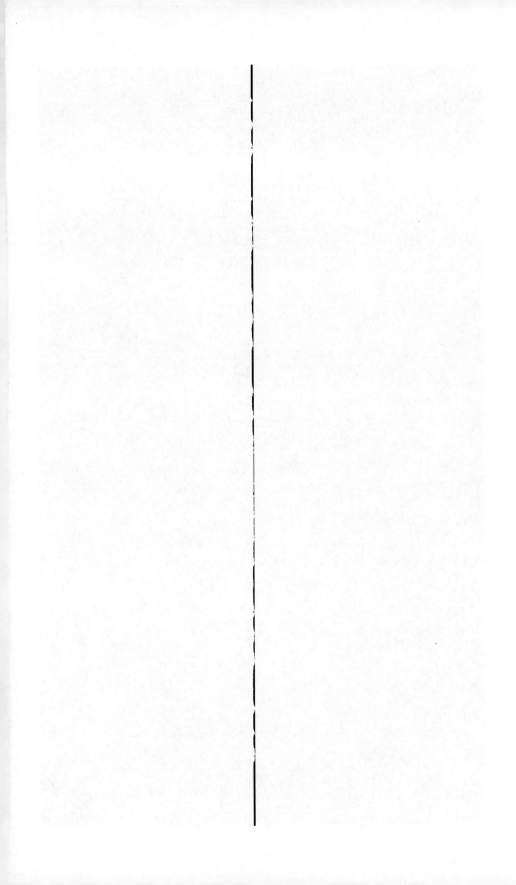

A PRACTICAL TREATISE

ON

ORGAN-BUILDING

BY

F. E. ROBERTSON, C.I.E.

THE ORGAN LITERATURE FOUNDATION
Braintree, Massachusetts 02184

ORGAN-BUILDING

ORGAN-BUILDING

This set is an unabridged republication of the original and is

available from

THE ORGAN LITERATURE FOUNDATION

Braintree, Mass. 02184

Text and Atlas, Price $35.00 prepaid for both volumes

A PRACTICAL TREATISE

ON

ORGAN - BUILDING

WITH PLATES AND APPENDICES

BY

F. E. ROBERTSON, C.I.E.

MEMBER OF THE INSTITUTION OF CIVIL ENGINEERS
PRESIDENT EGYPTIAN RAILWAY BOARD

LONDON
SAMPSON LOW, MARSTON & COMPANY
(LIMITED)
St. Dunstan's House
FETTER LANE, FLEET STREET, E.C.
1897

ML556
R649
1970
V. 1

PREFACE

To use the hackneyed phrase, the author of this work ventures
to introduce it to the public in the belief that it meets a want.
Judging from notes and queries in the 'English Mechanic,'
and the frequent introduction of the subject into amateur
work journals, it is one in which a very general interest is felt;
while how to keep an organ in order in India and the Colonies,
where a builder is not to hand, is a serious question. But
though the bibliography given in the last chapter contains a
list of 300 works, dating from the seventeenth century to the
present time, those in the English language are but few, and
none appear to fulfil the purpose of a handbook giving exact
particulars of the principles of construction.

Rimbault and Hopkins's classical work is indeed the
authority on the musical questions of temperament, &c., and
on historical matters; but contains no precise information,
even on the scales of pipes, from which an organ could be
designed, still less details of the structure. The small works
of Dickson and of Wicks, on the other hand, while they do
enable an amateur to build an organ of a particular type, are
not wide enough in their scope to serve as a general book of
reference. There is indeed the magnificent work of Töpfer, but
being in German, with foreign standards of measurement, it is
not very accessible or generally useful; while the 'Facteur
d'Orgues,' by Hamel, is, but for the extracts from Töpfer, more

curious than useful. It is also not up to date. The best information on organ-building accessible in the English language is that which has appeared from time to time in the pages of the 'English Mechanic'; but these notes and articles, scattered as they are over many years, scarcely supply the place of a handy book with tabulated information.

It is hoped, then, that this work will supply the information needed by the amateur builder, and enable those in charge of organs in foreign parts to keep them in order, while the special remarks as to organ construction for hot climates may be worthy the attention of builders, who little know what trials their work will have to undergo, even when built 'specially for hot climates.' The author now regrets not having made a collection of photographs of soundboards that have come before him for repairs, as a practical illustration of what has to be provided against, and an example of what will befall even the best work when put together on unsound principles.

As an organ, up to the foot of the pipes, is only a wind-distributing machine, it is simply subject to the ordinary laws of mechanics, and may fairly be considered as coming within the purview of the engineer. For the musical part, an experience of 25 years in repairing and building, with a keen interest in the subject, may justify the writer in expressing opinions which, in treating of such a matter, it is difficult to leave entirely colourless, even while fully admitting the justice of the maxim 'De gustibus,' &c. The reader will, it is hoped, accept this apology in advance, should any of the remarks on tone not agree with his own predilections.

It is sufficiently indicated in the chapters on the scaling of flue and reed work that they are mainly a review of what Töpfer and his editor, Max Allihn, have done in this direction, there being no other writers who have made any serious attempt to treat of this matter from a theoretical standpoint. The writer would have preferred to delay the completion of this work until he had been able to investigate the subject of reeds for himself; but, as press of work does not leave any near prospect of such experiments being undertaken, it is hoped that an account of what Töpfer has done will inspire some other person, with more leisure, to take up the subject systematically, or to publish what may already been done in that direction. An acknowledgment is due to Mr. Hope-Jones for particulars of his organ work, and to Mr. Henry Booth, of Wakefield, for many beautiful pipes and much valuable advice.

CONTENTS

LIST OF PLATES[1]

[1] In separate volume.

A

PRACTICAL TREATISE

ON

ORGAN-BUILDING

————◦————

CHAPTER I

INTRODUCTION

1. MANY of the more complete foreign works on organ-building begin with a certain amount of arithmetic, mechanics, and description of ordinary tools as an introduction ; but such a course is either too wide or too narrow, and the knowledge must be taken for granted. The reader need not be dismayed at the appearance of mathematics here and there in the following pages, as while such passages may be needful to develop a theory, the result has always been presented in a practical form. A little general advice to the would-be builder is not, however, out of place. Such a one must either be a competent carpenter himself or command the services of one, and a knowledge of metalwork in general will be very useful. A lathe, while always handy, is by no means a necessity, the ordinary outfit of tools and bench being quite sufficient, together with such special articles as are mentioned in connection with the different parts of the organ. But the tools and materials should be of the best, and be kept in perfect order, as 'good enough' will not do in organ-building. Two glue-pots should be kept—one for ordinary work, and the other for leather and fine work.

2. The shop being ready, the first point to be settled is the design, and here it is better to be modest at the start,

B

and if a big organ is desired, to begin with a small one until practice has brought some degree of perfection. Even then keep the design within the limits of time and money, and, it may be added, of space, both that it has to sound in as well as that which can be allotted to the instrument itself. Many an organ has been spoiled by 'just one stop more.' Before starting, make a careful plan of how all the pipes are to stand, as well as the necessary sections to show the arrangement of the action, and in most houses be careful to ascertain that the floor will safely carry the weight.

3. As to materials, let it be remembered that the best are always the cheapest in the end. Leather is always understood to be the white sheepskin specially prepared for organ-building, and no other will do. In buying it, state the exact purpose for which it is required—as bellows-ribs, for which stretched skins are used; or pallets and gussets, for which the thickest and softest is required; or pneumatic work, for which specially fine leather is necessary. Glue must be, for leather work especially, of the best procurable, and all wood perfectly sound and well seasoned, the quality being more important than the kind. Oak was used by the old builders, and there is nothing to beat it; but it is expensive and difficult to work. The sort of mahogany known as 'bay wood' is generally used for the best work, and very good work can be done with good, clean pine; in fact, good straight-grained yellow pine is as good a wood for pipes as can be desired. For hot climates teak is by far the best wood, but it appears to be unknown to English builders. It works well, and makes beautiful pipes. It is less affected by climate than any other wood, iron does not rust in it, and it is impervious to the attacks of insects; the only drawback being that its oily nature makes it a bad wood to glue, but the toothing-plane, chalk, and careful use of hot irons in gluing will get over this difficulty. Some stir a little red lead into the glue used with teak; but the advantage is doubtful, and heat, after all, is the principal point to insist upon to get sound glued work with teak, and indeed with every other wood.

4. In arranging the work it is well to rough out the wooden pipes first, and set the boards aside to season; then

the stuff for the bellows and soundboards, and next the frame, which can be completed. Then finish the bellows and put them in place, and then the soundboard and pipes can be joined up; and lastly the action, which is mostly in small pieces, can be made out of the off-cuttings from the other work. These being all the general directions, it is time to turn to the consideration of particular parts.

CHAPTER II

GENERAL DESCRIPTION OF THE ORGAN

5. A GOOD deal of ink has been shed upon the questions of temperament and the proper compass for the organ; but it is not proposed to examine these subjects, which may be regarded as practically decided. Before entering into the details of organ construction, however, it will be well to give a general description of the instrument, for the benefit of readers who have no previous acquaintance with the essential parts, and the points in which an organ differs from other instruments. An organ then may be defined as an assemblage of several instruments brought together under the control of one performer, with the peculiarity that, in addition to the keyboards or claviers played by the hands, there is another called the pedal, because it is played by the feet. While the claviers control the *notes*, the stop handles control the ranks of pipes equivalent to the different instruments, so that putting down a key will not produce any sound unless a stop belonging to that clavier is drawn.

6. Organs have various numbers of manuals, from one to four, each of which is, or should be, like a complete orchestra in itself, and of a timbre differing from that of all the others, though the same in range. Further, there are devices called couplers, actuated by draw-stops, which enable a manual to be played from another manual, or from the pedal, at the will of the player. An exceptional arrangement is found in the large organ at Ulm, which has *two* pedal claviers.

7. It is first necessary to explain the nomenclature of the notes of different pitch, with which we shall have a great deal to do. We shall follow the German nomenclature as

the most convenient, giving also the usual English
marking :

Length of open pipe	Mark	English mark	Pitch
32 feet	C_2	C C C C	The lowest note of the organ
16 feet	C_1	C C C	
8 feet	C_0	C C	The lowest manual key. Pitch C below a bass voice
4 feet	c^0	C	Tenor C
2 feet	c^1	c	Middle C
1 foot	c^2	c c	Treble C
6 inches and so on	c^3	c c c	C in alt.

Note.—The figuring changes on the C's, but in English works the change is
generally reckoned from the G's.

8. The manual compass of the organ now always begins
at C_0, the 8 ft. C, and extends to f^3, g^3, or a^3, while modern
concert and chamber organs extend to c^4. The pedal range
is invariably from C_1 to f^0. These statements refer to the
unison tone of the organ; but for reasons which will appear
hereafter, certain stops give a sound above the pitch of the
key put down, and also in large organs some stops sound
below the pitch, both on manual and pedal. Thus in a large
organ the C_0 manual key will command a pipe sounding C_1,
and even in a very large instrument C_2, while the C_1 key of
the pedal frequently commands a C_2 pipe. The object of this
is not to increase the range of notes at the command of the
player, but to improve the whole tone of the instrument by
the addition of harmonics and sub-harmonics. The *main
body* of sound will always be of the pitch indicated by the
note put down.

9. Fig. 169, Pl. XV., gives an ideal view of the arrangements
of one manual of an organ, and however many there may be,
the same details are simply repeated. The key, on being
depressed, merely opens a valve, which admits wind to the
pipes belonging to that note. The intermediate mechanism
may be electric or pneumatic, or a combination of both ; but
is generally a simple arrangement of levers. The chapter
on action describes the different varieties in detail, all that we
are here concerned with is the general principle. The different
shapes of levers are called ' back-falls,' or simple levers ;

' rollers,' or levers of which one arm is situated at some distance to the bass or treble side of the other, in a roller moving on a pivot; and ' squares,' of which one arm is set at right angles to the other, as the name indicates. The most complicated actions are built up of these simple elements. The valve opened by the key is called the pallet, and it admits wind from the wind-chest in which it is placed, to a groove or chamber over which the pipes are planted.

10. Here comes in the mechanism by which the performer controls the sounding of the different ranks of pipes, which are called stops. The same name is also loosely applied to the handles, properly called ' draw-stops,' which actuate the mechanism. The pipes stand upon what is unreasonably called the soundboard, on the under side of which are the grooves referred to above; but, instead of standing on the board itself, their feet are planted upon a board called the ' upper board ' a, being supported by the ' rack board ' b. See Figs. 163, Pl. XIV., and 179, Pl. XV., the latter of which shows a soundboard turned upside down, so as to give a view of the interior. Between the upper board and the ' table ' c, forming the roof of the grooves d, runs a movable slip of wood e, called the ' slider.' Through these three planks are bored the holes supplying the pipes with wind, so that if the slider be moved on one side, the wind is cut off, even though the valve may be open, and the pipes of that rank will therefore not sound. The slider is connected to the handle or draw-stop, within convenient reach of the player, who thus governs the admission of wind into the different ranks of pipes, and varies the sound from a mere whisper to the full thunder of the instrument. Between the sliders are slips of wood, f, called ' bearers,' which guide them, and carry the weight of the upper boards. On each draw-stop is engraved the name of the rank of pipes it governs, as well as the *tone-length*, or length of open pipe required to sound the note actually heard when the C_o, or lowest manual key, is pressed down. This is necessary for the guidance of the player, as the mere name— such as ' flute '—would not tell him whether the stop sounded the unison or an octave, or some other note above or below. A draw-stop labelled 8 indicates the manual unison, 16 an

octave below, and 4 an octave above it. The name of the
stop indicates the *timbre* that may be expected, and it is upon
the variety of contrasting tone provided by the builder, and
its judicious use by the performer, that the full glory of the
organ depends.

11. But as the organ gets larger, the number of stops
would soon be more than the player could conveniently mani-
pulate, even though the left hand may be spared for a
moment while the feet take the bass on the pedals ; and
therefore contrivances, called composition pedals, are employed
in all but the smallest organs.   These are pedals which, on
being pressed, arrange the stops of the department to which they
refer—in such groups as are generally applied to produce effects
of *p.*, *mf.*, and *f.*   They sometimes take the form of knobs
under each manual, which, when pressed by the fingers,
actuate a pneumatic or electric device ; and sometimes,
instead of a set combination, the mechanism is so arranged
that the player can build up certain combinations at will,
which take effect when he touches the pedal or pneumatic
piston.

12. The pipes belonging to one at least of the manuals are
generally placed in a box provided with movable shutters or
louvres in front, which are actuated by a pedal, so that the
sound can be made to die away and swell again at the will of
the player.   This effect is much abused by inferior players,
who, from force of habit, have even been known to pump away
at the swell while playing on another manual.   The object of
having different manuals is not to make more noise, but to
enable the performer to control entirely different qualities of
tone, and by playing with a hand on each, to contrast, as it
were, two instruments in the same harmony.   The principal
manual is [called the 'Great Organ' (though, indeed, the
modern tendency is to make the Swell quite as powerful), and
is the middle one in three-, and the lower one in two-manual
organs.   The uppermost of three or two manuals is, in
English organs, invariably the Swell, and the lowest of three
manuals is called the 'Choir,' the tone of this latter being
softer and lighter than that of the other two.   In German
organs, the second or upper manual is often the Choir or

'Oberwerk,' the Great being called the 'Hauptwerk,' and for small organs this course has much to recommend it. In large organs, a fourth manual, called the ' Solo,' is added above the others, and, as its name implies, is provided with stops of a commanding or special tone. In large German organs, the fourth manual was sometimes the 'Echo,' a name which sufficiently indicates the purpose. Everybody knows that the wind is supplied by bellows blown by hand, steam, gas, water, or even electric power. The pipes which convey the wind to the different departments of the organ are called ' trunks.'

13. By far the larger number of organs are built as described above; but there is another type of soundboard, considerably used in Germany, called the 'Ventil' soundboard, which has peculiar merits, and must, therefore, be recognised in the general description. In this type each rank of pipes has a little soundboard of its own, and each pipe a separate valve, so that when a key is put down, it opens as many valves as there are stops. The draw-stops, instead of controlling sliders, operate a valve called a ventil, which admits wind to the wind-chest, so that unless the stop has been drawn no sound is produced, though the pallet is open. Figs. 173, 178, and 180, Pl. XV., show some varieties of ventil soundboards, which will be further described in the chapter devoted to that subject.

14. So far, the organ is a mere wind producing and distributing machine, and we now have to consider the pipes. Of these there are two varieties, speaking on entirely different principles—one the flue pipes, of which the construction is simply that of the penny whistle ; and the other the reed pipes, of which the principal member is a vibrating tongue, admitting positive puffs of air to the body.

Flue pipes are both stopped and open, the effect of stopping the end being to lower the pitch an octave and to produce an entirely different quality of sound. They are generally made of metal and of wood, but good pipes can be made of paper. Most kinds are of uniform section ; but there are varieties which are narrower, and others which are wider at top than at the mouth, while others, again, are formed of two cones. Some wooden pipes are triangular in section, and some are bored out of the solid, like a flute. Pipes are to be seen that have their tops bent over like a chimney cowl. This makes no difference to the sound, and is only done when there is not room for their full height, or, in the case of reed pipes, to prevent dust from falling in.

Reed pipes are of two kinds—free and beating or striking reeds. A harmonium is a free-reed instrument, but without any pipe bodies; and a clarionet is a familiar example of a striking reed. The former are seldom used in English organs, but find favour abroad. The bodies of reed pipes are generally trumpet-shaped; but some of the more delicate are cylindrical.

15. The external appearance of the principal varieties of organ pipes is shown in Pl. XIII., where Fig. 139 is a cylindrical flue pipe, such as an Open Diapason, of which type are by far the greatest number of pipes in an organ. Fig. 140 is a taper pipe, of which the Spitz Flute is an example. Fig. 141 a Dolce, wider at top than at bottom. Fig. 142 is a Bell Gamba. Fig. 143 is a wooden pipe, which also can be varied by making it taper either way. Fig. 147 is a Trumpet, a reed pipe with a conical body; 145 is an Oboe, and 146 a variety of conical bodies sometimes used. Fig. 144 is a Clarionet, with a plain cylindrical body. Details of all these will be found in the chapters on the different stops and on the construction of the pipes; here it will be sufficient to give the name of the different parts. The terms ' body ' and ' foot ' require no explanation; the partition separating these parts is called the 'languid,' and the flattened parts above and below the mouth the upper and lower 'lips,' while the gap between the languid and lip through which the wind, admitted by the hole in the foot, escapes is called the 'wind-way.'

16. In a reed pipe the vibrating plate a (Figs. 11, 12, 13, Pl. III.) is called the 'tongue,' fastened by the 'wedge' b into the ' block ' c by jamming it against the 'reed' d, and that again into its hole in the ' block.' This block, which carries above it a socket to receive the body of the pipe, or the body itself, if a small one, is dropped into a foot piece e, called

the ' boot '; *f* is the tuning wire, which regulates the pitch by fixing the length of the vibrating part of the tongue as it is drawn up or down.

17. Fig. 286, Pl. XXVIII., gives a general idea of a three-manual organ with a reversed console, which is a much better arrangement than making the organist sit almost inside the organ, with his back to the choir. Fig. 286 is a cross section, Fig. 287 a longitudinal section, and Fig. 288 a plan. *a* is the Great Organ, *b* the Choir, and *c* the Swell. The pedal organ is arranged at the two sides; *d e f g* represent the pneumatic levers to the respective departments, *h h* are the couplers, and *k k* are roller boards. There are two sets of pull-downs to the Great and Swell, as two pressures of wind are supposed to be used. There are two sets of bellows with double reservoirs, so that four pressures of wind could be used if desired. The arrangement indicated would be suitable for a medium-sized organ with mechanical action; but large organs are as much as four storeys high, and there are several soundboards to each department, as one would be unmanageably large, and the tuner would not be able to get at the pipes. *l* is the ladder by which to reach the upper story—a detail which is often overlooked in planning, leaving the tuner to scramble about as best he can, to the imminent danger of the pipes and action.

18. Since the above was written an entirely new class of pipe has been invented by Mr. Hope-Jones, and named by him the ' Diaphone.' It is practically a tremulant applied to a pipe-body, and is therefore related to the reed type, the tone being between that of flues and reeds. The capabilities of this device have hardly yet been fully worked out.

CHAPTER III

ACOUSTICS, AS RELATING TO ORGANS

19. It is neither necessary nor possible to write a complete study of acoustics for reference in building organs; but facts connected with tone and tune will be better appreciated if the reader is familiar with the leading principles of the production of sounds. He will also have a clue to the vagaries of some organ pipes instead of groping in the dark, and will understand the reasons for the use of Mixtures and grasp better the details of tuning.

20. Sound is communicated by vibrations of the air. You cannot make a sound in a vacuum. A bell so situated will vibrate if struck; but, if no air surrounds it to take up the vibrations, no sound will be produced. A reed pipe does not sound by the vibrations of the tongue, but because they communicate movement to the air contained in the body of the pipe. A similar result would be obtained if the column of air were excited in any other way by regular impulses. That is the reason of the want of body in the sound of a harmonium; the vibrating mass of air is diffuse, but in the pipe a definite column is set in motion.

21. A clear conception should be formed of the nature of the vibrations in an organ pipe. It is apparent to the eye that the vibrations of a string are transverse, and that any particle partakes of them without longitudinal motion, just as a ship at anchor rises and falls with the waves without leaving its place. But the nature of the longitudinal vibrations of the sound wave in a tube, without any motion of the air mass as a whole, is not so immediately apparent. These vibrations can best be likened to the waves which pass over a field of corn under the action of the wind. In this case the motion is not up and down, but backwards

and forwards, and the wave effect is made apparent by the ears being more tightly packed in one part than in another. Imagine a row of men standing shoulder to shoulder ; a shove administered to the first will run along the line as each yields to the shock but recovers his place by the recoil from his neighbour, and it may be easily conceived that in a long line two or more such impulses may be in progress at the same time.

22. Of this nature are the air vibrations in a tube, which, once started by some shock, are propagated by the elasticity of the air. A tuning-fork held at the mouth of a tube condenses the particles of air in its immediate vicinity on the outward excursion of the prongs, and each particle so pushed communicates the shock to its neighbour, and thus vibrations set up in any way are propagated along the tube, a complete sound wave consisting of a pulse, of condensation and one of rarefaction. In the open air these impulses spread in every direction, and, as each sphere of waves has to set in motion more and more particles, they rapidly lose their force, and the sound will not travel so far as it does in a tube, where the size of the wave remains constant.

23. The nature of vibration, without actual movement of the air mass as a whole, can be well seen by placing a lighted candle in front of a tube filled with smoke, and making a loud noise, as by clapping together two pieces of board, at the other end. If dexterously performed, without throwing any air into the tube by the movement, the candle can be extinguished without the smoke being driven through the tube. The effect of windows being broken by the discharge of a heavy gun is well known, and a little reflection will show that the effect is not produced by an actual wind propelled from the gun, but by a wave or oscillatory movement of the particles of the air, which as a whole remains at rest.

24. To return to strings, there are certain phenomena of vibration which have to be studied. A heavy cord fastened at both ends, but not too tightly stretched, can, by regular impulses from the finger, be made to execute a simple pendular vibration throughout its entire length. The form of this vibration is known as the curve of sines, and how to

plot it is shown in Fig. 384, Pl. XLIV. If $a\,b$ be the length of the wave, and $c\,d$ its amplitude, divide $a\,b$ into any number of parts, and, drawing a circle with diameter $c\,d$, divide its circumference into the same number of equal parts, starting from the axis, and draw ordinates through the divisions. The ordinates to the curve will be equal to the corresponding ordinates of the circle. If, now, the impulses be increased, or if the cord be lightly touched in the middle, it will no longer make a simple vibration, but will divide into two loops and continue to vibrate regularly in that way, the central point remaining at rest ; and still further excitement, or touching the string at a point where a node should be, will cause its vibrations to break up into 3, 4, 5 . . . n segments, the limit to their number being the resistance offered by the stiffness of the string. The points of rest are called ' nodes,' and the vibrating parts ' ventral segments.'

25. Such a cord to give visible vibrations will have too slow a rate to produce an audible note; but the same facts can be verified on a musical string by putting a little strip of folded paper, called a 'rider,' on it, which will be thrown off in a segment, or vibrating part, but remains seated if placed at a node. It will also be observed that the rate of vibration increases as the number of segments; and if the natural rate of vibration of the whole string be observed, and it is then started from rest by impulses of double that frequency, it will at once assume the form of two segments. The formation of nodes is due to the passage to and fro of single pulsations, such as can be given to a cord by a single shake at one end—at the other the wave is reflected in the reverse phase, and the nodes are the points where these waves from both ends cross each other in an opposed sense, the crest of one against the trough of another. The single impulses which run backwards and forwards may be called the running wave, and the permanent shape of vibration the standing wave. The ends, being fixed, necessarily form nodes, and the period of vibration is the time taken by a pulse to travel two segments or whole wave-length, each segment being alternately the crest or hollow of a wave.

26. Now, it is not possible under the actual conditions

of a *musical* string to produce a simple pendular vibration; but the main wave is, so to speak, always overlaid with the ripples of several systems of secondary waves. This idea must not be taken literally, since the form of the wave is not that of the simple wave with ripples on its back, but may be so modified as to have apparently no connection with the original form. For instance, the wave shape of a violin string is given by Helmholtz as resembling straight-lined saw-teeth. The effect can best be studied by drawing a simple wave, and on the same axis subsidiary waves, with frequencies of 2, 3 . . . *n* times that of the primary, and with amplitudes diminishing as their vibrations increase, and then, from the algebraic sum of all these waves, plotting the resultant wave. This has been done in Fig. 336, Pl. XLIV., which is the wave form produced by the components drawn in Fig. 335. Fig. 338 is the wave form produced by the same primaries, but with a slight difference in phase as drawn in Fig. 337.

27. There is a mathematical investigation known as 'Fourier's theorem,' which proves that every periodic wave form can be resolved in one way, and in one way only, into simple waves whose vibration numbers increase in the ratios of 2, 3 . . . *n* to the primary wave. Now, since sound is produced by periodic vibrations upon the frequency of which the pitch depends, it follows that none but a simple pendular vibration will give a simple sound, and that the tone of a musical string contains as many really distinct notes as there are series of simple waves mathematically building up the resultant wave. Helmholtz has shown, both by analysis and synthesis, that the quality or timbre of a note depends upon the number and relative strength of these subsidiary sounds, which are called 'upper partials,' 'overtones' (should be 'upper tones'), or 'harmonics,' and, further, has explained all the phenomena of consonance and dissonance by their presence.

28. Another point regarding the sound wave remains to be noticed—that of 'phase,' an expression which describes the relation of the position of the waves to each other. If we draw two similar waves upon the same axis, and wish to

plot the resultant wave, it makes a very material difference whether we start drawing them with their nodes at the same place or not, and if at the same place, whether we put the crests and hollows on the same or on opposite sides of the axis.   In the last case, the waves exactly counteract each other, and the resultant is a straight line ; there is no vibration, and consequently no sound.   Nor is this effect impossible to realise in practice, though, to produce absolute silence from two sound waves they must be exactly similar in shape and opposite in phase—conditions a little difficult to secure. The experiment can best be performed by turning on its axis a tuning-fork held upright before the ear.   At four points in the revolution the sound will be a maximum, when the phases of the waves from the two prongs coincide, and at four points, where the waves are in opposite phase, it will die away.   The same effect can be produced in light by an arrangement which will reflect part of a ray in a different phase to the other part, the result being alternate bright and dark lines, proving that light is produced by waves.   Every organ-builder knows that two exactly similar pipes sounding together may interfere with each other, and produce a worse note than one alone.

29. In plotting the form of the waves of harmonics as described above, we should naturally start them all from one node ; but it will then occur to anyone to ask, How am I to know that the secondary waves are all to be drawn as starting from the same place, and with their curvature in the same direction as that of the primary ? because how they are arranged will obviously make a great difference in the shape of the resultant wave (and presumably in the sound).   The answer is, that it has been conclusively shown by Helmholtz with an apparatus of tuning-forks that the *phase* of the waves of the upper partials makes no difference to the ear. Although we may, with a primary and two secondary waves, obtain an infinite number of resultant waves by merely varying the phase, yet the ear will only, in any of those forms, recognise the presence of three simple pendular vibrations which build up the tone ; so that while a wave of a given form or mode of vibration must always produce the same

quality of sound, that quality may be produced by an infinite
number of shapes, provided they are built up of the same
elements with merely a difference of arrangement.

30. What has been said of the vibrations of strings applies
to the vibrations of a column of air in a tube, with the
difference that the vibrations are longitudinal instead of transverse. When it is considered that it is the amount of the
minute oscillations of the particles, and not their direction,
which determines the form of the wave, it will be seen that a
longitudinal vibration can be expressed diagrammatically by
a wave form, just as well as can a lateral one. Thus the
musical effects of an organ pipe are due to pulses of condensation and rarefaction, or waves of longitudinal vibration, the
exciting cause being near one end, and the other either stopped
or open. In the former case every pulse of condensation or
rarefaction is reflected back in the same phase from the end,
and as, right at the end, no longitudinal motion of the particles
is possible, there must be a node there, just as there is in a
string at the point where the vibrations are damped. At the
mouth, the place of excitement, we get the centre of a segment,
and a simple vibration will be as shown in Fig. 148, Pl. XIII.,
for the pipe of Fig. 149. (In these figures the mode of vibration is best shown graphically, as if it were that of a string;
but it is not intended to indicate by that any lateral oscillation
of the particles.) The width of the loop of the wave figure
indicates the amount of the oscillations to and fro of the
particles in that plane, this being a maximum in the centre
of a segment, and zero at a node. It was stated above that
the time of a complete vibration is that taken by a pulse in
travelling over a complete wave or two segments. This would
be four times the length of a stopped pipe; therefore the
vibration number of a stopped pipe is found theoretically by
dividing the speed of sound (the rate of travel of the pulsations) by four times the length of the pipe. The average
speed of sound in air may be taken as 1,120 ft. per second at
60° F., the exact amount depending upon the temperature
and barometric pressure. It is less in tubes, on account of
the friction.

31. It will be observed that the condition of a node at the

stopper limits the number of segments to the odd numbers
$\frac{1}{2}$, $1\frac{1}{2}$, $2\frac{1}{2}$, or 1, 3, 5 . . . so that a stopped pipe can
only have the odd-numbered partials, a fact which ex-
plains their dull tone. When overblown, a stopped pipe of
uniform section will consequently break into the second partial
or twelfth (see Fig. 148a).

32. Just a word must be said as to the numbering of the
harmonics, to avoid confusion. If the primary is the first
partial tone, the second will be that whose vibrations are
double, the third will be treble, and so on. But if the *upper
partials*—i.e. excluding the primary—are spoken of, the first
upper tone will be that whose vibration number is 2, and the
order of odd and even numbers will be reversed. The word
' harmonic ' is ambiguous unless it is explicitly defined, and
the writer intends to use it in the sense of ' partial tone,' the
primary being the first partial, or harmonic, and so on. Thus
the name of the partial and its vibration ratios agree ; but,
as sometimes used, the first, third, &c., harmonics are the
even numbered tones.

33. In the case of an open pipe, waves are reflected back,
but in the opposite phase, a wave of condensation arriving at
the end, communicates its pressure to, and loses it in, the
surrounding air, and travels back as a wave of rarefaction ;
and a rarefied pulse, being condensed between the superior
elastic pressures of the air in front and behind, travels back
as a condensation. Further, in this case, both ends of the
pipe form the centre of a segment, as shown in Fig. 150 for
the pipe of Fig. 151, so that the whole pipe-length is equal to
one segment, and the divisor for the vibration number is twice
the length of the pipe. There is thus a direct means of
calculating the length of any pipe required—say, a C_0 making
sixty-four vibrations per second will have a wave-length of
$\frac{1,120'}{64} = 17.5'$, or twice the length of the pipe, thus found to
be 8·7'. This, however, is purely theoretical, and supposes
that the diameter of the pipe is infinitely small, and for practical purposes a correction must be made for the diameter,
which subject will be treated of in the chapter on pipes. Thus
the pitch of a stopped is (approximately) double that of an

open pipe. The column of air in an open pipe can break up into segments represented by all the numbers 2, 3, 4 . . . *n*, as shown in Fig. 150*a*; they thus, when overblown, break into the octave, and their tone is richer in harmonics than is that of a stopped pipe.

34. Between open and stopped pipes there are all degrees of shading, from a slight shade over the top for tuning, to a stopped pipe with a hole in the stopper; but it is only for a slight variation in pitch from either a stopped or open pipe, that the speech remains good: shading the top of a pipe with a shade of more than half its depth, set down more than 45°, spoils the tone. The probable explanation of flattening the pitch by an obstruction at the open end of a pipe (or at the mouth) is that the wave is partly condensed, and its speed hindered. This seems corroborated by the fact that increasing the wind-pressure sharpens the pitch, the waves have greater energy to overcome the friction against the sides, and, as this action increases, the vibration becomes unsteady and the wave at last divides itself into two parts, doubling the number of vibrations, and sounding the octave (in an open pipe). Up to this point, increased energy of vibration builds up subsidiary vibrations on the main wave, and each of these produces its own tone or upper partial to the primary.

35. Why a flue pipe should sound, or rather, why the air blown from the windway against the upper lip should vibrate, is not exactly known. It does not vibrate at all unless it strikes in a particular way, as may be seen in the case of dumb pipes, and the mode of vibration, when it does speak, depends upon the way the sheet of wind reaches the lip, as may be seen by the difference in timbre produced by different adjustment of the mouth parts. The general explanation is that the wind passing just across—not necessarily against—the lip, causes a slight rarefaction inside by suction, and the moment this takes place the external air forces the sheet in and restores equilibrium, when the sheet recovers itself. The action of the bridge, or bar across the mouth, in a small-scale pipe, seems to confirm this view, since this appliance prevents a pipe from speaking the octave which without it will give no other note. Now, speaking the octave simply means that the

vibrations are doubled, and the presence of this little bar in front of the mouth seems to stop the excess vibrations, by hindering the inward-bearing draught from being so strong.

36. The three points to be considered in sound in connection with organs are: 1. Tune, or the pitch of a note, depending upon the *rapidity* of the vibrations. 2. Timbre, or tone, the *quality* of a note, as the difference between the notes of different instruments while sounding the same pitch. This depends upon the *mode* of vibration, or the presence of upper partials. 3. Intensity or simple loudness depends upon the amplitude of the vibrations, being proportional to the square of the amplitude.

37. Dealing first with pitch, it may be broadly stated that the pitch of a vibrating body, or the number of vibrations per second, is—

a. Inversely as the length, either of a string or pipe.

β. Inversely as the thickness of a string, and, to a certain extent, of a pipe.

γ. Directly as the square root of the tension in a string, to which corresponds the wind-pressure in a pipe.

δ. Inversely as the square root of the density of a string, to which in a pipe would correspond the effects of temperature and barometric pressure. The last is of no practical importance, but the former will be found to cause difficulty in dealing with organs.

The chapter on tuning will enter into details of how these theories are practically applied to the tuning of pipes; but the musical relations of pitch must be explained, as also what constitutes being 'out of tune.'

38. As stated above, the pitch of a note depends upon the number of its vibrations, always quoted at per second, which numbers are about sixty-four complete (i.e. outwards and back) vibrations per second for C_0, with double the number for each higher, and half for each lower, octave. An easy 'memoria technica' is that C_2, the 32 ft. pipe, gives thirty-two single vibrations per second. From this the number of vibrations of any note can be ascertained by doubling for the octaves upwards, and calculating for intermediate lengths in a way which will be explained hereafter. We generally speak of

double or complete vibrations. It has been stated that, on the average, the limits of sound audible to the ear are from 16 to 24,000 per second ; but this has been qualified by the statement that much depends upon the intensity as well as the pitch, acute sounds being audible up to 37,000 vibrations, if strong enough. Different ears have very different powers of appreciation in this respect, without any marked difference in the powers of hearing within a medium range. Some people, for instance, who are not the least deaf, cannot hear the top octave of the Fifteenth.

39. It is generally accepted that the limits of *musical* sound lie between 27 and 4,000 vibrations per second, corresponding to about A_2 and c^5 respectively, so that g^5, the ordinary top pipe of the Fifteenth, lies seven semitones above the limit. As for pipes below A_2, Töpfer has judiciously remarked that they delight the eye more than the ear. Helmholtz fixes the lower limit of audible tone at 31, and of appreciable pitch (by direct observation) at 40 vibrations, and says that lower notes than these are really appreciated by their harmonics. Of other musical instruments it may be noted that the lowest note, A_2, of the piano corresponds well with the limit in this direction, while the highest, a^4, gives 3,480 vibrations. The violin ranges from 193 to 3,500, and the average human voice from 82 (E_0) to 1,044 (c^3) over the whole range from bass to soprano. Extraordinary voices have been recorded from 61 (B_1) in the bass to 1,305 (c^3), and even to f^3 ; witness the part of Astrifiammante in the ' Zauberflöte,' which has reiterated notes of that pitch, though it must be remembered that the pitch of Mozart's day was much lower than it is now.

40. Having discussed the limits of musical sounds, we now turn to the relation which notes bear to each other, and to the reasons of dissonance. If two simple sounds, whose pitch differs slightly, are sounded together, beats are heard. If waves representing the vibrations are drawn, and the resultant plotted, it will be seen that they alternately reinforce and diminish the sound, and this waxing and waning causes a flickering of the note which is as disagreeable to the ear as the flickering of a light is to the eye. It is this flickering

which causes the beats or throbs heard when two notes are a
little out of tune, and the number of beats per second is the
difference of the vibration numbers, as can easily be verified
by plotting two waves of any given frequency. The ear can
count them as distinct up to four or five per second, but after
that they merge into a jarring sound, which becomes most
intense at the interval of a semitone, and disappears at the
interval of a minor third, so that in order to produce the
effect of a discord two simple tones must be within this
'beating interval.' As the number of beats for the same
interval is doubled for every octave up the scale, the dissonance does not depend upon the actual number of beats so
much as upon their relation to the vibrations of the notes.
But, to a certain extent, position in the scale does affect the
result, as a fraction of out-of-tuneness, which in a very low
note would produce a beat so slow as to be hardly perceptible,
would in a high one produce a rapid beat which could easily
be detected.

41. On this statement it may be asked : Why, if to produce
dissonance two simple tones must be within beating distance
of each other, does a fifth octave, or wide interval, sound bad
when out of tune? The answer is that the illustrious
Helmholtz discovered the physical basis of tone sensation to
be—that musical notes are not simple sound-waves, but
possess harmonics, and the sensation of discord is caused by
some of the upper partials of two notes getting within beating
distance of each other. It thus appears that except for the
interval of a tone and a semitone, there is not necessarily
any discordant interval, and that the harshness of a discord
depends *entirely* upon the number and strength of the upper
partials and the combination tones. Experience corroborates
this, as everyone who has played upon an organ knows how
very much less offensive a Gedackt is than a Gamba, when
both are equally out of tune, the reason being that the Gamba
is rich in harmonics, while the Gedackt has but few.

42. Taking the vibration number of the primary as 1, the
number for the upper partials are for the full series 2, 3,
4 . . . n, while under certain circumstances of constraint,
as in a Gedackt, only the odd numbers are present.

The series are as follows :

Ratio of Vibrations				Partial Tone
1	.	.	.	Unison
2	.	.	.	Octave
3	.	.	.	Twelfth, or octave fifth
4	.	.	.	Fifteenth, or double octave
5	.	.	.	Tierce, or third to double octave
6	.	.	.	Nineteenth, Larigot, fifth to double octave
7	.	.	.	Minor seventh to double octave
8	.	.	.	Third octave

Supposing only the first six of these partial tones present, and taking the interval of an octave, the bar below represents the simple tones that will actually be sounding, the notes being white and the upper partials black. These last are all concordant so long as the primaries are perfectly in tune ; but if a little out, there are three unisons to swear at each other.

With a stopped pipe, however, the case would be different, as the notes marked with a sign ($\times$) would be absent, so that there would be no partials within beating distance. Why, then, should a bad octave sound discordant on a Gedackt ? This introduces the subject of 'combination,' or 'difference tones,' as they are called. These are perceptible tones caused by the reinforcement of a certain number of vibrations of the two sounding notes which happen to coincide, as, for example, the well-known instance of the harmonic 32 ft. effect in the pedal organ, produced by a 16 ft. and its fifth, or Great Quint. The vibrations of these notes are in the ratios of 2 : 3, so that every second beat of the lower is met and reinforced by every third beat of the upper. The 16 ft. C_1 makes 32 vibrations, and the G_1 48, so that there will be 16 reinforced vibrations in a second, giving a distinct impression of C_2 sounding in addition to the primary notes. The number of vibrations of the combination tone is the difference between the numbers of the primaries.

43. Upon this principle depends the well-known thickening effect of a Quint or Twelfth ; it is as if a subdued sound, an octave below the lower primary, accompanied it, the shadow, as it were, of a 16 ft. tone on the manual. The combination tone of a fourth, where the vibration ratios are 3 : 4, is a difference of 1, or a twelfth below the lower primary, and so on for all the combinations of two notes up to an octave. Again, a combination tone can, with one of the primaries, make a second order combination; thus a note and its fifth, or 3 — 2, gives a difference of 1 for a first order combination, which, again, with the primaries, gives different tones of $3-1=2$ and $2-1=1$. These tones of the second order can be heard, and though the same theory will extend their number further, the results are too weak to be perceptible. Thus, although a bad octave on a Gedackt, say 100 and 202 vibrations, has neither primaries nor upper partials in collision, yet there will be a primary of 100 and a combination tone of 102, which *are* within beating distance, and therefore give the sensation of being out of tune, although with much less intensity than in a pipe sounding all the harmonics.

44. Everyone recognises that even a pure fifth is not so smooth an interval as an octave, and the presence of the upper partials, shown in the first stave of the bar below, ex-

plains the reason : the upper partial, *d*, of the fifth is within beating distance of two of the partials of the lower note. The second bar shows how the same chord would sound on a Gedackt, with the even harmonics wanting. The discord would be rather less, as there are only two upper partials within beating distance. An imperfect fifth sets all the upper tones of the open pipes beating and so increases the dissonance ; but it introduces no new elements of discord into the stopped pipes, so far as the *upper* partials are concerned, but sets the difference tones at variance in the manner explained above. There are many interesting details given in Helmholtz's great work on sound, which show that there is nothing absolute in musical theory, but that the concord or discord of an interval depends upon the *qualities* of the sounds of the different instruments playing them; as, for instance, that a certain interval is discordant with a clarionet playing the lower note and an oboe the upper; but no longer so when the positions are reversed, because in that case a certain discord is got rid of, owing to the fact that a clarionet has only the odd harmonics.

45. As a matter of fact, it is the intervals whose vibration ratios are the simplest which are the most concordant, and until the time of Helmholtz this gave rise to the somewhat fanciful explanation that the mind delighted in simple numbers. Thus we have, first, 1 : 2, or the octave, sounding when in perfect tune practically as one note. The next would be 1 : 3; but as this takes us outside the octave which has to be subdivided, we require the simplest ratios between 1 and 2. These would be $\frac{3}{2}, \frac{4}{3}, \frac{5}{3}, \frac{5}{4}$. We know that the ratio $\frac{3}{2}$ (meaning that the upper note makes three vibrations to two of the lower), called the fifth, is the most harmonious, and its connection with the second simplest ratio, 1 : 3, is that the latter represents the octave fifth. The next in order is the ratio $\frac{4}{3}$, called the fourth, which is the octave of the fifth below; for if the fundamental note be 1, the fifth below will be $\frac{2}{3}$, the octave of which is $\frac{4}{3}$. This interval is fairly harmonious, and is much used in tuning. $\frac{5}{3}$, or the major sixth, is a fairly simple ratio, and so is $\frac{5}{4}$, or the major third.

46. The Greek musical scale was developed entirely by a series of perfect fifths, bringing the notes within the compass of an octave; but it had the defect of very complex relations to the tonic, and a complex semitone, with a major third a whole comma sharp, and therefore unfit to be used in harmony. The modern major scale is constructed thus, taking *c* as the tonic:

Note				*c*	*d*	*e*	*f*	*g*	*a*	*b*	*c*
Ratio	.	.	.	1	$\frac{9}{8}$	$\frac{5}{4}$	$\frac{4}{3}$	$\frac{3}{2}$	$\frac{5}{3}$	$\frac{15}{8}$	2
Interval	.	.	.		$\frac{9}{8}$	$\frac{10}{9}$	$\frac{16}{15}$	$\frac{9}{8}$	$\frac{10}{9}$	$\frac{9}{8}$	$\frac{16}{15}$

$\frac{10}{9}$

$\frac{9}{8}$ is a major tone, $\frac{10}{9}$ a minor tone, and $\frac{16}{15}$ a semitone, and
·the difference, $\frac{81}{80}$, between a major and a minor tone is called
a comma.   Note also, that the lowest series of whole numbers
which will express our scale is—

| 24 | 27 | 30 | 32 | 36 | 40 | 45 | 48 |

47. This primitive arrangement of eight notes would, however, only permit of the execution of music in the key of C
major ; as if it were desired to transpose and take another
note, as *g*, for the tonic, we get the second semitone in the
wrong place, and to meet this have to introduce a new note
between F and G.   In theory, to raise a note to its sharp, the
vibrations are multiplied by $\frac{25}{24}$, the ratio of a minor semitone,
and divided by the same amount for the flat.   Therefore, if *f*
is sharpened (by multiplying the interval *e*—*f* by $\frac{25}{24}$), we get
the whole tone in that place, and the semitone between *f* and
g, where it is wanted.   But, properly speaking, the sharp of
a note is not the same as the flat of the tone above.   Thus,
c sharp is to *c* as $\frac{25}{24}$, while *d* flat is $\frac{9}{8} \times \frac{24}{25} = \frac{27}{25}$, or *c* sharp :
d flat : : 625 : 648.   Further complications would arise if it
were desired to use the minor mode, or other notes as the
tonic, and in short the translator of Helmholtz states that to
give just intonation there would have to be 72 notes to the
octave.

48. Instruments have been constructed with a large number of notes to an octave ; but these, called enharmonic organs,
have necessarily remained mere curiosities, and the system
formerly adopted was to distribute the errors over some few
scales, and leave the rest too bad to be played in.   Some old
organs, as at St. Paul's and the Temple, had double black keys
so as to give the sharps and flats separately.   The system now
universally adopted, called the equal temperament, is to divide
the octave into twelve equal semitones, so that the scale is
equally true, or untrue, whatever may be taken as the tonic,
and it is this ' tempering ' the intervals which constitutes the
great difficulty in tuning.   It is easy enough to tune a perfect
fifth or fourth, but very difficult to judge how much to falsify
them so that the errors shall be equally distributed.   There
is a very perceptible difference between a true and a tempered

scale to moderately acute ears, and it is to their just intonation that the violin and human voice owe much of their
superiority as musical instruments. It must, therefore, never
be forgotten in dealing with matters of tuning that the use
of twelve equal semitones in the octave is merely a compro-
mise, for the sake of using just that number of keys as
dictated for mechanical convenience, and that there is no
natural foundation for it.

49. Sedley Taylor gives to the nearest vibration the following comparison of the tempered scale (the upper line) and
the just intervals of the same scale :

c	c♯	d	d♯	e	f	f♯	g	g♯	a	a♯	b
264	280	296	314	333	352	373	395	419	444	470	498

c		d	e♭	e	f		g	a♭	a	b♭	b
264		297	317	330	352		396	422	440	469	495

The vibration numbers of the true scale are obtained by
multiplying that of the tonic by the vibration ratios assigned
above, while those of the tempered scale are obtained by multiplying the number started from (since any will serve as
a tonic) by $2^{\frac{n}{12}}$ where n is the 1st, 2nd . . . note. It
will be seen that the fourths and fifths are not much out,
but the thirds are bad ; still, the inaccuracies introduced are
no more than those which will soon develop themselves in the
pipe-work of an organ from the effects of dust, &c. ; only,
unfortunately, this further imperfection is quite as likely to
lead an already imperfect interval further from the truth
as nearer to it, so that too much care cannot be taken in 'laying the bearings,' or the tuner's error will be a third quantity
by no means negligible. In considering the deviations from
true tone, it must be remembered that they depend not upon
the absolute number of vibrations by which a tempered note
differs from a true one, since this is halved or doubled as the
octaves go down or up in the scale, but upon the ratio of these
vibrations to those of the adjacent notes.

50. We next proceed to the investigation of what causes
different qualities of tone or *timbre*, and this is closely connected with what has been said upon the subject of tune, as
it is upon the consonance of the harmonics that the sweetness

of a note depends.   It has been described above how no
musical sound is absolutely pure, the nearest approach being
in a tuning-fork, or a large scale stopped pipe ; and in reality
every musical sound is like a note on a large organ, with
several pipes speaking the harmonics as well as the fundamental note.   Up to the seventh harmonic they are all consonant ; but above this they get nearer and nearer, and
increase the dissonance, all above the eighth being considered
as mere noise.   At the sixteenth the partials are a semitone
apart, the interval of maximum dissonance.   Remembering
what was stated above about the formation of subsidiary
vibrations being checked by the stiffness of a string, it will
be understood why a very thin string, as in an old harpsi-
chord, gives a nasal tinkling sound as compared with a
piano, the strings of which are much thicker ; the thin
string develops harmonics well into the region of discord.
When it is found that a harmonium reed has easily recognisable harmonics up to the twentieth, it will be understood
why the tone of this instrument is so snarling and disagreeable.

51. Helmholtz studied the harmonics of a musical note
by means of a series of brass spheres called ' resonators.'   At
one point is a small nipple which is placed in the ear, and
opposite this is a short neck to receive the sound.   The
advantage of the spherical form is that it has only few and
faint partials of its own, and is, therefore, sensitive to its own
primary only, which it picks out with great accuracy from
among all the other partial tones.   Helmholtz gives the following formula for a spherical resonator—

$$n = a \sqrt{\left(\frac{3\,r}{8\,\pi^3\,R^3} \right)}$$

where n = the vibration number ; a = the speed of sound ; R
and r the radii of the sphere and of the opening.   His resonator for c^1 was 5·12″ diameter, with an orifice of 1·19″, and
for c^2 the dimensions were 2·76″ and 0·81″.   But any organ-
builder can contrive a set of resonators out of clarinet bodies,
tuning them exactly by the slides.   They are neither so
sensitive nor so accurate as the spheres, as they have upper

tones of their own, but for practical purposes they are sufficient.

52. In one experiment, Helmholtz used resonance tubes closed at one end, and with a circular hole in the lid at the other, and the dimensions were as given below for a pitch $a^1 = 440$. Such instruments can be exactly tuned by comparison with a fork. If shading (i.e. flattening) the aperture increases the resonance, they are too sharp; but if it diminishes, they are too flat. It is scarcely necessary to remark that the intervals must be true ones, and not those of keyed instruments. Flattening must be done by contracting the aperture; but sharpening may be done by opening the aperture, or reducing the volume by running melted wax into the end of the tube. Armed with a set of these, the qualities of tone can be studied in connection with the harmonics present. The influence of the upper partials can be well studied without any resonators by comparing a Sub-bass with a Violone (supposing always that the latter stop can be found, as the quality does not always accompany the name). In the Sub-bass but little is heard beyond the primary note, the pitch of which is quite uncertain; while the octave in the (properly voiced) Violone is so strong that the pitch can well be recognised right down to the bottom of the scale. The richest sounds are those which contain the first six partial tones well distributed, the absence of the even tones, or predominance of the odd ones, always producing a peculiar effect. Helmholtz mentions that in a Gamba or Geigen all the partials up to the sixth are strongly developed; but for a Diapason they were only recognisable up to the fourth, while for a wooden Diapason only the first three could be heard. This, however, depends upon the individual samples he experimented on, as a wooden pipe can be voiced to sound exactly like a metal one. Taper pipes have the peculiarity of sounding some of the partials from the fifth to the seventh stronger than the others. The Gedackts, as noted above, can only give the odd harmonics, a wide pipe having hardly any, while a narrow one may give up to the fifth partial. The Rohr Flute examined gave the fifth harmonic stronger than the others. But Helmholtz did not give his attention specially to organs, and

was even under the impression that free reeds only were used,
so that this extensive field for investigation is practically
unexplored.

SIZES OF RESONATING TUBES.

Note	Length	Diameters	
		Of Tube	Of Aperture
1. B$_0$ flat . . .	16·73	5·43″	1·24
2. b^0 flat . . .	8·27	3·23	0·93
3. f^1	4·61	2·56	0·63
4. b^1 flat. . . .	3·46	2·17	0·56
5. d^2	2·28	2·17	0·55
6. f^2	2·09	1·73	0·49
7. a^2 flat . . .	1·97	1·54	0·44
8. b^2 flat . . .	1·57	1·54	0·45
9. d^3	1·38	1·20	0·41
10. f^3	1·02	1·02	0·34

53. The theory of vibrations in pipes explains the reason
for the hole in the body of a harmonic flute; it helps to
abolish the node in the middle, and so enables the pipe to
speak its octave promptly, without employing an excessive
pressure of wind. Helmholtz's researches also throw a light
on the reasons for many things connected with voicing, as,
for instance, the fact that the more the wind is directed outward, the more cutting the tone. He shows that a smooth
tone is associated with a simple wave form and a sharp tone
with a jagged wave form, indicative of discontinuous action,
as in the case of the violin. Now the more the wind is directed outwards, the greater must be the jump of the return of
the stream after the inward draft has interrupted it, and
consequently the more discontinuous is the wave form. A
very great difference can be made in the tone of a pipe by
manipulating the wind in this sense; but there are so many
causes to influence the result that it does not seem the least
probable that voicing can ever be done by calculation.
Theory, however, will guide the voicer to a certain extent, as
indicating the reasons for particular qualities of tone. In the
matter of reeds especially, theory indicates that a shape of
tube which will reinforce the primary note or the consonant
partials will do much to modify the tone.

54. This hasty sketch of the salient points in acoustics, which have reference to organs, is necessarily very imperfect, and the reader is recommended to study Helmholtz's 'Sensations of Tone,' or Sedley Taylor's 'Sound and Music.' Blaserna's 'Theory of Sound' and Tyndall's 'Lectures' on the same subject are also profitable books to read.

CHAPTER IV

(a) PIPES—SCALE OF FLUE PIPES

55. BEFORE starting on the consideration of this subject, it is well to state explicitly that the figures and formulæ used are not employed in a strictly scientific sense. An investigation into the laws which govern the timbre of pipes is a useful help to the builder; but the conditions of their application are such as to preclude scientific accuracy. Let us by all means avail ourselves of the results of philosophical researches; but in employing formulæ, let it be clearly understood whether they are rational, or purely empirical, or whether they are mathematically accurate, and under what conditions. They may be useful enough for practical purposes, but their limitations should clearly be borne in mind. Any really accurate formula relating to the speech of organ pipes must take into account the temperature, the barometric pressure, the wind-pressure (in the pipe-foot, not at the bellows), and a host of conditions connected with the speaking parts which it would be practically impossible to express in a manageable formula, or even to reduce to figures.

56. For example: In speaking of a pipe, we say that the upper octave is half the length of the lower—a statement which is good enough to express the ratio roughly, for the purposes of the pipe-maker, but which is very far from being a scientific truth. In its naked form, it implies that if you cut a pipe in half it will speak the octave; whereas the truth is, that unless the pipe happens to be a very small scaled one, it will not speak at all, and even a small scaled one will require a rearrangement of the mouth parts which will materially affect the pitch. Thus it will be seen that, in saying that the ratio of pipes is one which halves or doubles on the octaves, the question of scales is implied, as if two stops are compared

which are not built to the same scale throughout, and a pipe of each is chosen, which, with the same dimensions, gives the same pitch, the upper and lower octaves of the two stops will not have the same dimensions in the diameters, and consequently in the lengths. It may be near enough, for practical purposes, to say that the length of pipes (with equal temperament) forms a geometrical series with half on the twelfth pipe; but it must be remembered that this is a broad, practical way of putting a relation which could only be scientifically expressed by a complicated formula, which would only hold good under certain specified circumstances.

57. As an example, let us consider the case of an Open

Note	N	$\frac{V}{N}$	P	L	L'
C_o . . .	64·66	8·83	0·50	7·83	7·83
C_o sharp . .	68·51	8·83	0·48	7·37	7·38
D . . .	72·58	7·86	0·46	6·94	6·97
D sharp . .	76·89	7·43	0·45	6·53	6·57
E . . .	81·47	7·00	0·43	6·14	6·21
F . . .	86·32	6·62	0·41	5·80	5·86
F sharp . .	91·45	6·24	0·39	5·46	5·53 .
G . . .	98·89	5·89	0·38	5·13	5·22
G sharp . .	102·6	5·56	0·36	4·84	4·93
A . . .	108·8	5·25	0·35	4·55	4·65
A sharp . .	115·2	4·96	0·34	4·28	4·39
B . . .	122·1	4·68	0·32	4·04	4·14
c^o . . .	129·8	4·41	0·31	3·79	3·91

Diapason with half-diameters on the 17th pipe, and pitch $a^1 = 435$ vibrations. Cavaillé-Coll's formula for length is near enough; it is $L = \frac{V}{N} - 2P$, where L is the length, V the velocity of sound, N the number of *single* vibrations of the note (the French usually reckon in single vibrations), and P the diameter of pipe. V has been taken at 1,142 ft. per sec., which must be divided by 2, as our N is given in whole vibrations. In the column headed L are given the approximately true lengths obtained by this formula, and under L' are given the figures obtained by halving the length for the octave and interpolating the intermediate lengths in a geometrical series. These last may do well enough to make pipes from, as a margin is always left, to be cut off in tuning; but they are far from being accurate in the mathematical sense of the word. It must, therefore, be understood that in speaking of this or that ratio for the diameters, &c., of pipes as compared with their lengths, we are discussing a practical, and not a strictly mathematical question. We assume, as a matter of conveni- ence, and for purposes of general discussion, that the lengths increase by double towards the lower and decrease by half towards the upper octaves ; but must not lose sight of the fact that this statement is only approximately true. To take the diameters into consideration would be a task of interminable complexity, since each scale would have to be treated on its own merits, and indeed, nothing would be gained, for the inaccuracies of practice and differences of winding, situation of pipes, &c., are as great as the errors caused by treating all kinds of pipes alike, so far as the ratio of lengths is con- cerned.

58. By the 'ratio' of the scale is meant the proportion which the areas of the pipes bear to each other in the succes- sive octaves, or, what is the same thing, the proportions of the linear dimensions of the double octaves. Thus, if the diameters of successive octaves are indicated by d, d_1, d_2, and n is the ratio of the scale, the diameters in terms of d will be

d, $n^{\frac{1}{2}}d$, $n\, d$, and the areas will be $\dfrac{\pi}{4} \times d^2$, $n\, d^2$, $n^2 d^2$, n thus

representing the ratio of the *areas* of the next, and of the *linear* dimensions of the double octave.

59. Inasmuch as the timbre depends mainly upon the ratio of the area to the length of a pipe, it might be supposed at first sight that the areas should vary as the lengths, and as these are in successive octaves as 1 : 2 (with the limitation mentioned above), the areas of successive octaves would then vary in the same proportion, and the linear dimensions of the second octaves would also follow the same rule. The scales given in Dom Bedos do, indeed, vary for different stops be- tween 1 : 1·935 (practically 1 : 2) for a Nasard, to 1 : 3·186 for a 32 ft. Untersatz—a variety so great that it would appear to be due rather to accident, or a recital of existing practice than to deliberate design, on any rational grounds, especially as his scales do not seem to vary in any regular

manner throughout, or according to the size or importance of the stops.

60. There are old German books on scales as far back as the 17th century (see Bibliography at the end); but Töpfer appears to be the first who has treated the matter systematically. He reduces the scaling within much narrower limits, and proposes for general adoption three scales only, viz. :

The ratio of 1 : 2·83 ($\sqrt{8}$), wherein the half-measure falls on the 16th pipe; the ratio of 1 : 2·66, wherein the half-measure fall on the 17th pipe; the ratio of 1 : 2·5, wherein the half-measure falls on the 18th pipe.

Of these Töpfer says : 1 : $\sqrt{8}$ is *the* scale, and his reasoning appears to be that, as the ration of 1 : 2 is an extreme in one direction, and 1 : 4 in the other, the geometrical mean $\sqrt{2 \times 4}$ will be the best scale, and we need not quarrel with the logic of this deduction, as the scales have met with general approval, though experienced voicers have their fancy for particular stops. Schulze gave his adhesion entirely to Töpfer's scales for flue-work, but not for reeds.

61. The writer has no desire to enter into the ' battle of the scales,' but only proposes to place before the reader what has been done in the matter. Since, for reasons given above, the whole question cannot be determined on a strictly mathematical basis, it may well be conceded that an experienced voicer can overcome singular irregularities in scaling ; while it may be urged that a regular scale will assist his labours, and enable artists of inferior skill to produce a tolerable result, and it seems reasonable to assume that a curve for the diameters should at least be *similar* to that for the lengths if it cannot be identical. Such a curve is given by Töpfer's method.

62. Before proceeding to a detailed consideration of how to draw scales, certain errors in works treating of the subject may be pointed out. They may fairly be called errors, in spite of the disclaimer in the last paragraph, since they produce results which are highly irregular without any advantages. Fig. 1, Pl. I., illustrates a scale given in one work. You are directed to rule up equidistant ordinates, making the first the diameter of the standard pipe, and if, say, the half-

measure is on the 18th pipe, mark off on the 18th ordinate half the height of the first. The next lot of 18 ordinates are to be half the distance apart that the first lot were, and another half-diameter is set off on the second 18th, and so on, drawing a straight line through the fixed points to get the intermediate dimensions. In the figure, the half has been taken on the 12th pipe. Another work recommends the scale shown in Fig. 3. Take a length equal to that of the longest pipe, 4' in the figure, and set off another 6" (why ?) on the base line. Then divide the 4' into 2'—1'—6", &c., successively, for the lengths of the several octaves, and erect 12 equidistant ordinates in each. Set off on the first ordinate the required dimension of the 4' pipe, and rule up a slant line from the end of the base for the dimensions of intermediate pipes.

63. Now, in both these scales there is a sudden jump, which cannot possibly be correct. In the first, the difference between the 17th and 18th pipes is double that between the 18th and 19th, if the half is taken on the 18th ; and in the second, the same jump occurs at the octaves. Clearly this cannot be right, and it remains to be shown how a scale can be drawn which will give equal gradation throughout. Readers whose mathematics are a little rusty need not be dismayed at the figures used in developing the theory ; the results will be presented in a form requiring nothing more elaborate than a foot-rule to make them available for ordinary work. What Töpfer virtually says on the subject of scale is, that, experimenting with pipes on Dom Bedos's scales, he found the results irregular and not satisfactory, both in respect of the actual range of scale and its division between successive pipes ; but that he found the proposed limits and graduation of scales satisfactory in practice after having developed the latter on a reasonable theory and having taken the former as representing a mean of existing practice.

64. Assuming that the lengths of pipes halve on the octaves, they follow a geometrical progression, the successive lengths being represented by the equidistant ordinates to a logarithmic curve, whose equation is $y = a.2^{\frac{n}{12}}$, n being the number of the pipe from that one whose length is a. Thus

the fifth pipe upwards would be $2^{\frac{5}{12}}$ times as long as the one from which the measure is taken, and the octave $2^{\frac{12}{12}}$, or simply $2a$ times as long. Reckoning downwards the index would be negative, as $a.2^{-1} = \frac{1}{2}a$. The other linear dimensions of the pipes should follow the same law, using a similar index for the curve, as $2^{\frac{n}{16}} - 2^{\frac{n}{17}}$ or $2^{\frac{n}{18}}$, as may be selected. Thus, with the first index, the double octave compared with the first pipe will be $2^{\frac{24}{16}} = 2^{\frac{3}{2}} = \sqrt{8}$, which is what Töpfer calls the ratio.

65. The practical application of these scales is as follows: Let D be the diameter or any linear dimension of the larger, and d of the smaller pipe; then—

$$d : D :: 1 : 2^{\frac{n}{m}} \qquad . \qquad . \qquad . \qquad . \qquad (1)$$

where n is the serial number of D, and m the number on which the half-measure is to fall, from which—

$$\log. D = \log. d + \frac{n}{m}\log. 2 \qquad . \qquad . \qquad . \qquad (2)$$

which formula gives at once the relative sizes downwards of any pipes on a given scale. Also the converse—

$$\log. d = \log. D - \frac{n}{m}\log. 2 \qquad . \qquad . \qquad . \qquad (3)$$

gives the sizes of the pipes upwards.

66. Another problem is, the measurement of any two pipes being given, to find the ratio in which they are scaled. We have from (2)—

$$\log. D = \log. d + z \log. 2,$$

putting z for $\frac{n}{m}$ the quantity to be found, and of which the factor n is known. Therefore—

$$z = \frac{\log. \frac{D}{d}}{\log. 2} \qquad . \qquad . \qquad . \qquad . \qquad (4)$$

and since $z = \frac{n}{m}$, $m = \frac{n}{z}$ and

$$m = \frac{n \log. 2}{\log. \frac{D}{d}} \qquad . \qquad . \qquad . \qquad . \qquad (5)$$

It may be as well to give some numerical examples of these formulæ, though really they are very simple. Take the case of (2) and suppose we want to know the diameter of the C_0 pipe of a stop whose c^1 is 2·12″ diameter, the ratio being 1 : $\sqrt{8}$, or half on the 16th pipe.

Then—   log. D = log. 2·12 + $\frac{24}{16}$ log. 2 and
$$\text{log. 2} = 0·301\ 0300$$
$$3$$
$$\overline{2)0·903\ 0900}$$
$$0·451\ 5450$$
Add log. 2·12   0·326 6063
$$\text{log. D} = 0·778\ 1513$$

the number of which is 6″.

67. The converse would be, if having a $C_0 = 6″$ diameter, we wanted to know the size of c^1 in the ratio 1 : $\sqrt{8}$. Then, by equation (3)—
$$\text{log. } d = \text{log. } 6 - \frac{24}{16} \text{ log. } 2.$$
$$\text{Log. } 6 = 0·778\ 1513$$
deduct $\frac{3}{2}$ log. 2 — 0·451 5450
$$\overline{\text{log. } d \quad 0·326\ 6063} = \text{number } 2·12.″$$

Finally, if we have $c^0 = 6″$, and $c^1 = 2·12″$, and desire to know in what ratio the stop is scaled, by (5)—
$$m = \frac{24 \times \text{log. } 2}{6}$$
$$\text{log. } 2·12$$

and—
$$\text{log. } 2 = 0·301\ 0300$$
$$24$$
$$\overline{7·224\ 7200}$$

also—
$$\text{log. } 6 = 0·778\ 1513$$
$$\text{log. } 2·12 = 0·326\ 6063$$
$$\text{log. } \frac{D}{d} 0·451\ 5450$$

and—
$$\frac{7·224}{0·451} = 16, \text{ the ratio sought.}$$

It must be observed that in this last case it is necessary, unless it is known that the pipes are made to some regular scale, to take the dimensions of *three* pipes, and see that the ratio between any two of them is the same, before you can be sure that the pipes are built to any regular scale at all. For instance, with the two irregular scales mentioned above, it would make a great difference which side of the break the test pipes happened to be measured. The reader should work out some examples to make himself familiar with the theory, but in practice he can get the dimensions ready made by reference to Appendix I., which gives the successive numbers and logarithms for the scale of lengths and for Töpfer's three pipe scales. Beyond the range given, the numbers have only to be doubled or halved; or, better still, all problems connected with scales can be directly solved by Fig. 10, Pl. II., where the dimensions of any pipe can be measured off, and from which a scale for any pipes can be traced, once the size of any one pipe and the ratio have been decided on. The scale can be extended to any size by doubling or halving from the part given.

68. It should now be pointed out that there are two ways of drawing a scale—one with equidistant ordinates and a logarithmic curve, as in Fig. 10, and the other where the base line is divided into logarithmic abscissæ, as in Fig. 2, Pl. I., when a line drawn from the first ordinate to the end of the base line will, by the principle of similar triangles, cut off the ordinates in the same ratio as that in which the base line was divided. This figure represents a Gedackt scale in the ratio 1 : 8, or half on the 15th pipe, and is constructed in the following way. Take any line AB, and bisect it in F. Divide B F into 15 logarithmic divisions, thus, C F = B F$^{\sharp\sharp}$, G F$^{\sharp\sharp}$, and so on. The first 15 having been set out, the remainder of the scale can be obtained by halving. Or the scale can be set out by taking the required logarithmic series to any scale, and setting off the consecutive numbers, to which end several logarithmic series that are likely to be useful in organ-building are given in the appendices. The base line being divided off, set up the ordinates, and marking off B D, the depth of the first pipe, join A D, then C E, &c., will give the successive depths in the ratio in which the base line was divided. Or the pipe taken may be any pipe, as the diagonal can be produced forwards to give larger dimensions than that started from. Both these

styles of scale have their advantages ; the latter is perhaps
more generally useful in the workshop, because, the base line
once divided in any ratio, any dimensions whatever in that
scale can be obtained by simply drawing a diagonal line. But
the equidistant ordinates are far the best for comparing
different scales, as it shows their deviations and irregularities
at once to the eye.

69. Another very simple way of drawing a scale with
sufficient accuracy for all practical purposes is to set off equidistant ordinates at any convenient intervals, as in Fig. 4,
Pl. I., and to mark on the first the dimensions of the largest
pipe, and half these dimensions on the ordinates corresponding
to the pipes on which the halves should fall, as shown by the
crosses. Through these points, taking three together, a fair
curve is to be drawn with a thin elastic strip of wood (called a
spline). If the half-points fall too far apart, others can be
interpolated by calculation. The scale illustrated corresponds
with Fig. 2. The writer has checked by calculation scales so
constructed, and finds them quite accurate enough. In
making the scales for wood pipes, it is recommended to set off
the double thickness of the planks below the datum, so that
the external dimensions can be scaled off at once.

70. From the above remarks, it will be understood that
no ordinates erected on a base line, divided for lengths, can
give what may be called, *pace* those who use them, a regular
scale. The linear dimensions must, from the geometrical
construction, vary as the lengths, or only differ therefrom by
an arbitrary addendum, and certainly it cannot be right that
the *diameters* of pipes should vary as their lengths, whatever
may be said in favour of proportioning the *areas* that way. A
very old, if not the oldest, plan is shown in Fig. 312, Pl.
XXXVIII., where the base line A B is divided for the lengths,
and A C being joined, the diameters of the octaves will diminish by halves. It was soon found that this would not do ;
so the practice appears to have been to set out the diameter
of the smallest pipe on its ordinate and to join that with the
first, the effect being to give an arbitrary addendum, as E F,
to the too rapidly diminishing diameters. Since it is just
as easy to draw a scale which gives a regular and known

progression, that method may safely be recommended for general adoption in preference to these devices.

71. Curiously enough, Töpfer has himself fallen into this very error, where in one place he shows how to set out the lengths of tongues in the ratio $1 : \sqrt{8}$, but the breadths and thicknesses as $1 : 2$. He directs the lengths to be set off on a base, which is consequently divided into a geometrical series, with half on the 16th pipe. On these dimensions are to be set up ordinates for the breadths and the half-breadths marked on the 24th ordinates, and joined by straight lines. This proceeding will not give a correct result for any except the dimensions actually set off.

72. One more proposal for scaling suggested by a writer in the 'English Mechanic' may be called the 'straight-line' scale, as it is directed to draw a straight line from the diameter of the first to that of the last pipe over equidistant ordinates. The enormous effect of this proposal in the middle of the scale can be seen by drawing a straight line in such a way in any of the curves given. Having due regard to the fact that, after all, scale must remain a matter of pious opinion, and due deference to the ability of the contributor who made this proposal, the writer begs to point out that a scale which assigns the same difference in diameter to two pipes 8 ft. long as to two $1\frac{1}{2}$ in. long, cannot surely be right. Since the timbre does depend mainly upon the relation of area to length, is it not reasonable to suppose that the *rate* of increase in diameters, &c., should bear some proportion to the *rate* of increase in length, instead of following an entirely different law? An actual solution of these questions will probably be obtained only by recording and comparing the shape of the sound-waves produced by different scales, as a permanent record, or by careful investigation with resonators throughout the range of a stop.

73. The ratio of the dimensions of successive pipes to each other may well be called 'relative' scale, and the choice of a dimension to start from 'absolute' scale, and the two points should always be considered together. If we take the lowest pipe as starting-point, a small-scaled pipe will naturally require a series which diminishes rather more gradually

than would be suitable for a larger one.   Thus, while Töpfer
professes to prove that the ratio 1 : $\sqrt{8}$ is the most perfect,
yet in most of the specifications given in his book he uses the
ratio 1 : 2·6̂6̂.   The ratio 1 : 2·5, which diminishes still more
slowly, is only suitable for Gedackts and Flutes, which should
avoid sharpness, particularly in the upper notes, where it is
likely to come in.   Even the ratio 1 : 3 could be used in some
such cases.

74. Hitherto scale has only been spoken of with reference
to the diameter or depth of a pipe ; but the same or similar
rules are required for all the dimensions which govern the
sound-producing parts, such as the height and width of
mouth, and its area as compared with that of the pipe body,
the area of the wind-way and that of the foot-hole.   These
dimensions react again on the diameters, so that, in choosing
the dimensions of a stop, all the circumstances must be considered together.   For instance, a C_0 pipe $4\frac{1}{4}$ in. diameter
can be voiced on a $2\frac{1}{2}$ in. wind to give a Diapason tone suitable
to a chamber organ, while the same pipe on a 4 in. wind
could be made into a fiery Geigen.   Again, the same diameter
of pipe will produce different results by merely varying the
mouth.   When spoken of without qualification, the pressure
is assumed to be 3 in., an average pressure for what may
loosely be described as 'ordinary' organs.   The reader must
not, therefore, feel disappointed that no absolute rules are
given for proportions of diameter, mouth, and voicing to meet
all cases.   In the judicious combination of these factors, and
of the different qualities of tone, lies the whole art of organ-
building, and no book can do more than illustrate the general
principles and give a few particular examples.   No formula
can be laid down to cover all cases, not to mention the variety
that exists in matters of taste.   The most useful exercise for
a student of the art is to take careful notes as to relative and
absolute scale in the organs to which he can obtain access,
with remarks on the quality of the tone, and reflections as to
what should be done to render it more perfect if found
defective.

75. The detailed list of the stops seems the most appropriate place in which to give what may be called limiting

dimensions for each. Here we propose rather to develop the principles governing the size of the different parts of a pipe. As the tone generally depends upon the area of body and the size of mouth, so far as construction is concerned,[1] it is immaterial what is the shape of the cross-section so long as the same proportions in these respects are observed. The standard width of mouth for a metal pipe is one-quarter the circumference, and from this it follows that a rectangular pipe, when the mouth occupies the whole front, should have the same depth as the diameter of the cylindrical one, and a width of one-quarter its circumference. Thus, taking a metal pipe of 3 in. diameter, the area is 7·07, and the circumference 9·42, of which a quarter is 2·355. If we make a rectangular pipe to correspond, dimensioned as above, we have an area of $3 \times 2{\cdot}355 = 7{\cdot}065$, and a width of mouth the same as above. But all mouths are not $\frac{1}{4}$ the circumference; they are sometimes as much as $\frac{2}{7}$ and as small as $\frac{1}{5}$, in which case a special calculation would have to be made if the rectangular pipe is required to have a mouth the full width of the front. As, however, there is no occasion for this, Fig. 9, Pl. II., will be found to supply all the information required for any variety of pipe, as it gives the widths corresponding to the quarter-circumference of a given diameter, and in dotted lines the width corresponding to $\frac{1}{5}$ the circumference. The $\frac{2}{7}$ mouth is almost exactly the side of the square, and in such a case it is sufficient to make the wood pipe square with the mouth the full width. Schultze preferred to make all his wood pipes square, with a mouth occupying part of the front, a good reason for this being that the unsupported width of plank is reduced to a minimum. Much of the quality of tone of a large pipe depends upon the planks being fully strong, and it is obvious that when all four sides are the same width, the best possible result as to firmness will be obtained, as in contrast to the case where, perhaps, the depth is twice the width.

[1] It is only in general terms that this statement is true. For the more delicate *nuances* of tone there *is* a difference between a rectangular and a cylindrical pipe of equal areas, mouths, and the same material. It is a fact that the exact quality of tone of a bored Travers Flute cannot be got out of a square pipe by the best voicer; but the difference is not one that would be appreciated by an ordinary observer, nor would it be appreciable below c^1.

76. Before dismissing the subject of equivalent metal and wood pipes—for this is practically what rectangular and cylindrical mean—it should be noted that where in the same stop a change is made from metal to wood, the wooden pipe should be about two pipes smaller than the metal one would have been. As the tone for the same size is slightly duller, the sharpness caused by diminishing the scale compensates for this. If this is done, and the proper proportions observed, it is possible to join wood and metal in *any* stop—even a Gamba—so that the junction is not perceptible to the nicest ear. Those who do not believe this statement (and they are probably many) can satisfy themselves by an inspection of Schultze's organ at St. Peter's Church, Hindley, Wigan, or any other of his organs where he has used metal and wood together.

The particular use of Fig. 9 is to convert the dimensions of a metal pipe into those of the corresponding wooden one. If, for instance, a wood bass is required for an open Diapason, take, on a rule, the diameter of the pipe at the change, and read off the corresponding width on that line; or if the pipe is to be square, read that dimension off on the proper line, and the mouth width on its line. So also for a Geigen, with a $\frac{2}{7}$ mouth, to get the size for the wooden pipe, read off the corresponding side of square, and make the mouth the full width. Or for a Salicional, which generally has a $\frac{1}{5}$ mouth, it can be made either square or rectangular, the width of mouth being taken from the $\frac{1}{5}$ line.

77. It has been generally stated above that the timbre of a pipe depends principally upon the diameter; but this must be qualified by a reference to the pressure of wind. The smaller the scale, the sharper the tone, but the stronger the wind also, the sharper the tone with the same diameter; therefore, by increasing the pressure alone, the note can be sharpened in timbre as well as in pitch. Hence the necessity for considering all the circumstances in settling the size of a pipe. Töpfer, who has made careful experiments in all matters connected with the speech of pipes, has laid down the following principles and voluminous tables, which, if not strictly applicable in all cases, are at least the only serious

information we have on the subject in a connected form. His coefficients also are deduced from actual experiments on pipes in organs, and not from samples, and on that account are more likely to be serviceable than would a purely theoretical discussion based upon data which cannot be realised in building.

78. The main principles which he lays down are as follows:

(a) With pipes of equal length, but different diameters, to produce the same tone, the quantity of wind must vary as their areas.

This statement, and all others of a similar nature, must only be held true within quite narrow limits, for it is impossible to get a similar tone from pipes of the same pitch, but very different diameters, by any process whatever.

(b) With pipes of equal areas, but different lengths, for equal tone the wind supply must be in the inverse ratio of the $\sqrt{}$ of the lengths.

This statement must also be received with caution. It is quite true for Töpfer's experiment, which was cutting a small scale pipe to half and quarter length, and noting the wind-supply required to produce an equal tone; but it might not hold good in any practical case, in which the mouths of two such different pipes would scarcely be identical.

79. The notation used in the following discussion is:

—	For the Larger Pipe	For the Smaller
Diameter	D	d
Length (double if a stopped pipe)	L	l
Area of cross section .	A	a
Mouth area	M	m
Wind supply	Q	q

Then $q : Q = \sqrt{L} : \sqrt{l}$, when D is constant . . . i.

and $q : Q = d^2 : D^2 = a : A$, when L is constant . . . ii.

and $q : Q = \dfrac{d^2}{\sqrt{l}} : \dfrac{D^2}{\sqrt{L}} = \dfrac{a}{\sqrt{l}} : \dfrac{A}{\sqrt{L}}$, when D and L vary . iii.

Then if n be taken as a numerical coefficient for the discharge, so that—

$$q = \frac{nd^2}{\sqrt{l}},\ \text{so also will}\ Q = \frac{nD^2}{\sqrt{L}}.\qquad\qquad \text{iv.}$$

Putting, further, a for the area of the windway, and V for the theoretical speed of the wind due to the pressure—

$$q \text{ or } Q = 0.8 \, a \, V \qquad . \qquad . \qquad . \qquad . \qquad \text{v.}$$

where 0·8 is the coefficient for friction, found experimentally to vary from 0·7 to 0·8, the larger pipes having less resistance than the smaller. The above equations and their derivatives give the relations between the wind supply and the pipes.

80. The mouth must next be considered in relation to variations in the length, diameter of area, and wind supply. The cases are :

(a) Wind supply and lengths equal, but areas different. In this case it will be found that if, as is usually the case, the width of mouth follows the diameters, the mouth of the wider pipe will have to be cut so much lower as to make its area pretty nearly equal to that of the smaller, so that in this case the size of mouth does not depend upon area.

(b) Equal lengths, but varying areas, and wind supply proportional to them. In this case the mouths will be proportional to the areas, and consequently to the wind supply.

(c) The same length and area, but different wind supply. Here the mouths must be proportional to the wind supply—a fact practically illustrated in voicing by a pipe overblowing when the wind-pressure has been increased until the mouth has been cut up.

(d) The same area and wind supply, but different lengths. Here the mouths are required to vary as the $\sqrt{}$ of the lengths —a fact which will be prominently brought to the notice of any person indiscreet enough to cut up the mouth of a pipe, in order to make it speak promptly, until it is known to be of the right pitch—i.e. length.

81. We have then the following expressions :
Equal length and varying wind supply

$$m : M = q : Q \qquad . \qquad . \qquad . \qquad . \qquad \text{vi.}$$

Equal wind and varying length

$$m : M = \sqrt{l} : \sqrt{L} \, . \qquad . \qquad . \qquad . \qquad \text{vii.}$$

Length and wind both unequal

$$m : M = q\sqrt{l} : Q\sqrt{L} \qquad . \qquad . \qquad . \qquad \text{viii.}$$

and if r be taken as a coefficient, such that $m = \dfrac{q\sqrt{l}}{r}$,

then also $M = \dfrac{Q\sqrt{L}}{r}$.   .   .   .   .   . ix.

And if for pipes the wind varies as the area, and in-
versely as $\sqrt{}$ of the lengths, $\dfrac{n\,D^2}{\sqrt{L}}$ from iv., can be

substituted for Q, from which in ix., $M = \dfrac{n\,D^2}{r}$. x.

so that in this case the mouths are proportional to the areas
of the pipes.

From v. the windway, $a = \dfrac{Q}{0\cdot 8\,V}$, so that if from ix. $\dfrac{r\,M}{\sqrt{L}}$ is

put for Q, then $a = \dfrac{r\,M}{0\cdot 8\,V\sqrt{L}}$.   .   .   .   . xi.

In every well-regulated scale, areas and mouths will vary
in the same ratio, so from ix., $q : Q = \dfrac{rm}{\sqrt{l}} : \dfrac{rM}{\sqrt{L}}$, so that if q is
put equal to Q, $m : M = \sqrt{l} : \sqrt{L}$, or the mouths vary as the
square roots of the lengths, when these are the only variables.
So if m varies, $q : Q = m : M$, or the wind consumption of
pipes of equal length varies as their mouth, or as their body,
areas.

And if the mouth area (and cross section) are constant,
$q : Q = \sqrt{L} : \sqrt{l}$, or the quantity of wind varies inversely as
the $\sqrt{}$ of the lengths.

82. For practical purposes, the equations most concerned
are $Q = \dfrac{n\,D^2}{\sqrt{L}}$ from iv., or, if the mouth is in question,

$Q = \dfrac{rM}{\sqrt{L}}$ from ix., and Töpfer conducted an elaborate series of
experiments to determine the values of these coefficients, of
which full particulars are given in his valuable work. It will
be sufficient to note his conclusions, remarking that the wind
pressure of the organ experimented on was 3 in. bare. The
Open Diapason for a not very penetrating yet powerful tone
gave n about the middle as 76, and the Geigen gave 93·4 for
a very energetic tone. In relation to the mouth, the Open
gave $r = 425$ at the middle, for a moderately fresh speech,

the variation being from 358 to 486, and the Geigen gave
458. The small scaled pipes gave an average of $n = 100$ and
$r = 487$, the exponent of the ratio of areas to mouths varying
rom 0·24 to 0·28. The tone of these stops was very stringy,
as well as strong and penetrating. In the stopped pipes the
average was $n = 92·5$ and $r = 332$. As to which of the two
coefficients is most useful—that is, whether the pipe should
be designed for a given tone from the mouth, or from the
diameter—Töpfer remarks that the wind stands in the closest
relation to the mouth, and can only be compared with the
diameter when that is scaled in an even ratio with the mouth.
In his experiments, the coefficients relating to the diameters
exhibited more anomalies than did those referring to the
mouth. It would seem better, then, to use the latter to find
the proper wind supply, and the former only as a check.

83. From the above-mentioned proportions, Töpfer pro-
fessed to show that the ratio $1 : \sqrt{8}$ is that which meets the
conditions of equal timbre (supposing always that his equations do really represent these conditions). For, from iv.,
$q = n\, \dfrac{d^2}{\sqrt{l}}$ is the relation between wind supply and pipe dimensions for an even tone, and assuming as he does that the
lower octave requires a double supply of wind, the equation
for the second lower octave will be $4\,q = n\, \dfrac{D^2}{\sqrt{4}\,l}$, so that
$4n\dfrac{d^2}{\sqrt{l}} = n\, \dfrac{D^2}{2\sqrt{l}}$, which reduces to $8d^2 = D^2$ or $d : D :: 1 : \sqrt{8}$.
But if there are so many assumptions in the whole train of
reasoning that it cannot be regarded as mathematical proof,
still we should be none the less grateful to Töpfer for the
empirical formulæ and coefficients established by so much
labour, from which some idea can certainly be obtained of the
proportions required to produce the wished-for result, and
which form a standpoint for further research, The tables he
has worked out for the three ratios have been recalculated in
English measures, and are given in Appendix VI., of which
any column can be used, starting at any place, to furnish a
series of numbers for any purpose of the given ratio as well
as that for which the columns are headed.

84. Assuming, as he does, that $1 : \sqrt{8}$ is *the* ratio which gives the most equal tone throughout the scale, Töpfer remarks that as circumstances may make other scales desirable, he gives two others, $1 : 2\frac{2}{3}$ and $1 : 2\frac{1}{2}$, which will give good results, and that any slight irregularity of tone caused by the scale can be remedied by a slight alteration of the mouth. In these he takes c^1 as the standard pipe of what he calls the 'normal diapason scale,' of the same dimension in each, and produces the scale upwards and downwards from that pipe. Thus the bass of the latter scales is successively smaller, and the treble larger, than in the first, and Töpfer proposes to remedy this supposed defect by using the ratio $1 : \sqrt{8}$ for the height of mouth, thus gradually raising it towards the bass, and lowering towards the treble, so that the same figures are used for the height of the mouth in all three scales. Whether his view is correct or not is not a matter of much importance, as in practice the height of the mouth would be adjusted to the taste of the voicer, and for each variation of wind pressure.

It will be observed that the column 'Width of Mouth' gives the width of a rectangular pipe whose depth is the same as the diameter of a metal pipe, and the column 'Side of Square' gives the side of a square of equal area to the circle, should that shape be preferred for the wooden pipe, thus putting into figures what Fig. 9, Pl. II., gives in the shape of a diagram.

85. As to the absolute size of mouth for different qualities of tone, Töpfer has, after experiment, made the following recommendations. The normal mouth for Diapason tone is a quarter of a circumference in width and a quarter of the diameter in height, its area thus being just a quarter of that of the pipe. For $\frac{1}{4} \times \frac{\pi D^2}{4} = \frac{\pi D}{4} \times \frac{D}{4}$, and the ratio of the height to the width is thus $1 : \pi$, or a little less than $\frac{1}{3}$.

With increasing size of the foundation work, the mouth area requires to be diminished to $\frac{2}{3}$, or even to $\frac{1}{6}$, of that of the pipe, retaining always the standard width, so that the heights will be respectively those fractions of the diameter, and will be to the widths as $2 : 7$ and $1 : 4$ nearly.

For delicate stops the mouth area may be one-fifth to
one-sixth that of the body, and in such cases the width is
better made one-fifth of the circumference, when the heights
will be respectively one-fourth and $\frac{5}{24}$, or, say, one-fifth of
the diameter, and their ratios to the widths as $1 : 2\frac{1}{2}$ and
$1 : 3$ nearly.

For flute work, on the other hand, the mouth area should
be one-third of the body area, when, with the standard width,
the height will be one-third the diameter, and its ratio to the
width as $3 : 7$ nearly.   There are exceptions to this, such as
the Travers Flute, which has a very small and peculiar mouth.
As a special case, a mouth two-sevenths the circumference is
used for Gedackts and for Geigens, and Schultze has even
used it in Diapason work, adding beards or fenders below the
mouth.   This width is near enough to be taken as the side of
a square wooden pipe, and is recommended where power is
required.   There is a difference of opinion among equally
competent authorities as to whether this extra width demands a
corresponding lowering of the height, as indicated by Töpfer's
theory.   The voicer had better follow the practice which he
finds succeeds best with him.   Wide mouths are always more
difficult to voice than medium ones.

86. Töpfer sums up the use of his coefficients n and r in
the following table, which gives the most useful limits of
wind-pressure and tone-quality; intermediate values can be
supplied by interpolation:

—	2·76 in.	Wind	3·7 in.	Wind
	n	r	n	r
For medium strength and sharpness .	74	376	85	432
Medium strength, but sharp . .	74	422	85	485
Strong and sharp . . .	82·7	422	95·4	485
Very sharp and strong . . .	82·7	475	95·4	548

He considers n as the coefficient on which to calculate the
wind consumption for *strength* in the equation $Q = n \dfrac{D^2}{\sqrt{L}}$, and
then equating to this $\dfrac{rM}{\sqrt{L}}$, with a number for r that corresponds to the desired degree of sharpness, M is obtained,

and the width of mouth being known, the height is found.
The process can easily be understood from the first two
entries in the table above. Here $n=74$ and $r=376$ for an
ordinary diapason tone; but should it be required to produce
a tone more approaching that of a Geigen, but of the same
strength, the larger number for r is taken, which consequently
diminishes M, the mouth area, and as the width remains
constant, the height is suitably diminished.

87. As an illustration, take the case of an Open Diapason
$C_o = 6$ in. diam., then $Q=74\frac{6^2}{\sqrt{L}}=376\frac{M}{\sqrt{L}}$. As we only want
M, we omit the solution for Q, and consequently at once
$M=\frac{74 \times 36}{376}$, and as the breadth of mouth is always a quarter
of the circumference, 4·71 in this case, the height $=\frac{74 \times 36}{376 \times 4·71}$
$=1·5$, or a quarter of the diameter. But if we take the
higher value for r, the height$=\frac{74 \times 36}{422 \times 4·71} = 1·34$, or $\frac{2}{9}$ the
diameter. This theoretical investigation is not altogether
useless, as presenting in an orderly way some of the principal
facts connected with the speech of pipes; but in practice
nobody is ever likely to calculate the amount of wind a pipe
should use, and from that deduce the width of windway.
The voicer would set the windway to suit his taste for loudness, and cut up the mouth to suit his idea of the sharpness
required. As an idea of the difference in tone due to wind-
pressure, Töpfer gives it that an Open Diapason C_o 6½ in. diameter has, if cut up ¼ the diameter, very little keenness on
a 2¾ in. wind, but gets quite stringy on a 3¾ in. wind. If
the pipe is cut up only $\frac{2}{9}$ the diameter, the tone is middling
strong and stringy on a 2¾ in. wind, and comes near overblowing at 3¼ in. This statement is very doubtful, as it is
not probable that such a large-scaled pipe would think of
over-blowing on a 3¼ in. wind, even with a $\frac{2}{9}$ mouth, when
voiced for a Diapason tone.

88. It should be observed, in using these coefficients, that
by reducing n absolutely, r is reduced in the same ratio,
though the mouth may remain unchanged; in other words, a

pipe, even with a low mouth, can be deprived of freshness by
plugging the foot.   A limitation of r should also be pointed
out—viz., that in very small scale pipes (not being Flutes) the
given values of r may produce a result for the height of mouth
greater than ¼-diameter, which quantity, however, must never
be exceeded.   In such cases, r must be supposed greater than
the table gives.   The average values given by Töpfer for n and
r for different stops and 3¼ in. wind are :

Stop	n	r	Stop	n	r
Open Diapason .	{ 83·2 { 101	{ 353 { 475	Gemshorn . .	67	404
			Spitz Flute . .	67	392
Pedal or large Open	72	455	Flutes . . .	{ 58 { 63	323
Geigen . . .	101	480			
Gamba . .	{ 77·2 { 117	{ 487 { 488	Quint . . .	63	404
			Quintadena . .	63	404
Viola . .	91	303	Gedackt . .	{ 75·6 { 83·2	{ 353 { 333
Salicional . .	91	480			
Violone . .	91	460			

The quantity for different wind-pressures must, of course,
vary in proportion to the theoretical speed of the flowing air,
as given in Appendix VII.   Finally, Töpfer derives from these
experiments an empirical formula for the diameter of the foot-
hole, which, converted for all dimensions in inches, is—

$$\text{Diameter} = \sqrt{\frac{1\cdot6536\, n\, D^2}{V\sqrt{L}}} = \sqrt{\frac{1\cdot6536\, r\, M}{V\sqrt{L}}}$$

where V is the velocity due to the difference in pressure in
pipe-foot and in wind-chest—a diminution which Töpfer considers permissible up to 0·452 in. for C_3 and 0·046 in. for c^5.

89. Cavaillé-Coll's formula for pipe lengths has been
alluded to above ; but as the question of length forms one of
the points to be considered in pipe design, it should be explicitly noticed here.   Theoretically, the length of an open
pipe is half the wave-length—that is, half the speed of sound
divided by the (complete) vibration number of the note ; but
this assumes that the pipe is infinitely small.   Töpfer has
made some suggestions for calculating length, based on the
observation of Bernouilli, that the node in a pipe does really
lie at a half wave-length (segment ?) from the *top*, whatever
the diameter, and that consequently the cause of deviation.

from theoretical length must be sought in the mouth and
other disturbing influences of the bottom half; but these calculations are not exact, and for practical use present no
advantages over a purely empirical formula, such as that of
Cavaillé-Coll, which gives, where L=length, V=velocity of
sound, N= number of single vibrations per second, P=depth
of square pipe, D=diameter, d=a smaller diameter as in a
conical pipe, $L = \frac{V}{N} - 2\,P$, $L = \frac{V}{N} - \frac{5}{3}\,D$, $L = \frac{V}{N} - \frac{D+d}{2}$.

For a stopped pipe, the length is found by subtracting a
quarter the theoretical wave-length from the length of an open
pipe of the same diameter.

90. Another form of the Cavaillé-Coll formula is given by
the translator in the English edition of Helmholtz—viz., for
a temperature of 59° Fahr., and a wind-pressure of 3¼ in.
dimensions in inches, to find the pitch in complete vibrations,
divide 20,080 by—

(1) For cylindrical open pipes, three times the length +
five times the diameter.

(2) For cylindrical stopped pipes, six times the length +
ten times the diameter.

(3) For square open pipes, three times the length + six
times the depth.

(4) For square stopped pipes, half the length of the open.

As 20,080 in. is the speed of sound increased by ⅓, it appears that this addendum has been made both to the speed
and pipe-length simply to get the correction for diameters in
round numbers. It is also noted that from 2¾ in. to 3¼ in.
wind the pitch rises one vibration in 300, and from 3¼ in. to
4 in., 1 in 400, and the following practical rule is given for
variation due to temperature—viz., the pitch number is P
$(1 \pm \cdot 00104 d)$; where P is the pitch number at a known temperature, and d the difference of temperature in degrees
Fahrenheit. The reason alleged for varying the formulæ
between square and round pipes is, that the flattening of the
lips affects the result (by diminishing the cube of the body);
but the principle does not appear to be followed in the case of
conical pipes, nor is any allowance made for the very appreciable

influence of the size of mouth, so that the formulæ can only be taken for quite rough approximations.

91. The tables for windway and wind consumption in App. VI. are calculated for a full Diapason tone, wherein Töpfer's coefficients of n and r are taken at 356 and 1,800 respectively. Töpfer completes his direction for pipe-scaling with a regular series of foot-holes, which are given as App. IX. Starting from any number, the regular order should be observed; the sizes are given in columns of octaves for whole tones, and the number marked with an asterisk is that assigned by him to c^1 of the normal Diapason measure. Looking at the three series of App. VI., it will be seen how the choice of a size of pipe to start with must influence the choice of the relative scale. If we start with a large scale in the bass, the more rapid diminution of the series $1 : \sqrt{8}$ is compensated by the actually larger size of pipes, while a more moderate absolute scale to start with demands the more gradual diminution of the two latter scales. The writer has a preference, based on considerable experience, for the middle scale, but does not find it necessary to vary the ratio of the height of mouth in the way proposed by Töpfer. It is quite sufficient to set the proportion of height to width once for all in the middle of the scale, and to preserve the same proportion throughout. The last scale, $1 : 2 \cdot 6$, is best suited for Gedackts and Flutes, which should be free from sharpness in the upper notes, though some experienced voicers do not like to vary the scales of different stops in the same organ.

92. Appendix V. is a selection of scales for different stops given by Töpfer. Those in the ratio $1 : \sqrt{8}$ are admitted by him to be very large, being after the model of Herr Haas, who had a preference that way, in the Basle Cathedral organ (what would he have said to the scales of English village church organs !). Those in the ratio $1 : 2\frac{2}{3}$ are more moderate, and may be called a fair average. Töpfer's own table only gives 5·8 in. diameter for C_o as the normal Diapason in the $1 : \sqrt{8}$ series, and $5\frac{1}{2}$ in the $1 : 2\frac{2}{3}$ series; but of these matters further details will be given in the chapter on Stops.

CHAPTER IV.—*continued.*

(b) *PIPES—SCALE OF REEDS*

93. If with flue pipes there is no rigid mathematical proof of the best scale, still less is this the case with reeds, where the acoustic properties of both the tongues and bodies have to be considered, and even, as will be seen further on, the feet of the pipes acquire in some cases an influence on the speech. It is well to get a general idea of the behaviour of reeds before going into the details of construction. First, then, a free reed, as in harmoniums, will give a musical note without any body at all, though, indeed, the note may not be worth much, from slowness of speech and want of body ; but a striking reed will not give any musical note without a body to act as resonator, and the note of this body must bear some definite relation to that of the tongue. The smaller a free reed is, the better it will speak without a body : but even in this class the influence of the body profoundly modifies the speech of the tongue, and becomes more necessary as that becomes larger and more powerful. The make of the reed pipe settles the shape of the body, which must have a comparatively small diameter in order to enter the block ; but from here it may expand gradually in a conical shape, as in a Trumpet, or cone with a bell, as in the Oboe, or at once into a cylinder, as in the Clarinet or Vox Humana.

94. In general terms, the laws respecting free tongues are as follows. The pitch depends upon the length (or, more correctly, to cover the case of loaded tongues, upon the radius of gyration) and thickness of the tongue, width having practically no influence. With equal thickness the pitch varies inversely as the square root of the length, and with equal length it varies directly as the thickness—that is to say, the

longer a tongue is, the fewer vibrations it will make in a given time ; but the thicker it is, the more vibrations.

Although Töpfer gives many tables for the size of tongues, he does not offer any formula for calculating the pitch or vibration period of a tongue, and it would appear that he started from some approved tongue, and deduced the dimensions of the others by the rule just quoted.

95. The formula for the vibration period of a flat bar or spring of uniform section, such as a free reed tongue, is given (in Weisbach's ' Mechanics ') as—

$$t = \frac{l^2}{h} \sqrt{\frac{4 \cdot 2579 \; r}{E \cdot g}},$$

where t is the time in seconds of a whole vibration, l=length, h=thickness, r=weight of unit volume, E=modulus of elasticity, and g=32·2 ft. × 12. Since E is generally given in

No.	Length of body	Note of whole pipe	Note of body	Difference	Wind Pressure	Pitch with constant pres. of 2·38 in.	Timbre
I.	II.	III.	IV.	V.	VI.	VII.	
	in.				in.		
0	—	278	—	—	2·52	278	Clear, sharp tone
1	18·5	275	340	65	2·45	269	Louder, but still sharp and unpleasant
2	19·5	271	315	44	2·8	267	Louder, but still sharp and unpleasant
3	20·5	266	297	31	2·88	263	Louder, but still sharp and unpleasant
4	21·5	261	287	26	2·92	247	Tone improves
5	22·5	256	278	22	3·12	249	Round good tone
6	23·5	246	269	23	3·21	239	Round good tone
7	24·5	235	260·	25	3·08	229	Tone becomes dull
8	25·5	225	251	26	2·94	220	Still duller and smothered
9	26·5	220	242	22	2·94	213	Rattling and weak
10	27·5	217	—	—	2·94	208	Rattling and weak
11	28·5	272	—	—	2·32	272	Over-blows, with pitch and timbre of No. 2
12	29·5	267	—	—	2·45	268	Like No. 3, but fuller

pounds on an inch area, the units must be taken in pounds, inches, and seconds. The factor 4·2579 is only applicable to the case of the slowest possible vibrations—viz., those answering to the fundamental note ; but this is, of course, what is required in practice. Taking the usual value of E for brass, the writer has compared the results of this formula with

Töpfer's tables for tongues; but the correspondence is not very close, the discrepancy, perhaps, being due to a wrong value of E, which is by far the largest factor; or Töpfer's tongues may not give the exact pitch of the pipe, allowing for the lowering effect of the body, a point explained hereafter. It would be necessary, before using this formula for tongues, to first calculate the E of the metal used, by counting the vibrations from a tongue of known dimensions; but, in any practical case, it is probably better to start with an experimental tongue. As for beating reeds, it is probable that the influence of the body in establishing the pitch of the pipe is paramount.

96. It is not the tongue itself which gives the note: a harmonium tongue set in motion by mechanical means, or a tuning-fork, gives only a poor note; the resonating body is the column of air, to which the tongue only serves as a regulator to establish a series of rhythmical vibrations. Naturally, therefore, a reed with a body gives a finer note than one without, because the vibrating air mass is larger and more compact. The curve of the tongue also modifies the note in the case of beating reeds. A straight tongue, that in shutting closed at once the reed, would give a hard and unpleasant tone; and tongues are always made with a gradual curve, for which, however, no measurements can be given, the execution depending upon the skill of the voicer.

To compare what takes place in striking and in free reeds, let us follow them from rest through a whole vibration, beginning at the natural position of the tongue, which in the striking reed is at the furthest point from the reed to which the draft draws it right up.

1. Phase. Slow motion of tongue from neutral position to outward limit—maximum air flow.

1. Phase. Tongue moves towards reed—diminution of air flow.

2. Phase. Tongue strikes and stops—wind stopped.

3. Phase. Tongue recoils outwards—wind flow begins.

On the other hand, the free tongue lies just above its reed, with the under surface clear of the upper surface of the reed, and the following phases are exhibited:

1. Phase.   Slow inward motion of tongue to rest—minimum wind flow.

2. Phase.   Outward motion—wind flow increases.

3. Phase.   Outward rest—maximum air flow.

4. Phase.   Return—wind flow diminishes.

97. A point of difference between free reeds without bodies, and striking reeds, is that the former do not alter their pitch with variations of wind pressure (this is not exactly true), but merely increase the amplitude of the vibrations, and thereby the loudness of the sound, while the latter rise in pitch with increase of pressure, just as do flue pipes. The ' Expression ' stop in harmoniums is merely a contrivance for cutting off the reservoir of the bellows, and allowing the feet to supply the wind direct from the feeders with varying degrees of pressure. The same contrivance could not be applied to the reeds of an organ, which would all go out of tune. The explanation of this is that the size of the free tongue is twice or three times that of a striking tongue, and thus opposes more inertia against any change. Further, the free tongue, swinging as it does backwards and forwards, acquires greater amplitude, and will resist any interference with its own vibration. The striking tongue, on the other hand, is not only weaker, but at every stroke its momentum is extinguished, and leaves the tongue ready to receive an impulse from the wind, which may differ in measure from the foregoing extinguished vibrations.

98. The puffs of air thus alternately admitted and cut off set the whole column in vibration ; but this is not a simple vibration as of a smooth wave, but a very complex one, giving harmonics, in which reeds are peculiarly rich. Indeed, it is to the superabundance of these and their relative intensity in the higher range that the snarling tone of harmoniums is due, as partial tones up to the 20th can be detected with a resonator, and some of these are within a semitone of each other and so create a horrible discord. Broad tongues have a better tone than narrow ones, being less influenced and twisted about by the wind, which thus causes complex vibrations and numerous and dissonant harmonics. Töpfer has made many experiments on actual reed pipes, using different

bodies to ascertain their effect on the pitch and character of
the note.   The table in § 95 shows the results of one made
with a c^1 Trumpet, to which 12 bodies, of the lengths figured,
were fitted.   All the bodies were 3 in. diameter at the top, and
their natural notes are given in the 4th column.   These can
be ascertained by using the tubes as resonators.

99. The results are better expressed in the diagram,
Fig. 51, Pl. VIII., where the ordinates give the lengths of
body reduced to one-fifth, and the abscissæ represent the vibration numbers.   Here it can be seen how the increasing length
of body compels the tongue to depart from its natural vibrations and deepen in pitch, until at No. 11 it will not stand any
more, but over-blows, and jumps back to nearly where it
started from.   The line $a\,b\,c\,d$ represents this series; $e\,f$
represents the curve of the lengths and vibrations of the
bodies and their own notes so far as the diagram reaches,
and $g\,h$ the line of theoretical wave-lengths.   The above
results were, however, obtained under the varying wind-
pressures given in column 6, as found to be most suitable to
each occasion ; but as for organ-work it is necessary to use a
constant pressure, column 7 gives this result, which is plotted
in the diagram as the line $k\,l\,m$.   From this diagram Töpfer
deduces that the points of favourable speech are indicated by
the correspondence of the pipe-tone (line $a\,b$) to the body-tone
(line $e\,f$), as the points 5 and 6 thereon lie nearest to and
follow the same curve.   The distance between the same
marked points on the lines $k\,m$ and a—d give the amount
of difference between the note of the body itself and that of
the whole pipe.

100. A point requiring investigation was that of wind
consumption, as possibly throwing some light upon the behaviour of the pipe.   It will be observed that it reached a
maximum at the point of best speech, fell off, and rose again
after overblowing in a second series.   The behaviour of the
tongue was investigated by means of a small mirror stuck on
its tip, which received and reflected light through a glass
window in the boot ; and the motion of this spark of light
gave a bright line on a screen, whose length corresponded
to the amplitude of the vibrations of the tongue.   From

experiment 0 to 6 this line held much about the same length
(1·29 in.) ; but at 10, where the tone had gone bad, it was
reduced to 0·98 in., returning to its original length so soon as
overblowing took place.   Thus it will be seen that the wind
consumption does not depend upon the amplitude of vibrations
of the tongue, since the wind differs considerably between 0
and 6, while the tongue movement is the same ; while from
6 to 10 the tongue movement varies by 27 per cent., but the
wind consumption only by 9 per cent.   The explanation is,
that the phases of vibration of the air column in the body
do not coincide with those of the tongue.   The wind consumption depends upon the difference in pressure inside and
outside the reed. If a condensation of the air column in the body
takes place at the moment of the tongue being opened, the
flow is opposed ; but if a rarefaction occurs at that moment,
it is hastened.   That the bottom of a reed pipe is a node, or
place of condensation, is proved by connecting the space
behind the tongue—the interior of the reed—with a wind-
gauge, when the movement of the water shows this to be the
case.   On this Töpfer likens a reed pipe to a Gedackt turned
upside-down and blown at the stopper, as the same experiment
can be performed by connecting that end with a wind-gauge
through a hole in the stopper.   A free tube will not produce
the result, because the rarefactions will balance the condensations ; but if a small slit in a plate be covered with a thin
membrane to act as a valve and allow the condensations only
to pass, the water column will be affected.

101. Thus the reed pipe is the reverse of a flue-pipe, and
there is no true analogy between the tongue and the sheet of
wind issuing from the mouth of a flue pipe, nor between the state
of the air column in each.   The air column in the open flue
pipe, set in motion by the sheet of wind, shapes a node in the
middle of its body, or, if a closed pipe, at the upper end.
With the reed pipe, the impulses proceed from the closed end
in a series of rarefactions and condensations, so that the
operation closely resembles that which takes place in a siren.
Töpfer illustrates the phases of a reed pipe by a diagram, as
given in Fig. 45, Pl. VIII.   Here at a is the reed open, a condensation at the bottom of the body, and an inward motion

from above. At *b* the reed is getting closed, the condensation has died away, and an outward motion begins at top. At *c*, the tongue has closed the reed, a rarefaction takes place at bottom of the body, and outward motion continues at top, and at *d* a neutral state returns below, with an inward motion at top.

Figs. 46 to 50 are Töpfer's representation of the relations between the vibrations of the body of air, of the tongue, and of the whole combined. In each the upper part indicates the vibration of the body, the middle part that of the wind impulses admitted by the tongue, and the lower part the combined impulses of the upper two. In Fig. 46 the vibration periods are as 3 : 4, in Fig. 47 as 4 : 5, in Fig. 48 as 1 : 1, in Fig. 49 as 5 : 4, and in Fig. 50 as 6 : 4. In Fig. 48 the resultant motion is regular, and the two sets of vibration strengthen each other. In Figs. 47 and 49 the maximum lies out of the middle of the wave, and this irregular shape indicates high, and consequently dissonant, upper tones. The same effect is intensified in Fig. 46, while in Fig. 50 there are two maxima of condensation, and the tone will rattle.

102. From the above, it may be concluded that the body of a reed-pipe should be of such a size that its own natural note, or period of vibration of the inclosed air-column (considering it as a cone stopped at the point), should give the note desired for the pipe, so that the tongue should act, not upon its own note, but upon that of the body (including the reed). But the natural period of vibration of the tongue must stand in a proper ratio to that of the upper part, since upon this concordance depends the timbre of the note.

As in the first series of experiments with bodies of equal upper size, the larger would be disproportionately small, and the upper equally big in comparison with the middle, and the tone might be expected to depend upon the angular opening of the cone, Töpfer conducted a second series of experiments with bodies all of which had an angular aperture of 7° 15', as set forth in the table on next page. The note of the tongue without a body was given in the last table as 278 vibrations.

Fig. 52, Pl. VIII., is the plot of the series, *a b* and *c d* being the curves of the body note, which, it will be observed, is itself

stated to over-blow—that is to say, Nos. 4 and 12 give the
same note, although the latter is double the length of the
former.   A deeper note can be detected in the longer body,
but the one entered is the predominant one; *e f* is the curve
of the pipe tone, which has two maxima of resonance and two

No.	Body		Note of Pipe	
	Length	Note		
	in.			
1	8·85	—	—·	Sharp tone
2	9·8	290	291	—
3	10·8	276	286	First max. of resonance
4	11·8	265	276	Tone dead and weak
5	12·8	—	291	—
6	13·8	- -	290	Over-blows
7	15·8	—·	287	A little fuller than No. 2
8	17·6	331	288	—
9	19·6	300	285	—·
10	20·8	285	277	—
11	21·8	274	271	—
12	22·4	265	265	Second max. of resonance
13	23·8	258	258	·-·
14	25·6	246	246	—
15	27·6	—·	295	Over-blows

periods of overblowing, and the same would occur at the three
or four fold lengths.   The first period of resonance is inferior
to the second in that the vibrating mass is smaller, and the
third recurring maximum would be better still.   It will be re-
marked that the curve of the body note only meets the curve
of the pipe note in the second or overblown series.

103. The deduction from this experiment is, that a striking
reed gives the best resonance for lengths of bodies which correspond to a quarter of the wave-length, or some multiple of the
same.   The natural note of the above pipe corresponds to a
length of 11·25 in., or a trifle more than that of the corresponding Gedackt.

An overlong wave-length divides itself into two shorter
ones, here at the lengths of 11·8 in. to 13·8 in., which split
into two of 6·9 in., giving the note of the short body, but with
a little more resonance on account of the double wave.
Again, at 26·4 in.—27·6 in, the wave divides into three of
8·85 in., the pitch jumping up to that note.

The overblowing is not determined by any hard-and-fast law; it depends upon the wind-pressure and the width of body (probably also the natural note of the tongue has some influence). Töpfer says that a wide body over-blows easier than a narrow one; but the writer has heard a contrary opinion expressed by experienced voicers, and the point has not been cleared up by actual experiment.

104. Töpfer also conducted experiments on free reeds, which are known not to require as long bodies as the other kind; but, on the other hand, to be very sensitive to the effect of the boot, a matter on which particulars will be given hereafter.

Two reeds were tried with the bodies of the last experiments, one an oboe, with a tongue tapering towards the point, a form which Töpfer holds to give it more elasticity; the other a clarinet, with narrow tongues of very elastic metal. Both of these are much less sensitive to external impulses than are the striking tongues, just as a free pendulum acquires greater momentum than one which is brought to a stand in the middle of every beat. This is well shown in the table attached.

No.	Body length	Oboe		Clarinet	
		Pitch	Timbre	Pitch	Timbre
	in.				
1	9·8	287	Good tone	289	Good tone
2	10·8	290	—	290	—
3	11·8	290	—	289	—
4	12·8	289	—	286	—
5	13·8	288	—	284	—
6	15·8	286	—	283	—
7	17·6	284	Tone heavy	280	Covered tone
8	19·6	281	Weak and hissing	277	—
9	20·8	281	Ditto	277	Low
10	21·8	281	Ditto	266	—
11	22·4	281	Dying away	266	Dying away
12	23·8	—	No note	—	No note
13	25·6	289	Clear and good tone as above	289	Dead, and slow speech
14	27·6	290	—	290	Clear tone

Here there is some difference in the behaviour of the two tongues. That of the oboe, possessing great strength, positively refuses to accommodate itself to the increasing length of body to a greater extent than nine vibrations, while that of the clarinet, though more accommodating, spoils and stops the tone altogether at just the same limit of length until, with a threefold length of body, the wave splits into three, and gives again a clear note of the original pitch. The striking reeds showed a far greater flexibility of adaptation to the note required by the body. Thus, free reeds will not tolerate long bodies, except of the right length, and partake of the timbre of reeds with none or very short bodies—viz., an excess of harmonics and defect of ground tone. For this reason it is probable that a spherical shape, which has few upper partials of its own, would be the most favourable for free reed bodies. These reeds also get easily out of tune with the rest of the organ, or more exactly, the rest of the pipes are more easily affected by changes of temperature than are the free reeds, especially those with none or short bodies.

105. Töpfer notices a peculiar construction of a free reed clarinet, tried by Herr Giesecke, in which the free end of the tongue is reversed—i.e. lies in the upper part of the boot, the idea apparently being that, as the free tongues resist the guidance of the air column, and as the condensations and rarefactions are strongest just at the node which lies at the bottom of the body, the nearer the free end of the tongue lies to that point the greater influence will the vibrations of the air column have on it. But it is not stated whether this construction was found to present any practical advantages.

106. While on the subject of the vibration movement in pipes, the reason of the demand of free reeds, especially broad ones, for large boots may be noted ; the details will be given further on. If a beating reed is tried without a body in a boot of variable length, the phenomena of lowering the pitch and overblowing when the tongue will stand no more are repeated as with a body. A small body will not make much difference ; but with a body of full length, the vibration of the more massive column has the mastery, and the boot can no longer govern the tongue. Thus the influence of the boot is not peculiar to free reeds as such, but because they are associated with very short bodies. The reason is, that there are waves of condensation and rarefaction in the boot just as there are

in the body, and when the waves of the latter have not pre-dominance, those of the boot, if their phases do not corre-pond—i.e. if the boot is of unsuitable length—will by their opposition spoil the symmetry of the vibrations of the tongue and weaken the tone.

107. Before proceeding to the actual scales recommended by different authorities, we should notice what theory has done on the subject. The most elaborate work has been done by Von Weber, who presents a formula of considerable com-plexity for calculating the length of bodies; but as it applies only to free reeds with cylindrical bodies, it is more a question of academical interest than a point of practical use to the builder. On such an obscure point as the speech of reeds, no information is unimportant, as, if not immediately useful, it may indicate the best path to follow. Weber's formula is this:

Let L = length of body.

n = the vibration number of a free tongue alone.

n_1 = the vibration number, when the pitch has been deepened by the body.

w = the weight of a square cm. of the tongue.

s = the speed of sound = 34,680 cm. per second.

$2g$ = the double fall of a body in the first second = 980·4 cm.

R = ratio of vibrating area of tongue to the upper area of the body.

k = the coefficient in Boyle and Mariotte's law = 1·375.

p = the atmospheric pressure in grammes per square cm. of tongue = 1032·8 gr.

The formula is—

$$\tan. \frac{\pi\, L n_1}{s} = \frac{(n^2 - n_1{}^2)\, \pi w s}{2g\, R\, k\, p\, n_1}.$$

Of the coefficients, $\dfrac{\pi\, s}{2g\, k\, p}$ is a constant, which may be called

A, and = log.$^{-1}$ $\bar{2}$·88343. Also $\dfrac{s}{\pi}$ is a constant, B, and

= log. $^{-1}$ 4·03293, therefore the equation reduces to—

$$L \frac{n_1}{B} = \tan.^{-1} \left\{ A \frac{w\,(n^2 - n_1^2)}{R\,n_1} \right\}$$

or
$$L = \frac{B}{n_1} \tan.^{-1} \left\{ A \frac{w\,(n^2 - n_1^2)}{R\,n_1} \right\}$$

108. Töpfer has made trials of this formula, and an example of an 8 ft. trumpet pipe may be given to illustrate the use of the formula.

Pipe-length	Cylindrical bodies			Pipe-length	Pipe note	Body note	Timbre, cone of 4° 45′
	0·59 in. diam.	0·79 in. diam.	Timbre				
in.				in.			
6·7	291	289	Loud tone	8·7	—	—	Sharp
7·9	297	286	—	9·8	286	272	—
8·7	285	270	—	10·7	277	258	Maximum of resonance
9·8	267	246	—	11·8	265	247	Diminishes
10·7	291	239	Sharp and snarling	12·6	288	—	—
11·8	289	286	—	13·8	286	—	—
12·6	285	281	—	15·7	281	—	Tone snarls
13·8	278	—	Tone fails	17·7	284	311	—
15·7	258	—	Coughing sound	19·7	275	280	Tone improves
17·7	221	—	—	20·5	296	270	Louder
19·7	—	—	No note	21·6	259	261	Good tone
20·5	—	—	—	22·5	252	253	Becomes dead
21·6	297	—	Heavy and slow	23·6	246	247	Dead and soft
22·5	—	—	—	25·6	233	233	Dead and weak
23·6	294	—	As the first	27·6	225	225	—

The body does not deepen the pitch of the tongue a whole tone, and n has been taken at 64 vibrations and n_1 as 61·5, so that $n^2 - n_1^2 = 314$. The area of the vibrating part of the tongue is 8·9 sq. cm., and that of the upper part of the body 162·7, so that $R = 0·054$, $w = 0·483$ grammes. Then—

$$\log. (n^2 - n_1^2)\ 314 = 2·49693$$
$$\log. w\ (0·483) = \bar{1}·68395$$
$$\log. A = 2·88343$$
$$\overline{}$$
$$\bar{1}·06431$$
$$0·52127$$
$$\overline{}$$
$$0·54304$$

$$\log. R\ (0·054) = \bar{2}·73239$$
$$\log. n_1\ (61·5) = 1·78888$$
$$\overline{}$$
$$0·52127$$

This, by reference to a table of log. tangents, is found to represent the angle 74° 1', which, in circular measure, is $\log.^{-1} 0{\cdot}11208$, so that we have—

$$
\begin{aligned}
\text{log. angle } & 0{\cdot}11208 \\
\text{log. B } & 4{\cdot}03293 \\
\hline
& 4{\cdot}14501 \\
\text{log. } n_1 \ & 1{\cdot}78888 \\
\hline
& 2{\cdot}35613
\end{aligned}
$$

which gives 227·06 cm. as the length. The actual length of the pipe experimented on is given as 228 cm. It will therefore be seen that, after all the trouble, the correspondence is not very close. Nor, indeed, could this be expected with a striking reed and conical body, from a formula framed on the conditions of a free reed and cylindrical body. Nobody appears to have attempted a formula for striking reeds, and there are circumstances, such as the difficulty of expressing the exact volume of the air mass involved, the elasticity of the tongue, and the wind pressure, which seem to render the attempt hopeless—a circumstance which, indeed, is the less to be regretted, as the minute measurements involved are rather out of the usual practice in organ-building.

109. The deepening of the pitch of the tongue by the addition of a body is explained by the opening of the tongue coinciding with the wave of condensation, and its shutting with the wave of rarefaction, so that its motion is somewhat retarded. The uncertainty as to what the value of n_1 should be, in any given case, is against the use of the formula for calculating lengths, and it would appear to be more likely to be useful to ascertain from the length and pitch of a given pipe the pitch of the tongue itself, for which purpose the formula would read—

$$ n = \sqrt{\dfrac{R\, n_1 \left(\tan. L\dfrac{n_1}{B} \right)}{A\,w}} + n_1 $$

Töpfer gives some figures of tongues tried this way, and the discrepancy between the pitch found by formula and the actual pitch appears to be about 5 per cent.

110. A purely empirical formula, which gives quite as good results as Weber's, is that known as Philbert's. In this, let W be the wave-length of the given note, L the pipe-length from tongue to top, D the upper and d the lower diameters (in this case the latter is the interior of the reed), then $W = L \dfrac{D+d}{D}$, or, since we generally want to find the length for a given pitch, $L = W \dfrac{D}{D + d}$.

From details given by Töpfer, it appears that Cavaillé-Coll's formula for reeds is more accurate. He takes d as the width of the slit in the reed for the real lower diameter of body. From experiments on several pipes, the average error of the Philbert formula is 3·3 per cent.; but that of the Cavaillé-Coll formula only 0·46 per cent., the latter also appearing more consistent in different sizes of pipes. These empirical formulæ will only apply with accuracy to pipe-work where the dimensions of tongues, reeds, holes in block, &c., are similar to those from which they were formed, and where the relative scale of the bodies is the same.

111. As a beginning towards establishing scales for the bodies, Töpfer gives a series of experiments with cylindrical bodies 0·59 in. and 0·79 in. diameter, and with cones of different angular aperture, the note desired, and presumably the tongue, being the same, c^1, as was used in the former experiments (the 7° 15′ cone series is the same). The natural note of the cylindrical bodies could not be ascertained; but the gaps in the series of the conical bodies are not explained. Their pitch could, however, be approximately calculated by one of the formulæ given above. In all these series the points of best resonance are where the pitch of the tongue, of the body, and of the whole pipe agree best, as can be seen from plotting a diagram. After passing the natural vibration number of the tongue, the body has it all its own way, and fixes the pitch of the pipe to its own pitch; but the tongue, struggling against strange periods of vibration, spoils the tone. It will be observed that as the body gets wider, so does the point of best resonance require a longer body; and the wider the body, the higher the pitch—exactly the reverse of what

happens with flue pipes. Thus, the 21·6 in. body of the smallest aperture gives a good note of 259 vibrations, while the next largest cone in the same length gives 271 vibrations, and has not yet got its best tone; while a cone larger still gives 276 vibrations.

Pipe-length	Pipe note	Body note	Timbre, cone of 7° 15′	Pipe note	Body note	Timbre, cone of 9° 45′
in.						
8·7	294	—	—	—	—	
9·8	291	290	Sharp tone	294	294	Sharp
10·7	286	276	Strong and clear	289	281	Broad and strong
11·8	275	265	Heavier and thinner	283	270	Diminishes
12·6	291	—	Over-blows	293	—	—
13·8	290	—	—	291	—	—
15·7	287	—	Thin and hollow	288	—	—
17·7	288	331	—	289	—	—
19·7	285	300	Tone improves	287	—	Stronger, clearer tone
20·5	278	285	—	284	—	—
21·6	271	274	Good trumpet tone	276	—	Becomes rounder
22·5	265	265	Yet better	269	—	Good tone
23·6	258	258	Good horn tone	263	—	Covered and weaker
25·6	246	246	Heavy and weak	252	—	Like military horn
27·6	295	—	Over-blows	295	—	Over-blows

112. According to Töpfer, the explanation of the wider body giving the higher pitch is, that conical reed-bodies act in some measure as Gedackts; that they, and resonators of a tube form, closed entirely on one side, and nearly on the other, oppose a resistance to the free-flowing air-wave, and, by hindering its motion, lower the pitch. Thus also the return wave in a conical body is always moving into a narrower space, and condensation is formed, as if another wave were opposing. With a wider opening there is less hindrance to the wave, its motion is quicker, and vibrations—i.e. pitch—increase, until, if wide enough, the pipe-wave will have the same speed as the theoretical wave, and the body half the theoretical wave-length as of an open pipe. But diminishing the size retards the wave and deepens the pitch, until, with a partly closed top, as (sometimes) in the Fagotto and Vox Humana, the length becomes that of a Gedackt, or even less.

In this respect Weber's formula is unsuitable for calculating the length of conical bodies, since it does not explicitly recognise the angle of the cone, but expresses the ratio between the areas of the tongue and diameter of a cylindrical body. Cavaillé-Coll's formula takes the upper and lower diameters directly into consideration.

113. From these ideas Töpfer makes a very interesting deduction, that he regards conical reed bodies as harmonic Gedackts, which will over-blow into the *octave*, and that, consequently, if a Gedackt were made conical it would also speak the octave when overblown. He cites an experiment with a wooden pyramidal body, in which is cut a slit, covered with parchment, and strewed with sand, the distribution of which, when the pipe is sounded, shows the numerous waves of condensation caused by the hindrance to the free-running wave. The trumpet has the second and fourth partials strongly developed, and over-blows into the octave. Töpfer made a Spitz-Gedackt by putting a trumpet body stopped at the end on a metal pipe cut down, and it gave the octave when strongly blown, and the shorter the body and narrower the scale, the easier it over-blew. This pipe is described as having all the harmonics, and giving an agreeable and very peculiar tone, much preferable to that of an ordinary harmonic Gedackt, which speaks the twelfth, and has only the odd partial tones. On the same reasoning, Töpfer says a cylindrical reed tube will behave like a cylindrical Gedackt; it will only have the odd harmonics, which give the peculiar hollow timbre of the clarinet, and the first series of experiments recorded above shows that the cylindrical bodies utterly refuse to speak with a double length, but the tone comes again with threefold length. This kind also follow the laws of flue-pipes, and the wider body gives the deeper pitch. In other respects, they, like conical bodies, require that for the best speech, the pitch of the tongue, of the body, and of the whole pipe should lie as near as possible.

114. To develop his theory, Töpfer next extends the series of body sizes which differ by 2° 30', by interpolating and fixing the lengths for, say, c^1 of 254 vibrations. This gives—

Angle	4° 45'	6° 0'	7° 15'	8° 30'	9° 45'
Length of body	22·2''	23·2	24·2	24·8	24·4
Difference from 26'', the theoretical length of pipe	3·8	2·8	1·8	1·2	0·6

The lengths themselves do not vary in any regular series ; but, by taking their differences from 26″, the theoretical length of pipe (half wave-length), we get the series given in the line ' difference,' which, allowing for small defects in the make of the bodies and in the experiments, can be recognised as a geometric series and amended and extended as—

Angle.	.	.	4° 45″	6° 1′	° 15′	8° 30′	9° 45′	11°
Difference .	.		3·8″	2·4′	1·5′	0·98″	0·63°	0·41″

Or, turning it into even angles for more convenient use, as—

Angle	.	.	4°	5°	6°	7°	8°	9°	10°	11°
Difference .	.		4·9″	3·5″	2·4″	1·7″	1·2″	0·82″	0·55″	0·41″

from which Töpfer presents the following table of lengths for $c^1 = 254$ beats :

Angle .	. 4°	5°	6°	7°	8°	9°	10°	11°
Length of body	21·5″	22·45″	23·6″	24·4″	24·8″	25·2″	25·5″	25·7″
Ratio of length to free wave-length.	.0·8109	0·8669	0·9077	0·9365	0·9546	0·9673	0·9788	0·9847

The use of this table is to find at once the length of a body when the pitch and angle of cone are given ; thus, for $a^1 = 435$, and body of 6° the wave-length is $\dfrac{1120}{2 \times 435} = 1\cdot29'$, which multiplied by 0·9077, the coefficient for 6° = 1·17′ as the actual length.

T. e shortest body that gives the note could be used for a reed pipe ; but it would easily get out of tune, and the tube of full length gives a finer tone, with more of the primary note ; such, therefore, are preferable for Horns and Cornopeans, but not always for Trumpets.

115. In scaling reeds, it is even more necessary than in flue work to see that the treble is not overpowered by the bass, as it labours under the disadvantage of smaller body and a less efficient wind supply, more pressure being lost by the small passages. Töpfer relates that Herr Giesecke made an experiment with double tongues in the treble. They do not, of course, give double the tone, which depends upon the air column of the body; but they do benefit it by giving a freer wind supply, which the greater stiffness of small tongues, as compared to their area, hinders. The device was

found specially advantageous with free reeds, and there was
no difficulty in getting both tongues to pitch.

Another method is to lengthen the bodies of the upper
octaves so that they over-blow, a practice introduced by
Cavaillé-Coll, who calls such pipes harmonic reeds ; the
treble, and even the quadruple, length may be taken. Of
course also, widening the scale helps the strength of tone, but
at the expense of unity of timbre—at least from the point of
view of Töpfer's theory, which demands the same angle of
cone throughout.

116. But it is a little disappointing to find that, after
nearly sixty pages of closely-printed theoretical discussion, of
which the above extracts give the barest outline, Töpfer
practically abandons all idea of enunciating a theory *à priori*
when it comes to giving scales to build from, and simply says
such and such diameters for the first and last pipe are found
in practice to be favourable, and we will interpolate the intermediate dimensions in a geometrical series and arrive at the
lengths by Weber's formula, tempered by the expedient of
making the bodies full long, so that they can be cut down
when voicing. He gives, in addition to his own scales, several
by different builders, of which he considered the result satisfactory, which will be shown in Pls. XXXIII. to XL., this
form of diagram being, in the opinion of the writer, much the
best for comparing scales. Any irregularity shows up at
once, and as there are a good many misprints in Töpfer's
tables, this automatic check is useful. Where the scale is at
all regular, an error can be corrected without any difficulty ;
but where, as in the case of the Vox Humana, the dimensions
are very arbitrary, it was sometimes a little difficult to make
out what was meant. In these diagrams the letters on the
lines show to what dimensions on the little sketch they refer,
and in all of them *l b t* refer to the length, breadth, and
thickness of the tongues. The dimensions are measured
from the base line to the curve in question by the scale given.
And to economise space, two pipe scales are given on each
diagram, one in full and one in dotted lines, corresponding to
the little sketches annexed. The full description of each
scale is given in the chapter on Stops.

117. The following table exhibits the principal features in the scaling of reed bodies by different artists, only Trumpets being dealt with, as the typical representatives of this kind of stop. The 'ratio' is the same as that referred to for flue pipes—viz., the ratio of the upper diameters in the double octaves.

Authority	Diameters		Ratio	Half measure on pipe
	C₀	c²		
	in.	in.		
Haas	5·41	2·4	1·5	41
Töpfer	5·45	2·4	1·5	41
Ditto free reed . . .	5·7	1·6	1·86	27
Cavaillé-Coll . . .	4·9	1·8	1·6–1·68	27
Giesecke . . .	4·9	1·6	1·77	29
Ditto	3·8	1·3	1·68	32
Sauer	5·4	1·9	1·65	30
Ladegast	5·8	1·5	1·94	25
Dom Bedos	5·9	2·0	1·6 ⎫	
Ditto	4·9	1·9	to 1·7 ⎭	irregular
Sonreck	5·35	1·7	variable	21 to 33
Schultze	5·25	1·9	1·65	30

Töpfer's scale is simply Haas's, which he approves, as favouring the upper notes which are naturally weak. Either this or Schultze's scale is a good one; in fact, among the regular scales there does not appear to be so much variety between those by different builders as there is in the case of flue pipes. It will be observed that the larger scales, as a rule, decrease in a quicker ratio than do the smaller.

For pedal stops, Töpfer (as well as other authorities) chooses a larger scale than the manual to get breadth of tone, and consequently the ratio of diminution in diameters is taken at a higher figure, 1 : 1·86, quite arbitrarily.

118. This ratio also Töpfer assigns, without any special reason, for the manual Trumpet with free reeds, as well as for the pedal work, thus showing a remarkable inequality between the scales for free and those for striking reeds, the curves of which cross. He expresses himself as satisfied with the free reed work in examples by Schultze, and in organs built under his own direction. But here also he makes arbitrary assumptions in settling the length of the pipes. He

says that with a deepening of one tone (the $n - n_1$ of Weber's formula) free reed pipes require just half the length of an open pipe of the same pitch, and do well therewith. Then he proceeds to say that further experiments (not given in detail) show that the tone is full and strong up to a deepening of a fourth, which will give a pipe of two-thirds the length of an open one; and finally he assigns a deepening of pitch of five notes in the pedal and two in the manual in calculating the lengths by Weber's formula. In one case, a striking reed, he makes out from an actual trial that the deepening of the pitch of the tongue by the body is 10 notes—a fact which, if accurately stated, seems to conflict with the theory about the best respective periods of resonance of tongue and body. The truth appears to be that if the co-efficient ‘deepening of tone’ in Weber's formula may be anything from 1 note to 10, it is better to recognise the fact that the formula is only useful for precisely the case for which it was designed, and to trust to experiment for the best length of body to produce the required timbre.

For cylindrical pipes, which are always of small scale, the difference in diameter between the first and last pipe is generally so small that it really does not matter much what the curve is; a straight line will, in most cases, be near enough.

119. In the matter of the scale of tongues, the laws affecting them as vibrating bodies were given at the beginning of this chapter. These, put into figures, using L, l for lengths, B, b for breadths, and T, t for thickness, give the following equations, wherein the capital letter is taken as representing the larger size, and N, n the vibrations belonging to the large or small letters respectively:

$$L^2 : l^2 = n : N, \text{ where T is constant}$$
$$T : t = N : n, \text{ where L is constant}$$

B does not affect N.

$\dfrac{T}{L^2}$ is then the ratio by which both dimensions vary, and by the addition of an experimental coefficient, $c = 559,873$, for brass tongues, becomes a general expression for the vibration numbers, so that $N = c \dfrac{T}{L^2}$.

Töpfer, of course, introduces his favourite ratio, 1 : $\sqrt{8}$, for the areas of tongues, which he says influence the timbre in the same way as do the mouth areas of flue pipes; but this appears to be pure assumption, and is not even strictly adhered to by himself. Nor do the tables for the length, breadth, and thickness of free tongues which he gives agree with their intention declared in the text; as, for instance, in a table for pedal stops, which professes to be based on the condition that the breadths shall be a quarter of the lengths, the latter vary from 2·7 to 3·7 times the breadths.

He gives scales corresponding to the three ratios for flue pipes, and apparently, as in them, takes c^1 as the neutral point, where the three scales coincide, since the areas of the tongues are about equal, being—

Ratio					L.	B.
1 : $\sqrt{8}$	.	.	.	.	0·95″	0·168″
1 : 2·6	.	.	.	.	0·82	0·188
1 : 2·5	.	.	.	.	0·72	0·26

Nor are the ratios of length to breadth of tongue constant in any series except the first, although it is to be gathered from his remarks that he considered it theoretically advisable; in fact, the only decided information that can be gathered from his theorising on tongues is, that with a suitable wind-pressure, increasing the width to a quarter the length improved the tone. This was for rectangular free tongues of uniform thickness.

120. In discussing actual scales, Töpfer points out the irregularity of those of Dom Bedos, and sets forth a series for tongues based on dimensions found convenient within the limits of C_2 and c^3, in which the lengths increase in the ratio 1 : $\sqrt{8}$, but the breadths and thickness as 1 : 2, so that the ratio of length to breadth varies from 1 : 2·3 at the treble end to 1 : 7 in the bass. The ratio of the areas of successive octaves is thus 1 : 2·38. The size of the c^1 tongues is fixed at 1·15″ × 0·33″ × 0·0154″. The reader can plot such a series for himself if desired. It should be noted that this table is based on the supposition that the pitch of the tongue will only be deepened one note by the body, as a deepening of two notes would have a marked influence on the timbre, and more

would injure it. This is the scale he appears to favour for ordinary trumpets, &c.; but he increases the size of the tongues for pedal-stops with striking reeds, as will be seen in the figures of scales. He also makes the upper area of body dependent upon the area of the tongue, as, for example, where he finds by experiment that a free reed trumpet gave good results with a tongue 1·07 in. × 0·81 in. × 0·22 in., and an upper diameter of 2·3 in.; but desiring to use his standard series of tongues, which have a larger area, he correspondingly increases the upper area of body to 2·89 in.

For oboes, clarinets, &c., Töpfer professes an unqualified adherence to free reeds, and recommends for the size of c^1, 0·965 in. × 0·388 in. × 0·0113 in., the lengths to vary in the ratio $1 : \sqrt{8}$, with $1 : 2$ for the breadths and thicknesses.

121. Judging from the general drift of remarks in Töpfer and in Helmholtz, and from the fact that Schultze, after visiting England, gradually abandoned free reeds, the truth as between them and striking reeds appears to be that the English builders always managed the latter well, by giving the tongues a suitable curve and thinness; but that the Germans, not being able to get a smooth tone, preferred the free reed. Nobody who has heard the reeds of good English builders would hesitate to prefer them to free reeds, except for some very special effect, which, indeed, if worth attempting, could doubtless be produced by an English artist from a striking reed. Töpfer certainly never heard a good English Oboe, or he would not have insisted on free reeds for that stop.

122. An item in the scaling of reeds which requires notice is that of the size of boots—a very important factor in reeds with short bodies. From numerous researches made by Töpfer and other advocates of free reeds, who are compelled to attend to this matter, it appears that the best size of boot is that which gives the note of the pipe; but an octave, or with very large pipes two, can be jumped over without material disadvantage. The interval of a fifth will also do, but not so well. Further, it has been observed that, beyond the boot, the wind-spaces in the soundboard groove occasionally affect the speech, and the pipe will not perform satisfactorily until the boot, even when itself consonant, is altered. Evi-

dently such a remedy is purely empirical, as the exact nature
of the disturbing factor cannot be ascertained. The best
rules for the boots of free reeds are :

In the 32 ft. octave the boots must begin with 8 ft. long.

In the 16 ft. octave the boots must begin with 4 ft. long.

For the 8 ft. pipes the boot should be half the length of an
open pipe of the pitch, subject to the possibility of having to
alter it arbitrarily to meet some influence of the air-passages.

123. English builders, who always use striking reeds,
make the boots of arbitrary sizes ; but Herr Haas, who conducted lengthy experiments, says they are improved by having
free reed sizes, the difficulty being the enormous length. He
also finds that from 32 ft. to 8 ft. pitch, striking reeds will do
perfectly well without any boots at all, being stuck straight
into the soundboard. From 8 ft. to 4 ft. he prefers quite a
short boot, and from c^0 uses the same sized boot as for free
reeds, cutting them when required in voicing.

He remarks, that if a trumpet be made with boots all of
one size, at some place or places in the scale the notes will be
spoiled, which places are where the note of the boot is discordant with that of the tongue. There certainly seems
sufficient evidence to make it worth while to attend to this
point, and see that the boot either has the note of the pipe, or
one far removed from it—and insignificant in power.

A free reed clarinet by Herr Ladegast has boots of the
following sizes :

Note					Length	Diameter
C_0	.	.	.	.	26·4″	2·68″
c^0	.	.	.	.	20·9	2·24
c^1	.	.	.	.	14·9	1·94
c^2	,	.	.	.	12·0	1·65

124. For the reeds themselves, it is difficult to see how
scales can be deduced mathematically ; but their proportions
exercise a decided influence on the tone, and it is reasonable
to assume that innumerable experiments have fixed the sizes
generally used as the most convenient all round. The writer
is not aware of any record of experiments on different sizes of
reeds, but has been assured by a competent authority that
any material deviation from the usual proportions is pre-

judicial. A cylindrical reed produces a thin and fiery tone, and in the upper notes the reed should be as small as possible. The usual practice is to give the reed $\frac{1}{2}$ in. for every foot of tone-length of the pipe, plus enough to secure it firmly in the block. Thus, a C_0 reed would be about 4 in. in clear length, and enter $\frac{3}{4}$ in. into the block, with a diameter of $\frac{9}{16}$ in. at the big end and $\frac{3}{8}$ in. at the small end; while the top note might have a length of about $\frac{7}{16}$ in., with a tail of $\frac{5}{16}$ in., and large and small diameters of $\frac{3}{16}$ in. and $\frac{1}{8}$ in. respectively. The opening in the reed is filed to suit the taste of the voicer, being generally from one-third the length for a weak to two-thirds for a strong stop, merging into the open reed. As for the blocks, they are generally cast in moulds in sets which serve for about half a dozen pipes, the largest being about $2\frac{1}{2}$ in. diameter, and the smallest 1 in. .

125. To sum up, it may be said that, though Töpfer and his latest editor, Max Allihn, have not succeeded in establishing any theory from which reed pipes can be designed, yet many thanks are due to them as the only people who (so far as the writer knows) have taken the trouble to publish the results of their experiments. Nor are their labours fruitless, for if their scales (which are not approved by competent judges) are not the best possible, yet the information they have collected throws a light upon the behaviour of reed pipes, and indicates the direction which further research into this most interesting subject should take. It is owing to the fact of there being no English translation that Töpfer's works are not more generally known and studied. Töpfer at least has explained why a striking reed will endure a considerable variation from the best length of body before it absolutely declines work, though the tone suffers all the time; and he has shown, to some extent, how to anticipate the best length, instead of taking an arbitrary size, such as the fifth or fourth, as used to be the custom.

126. A scale after Weber's ideas, as given in Hamel, is plotted in Fig. 299, Pl. XXXII., as a logarithmic scale in the ratio $1 : \sqrt{8}$, which can be used for any series in that ratio. There are seven scales, making a difference of an octave in size, of which, for the sake of clearness, only the middle—a

medium one—has been drawn throughout. These scales give the length and width of the tongues, and the diameter of the pipe and the thickness of tongues × 1,000 is found in Fig. 298, which also can be used for any scale in the ratio 1 : 2. These diagrams have been given more for the sake of the ratios for general use, than because the particular scales drawn thereon are recommended. The corresponding pipe-lengths are given in Appendix III.

Fig. 297, Pl. XXXI., is Schultze's scale for reeds.

CHAPTER IV—*continued*

PIPES: (c) MATERIALS

127. THE materials of which pipes are made are practically tin, 'metal,' zinc, and wood.   They can be made of any
metal, and of paper, and even of glass; but with the exception of paper, none of these other materials are worthy of
serious consideration.   The book on organ-building by Mark
Wicks gives full instructions for making paper pipes; but, as
they are held together by glue, they would be quite inadmissible for work abroad.   The writer has made big pipes of
paper with various styles of mouthpiece to try and get over
this difficulty; but none are worth description.   Such pipes
are very strong and light, and give a fair tone.

128. *Tin*—not to be confounded with tin-plate, which is
only tinned iron—is the best of all metals for pipes.   It is
light, strong, and of a lustre equal to silver, and less liable to
tarnish.   It also resists the action of the acids found in some
woods better than other metals do.   It is generally alloyed
with one-tenth lead, and as its specific gravity is only 7·3,
while that of lead is 11·4, it is easy to ascertain the amount
of base metal in a pipe.

129. 'Metal' is a very indefinite term, as it may mean
anything from very good stuff to pure lead, with antimony
and other abominations mixed with it to supply enough
rigidity to enable the pipes to stand up till the organ has
been paid for.   In Germany the general proportion is 25
parts of tin to 7 lead, down to half and half.   What is
known as 'spotted metal' is good; the best proportion is
95 lb. of tin to a cwt. of lead, and nothing worse should be
used.   Less tin will bring the spots, but they are small and
the lustre is poor.   At about these proportions there are

reasons for thinking that the metals form rather a chemical
combination than a mere alloy. The writer has seen, in a
book of advice on the purchase of organs, the statement that
no reliance can be placed on the appearance of spotted metal,
as it is easily imitated. This must surely be a mistake, as
diligent inquiry among those skilled in such matters fails to
corroborate the statement, and it is difficult to imagine any
way by which even a colourable imitation of spotted metal can
be produced.

130. Good metal, being more hard and elastic than lead,
gives a better tone to the pipes, particularly those of the
Gamba tribe; but it is more on account of durability, than of
tone when new, that what is euphoniously called ' good plain
metal' is condemned. A pipe made of a soft heavy metal
deteriorates from the day it is put up, the feet get bent and
wrinkled, and the accurate adjustment of the mouth-parts,
upon which the tone depends, is quite a matter of chance
after the organ has been tuned a couple of times. German
builders, as a rule, use very good metal, even in small organs;
but English builders are, or used to be, great sinners in this
respect.

A friend, associated in organ building with the writer,
once bought for 13l. a three-manual organ of no great age of
a cathedral in one of the Presidency towns in India. This
organ, built by a London firm who would consider themselves
a leading firm, was condemned as useless. The pipes were of
pure lead, and so thin that a $c°$ pipe could be easily ripped
right down by the fingers, and most of the feet had crumpled
up. On trying to voice the pipes after repairing visible
damages, no good tone could be got, and a careful examination revealed the fact that they were full of pin-holes, or
rather specks of dross which had perished, and through which
a pin could easily be stuck. The eminent builders would
doubtless have assured the purchaser that ' plain metal' was
good for tone, and it would have been interesting to get their
opinion on their pipes after twenty years. Without knowing
the cost of the organ, it is impossible to say that the bad work
was not the fault of the purchaser, who insisted upon more
stops than the price would cover; but the moral is, that in

the long run it does not pay a builder to accept such orders, as nobody who had seen such an organ would be likely to run the risk of getting another.

131. *Zinc, of proper substance*, is a fair material for large pipes, on account of its stiffness and lightness—qualities which sometimes tempt builders to make the pipes too thin; 18 B.W.G. is a fair thickness for an 8 ft. pipe. The metal does not seem to do well for pipes below 4 ft., though a German firm have turned out very fair pipes of all sizes by special machinery. These are nickelled for front pipes, but nickel does not stand in India. Zinc pipes should have metal languids and lips for purposes of adjustment, though the writer has made an 8 ft. octave entirely in zinc, but the pipes require to be most exactly made. There is a difference in tone at the junction between spotted metal and zinc, which is difficult to overcome.

132. *Wood.*—The sort of wood does not really matter so much as that it should be the best of its kind, well seasoned, straight in grain, and free from knots. Of all woods, a hard, straight-grained pine is, perhaps, the best for resonance. Oak is a good wood, but is not used (in England) nowadays, though magnificent specimens exist in old organs. Mahogany—the kind called 'baywood'—is good when thickness is not grudged, and nothing can beat teak for tropical climates. For the front boards or mouths of small pipes, pear-wood, cherry, and maple, or other smooth-grained woods, are excellent, and for such pipes as the Travers Flute, which are bored out of the solid, are essential.

133. A note of how to take the specific gravity of pipe-metal, in order to check the nature of the alloy, may be useful. Cut off a piece of the metal, and hang it from the scale-pan of an accurate balance by a thread or thin wire, and take the weight, first in air and then in water, by just submerging the piece, seeing that no air-bubbles are adhering; then, if W be the weight in air, and w the weight in water, the specific gravity will be $\dfrac{W}{W-w}$. Then, to find the relative proportions of each metal in the alloy of which the specific gravity is known: if L is

put for the weight of lead and W for the weight of the piece, and S its specific gravity, then $L = 2 \cdot 78 \times \dfrac{W\ (S - 7 \cdot 3)}{S}$. Töpfer gives the following table of specific gravities of different alloys, which will save the trouble of calculating:

Tin	Lead	Sp. gr.	Tin	Lead	Sp. gr.
3	1	7·9942	1	2	9·5535
5	2	8·1094	2	5	9·7701
2	1	8·2669	1	3	9·9387
3	2	8·4973	3	7	10·0734
1	1	8·8640	1	4	10·1832
2	3	9·2653			

134. The thickness for pipe walls recommended by Töpfer is given in Appendix IV., as well as the approximate weights of different stops; but these thicknesses refer only to tin, and the worse the metal the thicker it must be, thereby also the heavier, and the feet the less capable of bearing the weight. In large pipes the thickness may be taken for the mean, as the sheets may be rather thinner towards the top and thicker towards the bottom of the pipe.

For wooden pipes of pine, Töpfer gives the following thicknesses for foundation work. Softly-voiced stops, or those built of stronger wood, may do with rather less thickness; but no good tone can be got out of pipes with thin walls, or where the planks are spliced:

	C_2 in.	C_1 in.	C_0 in.	c^0 in.	c^1 in.	c^2 in.
Square	14·2	9·3	5·87	3·69	2·32	1·47
Thickness	2·9	1·93	1·34	1·05	0·7	0·5

It is also a good plan to reinforce large pipes by bands or frames at the nodes.

135. It is a curious but undoubted fact, that spotted metal and pure tin get softer with age. A pipe-maker will always prefer to let sheets of good metal lie a week or ten days before attempting to roll them up, and pipes twenty years old are distinctly softer than when they are new; and the writer has been assured by a very competent voicer, that pipes do lose their freshness of tone by age. This man had

also a word to say in favour of antimony metal, which he said had a worse reputation than it deserved, because pains were not taken to study the best proportions. With good spotted metal and tin, there need be no fear of the pipes crushing their feet, or getting full of holes.

CHAPTER IV—*continued.*

PIPES: (d) PIPE-MAKING

136. THE manufacture of pipes will be treated of in the following order—metal flue pipes, reeds, wood pipes. Although there is no great difficulty in making ordinary pipes, yet such a course cannot be recommended to the amateur. Pipe-making is a trade in itself, and those who follow it naturally attain a degree of perfection with which an amateur cannot hope to compete. Stops can be bought unvoiced to any scale required, for less than they will cost to make, taking failures into account. The principal plant required is a casting bench a little longer and wider than the sheets required, with a box and a melting-pot and furnace. The bench is shown in Fig. 121, Pl. XII., and should be of the solidity of a billiard table, and may be after the same fashion, with a slate bed. As pipes over 4 ft. long can be made in zinc or wood quite as well as in metal, an amateur need never require a table more than 5 ft. long and about 18 in. wide, and this can be efficiently and cheaply made by bolting together deals 1½ in. thick, and not less than 4 in. wide, the planks running lengthways, their edges forming the top of the table. The deeper they are the better, and timber need not be grudged, as it can be unbolted and used for other purposes when the owner has done with the table. The planks should not touch throughout their whole depth, but should be laid about ⅛ in. apart, with thin slips between them at the top side, so that the whole when planed off presents a smooth surface. So long as the table is solid and the top true, it may be built up in any way preferred.

137. Having, then, a good solid level table of a suitable size, it must be covered with some stuff, generally bed-ticking.

This can simply be tacked on to the sides of the table; but the best plan is to make a frame of 4 in. by 1 in. stuff, large enough to embrace the table loosely, and tack the ticking on to this. The weight of the frame will keep the ticking always well stretched on the surface of the table, whereas if tacked on to the table direct, the stuff would have to be ripped up and refastened every time it began to get loose. A casting-box and trough for waste metal have to be provided. The former is simply a stout box without a bottom, made of not less than $1\frac{1}{2}$ in. thick close-grained hardwood, such as pear or walnut. The front board slides in grooves, and can be raised about $\frac{1}{8}$ in. above the others, either by screws a a from a bar above it, as shown in the figure, or it can be jammed at the required height by screws in the sides. The bottom edge is bevelled on the outside as shown in section in Fig. 119, Pl. XII. The inside of the box will be about 5 in. to 6 in. wide, and 5 in. to 8 in. deep, according to the quantity of metal to be run. The sides, or sometimes one side only of the box, are furnished with guides, in which are two holes b b for pins, with corresponding holes in the table to secure the box while the metal is being poured in, so that it is jammed against the slip c screwed on the table near the end, in order to prevent the metal flowing out of the slit left by the front board.

138. When sufficient metal to cast a sheet has been poured into the box, the pins are drawn, and the box being slid rapidly down the table, the molten metal flowing out of the slit between the bottom of the front board and the table forms a thin sheet for the full length and breadth of the space traversed. The trough for surplus metal, d, is simply a little trough hung at the far end of the table, so as to be readily removable when the surplus has been caught. A more elaborate style of casting-box is shown in Fig. 119. It is provided with a metal reservoir, e, revolving on a hinge, f, supported and lifted by a bar, h, which runs across, and rests on the sides of the box. When the metal is in a fit state to run, the reservoir is inverted, the metal flows into the pouring part, and the box is started off at once on its journey down the table.

139. The arrangements for melting do not need a particular description; any iron pot that is large enough will do.

As the melting-point of lead is 612°, and that of tin only 442°, the lead should be melted before the tin is put in; and here it may be noted that the better the quality of the metal, the less damage need be done to the casting gear on account of the reduction in temperature. A little tallow and resin should be put into the melting-pot, and the mixture well stirred, on account of the very different specific gravity of tin and lead. To prepare for casting, give the box a couple of coats of the soiling used in soldering, which will preserve it; and if a plain box is used, put a sheet of brown paper under it to keep the ticking from getting burnt, and provide a pot or ladle to pour the metal with. Whichever is used—pot or reservoir—grease it well, and fill from the furnace, stirring all the time, and when the metal shows signs of getting pasty, pour it at once into the box, and draw the latter right away over the end of the table, returning to the furnace the surplus metal which has been caught in the waste trough, before it has time to set. When very long sheets are run, it is better to ease them up off the table at the two ends at once, or the sheet may pull itself in half in contracting. It requires a good deal of experience to judge exactly the right heat at which to pour; but, as a guide, it may be taken that the metal should brown, and not burn, a piece of paper plunged into it. The gate should be set a little wider than the thickness of the sheet, and the speed at which to traverse the box is a point to be learned by practice.

140. Rolling would seem to be the best way of finishing sheets; but it will not answer with tin, and the usual practice is simply to plane them. The old builders used to beat them. An examination of a pipe will show inside the marks of the cloth on which it was cast, the outside only being planed. This is done with an iron-soled plane, the blade being set more upright than in the tool for wood. It is scarcely necessary to remark that the strokes of the plane must always be taken away from the point of fixture of the sheet, which is clamped down under a batten. To keep the polish, the sheet must be well greased, and the grease spread after every stroke with the ball of the thumb, which is the best cushion, or a swab may be used. A finish is put on with a

steel scraper. Care must be taken to keep the sheet exactly
the same thickness throughout, or the tone will suffer. Some
prefer to plane the sheets after they are cut out; but there is
much risk of damaging the edges.

141. To cut up the sheets to size, a saw may be used for
thick ones; but a stout saddler's knife will do for all the
small pipes. Shears are not good, because they turn up the
edges. Fig. 120 represents a tool called a shave hook, which
is useful in cutting sheets. Two or three sizes will be
required, which can be bought or made out of round steel.
The sheets should be cleaned with soft soap and water, and
polished with whiting until bright. The most useful dimension for the scale of metal pipes in the shop is the circumference, and not the diameter, as the width of the sheets is
wanted; and a word must be said here on cutting out conical
forms, as for the feet. On the edge of a sheet set off $a\ b$,
Fig. 115, the slant height of the foot, and $b\ c$, bearing the
same ratio to $a\ c$ that the bottom diameter is required to
have to the top. From centre c describe arcs from a and b.
Take, on a narrow strip of metal or paper, the width of the
sheet for the pipe body, and bending it round the arc, set it
off as $a\ d$, and join $c\ d$; then $a\ b\ c\ d$ is the development of the
cone. Pipe-makers keep patterns ready to hand.

142. The next job is to get the languids ready. The
shape of these is shown in Fig. 117, both in plan and section.
They should be strong, so as not to sink and put the pipe off
its speech, and should be of the same metal as the pipe,
though too often made of lead. If of a baser metal than the
pipe, they had better be tinned to obviate the risk of burning
the sheets. For large languids it would be a good plan to
cast in an iron wire as thick as the languid will admit, or to
solder a rib across underneath. It will be seen from the
figure that the front of the languid is thicker than the back,
and a chamfer runs right round the top. They can be cast,
a lot at a time, in a trough made of two planks, as shown in
Fig. 116. Into this trough a number of wedges are stuck,
dividing off the different castings.

143. To prepare the parts for soldering they must be
'soiled' to keep the sheets from getting burned, and the

solder from flowing where it is not wanted. Prepare some thin glue or size, and stir in whiting, and this also requires a little judgment; if there is too much glue the soiling will chip off, and if there is not enough the soiling will not be strong enough. It should resist being scratched with the finger-nail. Rolling up a sheet is a delicate operation, and the difficulty increases much with the length. The best plan is, after having soiled the inside, to lay the mandrel on the sheet and slip a feather-edged lath under the edge, and so bring it up in a straight line to the mandrel, and then roll the rest. Never use the block of hardwood called the 'beater' in the way its name implies, or the sheets will stretch, and the edges become a beautiful wavy line; it is only used for pressing and smoothing the sheet down on the mandrel. An amateur will probably despair at first of ever turning out the beautifully clean and fine thread of solder such as is seen on the seams of an organ-pipe; but it is perfectly easy if done the right way. Soil the joint, and then, with a shave-hook or small plane, bird-mouth it with a *clean cut*, as shown in Fig. 118. Rub it down with a tallow candle, and tack the edges together with a drop of solder here and there; then, with the pipe rather on the slant, draw the soldering iron down at a suitable speed, and it will leave a clean job behind it. The whole secret lies in having a *clean cut*, and not a filed, scratched, or jagged surface, and the same applies to all soldering work.

144. A word as to the style of bit is here required. It should be of iron, not copper, of the shape shown in Fig. 114, and as heavy as possible, so as to keep up a uniform heat. The handle should be split and the ends tied together, so that the tang of the bit lies loose when the grip is slackened, and the· hold on the iron can thus be shifted by one hand. A good size for the head is 1⅛ in. or 1¼ in. square, and about 4½ in. long; the flat slanting face is used, and should be tinned all over, so as to hold plenty of solder, which can be made to flow as required by a turn of the wrist. In using tin, which melts so easily, care must be taken not to burn it by overheating the iron, which will also give the trouble of having to re-tin the bit on account of the solder being perished. A hint on

tinning the bit may not be amiss, as a beginner might find a difficulty in it.   File the face to be tinned quite clean and smooth, heat it moderately, wipe clean, and rub with sal-ammoniac, and then rub in the solder placed in a slight hollow on a clean hard brick or tile, using tallow and resin as a flux. The operation can be performed on a board, if required, the only essential being smoothness and chemical cleanliness.   Of course, the operation known as 'pickling' can be used; this is the chemical cleansing used on iron before it is galvanised, and consists in dipping in a bath of dilute acid and then in hot water.

145. The body and foot being soldered up, the flat of the upper and lower lips is easily formed by rubbing the metal down over a brass or hardwood cone with a flat filed on it, and then the mouth has to be formed by cutting away the gap with a shave-hook.   It must be left full low, to be cut up by the voicer; as if too high, there is nothing for it but to saw off the body of the pipe and re-solder it.   When the pipes get a little large the sides of the lip require to be slit with a saw, as all the stuff in the arc will not pack into the chord without bulging the pipe, and for the pipes in the 8 ft. octave the whole of the lip is a separate piece, soldered into a gap cut to fit. The lip-piece should be thicker than the rest of the pipe, and if made of pure tin, nicely burnished, will have a handsome effect.   The most effective mouths are what are known as 'French mouths,' shown in Fig. 104, Pl. XI., and in section in Fig. 105.   Here the edges of the gap are gradually raised with a burnisher, until the top of the lip stands well above the body of the pipe, the front shape being a rectangle, surmounted by a semicircle.   The rectangular portion is flat, and the semicircular part curves out to meet the raised edge.   The lower lip is a semicircle in front view, but particular care must be taken not to give too much curvature in the vertical section; the part just opposite the languid must still be curving towards it, and not lie tangential to it, as shown in the section.   The ordinary 'bay-leaf' mouth is cut out for large pipes; but it is not usual to raise the edges (see Fig. 31).

146. The body and foot having the mouths formed and adjusted to each other, the languids may now be placed. They, being previously chamfered and if necessary tinned,

will be soiled, as also the top of the foot, which will then be slightly chamfered. To keep a large languid in place until secured by two or three drops of solder, place a narrow strip of paper across the top of the foot held by the finger and thumb, and on it adjust the languid and tack it down with solder. Another way of adjusting the languid is to lay it down on a plank and touch on three drops of solder, by which it is supported on the foot until tacked down, and the drops are absorbed in the process of running the solder round. Some prefer to use rather more lead in the solder for languids than for bodies. The languids of very small pipes are made by soldering a strip of the right width and thickness to the foot; the rest is then nipped off, and the languid nipped round to fit the pipe with a pair of nose-pliers, rounded up to shape, and solder run round.

147. The languid being secured into the foot, this and the body have now to be joined, which is the most difficult operation of all, as a body crooked on the foot looks ugly, will probably jam some of its neighbours, and may spoil the tone. The parts to be joined having been soiled and chamfered as usual, and the windway noted as correct (it is better too large than too small), fit the two parts together, and pressing the foot by touching the body against the breast of the operator to keep them in position, secure them by a touch of solder on each side, pass the tallow candle over the chamfer, and, if a large pipe, add more drops of solder, then revolve the pipe under the bit, held at a constant angle, and the joint is completed. The beginner will probably find it necessary to get a friend to help him. To complete the pipe, the ears only require to be fixed; these are simple strips of the same metal as the pipe, and fixing them requires no particular description. Pipes of good metal, and well burnished, will retain their lustre a long time if lacquered. The best procurable should be used, the pipes perfectly polished, and then heated as hot as the hand will bear, and the lacquer run on with a big soft brush.

148. The general method of making pipes having been described, the particular arrangements required for different sorts should now be noted. The pipe described above is a typical open diapason, and has no accessories. But with a string-toned pipe a ' bridge ' in front of the mouth is required.

This is generally a simple bar or plate soldered to the ears in front of the mouth. A variety which does specially well for a strong tone, as a Geigen, is shown in Fig. 110, Pl. XI. Here the piece of metal is shaped like an angle-iron, and a curved piece cut out near the ears. Another arrangement is shown in Fig. 111, where a round bar of wood is used with a pin at each end resting in a notch in the ears, and kept in its place by a bit of spring wire soldered to the front of the foot. In pipes with a bell, as the Bell Gamba, it should be remembered that the bell cannot be soldered on till the pitch is known, as any sharpening must be done on the body, and not by cutting the bell. Note also that a bell which runs too far down the body spoils the tone.

149. For stopped metal pipes there are many ways of arranging stoppers, and to select a good plan is important, as the tone depends entirely upon the integrity of the stopper. For England almost any plan will do ; but such is not the case in hot countries. Turned wood stoppers covered with leather are a common device, but are not good, as their weight causes them to sink and put the pipe out of tune. Corks are better, but in India cannot be used for pipes above 1 in. diameter, as in damp weather they swell and bulge the pipe, and in dry weather shrink. Cork also has a grain, and alters more across it than along it, so that cork stoppers are only round under the precise conditions in which they were cut. A good plan is to permanently solder on the top of the pipe, providing large ears to tune with. The difficulty in getting at them for tuning is the only objection to this plan. For a Rohr Flute the little chimney is soldered into the lid. A simple box-lid, with paper or leather in the joint, does fairly well; but perhaps the best plan is to put the lid inside the pipe, with a wire sticking through it, and resting on an incline cut on the pipe top, as shown in Fig. 112. The stopper, of course, is leathered. When stoppers are applied to zinc pipes the surface on which the leather slides should be a band of pure lead, as leather seizes on mixed metal. The feet of large pipes should be at least 12 in. long, and, better, 18 in., not only for appearance, but because if the foot is too short the tone may suffer. The feet of small pipes, which are all of one length,

can be most economically cut out of a strip of metal whose
width is the length of the foot, the pieces for the feet being
set out heads and tails alternately, so as to waste no metal.

150. No particular difference exists in the making of zinc
pipes, except that the best flux for soldering them is hydrochloric acid, known as spirits of salt. Take a pennyworth,
put it into a wide-mouthed bottle, and drop in as much zinc
shavings as it will dissolve. When settled, strain off, and add
twice the quantity of distilled or clean rain-water, and a spare
bit of zinc to kill any excess of acid. Zinc is too stiff to work
cold, but is soft when heated. As, however, only large pipes
are made of zinc, and these require a proper rolling machine,
the amateur will probably not have much to do with them.

151. There is no difficulty in painting metal pipes should
the metal be so bad as to require concealment; but zinc pipes
require a good deal of care, or the paint will come off in large
flakes. The pipes must first be well cleaned, then served with
dilute hydrochloric acid, quickly washed over with hot water,
and painted at once. Spon gives an elaborate recipe as follows: 1 part chloride of copper, 1 part nitrate of copper, 1
sal-ammoniac, 64 water. When dissolved, add 1 part com-
mercial hydrochloric acid. Brush the zinc over, and leave
for 24 hours. The plain bath, however, does just as well.

152. *Reed Pipes.*—Although it is quite possible for an
amateur to make reed pipes himself right up from the raw
metals, yet such a course is not recommended. Even organ
builders do not always make in detail every part of their pipes,
but purchase reeds and tongues from the makers of such
articles, merely giving particulars of size. We will, therefore,
only briefly describe the making of such articles as should be
bought, and the amateur will find his hands quite full in
putting them together so as to produce a pipe which shall
speak intelligibly. For a reed pipe we have to provide,
besides the body and foot, or boot as it is called—which are
made in the same way as described for flue pipes—a block, a
reed, a tongue with wedge, and a tuning wire. To begin with
the block, shown at *a*, Figs. 11, 12, 13, Pl. III., this does not
vary in size for every pipe, as it has nothing to do with the
tone. Blocks are cast in certain sets which are used for any

stops, the only desideratum being that they shall be large
enough to take the neck of the pipe body and the tuning wire,
so that six or eight pipes in succession can have identically
the same blocks and boots. The blocks can very well be
turned in hardwood—in fact, they were so made in old
organs; but it is not difficult to cast them in a wooden mould,
using iron pins as cores, and soiling the mould to prevent it
getting burned. The big hole into which the body enters at
top, and the reed at bottom, is put as near the edge as it will
safely go, and the small hole for the tuning wire just gives
room for the crook of the latter to press against the reed.
The projection of the block behind the reed is to sustain the
latter against the pressure of the tuning wire, which in its
proper position rests on the tongue just at this place. The
pipe illustrated is a tenor C Oboe, and the diameters at the
top of the boot are, $c^0 = 1\frac{7}{16}$ in., $c^1 = 1$ in., and $\frac{7}{8}$ in. for c^2 and the
other pipes, dimensions which will be sufficient to guide any-
one desirous of making a set of blocks; but, as aforesaid, it is
much simpler to buy them. The reed or tube against which
the tongue beats is shown in position at d in the figures, and
separately in Figs. 19, 20, and 21, of which the first is what
is called a closed, and the last an open reed. Fig. 20 is a side
view, but the end of the reed is sometimes cut off square.
Open reeds give a more powerful tone, but are not in favour
in England. Figs. 14 to 17 show full size the tongues for
different stops, and in dotted lines the holes in the reeds which
they cover.

153. The reed is simply a brass tube, tapered so that it
can be firmly wedged into its hole, and closed at the lower end
by a plate soldered on, either square, or slanting a little
upwards. Continental reeds sometimes have the ends rounded
up. The average size of a reed is $\frac{1}{2}$ in. in length for every
foot of *tone*-length of the pipe, with enough surplus to fasten
it into the block (see par. 123). The reeds are made of sheet
brass from about 16 to 20 B.W.G., swedged up in an iron
mould; the joint comes on the flat part, and is not soldered.
Before commencing to make them, patterns in metal should
be prepared, to cut the brass by; they should be rolled up
and fitted exactly, and then flattened out and marked with a

reference number. The reed being made, it is turned, and the flat filed on it. This dies away at the top of the reed, leaving only just width enough for the root of the tongue to rest on, and at the bottom is arranged to give the size of aperture required. The flat must be finished dead true and smooth. An 8 ft. trumpet will, for example, require only twelve sizes of reeds, there being from three pipes in each at the bottom, where the size changes rapidly, to five or six in the smaller reeds, where the variation is less.

154. The tongues are made of sheet brass, hammered or drawn to make it hard and elastic, and filed or planed dead smooth. A good machine for planing can be made of two hard steel bars united by fine-threaded screws with large heads, and an index to gauge the thickness; the upper block forms a planer, having an edge set at the correct angle for brass. Drawing the tongues through this makes a better job than filing. Rolling should answer; but the writer does not know if it has ever been tried. To make tongues, take a strip of brass of the right thickness, and as wide as the length of the longest tongue, and mark off the tongues side by side, head and tails, and then score them off with any sharp-cutting instrument, keeping the sheet quite flat. When scored nearly through, they can be broken off; but they should not be sheared, or the edges will curl up and spoil them. To finish, put them into a vice with jaws of hard, smooth wood, and file or plane the edges with an iron plane to the exact size. If in the course of the operations a tongue gets kinked in any way, throw it away—it is spoiled. Finish the tongues on the finest emery-paper, killed and glued on a flat board. A handy vice for working tongues can be made by joining two pieces of wood with a leather hinge and a thumbscrew near the top, or two if the jaws are more than about 3 in. long. The tongues can be cut to shape by putting each into its place when in the rough, and marking off the outline of the reed, or they can all be finished to a scale. Some people prefer to dress tongues with a small hammer on a polished surface, and good work can be done this way, as the writer has succeeded in straightening and using crumpled tongues by this method in repairing an organ when no spare tongues were to hand.

The tongue, when finished, is sometimes made a little thicker at the root than at the tip. The curve is best produced by rubbing the tongue with a smooth steel wire, or even the back of a knife ; but this is a part of voicing, not of pipe-making.

155. As an easy means of avoiding harshness, the larger reeds are generally leathered in modern practice ; but the writer does not approve of the system, and it always gives trouble in hot climates. Probably a hardwood reed would do well in such cases ; or, better still, a more scientific way of curving the tongue would probably enable reeds to be voiced with certainty. The way to leather reeds is to clean them as far as can be seen, dip them in dilute hydrochloric acid (spirits of salt), and then, after cleaning in hot water, heat them on a hot iron till they can just be held. Roll the leather round them with the joint at the back, pressing it well down, and using *pure* gum-arabic or shellac as the cement. Down to and just beyond the tuning wire, the leather must be cut off the flat, and a piece of card of just the same thickness cemented on, otherwise the soft leather would yield under the tuning wire, and make a kink in the tongue. Then carefully level off the leather and card by rubbing on a dead-smooth file or emery-paper, and cut out the wind-hole with a sharp knife.

The wedge requires no description. It is made of hardwood, but metal wedges are best for hot climates.

A view of the tuning wire is given in Fig. 130, Pl. XII. It is made of unannealed steel wire, and the sizes may be 13, 14, and 15 B.W.G. for the 8 ft., 4 ft., and 2 ft. octaves respectively.

156. A free reed can be fitted in much the same way as a striking one, only that the reed must be wider, and preferably fitted with a face-plate to allow the tongue to play through it, the tongue itself being fixed in the block by a wedge, and tuned by a crook fitted exactly as in the striking reed. A better way of fitting free tongues is shown in Figs. 310 and 311, Pl. XXXVIII., where the tongue *a* is secured to a stout plate, *b*, by a couple of screws, *c c*, like a harmonium tongue. This plate is secured to the metal or wooden block *d*, or might even be stuck direct on to the side of the pipe body,

near the bottom, the whole then entering bodily into the boot. But the tuning apparatus makes a difference. In a harmonium, as the reader probably knows, the tongues are tuned by being scraped at the tip to sharpen, and at the root to flatten them; but this would not do for the organ. At the head of the tongue aperture in the plate is a rebate of the following size: At C_1, 0·47 in. wide and 0·08 in. deep; at C_0, 0·41 in. by 0·067 in.; and at c^1, 0·35 in. by 0·04 in. In this rebate slides a little bridle e, which is moved by two pins projecting from the crook f, which, by the elasticity of its wire, presses the tongue firmly down on the bridle, and so settles its vibrating length. Fig. 311 is a side view of the frame, and Fig. 315 a view of the crook. These bridles get too small to be used above c^2. It will thus be seen that a free tongue involves much more fitting than a striking one, and the workmanship must be very perfect; and as they thus have no advantages, either in tone or ease of construction, their use is likely to be limited to special cases, as pedal reeds for chamber organs.

157. Töpfer gives several examples of German practice in free reeds. Fig. 42, Pl. VII., represents full size the largest and smallest reed of a 16 ft. Posaune; Fig. 43 those of a serpent or Fagotto; Fig. 44 an 8 ft. manual trumpet; Fig. 40 a clarinet, and Fig. 41 an oboe. It will be seen that the reeds are just like those used in harmoniums, with the addition of the rebate for the tuning device; also that the area of the tongues is very much larger than that of the striking reeds. J. F. Schultze used *wooden* free tongues in an organ at Bremen, and the tone is not distinguishable from that of metal tongues. The orchestral clarinet has a straight wooden tongue, with a curved reed for it to beat against, and the same arrangement could, of course, be used in an organ pipe.

158. The body of a reed pipe is made just like that of a flue pipe, a conical body being cut out just like a pipe foot (see Fig. 115, Pl. XII.). Bodies under about 2 ft. long are soldered to the block, but for larger pipes the body is separate, and is stuck into the socket shown in Fig. 11, Pl. III. The socket for a cylindrical body is splayed out much more to take

the bottom of the body which is coned off, as in Fig. 144, Pl.
XIII.   Finally, it is necessary to note that reed pipes are very
often mitred to save height, and this does not the least injure
the tone.   It is also very necessary for outside pipes to mitre
them at top, so as to keep the dust out.   Fig. 122, Pl. XII.,
shows a pipe mitred at the bottom to gain height, and hooded
at the top to keep out dust.   Appendix IV. gives Töpfer's
weights for bodies of different stops in tin.   If of worse metal,
the weight must be proportionably increased.

Reed pipes with loose bodies require to have them supported by a rack near the top.   This is a piece of plank, with
holes cut to receive half the body, sloped so as to match the
length of the pipes, which are secured by tying with tapes, or
by a metal loop soldered on, which hooks over a stout pin
driven into the rack.

159. Wooden pipes next claim our attention, and for the
manufacture of these nothing more than ordinary carpenters'
tools is required.   The block is best made out of a piece of
scantling, reduced to the cross section of the largest pipe of
the series.   Cut off the first block about ½ in. longer than required, for a purpose that will appear hereafter; the block
may be any length that will give room for the throat, and a
piece strong enough to stick the foot in—say 4 in. for the first
octave, 3 in. for the second, then 2½ in. and 2 in., diminishing
gradually.   Plane the scantling down to the section for the
next pipe, cut off the block with the spare ½ in., and so on.
Builders always make the feet separately, and stick them
in afterwards; but the writer prefers to make them in one
piece, with blocks less than 1 in. thick.   The top of the block
should not be square, but inclined down in the pipe at an
angle of 30°, as shown in most of the sections of pipes.   The
two side boards should next be glued and screwed to the
block, the extra ½ in. being cut off and stuck between the
boards at the top of the pipe to insure the dimensions being
true.   Indeed, if the pipe is a long one, it is better to stick
two or three little pillars between the sides to keep them true,
for if a pipe is the least bit hollow in section it will never
speak well; but, curiously, it does not matter if it is a bit
bulged in shape.   The edges of the boards, and with them the

H

block, should now be shot perfectly true, and the front and
back boards may be put on. And here a word must be said
upon the process of gluing. A glued joint is all very well in
Europe, though even there it sometimes fails ; but in a tropical
climate the glue absolutely perishes out of a joint which
depends on it alone, and a well-made English pipe may after
a short time be picked up in four pieces. No pains, therefore, must be spared to insure a perfect joint for any climate.
The joint may be screwed down, and so true that the eye
cannot detect it, yet unless by means of the glue the two
planks vibrate as one body, no tone can be got out of that
pipe. Heat is the great essential to secure proper penetration
of the glue, and the best way to apply it in pipe-making is to
have a lot of scrap iron in lengths of about 2 ft., and any sections over 1 in. square, these to be laid, when hot, right along
the joint, and left there during and after the process of screwing down. Brads are not contemplated in decent work. The
writer uses a little iron tank filled with water, kept boiling to
heat the irons in ; but where gas is available, a little stove
might be contrived. For tropical climates and for teak, it is
a good plan to interpose a strip of leather in the joint, because
glue holds wood and leather better than wood and wood.

160. When the block and side boards have been faced up,
go over them and the other boards with the toothing-plane, a
tool which should always be used for work to be glued. For
a large pipe use screws, and do not be stingy with them, but
for small pipes it is best to wrap with string, and wedge, and
put the screws in afterwards. When dry, trim off the sides,
and cut off the bottom and the top with the piece in it.
Blocks are often made by gluing a ¾ in. strip of mahogany on
the face of a soft wood scantling, a practice quite inadmissible
for hot climates, where the block must be solid. Nor is it
good to splice in a mouthpiece ; if the front board is good
wood of a proper thickness it is quite unnecessary.

The pipe being made and cleaned, the cap and accessories
—in the way of ears, beards, and bridges—should be provided, and if the pipe is a Gedackt it will require a stopper.

161. A common, but vicious, practice is to make this out
of a bit of board, with a peg stuck into it for a handle ; but in

hot weather the pipe-walls will shrink, and be split where the plank of the stopper runs lengthways of the grain, and consequently does not alter. So in damp weather, the pipe-walls will expand more than the stopper does lengthways, and the joint being loose, the tone will be spoiled. Stoppers should always be cut with the grain, as they are for small pipes; in fact, the larger the pipe, the more necessary it is. For very large ones, they need not be carved out of the solid, handle and all; but they can be glued up round the handle, or made of a thin plate, cut *across* the grain. The stoppers should be quite smaller than the pipe, and packed to fit with leather strips. The writer has used felt lining in big pipes with much success; it makes a much better fit than a stopper with one thickness of leather. The corners and edges of the stopper should be arrised to prevent the leather getting cut, and in putting it in, a dab of glue should be put on the end of the stopper, which should then be pressed on the hair side of the leather, the other side and the interior of the pipe being well blackleaded. To test the fit in both directions, thrust the stopper cornerways into the pipe, as, if put in square, the fit might be tight in one direction but quite loose in the other. As nine-tenths of the ailments of stopped pipes are due to defective stoppers, too much care cannot be taken with them.

162. Another variety of block for large pipes must be described. When the pipe gets too large to have a solid block, it is made up of two planks an inch or more thick, checked into the sides, with the grain running across the pipe so as to give a smooth surface for the windway. The pipes shown in Figs. 22 to 25, Pl. IV., are built in this way.

163. After the pipes are finished they should be well coated both inside and out with two coats of good oil paint; the ordinary rough wood, with a little sizing smeared over it, by no means making the best of the material. For large pipes it has been the writer's practice to paint the trough formed by the sides and back, and all the front board except the part to be glued, leaving only the front corners to be done with a mop after the pipe is finished.

Regarding the thickness of planks to be used for pipe-walls, an ordinary Gedackt c° would require ¾ in. plank in pine or

$\frac{3}{8}$ in. in teak, and no pipe should have less than $\frac{1}{4}$ in. Such a pipe would be about $3\frac{1}{2}$ in. deep, and as the thickness of plank is a function, not of the length, but of the unsupported width of the pipe, this statement will give some idea of the sizes to be used. As the thickness depends upon the maximum unsupported width, the advantage of a square pipe is obvious, since it reduces the size to a minimum. Töpfer gives as the proper thickness for a full-scaled and toned pedal open 2·9 in., 1·9 in., and 1·34 in. for the C_2, C_1, and C_0 respectively; and though these thicknesses are more than are usually deemed sufficient, there can be no doubt that a good tone is not to be got out of old packing-cases glued together.

164. Having described in general terms the building of a wooden pipe, the different varieties of mouths which have to be provided for must now be noticed. Fig. 29, Pl. IV., shows the mouth of a Bourdon suitable to a chamber organ or a Lieblich Bourdon. The upper lip is left thick, and rounded off, and may be slightly arched. The block has been made of two plates, as described in par. 161, and is formed with an English mouth. Figs. 27 and 28 compare what may be called the English and the German style of mouth. The former leaves the block untouched, except for the notching, and the cap is hollowed out and the windway taken off it, and is set a little below the block. The latter has the throat slanted right up to the top of the block, off which the windway is taken, and the cap is left level. The former is better for soft, and the latter for loud Gedackts and flutes. The square-topped block is shown with the English mouth, because builders usually make them that way; but the slanting block shown in most of the pipe sections is much the best for every sort of pipe. The Bourdon shown in Fig. 29 is provided with ample ears and beard.

165. Fig. 30 shows the mouth of an open Döppel Flute, and a single mouth flute would be made in just the same way. Here the block is solid, and the throat is made by boring two holes through, and taking out the piece between. A slight slant is cut down the block, and the windway is taken off the cap. The top of the block slants down from each mouth towards the middle of the pipe.

Fig. 26 shows an entirely different class of mouth—that of a Salicional.   The block is in one piece, and the throat slopes right up to the top of the block, leaving a sharp edge.   The cap is slightly hollowed, and the windway is taken off it ; then a slant, something like the upper lip, is cut on the outside of the cap, and a bridge of peculiar construction fitted in, its exact position being fixed by the voicer.   It should be observed that the mouth does not occupy the whole width of the pipe, which is square, but is as much less as will give a width of mouth corresponding to one-fifth the circumference of a metal pipe.

166. Fig. 22 shows a wooden Open Diapason, which, if of small scale, requires a bridge to the mouth.   The type of bridge here figured is that generally used by Schultze, and is of a peculiar shape.   *a* of Fig. 23 shows the bridge looking from the foot, and *b* the same viewed from the mouth.   A plain cylinder is also sometimes used.   An Open Diapason voices well without cutting any windway at all, by using a flat cap bedded on a strip of leather of suitable thickness.

Fig. 24 shows a Violone pipe, which does not differ much from the style of the Open.   The windway of the cap may be a little more slanted outwards ; *a* shows the bridge.

Fig. 25 shows a Viol da Gamba pipe ; here also the mouth is not the full width, as a delicate tone is required.

167. Fig. 32, Pl. V., shows a wood Travers Flute (harmonic). These, if properly voiced, sound exactly like a real flute.   The bodies are turned out of some smooth-grained wood—cherry is good—or they may be planed up octagonal; the bore is then made and smoothed.   Then a slant is taken off one face with a plane, the mouth marked and cut, and a cork plug glued in to form the bottom of the pipe a diameter below the mouth.   The windway hole is bored and the cap and foot fitted.   The most elegant way of tuning these pipes is to spring *into* the bore a little rolled-up strip of tin-plate or thin sheet brass like a cartridge case, in just the same way as the tuning slide is put outside a metal pipe.

Fig. 37, Pl. VI., shows a flute, whose peculiarity consists in having a bead or cylinder, instead of an edge to the lip ; but it has no special merit provided the lip of a flute-toned pipe is left thick, as it always should be; just on the principle that a thick soft hammer will produce a softer sound than a hard thin-edged one on a string.

168. Fig. 33, Pl. V., shows another style of flute which gives good results, but does not differ materially from Fig. 34, which shows the French style of Travers Flute. The pipe may be either built up, or bored out of the solid, and the principal peculiarity consists in the wedge *a*, which tilts up the cap, so as to throw the wind against the upper lip, much in the same way as the mouth of a flute-player acts.

Very much akin to this is the Harmonika, a German contrivance, Fig. 35, Pl. VI. This pipe is also furnished with a wedge, *a*, and the mouth has ears *b b*, and sometimes a metal bridge, or shade, is put in front of the mouth, as shown by the dotted lines at *c*. The cap and wedge project over the mouth, and are adjusted in voicing; the higher up they are put, the sharper is the tone. Fig. 35A shows the style of windway for the four C's. The wedge for C_0 would be 0·15 in. thick in front, and 0·2 in. at the back, tapering down in the smallest pipe to the thickness of a sheet of paper. The lengths vary from $2\frac{1}{4}$ in. to $1\frac{1}{2}$ in.

Fig. 38 shows a style of mouth highly commended by an able writer in the 'English Mechanic'; the cap is plain, and set the least trifle *above* the block.

Fig. 36 shows the top G sharp of a Doppel Flute. Here the essential downward slant of the block is obtained by boring a hole at the junction of a pair of blocks, and then sawing them asunder.

Fig. 39 shows half-size a Violone pipe by Roosevelt, of New York, which has a cylindrical bridge.

169. These figures, and the descriptions above given, should be sufficient for the construction of any style of wood pipe, and it only remains to add that the number or note of the pipe should be neatly stamped near the mouth, and stencilled on the top, so that it can be seen when the pipe is in position. One point that was omitted above may be noticed here—viz., how to form the slant of the upper lip, for though it does not exactly affect the tone, yet it is as well to do it by rule. Make the slant part square, that is, for the top of the

slant, set off the width of the mouth above the upper lip. Then cut the slant down so as to run out to nothing at the bottom end of the board, and when the mouth is cut up the lip will be of a suitable thickness. The low mouth of a Salicional will be tolerably sharp, while the high mouth of a Gedackt will be thick, as it ought to be. Pipes requiring a keen tone should have the upper lip made quite sharp by the stroke of a chisel at the time of voicing. When round pipes cannot be conveniently bored in the solid, they may be made in two halves, scooped out, and then joined ; but there should be no difficulty in boring with the different sizes of auger-bits of a set, and finishing to the exact size with a rimer or expanding bit, which could easily be contrived.

Plates IV., V. and VI. represent the pipes half-size.

CHAPTER V

ORGAN STOPS

170. ORGAN stops may be considered as the instruments which make up a complete orchestra; from which it is obvious they must *first* be selected rather with a view to building up a harmonious whole, than for individual peculiarities of tone, a point which will be discussed further on. With the description of the stops is given a choice of scales and the wind-consumption, as a bare list of organ stops is of very little use. Only such stops are mentioned as are of real use in organ-building; mere fancy variations and antiquities are omitted.

A word must be said as to the naming of stops. Clearly the use of the name on the draw-stop is to intimate to the organist as nearly as possible the character of tone-colour it governs; and therefore certain names should indicate well-defined qualities as near as the personal equation of the builder will allow. But builders are often careless in such matters, and are content to make one name, such as Open Diapason, cover anything from a flute to nearly a Geigen. The writer has seen a coarse open wooden flute labelled 'Rohr Flute' (the stop had not been changed), and, to equalise matters, in another organ a real Rohr Flute with metal chimneys was labelled simply 'Flute.'

171. Stops have to be considered under the following aspects : (1) Tone-length—as whether they sound the unison to the note put down, or some other note, under which heads there are : *Foundation stops*, which give the note of the key, whether higher or lower in octaves; *Mutation stops*, which sound the harmonics to the note touched, as the fifths and thirds in different octaves, known as Quint and Tierce sounding-stops; and *Compound stops*, as Mixtures and Cornets,

which have several pipes to each note.　(2) In respect of tone
stops may be classified as : *Diapason tone*, of which the Open
Diapason is the exemplar ; *String tone*, of which the Gamba
is the representative ; *Flute tone*, the name of which is sufficiently definite, and under this head the covered stops will be
included ; *Reed tone* must have a classification to itself, not
because the pipes are made in a different way to the above
mentioned, but because there is a broad distinction between
the quality of all reed and flue work, quite independent of the
question of mere loudness.　Among reed stops themselves
there are great varieties of tone.

172. Rimbault also classifies stops as whole—half—incomplete—short and repetition, as well as accessory ; but it
seems hardly necessary to accord a formal recognition to im-
perfections, and in a properly-designed organ every stop
should go through, except, perhaps, stops imitative of orchestral instruments whose range is less than that of the organ,
and even these should be provided with a suitable bass on the
same draw stop.　As for couplers—they are couplers and not
stops, for there is an essential difference between *stops* and
stop-handles, and the only intelligible way of speaking of an
organ is by the former, though it is to be feared that organs
are too often appraised by the latter.

In respect of the classification by tone-length, the necessity
for stops sounding other than the unison is explained elsewhere, and here we need only remark that, in addition to the
name, it is customary and necessary to mark the tone-length
on the stop label, as the same name—such as Flute—may
indicate either the 8 ft. or unison, or 4 ft. or octave, or perhaps
some other length.

173. The writer considers the classification by tone as the
most important (though it is sometimes a little difficult to say
exactly under which category a pipe should be placed), and it
is under this heading that the detailed description of stops
will be given.　One of the commonest faults in English
organs is an utter disproportion between manual and pedal,
so it is as well not even to talk of ' pedal stops ' as a separate
order.　They will be referred to merely as a variety in tone-
length of the manual stop.　The French and German names

have also been given, and it is well to point out that these do duty for any tone-length, instead of being reserved for a particular pitch, as is usual in England. Thus an English organ with 16 ft. manual would be described as having a Double Open Diapason 16 ft., Open 8 ft., Principal 4 ft. ; and an 8 ft. manual as Open 8 ft., Principal 4 ft. ; while in Germany the description of the former would be : Principal 16 ft., Octave 8 ft., Octave 4 ft. ; and of the latter, Principal 8 ft., Octave 4 ft. And even this arrangement might be varied, and the stops labelled—Principal 16 ft., Principal 8 ft., Octave 4 ft. ; from all which variations in nomenclature the absolute necessity of indicating the tone-length may readily be seen.

STOPS OF DIAPASON TONE.

174. *Open Diapason* (a), 32 ft. tone on Pedal. *Double Open* ⟩ 32 ft. G., *Untersatz.* Fr., *Pédale de 32 ft.* ; *Grosse Principal, Montre* (when the pipes are in front). This stop is only found in the largest organs, and, having in view the fact that the limit of musical notes is about G_2, below which the pitch is only recognised by the harmonics, it seems very doubtful whether it is worth while to carry this stop any lower, especially as a distinct 32 ft. tone can be obtained by the combination of a Great Quint with the 16 ft. Open. This is called a ' Harmonic Bass.'

The lower pipes of the Untersatz are enormously costly in money, wind, and space, and are not always a success. The pipes must be of large scale, being a little larger than the 16 ft. pedal, which in its turn is a little larger than the Manual stop for fulness, and the very large pipes require an extra low mouth, since the absolute distance the wind has to reach is so great. Where the mouth in 8 ft. tone would be $\frac{1}{4}$ the diameter, it should not at 32 ft. be more than $\frac{1}{5}$, and in a square pipe with full mouth proportionately lower, to keep the same relation of mouth to body area, though some dispute this, and would keep the height of mouth constant for the same wind, whatever the width.

Some builders go up to 24 in. by 20 in. with a mouth $5\frac{1}{2}$ in. high ; but 19 in. diameter would be a more moderate scale for a maximum in the ratio $2\frac{2}{3}$. The bore would be 3 in. and wind consumption 1,670 c. in. per second. For a minimum scale $15\frac{1}{4}$ in. by 12 in. in the ratio $2\frac{1}{2}$. Bore $2\frac{1}{4}$ in., wind 915 c. in.

To be a success, this stop should have a soundboard of its own, and the planks should be very thick and sound. This, and not making the pipes as big as a culvert, is the way to get tone out of them.

175. (*b*) 32 ft. tone on Manual. Double Open, 32 ft. G., Manual-Untersatz. Fr., Grosse Principal, Montre de 32 ft. A very rare stop, and should follow the scaling of the 8 ft. stop. There is one down to c° in Schultze's organ in Doncaster Church.

176. (*c*) 16 ft. tone on Pedal. *Open Diapason*, or *Double Open*, 16 ft. G., *Principal-Bass*. Fr., *Grosse Principal, Prestant, Montre*. Sounds C_1. This is the foundation-tone of the pedal, and the pipes should have a rather larger scale than the manual, not for loudness, but for fulness.

For a very large organ, C_1 might be $11\frac{1}{2}$ in. by 9 in., mouth $2\frac{1}{4}$ in. high, ratio $2\frac{2}{3}$, bore $1\frac{3}{4}$ in.; wind supply 800 c. in.; but a better scale would be $10\frac{1}{2}$ in. by $8\frac{1}{4}$ in., mouth $2\frac{1}{4}$ in., ratio $2\frac{1}{2}$, bore $1\frac{3}{4}$ in., wind 730 c. in. For a smaller organ, $7\frac{3}{8}$ in. by 6 in., mouth one-third the width, bore $1\frac{3}{8}$ in., wind 410 c. in.; the tone to be kept stringy, but full. These scales may be smaller than those mostly affected by English builders; but if properly built, voiced, and planted, they are perfectly efficient, and give an excellent tone. The feet are not supposed to be plugged.

It is, of course, a matter of taste what the scale, on which the tone so largely depends, should be, and some people may like the thick, tubby tone produced by the monstrous scales found in many English organs; but the writer prefers the more melodious note produced by a moderate scale. It is probable that the origin of these large scales is to be found in the attempt to make up in a few pipes for the want of an effective pedal department, and that they have been continued from mere force of habit and the curious idea that making windows shake is grand music. As pointed out in Rimbault and Hopkins, they are never used on the Continent.

177. (*d*) 16 ft. tone on Manual. *Double Open*, 16 ft. G.,

Principal. Fr., *Principal, Prestant, Montre.* Sounds C_1. This is, in a large organ, the foundation from which all the other stops are scaled; but as it only follows the principles of the 8 ft. Open, the scaling will be given under that head.

178. (*e*) 8 ft. tone on Manual. *Open Diapason,* 8 ft. G., *Principal,* 8 ft. Fr., *Prestant, Montre.* Sounds C_0. This stop is the foundation of the whole organ. Upon its worth depends that of the whole instrument, and its scale decides that of all the other stops in the organ except the string and flute stops. Too much care, then, cannot be exercised in selecting the best proportions and tone for each individual case. For a large instrument the Open should be full, but never lose its freshness and become tubby; and for smaller ones it should be melodious, with power suited to the rest of the organ. It is not uncommon to find instruments in which the Open bears no sort of proportion to the other stops, but when drawn simply swallows them up. A good average rule is to make the Pedal Open three pipes larger than the first Manual Open, and any second Open three pipes smaller, voicing at the same time for a distinctive quality of tone.

The writer is of opinion that 6 in. diameter for C_0 is the biggest scale that should be used (for 3 in. wind) scaling in the ratio $1 : \sqrt{8}$. This would require a bore of 1·1 in., and a wind-supply of 310 c. in. per second. He can state from experience that $5\frac{1}{2}$ in. adequately voiced is ample for the C_0 of an organ of 30 stops in a large church. Schultze used $5\frac{3}{4}$ in. diam. in the ratio $1 : \sqrt{8}$ as a *full* diapason scale. When pipes are made much larger than these sizes, they must inevitably, if properly winded, be so much louder than the other stops as not to blend with them, and if not winded up to their size, they give a tone quite wanting in the richness that should never be absent from the true Diapason.

179. As it would be difficult to improve on Schultze, we will note here that if $5\frac{3}{4}$ in. diameter at C_0 is taken as the standard for all except the very largest organs, and the ratio of $\sqrt{8}$ is used, we shall have a c^1 2·03 in. diameter, and C_1 will be 10·8 in., and C_2 18·2 in. If the ratio $1 : 2\frac{2}{3}$ is used, in which the half falls on the 17th pipe, we shall have $C_2 = 17·1$ in., $C_1 = 10·5$ in., and $c^1 = 2·16$ in.

The standard mouth for the Open is $\frac{1}{4}$ the circumference in width, and $\frac{1}{3}$ the width, or more exactly $\frac{1}{4}$ the diameter, in height; but Schultze obtains a very good effect from quite small scales by using a mouth of $\frac{2}{7}$ the circumference, with beards up to about 9°.

For smaller organs, $5\frac{1}{8}$ in. diameter in the ratio $2\frac{2}{3}$ would do well, with a bore of 1 in. and wind-supply of 245 c. in. For sweetness, rather than power, reduce the width of mouth to $\frac{2}{8}$ the circumference.

For a chamber organ on a $2\frac{1}{2}$ in. wind, $4\frac{1}{4}$ in. diameter will be found sufficient. Bore 0·9 in. and wind 200 c. in. When there are more than one Open in the organ, there should be difference in the quality of tone, as well as in mere loudness.

180. Töpfer practically recommends 2 in. diameter for c^1 for ordinary church organs, whatever the ratio. This gives at C_0 5·6 in. for the ratio 1 : $\sqrt{8}$, and 5·3 in. for ratio 1 : $2\frac{2}{3}$. He quotes the 16 ft. Open in the Basle organ by Haas, as the scale of a man given to large scales for a very large building. The C_1 is 10·2 in. diameter, and the C_0 $6\frac{1}{4}$ in., a size that may be found in village church organs in England. The C_1 of this organ has a bore of 1·4 in., and the height of mouth is only $\frac{1}{5}$ the diameter, on account of the very large scale. The size for C_2 would be 18·9 in. to correspond. In the Leeds organ there is a $6\frac{1}{4}$ in. Open on a $8\frac{3}{4}$ in. wind; but this would be too much for any ordinary organ.

It will be convenient to assemble, for ready reference, the scales scattered about in the above remarks, as too much thought cannot be given to the decision of a point on which the whole musical character of the organ depends. The diameter of a metal pipe is, it will be remembered, equivalent to the depth of a wooden one to produce the same quality of tone:

C_2	C_1	C_0	c^1	Ratio		
in.	in.	in.	in.			
24	14·75	6·75	2·19	various	Different English organs	
18·9	10·2	6·25	2·35	$2\frac{2}{3}$	Absolute maximum, Töpfer	
17·6	10·5	5·6	2	$\sqrt{8}$	Ordinary Scales,	In all these the
15·9	9·8	5·3	2	$2\frac{2}{3}$	Töpfer	pedal is made
18·2	10·8	5·75	2·03	$\sqrt{8}$	Full scale, Schultze	three pipes
16·5	10·1	5·5	2·06	$2\frac{2}{3}$	Recommended by writer	larger than the manual
—	9·6	5·2	1·95	$2\frac{2}{3}$	Open for second manual or small organ	
—	8·0	4·25	1·6	$2\frac{2}{3}$	Chamber scale	

The reader should have no difficulty, from the examples given above, in suiting himself with a scale for any size of organ.

181. *Principal*, 4 ft. G. and Fr., *Octave*. Sounds c°. This is really the Open in 4 ft. tone, and should be bright and clear, voiced with reference to what is below as well as above it. It may be the same scale as the Open, or a pipe smaller.

182. *Twelfth*, 2⅔. G., *Quint*. Fr., *Quinte, Nasard*. Sounds g°. From the relations of the 'combination tones,' as described in the chapter on Acoustics, all Quint stops have a peculiar thickening effect, and, if too predominant, produce a disagreeable effect, and especially should they be kept from obtruding themselves in the lower part of the scale. It is, therefore, more important to keep the tone quiet and as fluty as possible in the bass, by voicing, than to reduce the scale, which should be that of the Open, but with a smaller mouth, ⅕ or ⅔ the circumference. The upper notes may be voiced keener. This stop should never be used without the Fifteenth to cover it, and consequently, if the convenience of the player is consulted, rather than the desire to increase the number of stop-handles, it should be placed on the same draw, which is then labelled Rausch-Quint (q. v.).

183. *Fifteenth*, 2 ft. G., *Octave* or *Super Octave*. Fr., *Doublette*. Sounds c¹. The scale should be a pipe or two smaller than the Open, and the tone not too screaming—a common fault. The mouth should be kept low, and the tone keen and bright—a remark which applies to all small pipes. A screaming tone is produced by cutting the mouth too high and voicing up to that. This stop always goes through; but, to tell the truth, the last half-dozen pipes are very little use, and it would probably be an improvement to repeat from c⁵.

The Fifteenth is the smallest stop that should be dignified by a draw to itself, though a thing called a Sifflöte, 1 ft. tone-length, has been so placed. There are also to be found in old organs the *Tierce* 1⅗, G. and Fr. *Tierce*. Sounds e¹. A Tenth or Double Tierce, sounding e°, is a rare stop found on few organs on manual and pedal. *Nineteenth*, 1⅓; F., Larigot, the octave twelfth.

184. We next take up the Compound Stops, as they are really members of the Diapason work.

Quint Mixture, $2\frac{2}{3}$. G., *Rausch-Quint.*—A Twelfth and Fifteenth on one slider, the most appropriate way of placing them. Both ranks run through without a break, though, where space is an object, it is admissible to admit the lowest four, or even six, pipes of the Twelfth rank.

Here it should be explained that, as most of the pipes in compound stops are smaller than the Fifteenth, they cannot be carried right through, as the pipes get too small; it is, therefore, necessary to repeat the octaves, taking care to arrange the breaks, as they are called, so as to be as little perceptible as possible.

185. *Mixture.*—Like many other names of stops, this word is used rather indefinitely. In the first place, it is the generic term for all compound stops; but, strictly speaking, it means the principal compound stop, made up entirely of fifths and octaves. The tone-length is not invariable, as it depends a good deal upon whether the organ has a separate Twelfth and Fifteenth. For instance, a not uncommon arrangement in small German organs is to put, after the 4 ft. work, a III. rank Mixture of 2 ft. tone, thus :

$$C_o \text{ has } \qquad c^1 - g^1 - c^2$$
$$c^2 \text{ has } \qquad c^2 - g^3 - c^4$$

For a VI. rank Mixture the following is an ordinary combination :

$$C_o \text{ has } \qquad g^0 - c^1 - g^1 - c^2 - g^2 - c^3$$
$$c^0 \text{ has } \qquad c^1 - g^1 - c^2 - g^2 - c^3 - g^3$$
$$c^1 \text{ has } \qquad g^1 - c^2 - g^2 - c^3 - g^3 - c^4$$
$$c^2 \text{ has } \qquad c^2 - g^2 - c^3 - g^3 - c^4 - g^4$$
$$c^3 \text{ has } \qquad g^2 - c^3 - g^3 - c^4 - g^4 - c^5$$

But if there are other compound stops with breaks on the 'c's,' the repeats of the Mixture should be put on F sharp.

To reduce the ranks of Mixture, drop the lower ones, and to increase them, as is sometimes done, up to VIII., add upwards in 'c's' and 'g's' as far as size will allow. The stop is made to Diapason scale, or, according to some, there should be a difference in size of a pipe between the several ranks. Screaming Mixtures are so objectionable, especially when fluty as well as loud, that many builders omit them from organs whose size demands them. But there is not the slightest occasion for a Mixture to be offensive in an organ of any size, as those can testify who have heard the *five*-rank Mixture in Mr. Audsley's chamber organ, the effect of which was charming, though the organ was not at all a large one (see specifications); but then the Mixture was of small scale, and as carefully voiced as if each rank was a Solo stop—not made by the yard and cut off in slices.

186. *Sesquialtera*, $2\frac{2}{3}$.—This is another name which has been loosely used. Properly speaking, the Sesquialtera is a two-rank stop, sounding the Twelfth and the Tierce, the interval between which is a major sixth, hence the name. Such a stop goes through without a break. The name, however, is extended to mean a compound stop of thirds, fifths, and octaves, examples being found up to V. ranks, the notes for which on C_o would be e^1—g^1—c^2—g^2—c^3. The scale should be full, the mouth small, and the tone not too predominant, and there is no harm in leaving out four or five of the Tierce pipes in the bass.

187. *Cymbal.*—This is really a second Mixture of smaller scale, and in most cases of higher pitch—for instance, with a IV. rank Mixture of g^1—c^1—g^2—c^3, if a second compound stop were wanted, it might be a III. rank Cymbal of c^2—g^2—c^3. The composition of a VII. rank Cymbal would be—

C_o has .	.	. $c^1 - g^1 - c^2 - g^2 - c^3 - g^3 - c^4$
c^o has .	.	. $g^1 - c^2 - g^2 - c^3 - g^3 - c^4 - g^4$
f^o has .	.	. $f^1 - c^2 -- f^2 - c^3 - f^3 - c^4 - f^4$
c^1 has .	.	. $g^1 - c^2 - g^2 - c^3 - g^3 - c^4 - g^4$

and so on, dropping the larger ranks as their number decreases. The pipes of this stop being all very small, it should have Diapason scale, and screaming should be carefully avoided.

188. *Sharp: Scharf: Acuta.*—This is a stop of fifths, thirds, and octaves of small scale and sharp tone, suitable to the second manual. It has various numbers of ranks and different pitch. A VII. rank would have—

C_o has .	$g^1 - c^2 - e^2 - g^2 - c^3 - g^3 - c^4$
$F_o\sharp$ has .	$f^1\sharp - c^2\sharp - f^2\sharp - a^2\sharp - c^3\sharp - f^3\sharp - c^4\sharp$
c^o has .	$g^1 - c^2 - e^2 - g^2 - c^3 - g^3 - c^4$

and so on, with a break on every c and f sharp. For fewer ranks omit the upper ones.

189. *Furniture.*—A French stop, also found in English organs. It appears to be the second or third compound stop where more are wanted, and is smaller than any of the others. It has various pitches and compositions.

Tertian.—A very rare stop. It has a Third of 1⅗ ft. length and a Fifth of 1⅓ ft.

190. *Cornet.*—A compound stop found in most old organs, but in very few modern ones. It is a complete little organ in itself, as the proper definition of a cornet is a compound stop of 8 ft. tone, containing the unison, either stopped or open, the Principal, Twelfth, Fifteenth, and Tierce. It should have a wider scale than the Open Diapason, and go through without a break; but it seldom ranges below c⁰, nor in English organs below c¹, nor does it always start at once with the full number of ranks. The stop is also called 'Mounted Cornet,' from the fact that it often stands on a little sound-board of its own, supplied by wind through a conveyance pipe from the slider in the main soundboard.

String-toned Stops.

191. *The Gamba.*—The string-toned stops, of which the Gamba is the chief, are just as important as the Diapason work, and should be introduced next after it, for are not the strings the backbone of the orchestra? This quality of tone has been most unaccountably neglected by English builders, and may be said to have been introduced into this country by Schultze. Even now a full use is not made of this necessary ingredient in tone-colour, and a so-called Gamba by an English maker often could not be recognised by its tone. They are also frequently slotted, a practice which is destructive of the true Gamba tone, and which makes much more difference than might be expected. Slotting imparts a peculiar hard or horny quality of tone, and should never be employed unless that quality is deliberately wished for. It is, after all, a matter of taste; but the writer finds that quality to be very wearying. If any reader has a slotted string-toned stop, let him try soldering up the slots of half a dozen pipes, and cutting them to the proper length, and it is probable that he will

I

convert the rest of the stop. The cutting away the back of front pipes has not the same effect as slotting, because the superfluous length is so completely cleared away that it is as if it did not exist.

192. The true Gamba is a small-scaled stop of a strong and pungent tone. It should be voiced up as much as it will take without becoming harsh, so that it is by no means a soft stop. It imparts a richness to the general organ tone that can be got in no other way, and in combination has the effect of reed work. There is not much variety in the scale, as a special quality is required that can only be got by a small scale. It is found in both 16 ft. and 8 ft. tone as—

(a) *Violone*, 16 ft. G., *Violon-Bass*. Fr., *Gamba*, 16 ft.—A Pedal stop. This is the Pedal to the string-toned stops, and should be simply a Gamba of full scale in 16 ft. tone; but stops labelled with the name are found of curious scales, the mere mention of which is enough to show that the true Gamba tone is absent. Schultze's usual scale was $5\frac{1}{2}$ in. square for C_1, and anybody who thinks that he can improve upon that master's work in string-toned (or, indeed, in any) stops should visit the organ in St. Peter's Church, Hindley, Wigan, the Violone of which is $5\frac{3}{8}$ in. square at C_1. The magnificent tone of the string stops in this organ will be a revelation to most people, as also the fact that the keenest tone that can be wished for is obtained from wood pipes, and that the junction between wood and metal in such stops as the Gamba cannot be detected by the nicest ear. It is generally supposed that string-tone cannot be obtained from wood pipes, and that metal gives quite a different tone; witness the common practice of labelling 'Metal Open' and 'Wood Open.' But there would be no difficulty in matching the tone with the materials reversed.

A very good writer in the ' English Mechanic ' gives 7 in. by 5 in. at the mouth, and $8\frac{1}{2}$ in. by $6\frac{1}{2}$ in. at top, with a mouth cut up half the width, as a Violone scale; but the scale is rather large, the mouth much too high, and the taper more trouble to make than a plain pipe, and *not* good for the tone. The writer has used as much as $5\frac{3}{4}$ in. square (on a 4 in. wind) for a Violone in a fairly large organ, where a

Major Bass could not be placed, and the result was satisfactory, giving a good fulness of tone without losing the 'bite.' He believes that a Violone has been made as small as 3 in. square at C_1, but has not seen one so small,

Töpfer's scale is 6·25 in. diameter for C_1 in the ratio 2⅔, wind 270 c. in., and bore 1·1 in., the mouth cut up ⅖ the diameter.

Violone pipes should, if possible, have a clear look out of the organ, as they are very sensitive. When a pipe will not speak properly, sometimes turning it round will set it right. They sometimes go off their speech in places where they do not seem at all crowded.

193. (b) 16 ft. Manual tone. *Contra Gamba.*—A rather rare stop, but might be used more often to much advantage. There is a beautiful example in the Hindley organ, of which C_1 is 6¼ in. by 5 in., with a mouth 1 in. high. The scale is rather large, and the voicing is kept down so as not to make the stop too prominent.

194. (c) 8 ft. tone. *Gamba* on the Manual, and *Violoncello* on the Pedal.—Töpfer recommends for C_0 3·4 in. diameter in the ratio 2⅔, with bore 0·72 in., and wind consumption 122 c. in., mouth 0·85 in. high. Or 3½ in. diameter in the ratio √8. Schultze made Gambas up to 3⅜ in. diameter, and an English voicer, unsurpassed at this class of stop, made his C_0 only 3 in. diameter, and increased the scale one pipe at each of c^1, c^2 and two pipes at c^3, g^3.

This class of stop is not much used above the 8 ft. pitch (and not enough there, in England), but, to complete the string family, a 4 ft. Gamba might be introduced after the Principal.

195. *Terpodion.*—This is verging upon the fancy stops, but merits a description, as the tone is as near an approach to that of a reed as can be got from a flue pipe. The stop was first made by Schultze for the Doncaster organ, and is a Gamba with a very wide, low mouth, and exceedingly keen tone, rather slow in speech. Such pipes are an awful trouble to voice *keeping the tone*, though easy enough if cut up recklessly.

196. *Violin Diapason,* 8 ft.　G., *Geigen.*—This stop is on

the borderland between the Diapason and string work; but its name places it in the latter category. It forms the second Open, or the Open of the second manual, on all German organs, and has a perfectly definite tone, partaking of the fulness of the Open and the fire of the Gamba; but most English examples are wanting in character. The anonymous author of a very excellent little work on voicing and tuning (evidently a practical man) well exemplifies the reason for the failure of the average English Geigen, when he describes it as 'one pipe smaller than the Open, and rendered reedy by a slot.' He had evidently never heard a real Geigen. It is, of course, a matter of taste whether the hard, horny tone produced by slotting is desirable; but the stop described is not the least like the Geigen, either in scale or treatment, and should be called a Horn Diapason.

Schultze's full scale with a $5\frac{3}{4}$ in. Open was $4\frac{1}{2}$ in. diameter for C_o of the Geigen, or five pipes smaller, and this is also the scale given by Töpfer. The height of the mouth would be 1·08 in., wind 215 c. in., and bore 0·95 in. This stop, as well as the Gamba, requires a bridge in front of the mouth, and the great octave of both can well be made in square wood pipes. The writer recommends a $\frac{2}{3}$-wide mouth for the Geigen; this style is more trouble to voice, but produces a magnificent tone.

197. *Bell Gamba*, 8 ft.—This is a very beautiful stop, of a soft stringy tone, and, as its name implies, is of conical shape, surmounted by a bell. The stop does not generally go below c°, and should then be completed by ordinary pipes. Some people would not scruple even to put stopped pipes. There is a fine example down to C_o by the late F. Booth, of Wakefield, in Brunswick Chapel, Leeds.

A fair scale would be, for c¹, diameter at mouth $1\frac{3}{8}$ in., at neck $\frac{3}{4}$ in., at top of bell $1\frac{1}{4}$ in., with a length of body of $21\frac{3}{4}$ in., and of bell $3\frac{3}{4}$ in. Bore only $\frac{1}{8}$ in., and mouth cut up $\frac{1}{4}$. The bell has throughout the scale the same proportion to the body. This stop has more satisfactory examples in English organs than any other of the Gamba tribe.

198. *Viol da Gamba*, 8 ft. Also *Viola, Viol d'Amour.*— This name is sometimes used for the last-named stop, or even

for the Gamba; but it is better to use the distinctive names
of Gamba and Bell Gamba for those stops, and reserve that
of Viol da Gamba for the softer members of the Gamba
species. There is a good deal of variety in the scale and
voicing of this stop, according to the place it occupies in the
organ, but it may be taken as midway between the Gamba
and Salicional. The scale may be from 3 in. to $3\frac{1}{2}$ in. diameter at C_o; wind about 90 c. in., and bore 0·65 in. Mouth
from $\frac{1}{4}$ to $\frac{1}{6}$ the circumference, according to scale and strength
required (the larger the scale the smaller the mouth should
be). The area of the mouth should be about $\frac{1}{6}$ that of the
pipe section. It can be made as small as 2″ diameter at C_0.

199. *Keraulophon*, 8 ft.—We now come to a stop that is
legitimately slotted, it having, as the name implies, a horny
tone. The stop has about the scale and strength of the Viol
da Gamba, the peculiarity consisting in a tuning-slide with a
hole pierced in it about one diameter below the top, the hole
being $\frac{1}{2}$ in. diameter at $c^°$, diminishing to $\frac{1}{8}$ in. at the smallest
pipe. In some examples there is merely a slot in the pipe
with a tuning tongue.

200. *Salicional, Dulciana, Vox Angelica.*—These stops are
the most delicate in the organ, and the distinction is only one
of name. The amount of tone to be given, whatever the name
may be, must depend upon the place in which the stop is to
be heard. These stops should never be slotted, as it destroys
the velvety quality of tone that should distinguish them.
The writer has been insistent upon this matter of slotting, as
it is so commonly done without any attention to its evil effects.
In many cases it is probably done simply for convenience in
tuning these small-scale pipes, which are very indifferent to
the action of the tuning-horn, which also is liable to damage
their delicate mouths. The proper remedy is to furnish them
with slides, which project just above the top of the pipe.

If there be any shade of difference between these stops, it
is that the Salicional should be beautifully soft and stringy,
yet not without fulness, the Dulciana quiet and a little less
reedy, and the Vox Angelica the thinnest of all, on account
of its extremely small scale. The mouth of the Salicional is
sometimes slightly arched (Töpfer recommends this), though

it is probably only fancy, and a French style has the Gamba scale, with the diameter at top reduced to a half.

Töpfer's scale for the Salicional is 3·13 in. diameter at C_o, ratio 2⅘, mouth 0·82 in. high, wind 74 c. in., and bore 0·6 in. The mouths of all these stops are usually only one-fifth the circumference, and the mouth area one-sixth the body area. The Dulciana is made to the same scale, and the Vox Angelica two pipes smaller. Such small scales and delicate winding render the pipes very sensitive: the least thing puts them off their speech, and the writer recommends as much as 3½ in. diameter at C_o as a very good scale, as with a small mouth and suitable voicing a most beautiful tone can be got from such pipes, while they are not nearly so troublesome as the very small scales.

The common practice is to discontinue these stops at c^o and groove them into a Gedackt ; but a greater mistake could not be made. The C_o of the Salicional is one of the most beautiful notes in the organ—soft and stringy, yet distinct—and it cannot be replaced by any other stop. It also produces a beautiful effect in the 16 ft. octave.

One or two Dulcianas out of tune are called a ' Voix Céleste '—a gross libel on the harmony of the spheres.

201. *Gemshorn.*—This stop is generally found in 4 ft. tone; but there are examples of it in the 8 ft. pitch. It has a light, piping tone, slightly reedy, and is generally used as the 4 ft. stop instead of the Principal on the second manual of small organs, or in addition to the Principal in large ones. The scale must have some reference to that of the foundation stops, and may range from 4½ in. to 5¼ in. diameter at C_o, the top being only one-third the diameter of the bottom ; bore 0·9 in., and the wind 186 c. in. ; mouth cut up ¼ the diameter. This stop is not strongly marked as to string tone, but belongs to this family rather than to any other.

202. *Fugara*, 8 ft.—This is a German stop, not used in England. It is really a Gamba of lighter tone. C_o may be 3¾ in. diameter, mouth 0·9 in. high, bore 0·8 in., and wind 128 c. in.

FLUTE WORK.

203. Under this heading are all stopped pipes, and such open ones as give a dull or fluty tone as distinguished from the mellow, yet fresh, tone which should characterise the Diapason work, and the keenness of the Gamba family. The most important member is unquestionably the Stopped Diapason or Gedackt, and there is no stop in the organ about the scale and different proportions of which opinions vary so much. We have—

(a) 32 ft. tone on Pedal *Sub-Bass*, 32 ft. *Untersatz.*—Of this stop Schultze has recorded his opinion that it is not worth the wood it is made from. If the lower pipes are cut up high enough to keep the Twelfth out, the wind will not reach, and when more wind is given the Twelfth comes in, and, after all, the note is not worth the trouble and expense when you have got it. It is certainly better not to attempt to carry this stop below A_2, and it must be of full scale. Töpfer gives $12\frac{3}{4}$ in. square at C_2, with a bore of 2·1 in. One or two pipes larger than the 16 ft. stop would be suitable.

(b) 32 ft. tone on Manual. *Sub-Bourdon*, 32 ft.—A very rare stop; the same remarks apply.

204. (c) 16 ft. tone on Pedal. *Sub-Bass*, 16 ft.—This stop is almost invariably called Bourdon in English and in French organs, while in German organs that name is reserved for the Manual stop, a usage which seems preferable. A very ordinary English scale is 9 in. by $7\frac{1}{4}$ in. for C_1, and some advocate even a larger scale. Dr. Haynes, in his book of advice to organ-buyers, says, with reference to the Bourdon, 'insist upon having the C_0 13 in. by $11\frac{1}{2}$ in.,' and adds that those monstrous pipes, known as 'Haynes's tubs,' give almost as good a tone as an open pipe. Making all allowance for difference in taste, it is impossible that a stopped pipe, with only the odd harmonics, and very little of them, with such a scale, can give a tone in the least approaching that which is desired from an open pipe. Noise or thump there may be, but *tone*, in the sense the writer understands it, is simply impossible. It would, of course, be possible to make an open pipe nearly as dull as such Bourdons, but then it would no longer be an Open, but a tub.

The writer considers 8 in. by $5\frac{3}{4}$ in., with a mouth cut up $3\frac{3}{4}$ in., as a very sufficient scale; $6\frac{1}{2}$ in. square, with mouth cut up 2·11 in., and wind consumption 320 c. in., makes a very good Sub-Bass for ordinary organs, and the scale might be increased to 8 in. square, mouth 2·6 in., and wind 500 c. in. for a very powerful stop. Töpfer advocates the ratio 1 : 2·5 for Gedackts, but Schultze always used the same scale as for the foundation work.

205. (d) 16 ft. tone on Manual. *Bourdon*, 16 ft.—A fair scale for this would be $6\frac{3}{8}$ in. by $3\frac{3}{4}$ in., mouth $3\frac{1}{8}$ in. high, and any size from this down to a Lieblich Bourdon of 5 in. by $3\frac{3}{8}$ in. can be used. It should be noted that the covered stops below the unison require an 8 ft. stop to be drawn to help them.

206. (e) 8 ft. tone on Manual. *Stopped Diapason*. G., *Gedackt*. Fr., *Bourdon*, 8 ft.—This stop may be found of all sorts and sizes, from 4 in. square down to 3 in. by $2\frac{1}{2}$ in. Fair average scales are $3\frac{3}{4}$ in. by 3 in., $3\frac{1}{4}$ in. by $2\frac{3}{4}$ in. It is a good plan to make this stop of different scales on different manuals; thus, in the Hindley organ the Gedackts on Great, Swell, and Choir are respectively $3\frac{7}{8}$ in. by $2\frac{7}{8}$ in., mouth 2 in., and 3 in. by $2\frac{1}{8}$ in., mouth $2\frac{1}{4}$ in., and $3\frac{1}{8}$ in. by $2\frac{1}{8}$ in., mouth, $1\frac{1}{2}$ in., the wind of the last being a bare 2 in. The trebles of these stops are metal, and measure at c^1: Great $1\frac{1}{2}$ in. diameter, mouth $\frac{1}{4}$ the circumference, and $\frac{9}{16}$ in. high; Swell $1\frac{5}{16}$ in., mouth $\frac{1}{4}$ circumference, and cut up $\frac{5}{8}$ in.; Choir $1\frac{3}{16}$ in. diameter, mouth $\frac{1}{2}$ in. high and arched.

Not only has there been great contention over the scales of the covered work, but also over the voicing; the general English plan being to make a very large pipe, which requires low mouth, and then to plug the foot almost up to prevent the pipe speaking the Twelfth: while the German plan of moderate scale, high mouth, and full winding commends itself to the writer as the most reasonable, and is gradually making its way in England.

The absence of the even harmonics gives a peculiar quality to the tone of the covered stops, which are often very dull;

but a well-voiced Gedackt is very liquid and pleasant in the treble, and has the most refined tone of all the flute tribe. Covered pipes of more than 1 ft. actual length are generally made in wood, but sometimes in metal, and then there is trouble with the stoppers, as will be seen in the section on manufacture.

207. *Rohr Flute.* Fr., *Flûte à cheminée.*—This stop is simply a Gedackt with a hole in the stopper, and the name is derived from the German 'rohr,' a reed, alluding to the reed-like tube or chimney projecting from the top of the stopper when in metal. The tone is rather more liquid and clear than that of the Gedackt. The stop is found in 16 ft., 8 ft., and 4 ft. tone, the latter being the most common. The top octave in 4 ft. tone should be of open pipes, as such small stopped ones are no good, and will not stand in tune. A moderate scale is best for this stop; but the same variety is found as in the Gedackt. The chimneys are not usually carried below $c°$, and are generally 4 in. by $\frac{3}{8}$ in. at that note, diminishing to $\frac{1}{2}$ in. by $\frac{1}{8}$ in. Töpfer recommends a quarter the diameter of pipe for the bore of the chimney, with a length half that of the pipe. The larger the chimney the more open the tone.

A variety of this stop, with chimneys about double the ordinary size and a lower mouth, is called the *Clarinet Flute*, but the writer has never heard one that at all resembled the clarinet, except in name. But a combination of such a covered stop on the Great, with the Swell Rauschquint (shutters being closed), *does* give a very fair imitation of a clarinet, if not carried too low in the scale.

208. *Quintatön.*—This stop is found in both 16 ft. and 8 ft. pitch, and is so called because it sounds the twelfth or octave quint as strongly as the ground tone. It is found in many Continental organs, and has a peculiar tone, the liking for which is a matter of taste. Schultze did not care about this stop, though it is much used in Germany. It is often made to an ordinary Bourdon scale in wood, with a very low mouth to favour the harmonic; but this is apt to make the tone hard, and the end is best attained by making the stop of small scale, preferably in metal. Töpfer gives for C_1 only

4½ in. diameter, bore 0·9 in., wind 202 c. in., mouth cut up
1·42 in., and recommends it as the first 16 ft. manual stop on
account of its doing well in combination.

209. *Quint* or *Great Quint.*—A stop of 10⅔ ft. on the
pedal and 5⅓ in. on the manual. There is an example of a
21⅓ ft. quint on a 32 ft. pedal by the elder Schultze. This
stop must by no means be confounded with the Quintatön,
with its obtrusive tone. As it sounds below the first upper
partial, it must be most carefully used, and the tone kept
quite dull. It is best made in wood of a full Gedackt scale,
or as an open flute, very softly voiced. G_0 may be 3¾ in.
square, bore ¾ in., wind 130 c. in.; but the scale should really
be selected with reference to that of the Diapason. Töpfer
gives for open pipes a diameter up to 5 in., mouth 1 in., and
wind 200 c. in.; but the writer recommends a mouth only
one-fifth the circumference, so as to help to keep the tone
quite soft and quiet. As explained in the chapter on Acoustics,
this stop gives perceptibly a *resultant tone* of an octave below
that of the foundation stop with which it is drawn.

210. *Doppel Flute.*—This is simply a Gedackt with two
mouths, though the stop is sometimes made open, when it is
called ' Biffara.' Although the tone does not seem to differ
much from that of the Gedackt, and is scarcely louder, yet in
combination it gives much more ' body' to the organ tone.
A very beautiful example by Roosevelt has c°, 3 in. by 1¾ in.,
and, as a rule, the double mouth is not carried below this
note. Töpfer recommends for C_0, 8·35 in. by 4·15 in., with a
mouth arched up from 1·04 in. to 1·38 in., wind supply
265 c. in. (see Figs. 30, Pl. IV., and 36, Pl. VI., for an open
and for a stopped example).

211. *Spitz-Gedackt.*—If a Gedackt be made conical, it has
the peculiarity of over-blowing into the octave, and consequently has the even harmonics. Töpfer recommends this
stop as having a peculiar and pleasing tone; but the writer
has not been able to find any scale which gives a tone
answering to this description, the quality being very windy.
There is probably no existing example of the stop, and those
curious in such matters may profitably experiment upon it.

212. *Zauberflöte.* — A harmonic Gedackt sounding the

twelfth of its proper note. The writer only knows of one example—viz., in the organ by Michell and Thynne which was in the Inventions Exhibition at South Kensington, and is now in Tewkesbury Abbey. The stop was figured as of 4 ft. tone, but the pipes are of threefold length, and there does not appear to be any such special merit in the tone as to justify the trouble and expense of the extra-sized pipes.

213. The list of covered stops being now complete, we turn to the open stops of more or less fluty tone, beginning with *Spitz Flute*, 8 ft. This stop is really on the border-land between the Diapason and the flute work, since it is used as the Open for the Choir, or as a second Open on one manual. The tone is soft and light, owing to the conical shape, and the voicing should suit the general character of the Diapason tone. A good average scale would be for C_o, $4\frac{1}{2}$ in. diameter at mouth, top two-thirds, or half the bottom, bore 0·8 in., wind 134 c. in., and the mouth cut up 1·12 in.

214. *Hohl Flute*, 8 ft. and 4 ft.—This is a most useful member of the flute tribe, and gives, as its name implies, a powerful hollow tone. The scale varies a good deal, according to the size of the foundation stops. The Hohl Flute is made in metal and in wood, and when in the latter material has sometimes devices for increasing the width of mouth, and thereby the breadth of tone. Fig. 8, Pl. I., shows one of these, a slant mouth, which is also cut up rather high. Schultze sometimes made his Hohl Flutes triangular, c° having sides $2\frac{3}{4}$ in., and a mouth $1\frac{1}{4}$ in. high, and arched. The bass octave is generally made of stopped pipes. The scale may range from $2\frac{1}{3}$ in. to $3\frac{1}{2}$ in. square, at bore 0·62 in. to 0·87 in., and wind 83 to 163 c. in. per sec. The English *Clarabella* is practically a soft Hohl Flute, and is often made the same size as a Gedackt of the same *length*, with a mouth cut up only $\frac{1}{4}$. The mouths of this and of covered stops are often inverted.

215. *Harmonic Flute*, 8 ft. and 4 ft.—This is also a principal member of the flutes, and has a very full fluty tone. As the name implies, it sounds the octave, having a hole in the middle of the body to insure prompt over-blowing; the double length only goes down to c¹, and the 8 ft. octave is generally

composed of stopped pipes. The scale varies a good deal, from $2\frac{3}{4}$ in. to $3\frac{1}{2}$ in. diameter at c°, in proportion to the scale of the Open. It is often made the same scale as the Open, with a mouth one-fifth the circumference in width, and cut up one-quarter, with an arched upper lip. The stop is also used in 2 ft. tone, as the Harmonic Piccolo; but the writer does not recommend this class of tone in small stops.

216. *Travers Flute : Flauto Traverso*, 8 ft. and 4 ft.—This is also a Harmonic Flute, of which the pipes are made of solid wood (see Fig. 32, Pl. V.). When well voiced the tone exactly resembles the 'lip' of a real flute. The figure shows full size the c³ sharp pipe. Fig. 33 shows the mouth recommended by an able writer in the 'English Mechanic'; the mouth is semicircular, and the bottom, which has a slight bevel, is the width of the pipe above the block. Fig. 34 shows another form, of which the scale is a square whose side is $\frac{1}{16}$ the length of the pipe, or a rectangle of equal area, thus making the diameters vary as the lengths, an arrangement which is not to be recommended. The pipe figured is 10 in. long. An ordinary scale for a Swiss Flute is $2\frac{11}{16}$ in. by $1\frac{5}{8}$ in. for c°. The bass of this stop can very well be made in ordinary open wood pipes, gradually increasing the size of the mouth.

Töpfer recommends for the Travers Flute the following scale; but the writer cannot find any advantage to compensate for the extra trouble in boring taper pipes:

Note	Lower diameter in.	Upper diameter in.	Diameter of mouth in.
c¹	1·36	0·97	0·68
c²	1·04	0·75	0·55
c³	0·72	0·57	0·44
c⁴	0·54	0·41	0·28

The mouths are round, and covered about one-third by the mouthpiece, like that of the Harmonika. Below c¹ the mouths are half-round, and the pipes speak their ground tone. C_o is made 3·3 in. square, and slightly taper, like the solid pipes.

217. *Dolce*, 8 ft. and 4 ft.—A stop of soft and bright tone, which has an individuality caused by the pipe being larger at top than at bottom. It may be made at C_o $3\frac{1}{2}$ in. to $5\frac{1}{4}$ in. diameter at top, and $2\frac{1}{3}$ in. to 3·4 in. at bottom, the mouth

being only one-fifth the circumference, and from a quarter to one-third the width in height, generally arched. Bore 0·57 in., and wind consumption 65 c. in. per second.

218. *Harmonika*, 8 ft. and 4 ft.—A German stop much commended by Töpfer. It will be seen from Fig. 35, Pl. VI., that it much resembles the Travers Flute, from which it differs in not being harmonic and in being much quieter in tone— in fact, more resembling a Salicional. C_o may be 2·9 in. square, and slightly taper. The mouth varies according to the amount of tone required, from a half to a full round, and from half to the full width of the pipe, and is provided with ears, $b\,b$, and, if necessary, with a bridge or fender, c, to prevent over-blowing. The rest of the details are given in the chapter on Voicing. A good deal of fun can be got out of voicing these pipes, as they are most troublesome; but they make a very beautiful solo stop when well done. The stop has been carried down to C_1, which is 4·3 in. square.

219. Among other curiosities may be mentioned a flute with a round bead instead of a lip, Fig. 37, Pl. VI., which gives a very excellent fluty tone, for which the thick lip is suitable, as is mentioned in the chapter on Voicing.

Any flue stop can legitimately be brought under one of the foregoing heads, which comprise all the really distinctive qualities of tone; but it would be difficult to catalogue all the fancy names used, such as Wald Flute, Celestina, &c., and similar names peculiar to Continental organs. One fancy stop worth mentioning, however, is the Echo Oboe in wood, made by Schultze for the Armley organ, the scale of which is $1\frac{1}{2}$ in. by $\frac{3}{4}$ in. at c^1, with a bridge, as shown in Fig. 22, Pl. IV., and the tone quite soft but very reedy.

220. The list of reed stops is not nearly so long as that of the flutes, and comprises only two main varieties, the Trumpet tribe, with conical bodies and generally wide scale, and the softer stops with smaller scale and mostly cylindrical bodies. The difference between free and striking reeds is one of de-tailed construction, since both of the above classes of pipes are made with both styles of reeds, though the free reed has never been a favourite with English builders. It was used by Schultze, but given up by him, and he said the tongues were

always liable to break. Certainly free reeds, from their construction, can never have the fire of the others ; and on this
account are only suitable for small buildings and soft stops.
Töpfer considered that all Oboes and Clarinets should have
free reeds ; but he probably stands alone in this opinion, and
certainly there is no need to desire anything better for such
stops than the *best* class of English work in striking reeds.

221. To begin with, then, we have the Trumpet in both
32 ft. and 16 ft. tone on the Pedal, called *Trombone*. G.,
Posaune. Fr., *Bombarde*. Also in 16 ft. and 8 ft. tone on the
Manual, and as the *Clarion* in 4 ft. tone. An example in
64 ft. tone, and carried right down to C₃, is found in the
Sydney Town Hall organ, by Messrs. Hill ; but, considering
the natural limit of musical notes, it is very doubtful whether
such a stop is worth the money and room.

Fancy names, such as Tuba, Ophicleide, &c., are used by
some builders ; but the stop is practically a Trumpet, the
name Tuba, however, being generally reserved for a stop on
the solo manual, on a specially high pressure, sometimes as
much as 20 in., and never under 6 in. Very high pressures
are apt to render the tone coarse, and 10 in. is enough for all
ordinary purposes. Whatever the name or pitch may be, the
Trumpet, however loud, should be mellow and not hard, with
a peculiar clang which demands rather a curly tongue ; and
they are all the better for increased pressure, or a double
length of body in the upper notes, and this lengthening may
again be repeated. The tongues of the C's of a good English
example are shown in Fig. 15, Pl. III., and the scales have
been discussed in the chapter on Reed Scales, and in Plates
XXXIX. and XL. The bodies are always conical, and nearly
the length of an open pipe. Fig. 147, Pl. XIII., shows the
general aspect of a Trumpet pipe.

222. A free-reed Trumpet would have a body about half
the length of an open pipe ; but this advantage is somewhat discounted by the long boots which this class of stop
demands.

Of the figures, Fig. 303, Pl. XXXIV., gives in full lines a
Trumpet by Herr Ladegast, and in dotted lines one by Herr
Sauer, of which two the latter would be best in the treble ;

and Fig. 302 gives a large and a small scale Trumpet by Herr Giesecke.

Figs. 319 and 320, Pl. XL., give Töpfer's scales for a Trumpet and for the corresponding Pedal stops, and Figs. 304, Pl. XXXV., and 307, Pl. XXXVI., give Töpfer's free-reed scales for Trumpet and Posaune. Fig. 305, Pl. XXXV., is Cavaillé-Coll's Trumpet scale in full lines.

In these figures, where the length given is that of the body, the dimension ticks are so placed; but when the calculated length of air column is given, which includes the reed, the length is shown by ticks as reaching below the bottom of the movable body.

The larger tongues of the Posaune have often a lump of solder run on to their end, to render them more amenable in voicing.

223. *Horn.*—A stop very similar to the Trumpet, from which it differs in having a body a little larger, and a straighter tongue. The tone differs from that of the Trumpet in not having the clang that should characterise that stop, and from the large body it is fuller and smoother. The difference in scale being the only variation perceptible to the eye, it is not necessary to illustrate this stop.

224. *Cornopean.*—There is scarcely any difference between this stop and the last; but where the two are found together, its tone is a trifle smoother, and less powerful than that of the Horn. The scale is a little less than the Trumpet scale of the same organ.

225. *Oboe.*—A reed stop of quite moderate strength and thin tone, found in most organs. It should, of course, imitate as nearly as may be its orchestral namesake. Fig. 17, Pl. III., shows the tongues full size, and Fig. 145, Pl. XIII., represents the general shape of the pipe. The top has usually a cover, of which half is soldered to the body, leaving the other half as a shade, which can be bent up and down for voicing purposes. The instrument it is supposed to imitate has only a treble range, but as it is against the correct principles of organ-building to put in incomplete stops, this one may be considered as completed by a Bassoon, and as a matter of fact a slight change of scale from c° down is often given.

A scale that can be specially commended is that given in full lines in Fig. 309, Pl. XXXVII. The original was a most beautiful stop, built for the writer by Mr. H. Booth, of Wakefield. The great octave is really a Fagotto with plain conical bodies, the Oboe shape only beginning at c°. An ordinary English scale is shown in the same figure in dotted lines. Towards the top notes the bodies become a plain cone again, as there is not room for both the neck and the bell, and the tone is not perceptibly changed in that high part of the scale. Some builders have made the Oboe conical throughout, as in Fig, 300, Pl. XXXIII. Here the bodies are covered at top by a flat plate with a little voicing slit with a curled-up tongue, either in the plate or in the body at top. The ordinary style is the best. It is useful to know that the Oboe, having only a thin tone, will do very well in the bass with bodies of only half length. The same can at a pinch be done with Horns and Trumpets; but they lose in fulness of tone, which can ill be afforded.

226. *Bassoon, Fagotto,* 16 ft. and 8 ft., on both Manual and Pedal; called *Contra Fagotto* when in 16 ft. tone.—As noticed in the last paragraph, the bass of the Oboe (also of the Clarinet) is really a Bassoon. A small scale by Cavaillé-Coll is given in dotted lines in Fig. 305, Pl. XXXV. Another, a large scale for a free reed, by Töpfer, is given in full lines in Fig. 317, Pl. XXXIX. The opening of the upper cone should be about one-third the diameter of the body in the bass, and increase gradually towards the upper notes as much as is required for equality of tone. In the smaller pipes the top cone becomes a flat plate, like the cover of an Oboe. The dotted lines of this figure give the dimensions of a smaller scaled Fagotto or Clarinet, or the scale of the Oboe bass in Fig. 309, Pl. XXXVII., produced downwards, or a Clarinet scale may be used.

227. *Clarinet,* also called *Krummhorn* (i.e. crooked horn), hence the corruption *Cromorne* and *Cremona,* is a treble stop, imitative of its orchestral namesake. Töpfer's scale for a free-reed Clarinet is given in Fig. 317, Pl. XXXIX., and Herr Haas used, according to Töpfer, the enormous scale of 5⅜ in. diameter for c¹, or 4⅛ in. as a middling scale, these dimensions

being the upper diameters of the conical bodies shown in the figure. The bodies have the reversed cone and voicing lid, as for the Bassoon, which Töpfer treats as the same stop.

Fig. 300, Pl. XXXIII., shows in dotted lines a Clarinet scale by Herr Giesecke. This and other cylindrical Clarinets should be provided with slides for tuning, and are much best mitred, so as to keep dust and dirt from falling on the tongues. The dotted lines in Fig. 306, Pl. XXXVI., are a scale for a conical Clarinet by Herr Sauer, while the full lines give a scale of Schultze's, which can safely be recommended. The tongues of this stop should be straight and close to the reed. A set are shown in Fig. 16, Pl. III.

To give the true woody timbre, the stop should be placed in a box made of a light frame with $\frac{3}{16}$ in. pine panels, in which three or four sound holes, about 6 in. diameter, are cut, and then covered with soft leather. The top of the box should be hinged, so as to get at the pipes, and a hinged panel at the bottom for tuning, as in a swell-box, can be propped open at such an angle as to give the desired strength of tone. The Clarinet can be carried down to C_1, and then bears the same relation to the reed work as the Bourdon does to the flues, and a number of fine combinations can be got from it. The low notes are very difficult to voice, but they are worth the trouble.

228. *Vox Humana*, 8 ft.—An entirely fancy stop, useless in combination, and therefore only to be added when all foundation work has been satisfactorily provided for. It requires a soft Bourdon to be drawn with it, and should be used with a Tremulant; and is all the better for being placed in a swell-box of its own, and, if possible, right away from the rest of the organ, as is the case with the celebrated stop at Fribourg, which owes much of its effect to this circumstance.

This stop used to be made in many queer shapes—with cones, reversed cones, and pepper-boxes—but is now always made cylindrical, with small, short tubes. The tongues of a good English example are shown in Fig. 14, Pl. III., and the scale is given in Fig. 313, Pl. XXXVIII., the lengths repeating at c^2. Töpfer's scale is given in Fig. 318, Pl. XXXIX., and he recommends a sliding cap, partially covered, for voicing.

K

The tongues should be weak and thicker under the tuning wire than at the end, and the two lower octaves of reeds should be leathered.   This practice, indeed, is useful with the Oboe and Clarinet, but is used to a different extent by various builders.   For hot or damp climates leathering is inadmissible, and the voicer must do his best with the bare metal, or try wood.

229. There are other reed stops, such as the Euphone, a sort of Vox Humana ; the Physharmonika, a free reed with two tongues; the Æoline, a delicate stop; the Musette, and the Cor Anglais—all free reeds found in foreign organs. Most of them have none, or but very small bodies, and are not recommended.

230. A few words on the general question of organ-stop nomenclature may not be amiss, as at present stops are often loosely named, and new names are introduced without due cause. Mr. Audsley, in the columns of the ' English Mechanic,' has advocated Italian as the proper language to use, it being the language already in general use for musical terms.   The choice seems unfortunate, for, if Italy was first in the musical field, Germany is supreme in the masters she has produced, and, particularly in the matter of organs, the writer doubts if a decent organ has ever been built in Italy, while until quite recently the Germans stood first, without any question, and have twice taught organ-building to England.   The German terms are also concise and descriptive, and the writer urges a more consistent nomenclature of stops, based on German lines.

The Diaphone.

231. Since this chapter was written, the inventive genius of Mr. Hope-Jones has rendered it necessary to place the above stop as a class by itself, since it is neither a reed nor a flue-stop, though it partakes rather of the nature of the former.   The best description of it is a Tremulant applied to a reed body, and giving a tone capable of all modifications between reed and flue-tone.   In the chapter on Acoustics, it was described how sound is produced by any regular vibrations of a column of air, and it is clear that a Tremulant of sufficient

speed attached to a resonator will yield a musical note, the
quality of which will depend upon the details of the vibrating
orifice and of the body. Fig. 333, Pl. XLIV., is a diagram-
matic representation of a Diaphone; *a* is a chest attached
to the bottom of a pipe body, and connected to the soundboard hole. Between the chest and the body are two holes,
one covered by a small motor, *b*, and the other by a valve
attached to the tail of the motor, the collapse of which opens
the valve; in the normal state the motor is held open by the
flat spring *d*. When the touching of a key lets wind into *a*,
the motor collapses, and opening *c*, lets a puff of wind into
the pipe, but only a puff, because the action of the spring,
and the increase of pressure in the body, enable the motor to
open again, and cut off *c*. This is only an outline of the
device, the full capacities of which are not yet developed.
Variations in the nature of the cut-off and in the size of hole
will produce great varieties in tone, and the field covered by
this class of stop is a very promising one, especially for pedal
stops. One great advantage for the Pedal is the ability to
make one rank of Diaphone pipes serve for all degrees of
loudness within the range of the wind-pressures supplied to
the organ, for the pitch is not the least affected by pressure.
One Diaphone may, therefore, have two or three draws, provided they supply wind of different pressures, and all degrees
of effect can be produced, from a Fagotto up to a Tuba.

CHAPTER VI

SOUNDBOARDS: (a) SLIDER SOUNDBOARDS

232. THE soundboard is mechanically, perhaps, the most important part of the instrument, as it is the most difficult to make and the most subject to derangement. The name is quite misleading, as the function of the soundboard is to distribute the wind to the pipes at the will of the player. The ordinary, or slider soundboard, will first be described, then improvements on it, and after that the most usual types of ventil soundboard.

233. As a general description of a soundboard has already been given in Chapter II., we may proceed at once to practical details. The first thing to do in designing an organ, big or little, is to see if there is room to plant the pipes and to plan out how to stand them. The most natural, and in some respects the best way, is to plant them semi-tonally; but few situations will allow of this, and where there are show-pipes symmetrically placed, the conveyances get rather long. Some pipes also do not like their neighbours in pitch planted next them, and do better when placed at alternate ends of the organ.

For a medium-sized organ, such as for a chamber or small church, the most favourite plan is to alternate the pipes of the first octave, or thereabouts, and arrange the rest semi-tonally; while for a larger instrument the pipes throughout are alternated, with the smallest in the middle, and a passage board between the two halves of the soundboard. For very small organs, again, there are eccentric plans, such as distributing the great octave through the length of the soundboard arbitrarily, between the smaller pipes, so as to get the large pipes in front and over their wind.

234. In planning, reference must always be made to the space available for show-pipes; in chamber organs especially it is a necessity that all the larger pipes should stand facing out of the case. Schultze did not altogether approve of putting speaking pipes in front, because there is a decided difference in tone between them and those inside, and because long conveyances are always objectionable.

The only way to safely plan a soundboard or a front is to do it full-size, with paper or zinc patterns of the pipes, using boards jointed up for a drawing-board, or stout cartridge-paper gummed together. Begin with the smaller pipes, and so long as they take up less room than the necessary bars and grooves (generally about c^1), patterns will not be required. The tenor octave is usually the critical one, as, though the pipes of the first octave are larger, more are planted out.

In planning, it must be made an absolute minimum that no pipe must be nearer than its own diameter to another; but this is quite an extreme, and cannot be applied to a whole rank of pipes without spoiling the tone. Too much room cannot be given for pipes to speak into, and it may be taken that, if putting a pipe into its place lowers its pitch, the tone will suffer.

235. There are, however, differences between the different stops as to the liberties that may be taken in this respect, the flute stops being much less sensitive than those of string tone. If a pipe of the latter class speaks badly, try it in a place by itself, and if it then speaks well, overcrowding has spoiled it. Even without apparent overcrowding, there are little indulgences that must be made for this class of stops in planting them, such as not to put the Gamba next the Open, or some of the pipes will be sure to give trouble. The same applies to the Pedal, though if the pipes are of wood there will be less trouble, possibly because in a wooden pipe the stream of wind is more firmly directed than in a metal mouth. Curiously, it is rather a good thing to have the mouth of a Bourdon somewhat shaded, and Schultze has, in some of his organs, planted them with the mouths looking, not outwards, as usual, but sideways, each towards his neighbour's back.

236. To arrange the front pipes nicely, it is better to use a separate slider on the cheek of the soundboard, as shown at *d*, Figs. 163, Pl. XIV., and 176, Pl. XV., than to have conveyances from the holes in the table wandering about among the feet of the pipes. Even two sliders can be so placed in quite a small soundboard. For pipes at the ends of the organ, a good place for the special slider is on the *bottom* of the grooves, behind the windchest—in fact, for conveyances, a slider can be stuck on wherever convenient, and need not be restricted to the usual place on the table. In arranging the order of the stops, also remember to put two together if they are to have a common bass (grooving), and the same in the case of two soundboards, as shown in Fig. 164, Pl. XIV., where *a* is a pipe foot, receiving wind from the other soundboard through the valve *b*, its own back-pressure valve, *c*, being closed, to prevent other pipes on that groove from sounding. The valves can be a simple flap of leather, but care should be taken to make them and the conveyance pipe of ample size, or the pitch of the pipe will be different when fed by both valves to what it is when only one is open. If the pipe gets all the wind it can use from either of the supplies, it can make no difference whether both are blowing together or not.

237. No very useful information can be given as to the general size of soundboards, since so much depends on the scale of the stops and the relative proportions of length and breadth of the soundboard; but, roughly, it may be taken that five stops will require a board about 6 ft. by 1 ft. 9 in., and ten stops about 8 ft. 3 in. by 4 ft. 3 in., while some sizes of soundboards for small organs are shown in the figures.

238. While planning the soundboard so far as the pipe-room is concerned, we must also get forward the calculations for the size of the pallets and grooves. Here a knowledge of the laws which govern the motion of fluids is essential, as the most hazy ideas are to be found among people who build organs—such as that a big trunk does not compress the air, and a small one gives it force.

Air, like water, can only flow through a pipe by losing head or pressure; consequently, however little air is used, and however big the connecting pipe, the pressure in the wind-chest must be *something* less than that in the bellows, and as more and more air is used, the pressure diminishes to the extreme case of no pressure at all—viz., the trunk discharging into the open air, with the windchest cover off. At the other extreme, no leakage or use, the wind in the chest will stand at the same pressure as it does in the bellows. Between these two extremes the loss of pressure depends upon the speed with which the wind has to travel through the trunk.

Now, as organ pipes are voiced for a particular pressure of wind, they will not speak so well with any other ; consequently, as the demand increases, we should be able to increase the area of our trunk so as to keep the speed, and therefore the pressure, constant; and as this cannot be done in practice, we must get as near it as possible, and fix the area of all our air passages so large that the velocity required to supply the maximum consumption is such, that to cause it will not demand a loss of pressure greater than experience shows the pipes will stand, without obvious fluctuations in tone.

239. Töpfer has made very careful experiments on this subject, and his results are given in the subjoined table. The theoretical speed is that due to the head, or difference in pressure between the two ends of the communication, whether trunk or pallet-opening ; but on account of friction a co-

TABLE OF SPEED OF WIND IN PALLETS AND GROOVES.

| Note | Inches per second | | | Loss of pressure in 10ths of an inch |
| | Actual speed | | Theoretical speed | |
	Pallet	Groove		
	In small instruments			
C_0	233	379	537	0·433
c^0	181	288	414	0·273
c^1	133	212	304	0·137
c^2	192	148	211	0·079
c^3	60	93	134	0·039
	In large instruments			
C_0	268	427	610	0·55
c^0	208	330	472	0·35
c^1	156	249	356	0·195
c^2	112	177	254	0·118
c^3	75	118	170	0·039

efficient has to be applied, which he gives as 0·44 for the pallet opening, and 0·7 for the groove passage—that is to say, the theoretical speed has to be multiplied by these coefficients to find the actual speed through the apertures. The figures given in the table are the actual speeds permissible in different parts of the scale, without damage to the speech of the pipes.

240. As much of the crispness of the organ tone depends upon the precise admission and cut-off of the wind supply, this part of the mechanism is one upon which some further investigation might well be expended, and systematic experiments conducted upon the effects of different kinds of action. Theoretically, the pressure should rise at once to a maximum on touching a key, and drop to zero the instant the key is released. Graphical diagrams of what goes on in the groove could be obtained by a device similar in principle to the steam-engine indicator, and from these the best form of pallet could be determined. A perfect pallet would be one of maximum area and minimum rise, so as to give instantaneous admission and cut-off; but mechanical considerations of warping and difficulties of fitting restrict the length of pallets. Beyond the pallet also, the space to be filled with wind should be a minimum, in order to obtain a sharp admission and cut-off, and a ventil soundboard naturally fulfils both these conditions much better than any slider soundboard can do.

241. The first step is to find the wind consumption of the pipes which have to be supplied. This is given, on the authority of Töpfer, in Appendix V., or can be ascertained by experiment for any particular case; and, having the consumption of any one pipe, that of the others can be obtained from Töpfer's succession of numbers for the different scales, given in Appendices VI. and VII. The notes assigned to the quantities given are for what Töpfer calls the normal for the Open Diapason; but the table can be used by starting from any note whatever, and if the exact number cannot be found to start from, the nearest, or a mean, can be taken, as extreme accuracy is not required. Having found the consumption for each note, $\frac{1}{16}$ must be added to allow for loss in the sliders, and the sum gives the total consumption to be

provided for each note, which, divided by the permissible speed, gives the area required.

242. Let us take, for example, an organ of the specification given below, and write against each stop the wind consumption. Above c^1 it is not necessary to calculate individual stops, as the minimum groove is almost sure to be larger than is required. When the sum total for any note falls within the figures given in the tables, it is not necessary to fill in the detail stop by stop, as the totals can be written down direct from the progressive numbers in the table. There are not many varieties of reeds, and they do not consume much wind, so for them the subjoined short table will be found sufficient :

	C_o	c^o	c^1	c^2	c^3	
Trumpet	195	72	63	35	20	
	248	142	80	45	26	
Oboe and Clarinet	155	88	50	29	16	Cubic in. per sec.
	219	124	65	35	19	
Vox Humana	124	65	35	19	10	

WIND CONSUMPTION OF AN ORGAN IN CUBIC INCHES PER SECOND.

Great	C_o	Swell	C_o	Choir	C_o	Pedal	C_1
Open Diap., 8 ft.	275	Bourdon, 16 ft.	300	Lieb. Ged., 8 ft.	145	Major Bass, 16 ft.	565
Gamba, 8 ft.	122	Geigen, 8 ft.	202	Salicional, 8 ft.	74	Violon Bass, 16 ft.	250
Harm. Flute, 8 ft.	220	Hohl Flute, 8 ft.	220	Travers Flute, 4 ft.	175	Posaune, 16 ft.	400
Principal, 4 ft.	149	Principal, 4 ft.	150	Piccolo, 2 ft.	98	—	
Harm. Flute, 4 ft.	108	Gemshorn	100	Clarinet, 8 ft.	170	—	
Rausch Quint	188	Mixture	188	—		—	
Trumpet, 8 ft.	220	Oboe, 8 ft.	170	—		—	
	1,282		1,330		662		1,215
Add $\frac{1}{16}$th	80		83		41		76
Total C_o	1,362		1,413		703	C_1	1,291
„ E_o	1,030	—	1,160	—	575	G_o	912
„ G_o	878	—	1,005	—	493	—	
„ c^o	673	—	775	—	376	—	
„ e^o	551	—	625	—	305	—	
„ g^o	470	—	538	—	264	—	
„ c^1	360	—	370	—	203	—	
Total	5,324	Total.	5,886	Total	2,919	Total	2,203

243. We are now in possession of the quantities of air required for each note, and can find the areas required. Take C_o of the Great, then the pallet area should be $\frac{1362}{235}=$ 5·8 sq. in. Now the area of the pallet opening will, with a rise of $\frac{1}{2}$ in., be two triangles of a base of $\frac{1}{2}$ in., and whose height has to be determined, or, in other words, it will be the area of a rectangle of $\frac{1}{2}$ in. on one side, the other being found

to be 11·2 in., which is the effective pallet length.   The front opening of the pallet cannot be reckoned, because air has already been assumed to be flowing in, right up to the end, so that space has been accounted for.   Next, if the width of groove is less than 1 in., we must take the half-width, and not the pallet-rise, as the effective dimension.

244.   Next, as to the depth of groove.   We require an area of $\frac{1362}{379} = 3·6$ sq. in., which, divided by the width of groove, gives the necessary depth.   The same process should be gone through for all the C's, and any desired intermediate dimensions interpolated in geometrical progression.   The dimensions so calculated are the *least* that should be given, but there is no harm in giving *more*.   It is not advisable to make a single manual pallet opening more than $1\frac{1}{4}$ in. wide, or more than 14 in. long, and if these dimensions are not sufficient, two pallets should be used, and some relief mechanism will be required, or the touch will be too heavy. It must also be noted that a groove over an inch wide requires the pallet-rise to be increased accordingly.   For this reason, if the manual pallet-rise is set at $\frac{1}{2}$ in., there is nothing to be gained by putting in a bigger groove than 1 in., as, if the air entrance on each side is only $\frac{1}{2}$ in., more cannot be got in by making the face of the groove any wider, and the weight of the touch will be uselessly increased.   In any case, it is better to have two moderate pallets than one large one ; and where a delicate pipe, such as a Salicional, is put on a very big groove, it may be necessary to provide an escape valve to let the air out directly the pallet closes, or the sound of the pipe when sounding alone will die out with a smear instead of stopping sharp.   It is better to take out the size of a pallet in length than in width.   The treble bars and grooves of quite a small organ may be reduced to $\frac{1}{4}$ in. each ; but for a large organ they should not be less than $\frac{3}{8}$ in., whatever calculation may assign.

245.   Having both the patterns of pipes which have to stand on top, and the widths of grooves and bars which lie under the table, we can combine the two and space out the soundboard.   First see how far down the small pipes will stand on the minimum groove.   Then space off the patterns,

making grooves and bars gradually wider than the minimum, to fill up the necessary space, until, somewhere about the tenor octave, it will be found that the pipes gain so much on the grooves, that either pipes must be planted out or false grooves introduced. When all have been disposed of, not forgetting an extra stout bar about every foot among the thin ones, and space for false grooves to permit of expansion, spoken of below, the scheme should be transferred to a rod, marking the grooves with their numbers and a red score down their centres. The widths of slides and bearers should also be marked off on another face of the same rod. It will probably save mistakes to finish a full-sized plan of the soundboard, showing all pipes conveyanced on the board, and the conveyances to the pipes off it.

246. The ordinary way of making a soundboard is to glue up sufficient width of $\frac{5}{8}$ in. stuff to form the table, on this to glue the bars, with little slips called 'filling-in' between their ends, and, when finished, to trim all off and glue on a cheek, as in fig. 165. But this style of manufacture sins against the laws of Nature, inasmuch as the grain of the table runs across that of the bars, and when the wood shrinks, as it will, something *must* go. That something is, of course, the table. No amount of seasoning will prevent wood from altering under hygrometric changes, and the only way to make a sound table is to dodge the expansion and contraction, which can easily be done by having a separate narrow table for each stop, as shown in Figs. 176 and 179, Pl. XV. This provides for expansion in the width of the table; but, as the motion of the bars and fillings is restrained by the tables which run lengthways across them, a false groove should be left about every 15 in., and the filling in it split with a saw; thus the soundboard is free to move in both directions without damage.

247. Now for details of construction. First get out the cheeks, from $1\frac{1}{2}$ in. to 2 in. thick, and the requisite depth; mark off all the bars, and cut a mortise for each $\frac{1}{4}$ in. deep. Next get out all the bars, and, when planing the pallet-edge, mark the way the grain runs, so that it may all face one way, or there may be trouble when cleaning off the surface for the pallets; then true up one end, and, cramping all the bars

together, saw and plane off the other ends.   Then build up
the bars and cheeks into a frame like Fig. 179, Pl. XV., remembering the marks which indicate the direction of the
grain of the bars, and screw the cheeks to all bars thick
enough to hold a screw,   Then between the places for the
tables glue in the fillings *l l*, and clean off the whole.   The
grain of these fillings should, strictly speaking, run lengthways of the table; but they are more trouble to make that
way, and the writer has found the usual way sufficient, with
the aid of false grooves.   The tables should be leathered
underneath, and then screwed down ; gluing is not absolutely
necessary.   The fillings *f f* for the pallet tails should now be
put in, and that side of the soundboard cleaned off.

248. The windchest should next be fitted by putting on
the windbar *g*, Fig. 176, Pl. XV.   This is a good stout bar,
$4\frac{1}{2}$ in. to 6 in. deep, so called because the windtrunk often
joins on to it.   It helps the cheeks to sustain the not incon-
siderable load of the pipes, or indeed, with the usual style of
cheek just stuck on for ornament, it has all the work to do.
The windchest in most organs is only wide enough to hold the
pallets, and about $4\frac{1}{2}$ in. deep; but bearing in mind what was
said above, that an unlimited wind supply is the only perfect
one, it would seem as if the best plan were to make the wind-
chest the full width of the soundboard and 6 in. deep, which
latter dimension also gives more room to get at the interior.
When the ends, which should be dovetailed into the windbar,
and the bottom are fixed, the front board should be seen to,
and if the soundboard is anything more than quite a small
one, it is better to make the board in two halves, butting on
a piece dovetailed into the bottom board and the cheek, which
also has the advantage of supporting the bottom board, on
which the pressure of the air amounts to a good deal.   The
joint is made with a leather strip, and the usual practice is to
screw on the front boards with common screws, but a butterfly
nut is a much neater job, especially if slots are used in the
board instead of holes, as shown at *g*, Fig. 163, Pl. XIV., as
then the board can be removed by merely slacking back the
nuts.

249. The spring rail *h* and thumping-rail *k*, Fig. 179, Pl. XV.,

have now to be fitted. The former receives the ends and
guides the tails of the springs; the flat part may be 3 in. by
$\frac{1}{2}$ in., and the T-piece on it 1$\frac{1}{2}$ in. by $\frac{1}{4}$ in. of hard wood.
A punch-mark is made on the flat part for the noses of the
springs to rest in, and a saw-cut is made about half-way
down the T-piece to act as a guide to the spring tails. This
cut should be chamfered out like a V, so as not to grip the
springs. The positions of the springs can be obtained from
the rod on which the groove (and therefore the pallet) centres
were set out. The rail is secured to the bars by long screws
at intervals, at such a height as to fit the springs; these, with
the pallets, can thus be finally adjusted before the bottom
board is put on.

The thumping-rail is simply a slip about 1$\frac{1}{4}$ in. deep and
$\frac{1}{2}$ in. thick, with the top lined with felt. It lies about 1 in.
below the front of the pallets, and prevents them being pulled
off their pins; it is simply sprung into two mortises in the
end boards, or fastened in some way so that it can easily be
withdrawn. The windtrunk-hole can now be cut either in
the wind-bar, end-plank, or bottom board, as most convenient; and the rough work being now finished, the pieces
of the wind-chest may be taken off and the joints leathered
ready to go back, as they had better not be glued to the
soundboard.

250. The face of the latter can now receive a final touch
from the smoothing-plane, ready for the pallets. And here
we must join issue with English builders on their method of
gluing down pallets by their tails. What would be thought
of the builder of any other machine if, after providing a door
to get at them, he fixed the valves so that they could not be
removed, it being quite as easy to make them removable?
Yet this is the case with the organ pallet. It is quite as easy
and no more expensive to make pin pallets, and the writer
can vouch from an extended experience that they are not the
least liable to get out of order, while, in case of necessity, the
whole of the pallets can be withdrawn in a few minutes
without inconvenience, or any one pallet can be removed
without interfering with its neighbour. Such occasions may
not often arise in England; but they do abroad, and, in any

case, to glue the pallet to its seat is mechanically indefensible. While the above operations have been going on, and until the pallets are finally fitted, it is well to protect the bars by a thin board nailed over them.

251. Pallets are from 1 in. to $\frac{5}{8}$ in. thick, and are generally sloped down towards the tail end. They should be of a light, straight-grained wood, and are all the better for being varnished. If split out of a plank instead of being sawn they are not nearly so liable to cast, and even the work of the best builders is liable to warp in hot climates. A neat way of making them is to joint up the pieces out of which they are to be made into a plank, and then shape out the front and back right along the edge, Fig. 161, Pl. XIV. The joints must not be allowed to come into a pallet, or it will certainly warp. Having split or sawn out and planed the pallets to the right width, a lap of $\frac{1}{8}$ in. on each side of the groove, the centre should be marked along the face and back with a little gauge like a parallel ruler, with a marking point in the centre of the arms. The pin mortises can then be made (not too tight), and a punch-mark on the back of the pallet for the spring nose to rest in, which mark should really be in the centre of gravity of the pallet and action hanging on to it; but as it is difficult to ascertain this, it is generally put a little in advance of the centre of gravity of the pallet itself; but some prefer to put the spring behind the centre, in the belief that it holds the heel better. The leather hinge does sometimes make trouble. The pins are best made of $\frac{1}{8}$ in. brass wire—key pins do very well, and they should project about 1 in. from the bars. The usual plan is to put a thin pin on each side in line with the pull-down; but one stout pin is better than two thin ones. The pin mortises should be quite smooth, and should be blackleaded. The pull-down eye should be $\frac{3}{4}$ in. or 1 in. from the front, and may be a brass wire staple or a piece of whipcord, glued and wedged in.

252. Pallets are leathered with two thicknesses of the thickest and softest leather, or with felt and leather. To prepare the leather, the hair or shiny side must be well roughened to make it hold the glue, the best tool for this purpose being a small-toothed saw freshly set. Cut a strip of

leather as wide as the pallets are long, and lay it rough side
down on a board. Rub the glue into the pallet face (previously
roughed with a toothing-plane) until it foams, which prevents it
soaking into the leather and making it hard ; press the pallets
down with a sliding motion to expel all air, and bed them with
a tap from a hammer. Do this throughout the length of the
strip, and when the glue is perfectly set, cut off the pallets.
For the second layer, the glue must be rubbed on the leather
until it foams—this being especially necessary with felt. To
give them a good face, glue a bit of the finest emery-paper on
a board, and rub it down with whiting, and gently stroke the
pallet on to it, so as to level off the leather, and fill the pores
with whiting. To set out the pull-down holes in the bottom
board, make a diagram of the position of the pull-down eye
with the pallet shut, and with it open, and take the mean
distance from the front of the soundboard as the line for the
pull-downs, and be most particular to get the holes exact, or
they will wear oval, and the pallets will stick.

253. The position of each hole is marked along this line
from the rod with the groove centres marked, which was prepared for setting out the soundboard. The holes in the
bottom board should be $\frac{1}{4}$ in. diameter and burned out, a
strip of leather with the soft side out having been first glued
underneath. To make the communication air-tight, a strip
of stout sheet brass about $1\frac{1}{2}$ in. wide is taken, and a centre
line scribed on it, along which holes are drilled at the proper
distances with a watchmaker's drill, set so as to be just an
easy fit for a No. 18 or 19 wire, which should be brass or
phosphor bronze of the best quality. These holes should have
the edges rounded off with a large blunt drill, and a few more
should be made along the edges of the strip through which
to tack it into place, where it is finally secured by screwing
over it a couple of stout beadings, which also serve to protect
the pull-downs from injury (see Fig. 176, Pl. XV.). The best
way to insure exactness before finally fixing the strip is to put
two pallets at different ends of the soundboard (or of the strip,
if it does not reach all the way) half-way open, and, having seen
that the soundboard is level, hang a plumb-bob by a fine
thread from the pallets, and so adjust the strip. Schultze

liked separate pull-down plates, a brass washer to each hole, adjusted by the plumb-bob and secured by a bit of leather glued over it.

254. Before the pallets can be finally put in, the sliders and other gear on top of the table must be fitted—indeed, the description of this work should have preceded that of the under part of the soundboard, as it is generally done first. We left the top of the soundboard when the tables were screwed down; the screws, be it observed, must be well countersunk. The sliders and bearers, as the strips between them are called, must be first got ready, as well as the upper boards, and the rack-boards which support the pipes. The sliders and bearers can be of $\frac{3}{8}$ in. teak or mahogany, but the wood must be perfectly straight in grain and free from flaws. The upper boards should be $1\frac{1}{4}$ in. and the rack-boards $\frac{1}{2}$ in. or $\frac{5}{8}$ in.

Plane off the tables perfectly true, using a good straight-edge, and having trued up one side of the sliders and bearers, screw them down with small countersunk screws, so as to be perfectly solid on the table, and then true. up the other side. The upper boards can then be fitted, and to insure the pipes being truly vertical, screw on the rack-boards, and bore the holes for the rack-pillars at once, so that the exact position of the boards can always be restored by sticking a peg or two in the holes.

255. Next mark along the rack-boards the centres or spaces of the grooves from the setting-out rods, and from the plan of the soundboards mark off the position of the pipes, and take a final look to be sure that two holes do not run together when the slides are drawn, or a pipe will speak with the stop shut. Then with a fine drill, carefully held exactly plumb, drill the pipe-centres through the rackboards into the upper board, and, removing the rackboards, mark the position of the holes with a pencil-cross, and bore the holes at leisure. When working in a dark wood, such as teak, it is a convenience to give it a coat of white size, so that marks can easily be seen.

As we get towards the larger pipes it will be found impossible to keep them all within the width of the slider, as shown in Fig. 170, Pl. XV. To meet this case, the holes must be slightly conveyanced; the direct pipe hole will not be bored right through the upper board, but a fresh hole will be started within the limits of the slider, and the two connected by cutting out a channel. A $\frac{1}{4}$ in. strip glued over such places, with the holes for pipe-feet re-marked and bored again, completes the operation.

256. With reference to the holes in the slider and table, it should be specially noted that they should never be less than $\frac{1}{4}$ in. or $\frac{3}{8}$ in. It is quite a common practice to make them very small in the treble, to match the pipe-foot hole, with the result that, unless the draw of the slider is mathematically exact—a thing it is impossible to insure—the pipes will be most abominably out of tune. Plot two sets of holes, one of $\frac{1}{8}$ in. diameter and one of $\frac{3}{8}$ in. with an error in position of $\frac{1}{16}$ in. only, and the reason will be evident.

As to the lap required to cut off the wind, $\frac{1}{8}$ in. is sufficient in good work, but the more margin that can be given the better. When holes of more than 1 in. diameter are required, it is better to make them rectangular, so as to avoid giving the slider an excessive travel.

The rack pillars are simply little wooden pillars as shown in Fig. 163, Pl. XIV., and may be put about a foot apart. They are sometimes made with a screw cut on them at the upper end to take a wooden nut to jam them down; but this is not necessary if they are a good fit in the top and bottom holes. The longer and wider the rackboards are, the stiffer they will be, as the pillars are sure to incline slightly in different directions, but still enough to pull against each other.

257. When the holes are bored they should be burned out with a hot iron to get rid of all chips, and a countersink should be made in the upper board, for the pipe feet, with a rose bit or hot iron. To finish the moving surfaces, they should be rubbed down with a bit of fine emery paper glued on a board, and large V-shaped channels should be cut between all holes in the table and upper board, as shown in Fig. 163, and a similar channel scored all along the edge of the slider. The object of these channels is to intercept any wind that may escape between the slider and either of the adjoining surfaces, and prevent it getting into a neighbouring pipe. Generally

L

these channels are mere scratches, and can hardly do what they are supposed to; they should be cut out with a broad chisel, and not merely scratched with a scoring tool.

The writer always splits sliders with a fret-saw down the middle between the ranks of holes, with the object of avoiding the evil effects of warping, as shown in Fig. 177, Pl. XV., from which it will be seen that halving the width of a plank with a certain degree of curvature much more than halves the disturbance from level caused by warping.

It is well not to make the upper boards too long, so as to guard against warping. When the surfaces are all finished, they should be brought to a brilliant polish with blacklead, and, before replacing the bearers, they should have a strip of thin cartridge-paper pasted on them, to give the necessary freedom of motion to the sliders.

258. It used to be the fashion to line the table or sliders with leather, but the practice has gone out. The advantage of course is, that they are a good deal more air-tight than an ordinary slider: but the fitting requires great care, and for the first six months the sliders are very stiff. Being more air-tight, the addition for loss of wind in sliders may be omitted or diminished, and the pipes stand better in tune during hygrometric variations.

259. The holes for the pipe feet in the rack-boards can now be bored. Mark on the pipe feet with a gauge the position of the top of the rack-board, calliper the diameter there, and mark it on the hole; a special calliper, with a pointed leg, to give half the measure of the calliper end, is convenient. The holes are then cut out with an expanding bit made for this purpose, and finished with a rasp. And here it may be observed that the holes must be quite a loose fit *across* the grain to allow for shrinkage. If this is not done the plank will contract, and lift the pipe-feet a little, so as to leave them loose in their holes. The rack-holes for all pipes above 3 ft. long should be leathered, and all pipes above 4 ft. long should be supported by a stay at top. These precautions are usually omitted; but that does not render them any the less desirable in high-class work.

260. Whether the top or bottom of the sound-board is

finished first, the other side must be covered to protect it from injury, and the finishing touches should not be put until all the dirty work, such as burning holes and clearing away chips, is complete.

To finish the inside of the wind-chest, glue leather or American cloth over the bars and fillings up to the heel-pins, and cover any joints that may possibly leak with a strip of leather, and, finally, put in the pallets and springs. These last are made of hard brass or steel wire, usually the latter, 18 gauge, and can be bought, or made by the simple device shown in Fig. 154, Pl. XIV. Mark a triangle about 5 in. on the side, and put at the apex a wooden peg to form the eye of the spring on, and at the other angles a screw. The wire is gripped against one of the screws with a plier, twisted twice round the peg, and then led away to the other screw, against which the nose of the spring is turned up, and then cut off. It requires a little practice to make neat springs, and after they have been roughed out they should be 'set,' as shown at a in the figure, to get both arms into one plane, and the arms should be dressed to a slightly concave curve with a small hammer. The length of base of the triangle must depend upon the depth of wind-chest or distance of spring-rail. It is easy to try a couple of springs, and shift the screws if not satisfactory. A convenient tool for putting in and taking out springs is shown in Fig. 131, Pl. XII. It is easily made out of a bit of brass or zinc sheet, and the method of using it is so obvious as to require no description.

261. When it is seen that the pallets all bed fair, and springs work well, the bottom board can be put on and the pull-downs fitted. Some make the hook at the upper end of the pull-down first, and then, unhooking it, form the eye outside, and join up again. Another way is to form the outer eye first, and cut the pull-down to such a length as will reach right up to the grooves. Push it in and adjust the eye just clear of the brass plate, taking care that the beginning of the bend is really clear, or a most unpleasant sticking of the hole will be the frequent result. Having adjusted the eye, seize the pull-down with a pair of pliers just at the level of the pallet loop, bring them down to rest on the bottom board, and

turn the end of the pull-down over at right angles with the
finger, and finish at leisure into a hook. The outer eye
should be bushed with a bit of cloth or leather to prevent the
tracker wire from clattering. The thumping rail can now
be put in, the front boards screwed on, and the job is
complete.

262. Before dismissing the subject of sound-boards, it is
well to give some idea of how to calculate what the touch is
likely to be, and to show what influence the wind-pressure
has on it. Every inch of water on the gauge is equivalent to
a pressure of ·0·58, or, say, ½ oz. per square inch. This,
multiplied by the weight of wind of the organ, gives the
pressure per square inch of pallet area, which area may be
taken as all the aperture and half the seating. This total
area, multiplied by the pressure per square inch, gives the
total pressure *at the centre* of the opening, and the pressure
on the pull-down is less than this by the amount of leverage.
Take the following numerical example—pallet length over
groove and one seat 12 in., width over groove and one seat
1·2 in., heel pin to pull-down 10·5 in., and to centre 6 in.,
wind pressure 3 in.

Then we get (wind pressure 3 in. × 0·58 oz.) × (area
12 in. × 1·2 in.) × $\left(\text{leverage } \dfrac{6}{10\frac{1}{2}}\right) = 14\cdot3$ oz. on the pull-
down. Further, as the pallet rise is ½ in. at pull-down and
key fall only ⅜ in., we must increase this by the ratio ⅘,
making altogether a very heavy touch, as 8 oz. is quite
enough, and we have still omitted the resistance of the spring,
which is a doubtful amount, as it depends upon the strength
of the spring and the counterbalancing weight of action.
There is also a further resistance due to friction, though in
a well-made action this will be but small. The different
devices for lightening the touch will be treated of under the
head of Action.

263. As all the pipes cannot stand upon the soundboard,
arrangements must be made for planting them out. The
simplest is a pipe from the hole in the upper board called a
'conveyance,' and generally made of pipe metal. These conveyances, and the holes they spring from, must always be

made amply larger than the hole in the pipe foot to avoid loss of pressure from friction, and it was noticed above that it was better to start them from special sliders, than from among the pipe feet on the upper board.   But it sometimes happens that the show-pipes are too far from the soundboard, and often, in the case of an old organ, that there is not room to get in adequate conveyances.   In such a case, the device shown in Fig. 157, Pl. XIV., is good, where, instead of a large conveyance taking wind direct to the pipe foot, a small pipe is used, which inflates a motor, *a*, or a diaphragm might be applied ; *b* is a chamber filled with wind, which, when the valve *c* is lifted by the motor, rushes into the pipe foot at *d*. The details of construction of such a chest will appear under the head of Ventil Soundboards.

264. Fig. 163, Pl. XIV., shows the usual way of moving the sliders at the end of the soundboard ; but the writer prefers to carry out the table to the full length of the sliders, in order to secure them from damage.   Here the table is slotted to allow the levers to pass through it, and the upper boards also completely cover the sliders.   The travel of the sliders is controlled by a stud in the table, working in a slot in the slider.

Note.—Since the above was in print the writer has seen another instance of the failure after one year in India of a soundboard by a good English builder. He had been informed of the method of construction described in paragraphs 246, 247, but instead of putting separate fillings-in between the bars, ran a slip checked into the bars the whole length of the soundboard, with the result that the slips shrank in the hot weather, and there was a running throughout the soundboard.

CHAPTER VI—*continued*

SOUNDBOARDS: (b) VENTIL SOUNDBOARDS

265. HAVING described the construction of an ordinary or slider soundboard, we must next take up the construction of the ventil soundboard, where every pipe has its own valve; and, in this branch of the subject, the difficulty is rather to know what to omit than what to put in, as there have been so many forms invented. They all, however, follow substantially the same lines, and a description of the principal types will enable the reader to devise endless combinations.

A ventil soundboard has two particular advantages. Firstly, as each pipe has its own valve, no leakage of air takes place as in the sliders to waste the wind, and sometimes cause a running. Secondly, as each pipe has its own wind-supply, it always speaks in precisely the same way, no matter how many stops are drawn. Now, with the most liberal pallet and groove dimensions, this can scarcely be said of any slider soundboard.

The stop action is much more manageable, as there are no slides to stick and make trouble, but only a small valve to be opened. Consequently, the connections can be much slighter—a mere tracker will do—and combination arrangements can therefore be applied with much greater facility.

266. Fig. 173, Pl. XV., shows the original form of ventil soundboard that has been much used in Germany. The construction is simple and not liable to deterioration from climatic effects; most of the work consists in boring holes. The bottom pieces *a a* have valve holes of the required size bored nearly through, and again from the side to join the first hole. A $\frac{1}{4}$ inch or $\frac{1}{8}$ inch hole is bored from the bottom for the valve-stalk to play through. The partitions *b b* have a cor-

responding hole bored in from the side, and the pipe-hole is bored down from the top through the covers to meet it, *c c.*

The width of each chest is regulated by the plantation of the pipes, and the depth should be sufficient to give a more than ample supply of wind, and thus prevent its disturbance when many notes are struck at once. The rackboards stand above, as in an ordinary standboard.

This type is called in Germany ' Kegellade ' (cone-chest), from the circumstance of the valve being often a little porcelain cone. A plain mushroom valve can also be employed ; the stalk of the valve passes through a hole in a brass plate, like the pull-down of a slider soundboard. The windtrunk lies over the middle or one or both ends of the soundboards, as most convenient, with a hole calculated, as in the case of a pallet, to give an ample supply of wind, the valve or ventil being worked from the stop-handle by pneumatic or mechanical devices.

267. Fig. 178 differs only in each chest being separate, so as to be easily removable. Fig. 180 is a somewhat similar arrangement used by the writer, which saves a corner for the wind to turn, and a rackboard, the chest-cover performing that office. This arrangement has also the advantage that the tuner can put his foot between the ranks of pipes, as the rackboard forms part of a solid box. The pipes of different stops stand back to back, and cannot help having plenty of breathing room. This, which may be considered a disadvantage as ' wasting ' room, is a positive advantage, since it is an automatic check on overcrowding, which might have been applied with great advantage to most existing organs.

The best type of valve to use is a mushroom valve, working between four guide-pins, and as it is difficult to guarantee an absolutely correct fit in valve-head, stalk, and plate, the head should be flexible, so as to close the hole properly even if the stalk is not square. Fig. 126, Pl. XII., shows a stalk terminating in a broad button, *a*, on which thick soft leather is glued, and this again glued to the leather of the valve-face, the elasticity of the leather allowing the valve to rock on the stalk.

Töpfer suggests that the valve-face should be spherical, so that it would always fit the hole, whether the stalk were tilted or not ; but the writer is not aware of any practical example of this device, the leathering of which would be a difficulty. It would also be necessary to determine by experiment the least amount of curvature that would do, or there might be trouble from the wood shrinking more in one direction of the grain than another, when the face would be no longer spherical, this consideration affecting the holes also, which certainly do not remain circular.

·A better arrangement than four guide-pins round the body of the pallet is to have two, with a little wooden guide fixed to the top of the pallet, as shown in Fig. 126. One of the pins works in a slot, as if two holes were used the guides would be apt to bind unless the pins were dead true.

268. Action generally is described in the chapter devoted to that subject; but the application to this form of sound-board can best be described here, as it concerns the arrangement of the soundboards.

Figs. 91 to 94, Pl. XI., show a type with roller action. Fig. 91 is a longitudinal view, where a_1, b_1, c_1, &c., are the stalks of the valves of successive notes, the successive stops being shown in the section, Fig. 94, as A_1, a_1. These stalks, for the sake of adjustment, end in broad buttons, which are lifted by the arms of rollers, $z\,z$, which lie across and under the soundboard, and are carried by checks $v\,v$, Figs. 92, 94. As it would take too great a length of soundboard to make every roller clear of the next note, they are arranged in two tiers, and the stalks of the valves, operated by the lower tier, pass through holes in the upper arms.

The counter-arms, $y\,y$, of the rollers are pulled down by trackers, a_2, b_2, c_2, &c., either from an ordinary form of action, or from a special form of roller-board shown in plan in Fig. 93. Fig. 92 is a plan of the upper roller-board, and shows how the trackers are arranged in two lines, A, B, to clear the arms of the two tiers of rollers. The valve-stalks might also be arranged the same way, instead of passing through the arms.

The lower set of rollers is carried in a frame, and the arms $w\,w$, which pull down the trackers a_2, b_2, are set askew and on top of the roller, so as to project over the cheek t of the frame, and end on the two lines A B of the trackers. The vertical arms, $s\,s$, of these rollers are pulled by the horizontal trackers, a_3, b_3, c_3, &c., from the keys or intervening action. These trackers may either be round, terminating in the usual screw and nut, as shown in elevation, Fig. 91, or they may be flat trackers of a special form, shown in Figs. 93, 94, 97, the last giving the detail of a slot which engages on a pin in the roller-arm. The shaded part of the tracker in Fig. 97 represents cloth glued over it to prevent splitting.

269. Another form of action with squares is shown in Fig. 100, Pl. XI., where a a are the valve-stalks of one note on successive stops, ending in buttons as in the last case, and lifted by squares b b; c is a tracker which runs along all these squares, and is pulled back by a square, d, worked by e, a tracker from the action; f is a spring to return the action. The best form of tracker for this style is a flat one with holes above the centre, in which engage little brass pins driven into the squares. On account of the great number of parts, the adjustment of these types is tedious, and they are more liable to cipher than the ordinary action; but then it must be remembered that a cipher only disables the stop on which it occurs, and not the whole of the clavier, as in the case of a slider organ.

270. Fig. 153, Pl. XIII., shows in section quite another style of action, which does fairly well. Each chest is provided with pallets a a, which hang from levers b b, and the tracker c draws all open together, the pallets being adjustable by the nuts d d. The wire tracker passes through the ordinary brass pull-down plate, and the action is accessible by removing the bottom boards. Care must therefore be taken to have plenty of room to get at it, and the trackers to one department of the organ cannot pass under the soundboard of another, unless there is room to put a passage board over them.

To lighten the touch a pneumatic lever can be used, as shown in the figure. Here e is the motor, and f the square connecting the action. The lever arm g is left a little slack against h, so that the supply valve k can close before the exhaust l opens, and so waste of air is avoided. The moment the lever touches h, the pressure in the chamber causes e to collapse, and drag the tracker over. Valve k should have very small travel, and large area; it is closed by a spring, *m*, as shown in Fig. 152, which is a top view of the valve.

271. A somewhat similar arrangement, which has been used in small organs, is shown in Fig. 218, Pl. XIX., where a single tracker, *a*, of wire or wooden rod runs through pull-down plates or purses between the different chests. On this, pallets *b b* are set by jam-screws *c c* or by glue, so that the whole open together. The difficulty of adjustment prevents this type being used for more than a very few stops, but it is said to give a nice touch.

272. Fig. 219 shows a simple arrangement of ventil sound-board; the pallets are pushed open by stickers, worked by levers *a a*, the bottom ends of which, it will be understood, are pinned to a tracker. Fig. 220 is a very similar arrangement, believed to be that in use in the Albert Hall organ.

Fig. 221 is a peculiar form, where the valve is a ball lying in a cone, and pushed up by stickers worked by squares in the usual manner. This does not seem a desirable type, as the wind-supply would be but small, unless the valve had such a lift as would make the action difficult to work.

273. In all. the above-described forms of soundboard it will be seen that the key opens all the valves of a note; but that the sounding of the different stops is controlled by the draws, which open the valve admitting wind to the chest, which valve is called a ' ventil '; hence the generic name of this class of soundboard. There is, however, another species of soundboard of which several types have been made, prin-cipally in Germany, which can hardly be called ventil sound-boards, because the wind is always in the chest, the sounding of individual stops being regulated by a mechanical ' hit-or-miss ' arrangement operated by the draw-stops.

One such soundboard is shown in Figs. 216, 217, Pl. XIX. Here the pipe-wind is controlled by hanging-valves *a a* cover-ing holes in blocks *b b*, affixed to the table. A tracker, *c*, runs along the soundboard, and is pulled forward by the square and tracker *d*, and returned by the spring *e*. Upon the tracker are bell-cranks *f f*, one for each stop, and a lath *g* lies under each. This lath is attached to a parallel motion, *h*, so that, by the pulling out of the draw-stop, it rises by being pulled to one side, or pushed by a toggle. The first two laths in the figure are up and the third is down, so that when the key pulls the tracker *c* forward, the bell-cranks, whose tails are held up, engage and open the valves; while the third, whose tail is not supported, will miss the valve, and the stop remains silent.

274. Finally, directions for calculating the dimensions must be given. The section of the wind-chest must obviously be greater than that of a trunk to supply that particular stop, as if fed at one end it is virtually a trunk. The ventil must be of ample dimensions, calculated as a pallet, and, lastly, each valve must be regulated on the same principles. Most of the valves above c° will be a great deal larger than is necessary; but the size should be checked by calculation directly it gets near that of the foot-hole. Clearly, the area of the ring given by the lift of the valve must not be less than the area of the hole, and a lift of a quarter-diameter will do this; but it is safe to give a little more to allow for friction under the valve. So that, dividing the wind-supply by the permissible speed (see paragraph 243), we select from a table of circle areas the diameter necessary for the hole, and give a lift of a little more than a quarter that amount.

But, supposing that for some reason the required lift cannot be given, we must find the circumference which will, with the permissible lift, give the desired area, and then from a table of circumferences find the diameter.

Thus, supposing for a pipe requiring 300 c. in. of wind per second we can only manage a valve lift of $\frac{1}{4}$ in. Dividing by 200, the permissible speed, we get 1·5 sq. in. as the area required; and, dividing this by $\frac{1}{4}$ in., the lift, we get a necessary length of 6 in., which, by referring to a table, we find requires a 2 in. hole. Had we taken it for granted that the bore of the hole was the only criterion, we should have made it $1\frac{3}{8}$ in., and, consequently, too small; as, if made of that diameter, the valve would have required a lift of not less than $\frac{11}{32}$ in., or $\frac{3}{32}$ in. more than could be got.

CHAPTER VII

BELLOWS AND TRUNKS

275. AFTER deciding upon the stops, and before the sound-boards plans are completed, it is well to see what size the bellows must be, as it is no use to try and cut down the size of the soundboards below that of the bellows over which they will probably stand. A common rule of thumb is to allow 2 sq. ft. of bellows area for each stop; but the only proper way is to calculate the size required, and it does not give much trouble.

To take the case of the organ referred to before, we find the total consumption to be:

Great	.	.	.	.	. 5,264 c. in. per sec.
Swell	.	.	.	.	. 5,886 „ „
Choir	.	.	.	.	. 2,919 „ „
Pedal	.	.	.	.	. 2,203 „ „
Total	.	.	.	.	. 16,272 = 9·5 c. ft. per sec.

It may first be observed that the bellows should be as near square as possible, so as to obtain a maximum capacity with a minimum of material and of disturbance from the ribs. This, with the usual two-feeders, will require each to supply $4\frac{1}{4}$ c. ft. per sec., and their shape will, with a square bellows, have a length approximately double the width. But as 26 strokes per minute may be taken as a maximum speed, the theoretical supply, $4\frac{1}{4}$ c.f., must be multiplied by $\frac{60}{26}$ to give the capacity for a single stroke = 9·8 c. ft. in this instance. With a play of 9 in. the area of a parallel feeder would have to be $9·8 \times \frac{12}{9} = 13·1$ sq. ft.; but if the feeder is hinged as usual, the contents will only be one-half, and the area must be 26·2 sq. ft. Calling the width x, we get it from the equation $x \times 2x = 26·2$, from which $x = \sqrt{\dfrac{26·2}{2}} = 3·6$ ft. and the length will be double this, 7·2 ft. ; but as this is not clear air-space, on account of the intrusion of the ribs, we must add to the length, say, 0·2 ft., making it 7·4, and to the width 0·3 ft., making it 3·9 ft. The width of the bellows will be the length of the feeder, and its length the width of the two feeders plus, say, 0·25 ft., for the clearance between the feeders, so that a bellows of 7·4 ft. × 8 ft. = 59·2 sq. ft. will be required, while by the 2 ft. per stop rule we should only have had 44 sq. ft.

276. Bellows should never be *less* than the above calcula-tion shows, and it is never a waste of money to make them larger, as the only perfect bellows is one which is infinite in area. It would even be better to allow only 20 strokes per minute, as above that speed the blower is likely to thump.

For practical purposes the above operations can be ex-pressed in the simple formula, $w = 12\sqrt{c}$, where w is the width of a hinged feeder whose breadth is half the length, and c is the supply per second required from one feeder (half the total consumption) ; but the allowance for ribs and space between the feeders must be added as above to get the actual size.

Having settled the size of bellows to a standard shape, it is a matter of simple multiplication to convert it into any other that the conditions of the space may impose ; and one further note as to shape must here be made—viz., that it is desirable not to make both feeders exactly alike (in a bellows blown by hand), but to take a few inches off the width of one and add it to the other, as shown in Fig. 200, Pl. XVI., so that the feeder, which is raised on the downward stroke of the lever, when it is assisted by the weight of the blower, is larger than that lifted on the up stroke.

277. When feeders are not hinged, but open like a con-certina, they are called French feeders, and have the advan-tage of giving double the supply furnished by the other type, in a given area. This class is generally used where the organ is blown by power, and their size can be calculated on the lines given above, from the number of strokes per minute the motor is capable of making. The reservoirs may follow the rules given above.

To calculate the power required to work a bellows, only simple leverage problems are involved. The French feeder driven horizontally is a simple case. Here the weight to be moved is made up of the dead weight of the parts, and the active resistance of the ribs by their stiffness and friction, which must be ascertained by experiment, and the air pressure which may be taken at 5·2 lbs. per square foot for every inch of water gauge. The total load being thus known, and the speed at which it must make a stroke of determinate length to supply the most wind that can be required, the necessary force can be calculated from the equations of motion. If W be the direct resistance to be overcome (in lbs.), w the dead load of the moving mass balanced or supported, which only opposes the motive power by inertia, $t =$ time in seconds in which $d =$ distance moved in feet and $g = 32\cdot2$, then the *accelerating* force f required to move the load in the given time is found from the formula $f = \dfrac{2d}{gt^2}(W + w)$. Observe that f is the force required in *excess* of the direct resistance to give the speed, so that $F = f + W$ is the *total* force required to move the machine, and this value only applies to the length of stroke of the load. Correction must be made for leverage if the driving force has a different length of stroke.

Also in practice considerable allowance must be made for friction, and t must be reckoned liberally on account of the pause between the up and the down stroke.

278. Where there are two French feeders driven vertically by a balance lever, w will be the dead weight of the whole mass in balance, and W the air-pressure and friction as before, for though the two feeders may be in balance, their inertia affects the speed of stroke.

279. The common case of two-hinged feeders is the same as the last; with this difference, that the centre of motion must be taken as the centre of figure of the feeder, and the space as that through which this point moves. That is to say, allowance must be made for the leverage obtained at the point of suspension of the pulling rods, if the weight is ascertained there.

As an example, suppose a pair of feeders, each $4' \times 3'$ with the hanger $5'$ from the hinge, wind-pressure $4''$, and speed required 20 double strokes per minute. Let the stroke of the hangers be 9″ and the dead weight of each feeder and moving parts 30 lbs.

Then the air pressure is $4' \times 3' \times (4'' \times 5 \cdot 2$ lbs.) acting at the centre of the feeder or 2′ from the hinge with, say, 6 lbs. for friction, and as the hanger is 5′ from the hinge the resistance at the hanger will be less in the ratio of $\frac{2}{5}$, or the pull on hanger to balance the wind-pressure $= \frac{2}{5} (4 \times 3 \times 4 \times 5 \cdot 2)$, which, with 6 added for friction $= 102 \cdot 2$ lbs. $= W$.

Of the dead weight the hinge takes $\frac{3}{5}$ths and the hanger $\frac{2}{5}$ths on $W = \dfrac{2 \times 6}{5}° = 24$ lbs., t for each single stroke would be $1\frac{1}{2}$ sec., but to allow for the pauses take 0·75 sec. as the actual time of motion, then $f = \dfrac{2 \times 0 \cdot 75 \times (102 \cdot 2 + 24)}{32 \cdot 2 \times 0 \cdot 75^2} = 10 \cdot 5$ lbs. required over and above the 102·2 of direct resistance. Suppose, further, that the hangers are 3′ 6″ apart, with the handle pivot midway, and that the blower stands at 5′ from the pivot, he will have to apply a force of $\dfrac{1 \cdot 75 \times 113}{5} = 89 \cdot 5$ lbs.

Or, if it is desired to use a water engine of 12″ stroke, the net pressure on the piston must be $\dfrac{9 \times 113}{12} = 85$ lbs. nearly.

If it is desired to convert F into horse-power, multiply it (in pounds) by the number of feet through which it has to act in a minute and divide by 33,000; but remember that in ordering a motor for a bellows it is well to have plenty of power up your sleeve, as things do not always work to perfection; and remember always to reckon the weights and distances through which they are moved at the same place, as the work to be done is the product of a weight into a distance, and if you increase the one you diminish the other.

The smaller the cylinder of a hydraulic motor, the longer must be the stroke; but the quantity of water used will be the same, whatever the proportions.

280. Where parts of the organ are a long way from the main reservoir, it is well to have a subsidiary one close to the soundboard, as in the case of a divided organ, where the departments on the side away from the feeders require a full-sized reservoir for their use.

Where the floor space in the organ is limited, a double-storeyed bellows can be used, as shown in Fig. 233, Pl. XX., where *a a* are two ordinary bellows with their parallel motion joined by an extra floating frame *b*, the parallelism of the whole being secured by the large parallel motion which would need to be stronger than ordinary, as it has a double load to carry.

281. To get the wind from the bellows to the windchests, trunks are required, and here again it must be repeated that the only perfect trunk is that in which the wind would suffer no variation of pressure whatever the fluctuation in consumption, and which consequently would require to be infinitely large. The best shape is circular, as causing the least friction; but as trunks are generally made in wood, the next best shape – the square—should be chosen. The ordinary shape of a narrow rectangle is the worst possible, and is only used for the sake of convenience in attachment to a narrow trunk-band. But Fig. 185, Pl. XVI., shows how a square trunk can easily be led out of a shallow trunk-band by using an amply large junction-piece.

282. An actual speed of 112 in. per sec., giving a loss of pressure of $\frac{1}{70}$ in., may be allowed through the trunks. So, to determine them for the organ under consideration, we have the following calculation for minimum areas—and the larger the trunk the better; so the preferable arrangement here would be to take out a main trunk of 150 sq. in. area, and lead the minor branches from it as required:

Department	Consumption Speed	=	Area
Great . .	. $\frac{5,264}{112}$.	.	47·0 sq. in.
Swell . .	. $\frac{5,886}{112}$.	.	52·6 sq. in.
Choir . .	. $\frac{2,919}{112}$.	.	26·0 sq. in.
Pedal . .	. $\frac{2,203}{112}$.	.	20·0 sq. in.
Total .	. .		. 145·6 sq. in.

283. Many—we had almost said most—organs are deficient in wind supply, both in respect of bellows and of trunk

area, and to obviate this a concussion bellows is supplied to
the trunks. This is merely a small feeder, the board of which
is pressed by a spring so adjusted that the bellows remains
half-open when the pressure is normal. On a sudden draught
and consequent diminution of pressure, the spring forces down
the bellows and supplies wind, while a sudden increase of
pressure caused by the inertia of a descending reservoir suddenly checked causes the bellows to yield, and, by thus giving
more room, tends to equalise the pressure. The writer is not
in favour of concussion bellows, and prefers using large reservoirs and trunks, with springs under the weights. Cases have
been known where the addition of a concussion bellows has
made matters worse instead of better : this is caused by the
natural period of vibration of the air column in the trunks
synchronising with that of the spring, and can be cured by
adding a blank chamber to the trunks, so as to alter the
volume of the enclosed air.

284. Before going into the details of construction, a word
may be said as to the shape of the bellows and the ribs.
Although the best form is a square, bellows are generally made
oblong to suit the exigencies of space ; but the square form
should be striven after. Fig. 127, Pl. XII., shows a bellows
with two inward folds, and Fig. 128 one with an outward and
an inward fold, as usually constructed. The reasons for this
arrangement are not clearly given in Rimbault and Hopkins,
where it is said that the inward ribs, pressing forward wedge-
fashion into the confined air, give it more force, &c. The real
state of the case can be seen by looking upon the ribs as
something in the nature of a toggle-joint, where the vertical
components of the pressure of the air on the ribs by symmetry
balance each other ; but half the horizontal pressure acts
against the apex of the toggle, as shown by the arrows in
Fig. 128, and if the ribs are inward folding helps to sustain
the load of the top board, but if they are salient ribs, tends to
draw them down.

285. The exact solution is as follows (see Fig. 129). Let
W be the weight of the top board, whose area is $l \times b$, $c =$ the
width of a rib, $h =$ the vertical height of a fold, and $n =$ the
number of folds in the bellows ; then the total height of

M

bellows is $n\ h$, and let $V =$ the volume of air enclosed, and $a =$ the angle the ribs make with the horizontal.

Then, by the principle of work, for a small variation of volume $d\,V$ at pressure p, the energy supplied is $p \cdot d\,V$, and work done, $W \cdot d\ (nh)$ by the movement of the top board through the small distance $d\ (nh)$. Thus—

$$p \cdot d\,V = n \cdot W \cdot dh . \qquad . \qquad . \qquad . \quad (1)$$

For simplicity, omit consideration of the ends, as if the bellows were infinitely long, or as if the ends were vertical: then—

$V = nh \cdot bl - nh \cdot l \cdot c \cos. a$, and

$$h = 2c \sin. a, \text{ and } dh = 2c \cdot \cos. a \cdot da$$

$\therefore V = 2\,n \cdot l \cdot c \cdot \sin. a \,(b - c \cdot \cos. a)$

$$= n \cdot l \cdot c \,(2b \cdot \sin. a - c \cdot \sin. 2a)$$

$d\,V = 2n \cdot l \cdot c \,(b \cos. a - c \cos. 2a)\ da$

$\therefore$ from (1)—

$$p = \frac{W \cos. a}{l \,(b \cos. a - c \cdot \cos. 2a)}$$

which gives—·

For $a = 0$ . . . $p = \dfrac{W}{l\,(b - c)}$

,, $a = 45°$ . . $p = \dfrac{W}{b\,l}$

,, $a = 90°$ . . $p = 0$,

p being thus a maximum with bellows on the point of closing, normal only when they are half open, and a minimum when the ribs are fully expanded.

Applying this to a practical case, take a bellows 8 ft. square with ribs 5 in. wide, opening up to 30° with the horizontal. Here $b = l = 96$ in., and $c = 5$ in., while $\cos. a = \dfrac{\sqrt{3}}{2}$, and $\cos. 2\,a = \frac{1}{2}$, so that—

$$\text{Max. } p = W \frac{1}{96 \times 91} = W \frac{1}{8736}$$

and

$$\text{Min. } p = W \frac{\dfrac{\sqrt{3}}{2}}{96 \left(96 \dfrac{\sqrt{3}}{2} - \dfrac{5}{2}\right)} = W \frac{1}{8939}$$

or a variation of $2\frac{1}{4}$ per cent., say, 0·06 in. on a 3 in. wind, an amount of disturbance far less than is generally due to other causes.

286. For readers who do not understand the calculus, the following solution is offered. In Fig. 129, bd represents the direction of wind-pressure on the rib. By symmetry, the pressures at the point a balance, and the result is vertical as ab. The resultant of the force at e must pass through b, the intersection of forces bd, ab, and bf will be the vertical component of eb, representing the disturbance it exercises on the top board. Consequently, if bd represents the magnitude of P, the pressure per unit of length of rib, half of ab, cb, or bf will represent on the same scale those forces both in magnitude and direction, and clearly $a = 45°$ is the only position where the disturbing force on the top board is zero. For $a < 45°$, bf will act downwards, as drawn, thus increasing the calculated pressure, and for $a > 45°$ it will act upwards, thus diminishing the pressure, the maximum being with bellows down, when the extra pressure is $\frac{1}{2}$ P per lineal unit of rib for one side; and the mimimum when the ribs are in the same line when they carry all the weight of the top board. These results agree with those found above, and can be expressed in the following formula:

Let bd, as before, represent P, the pressure on the rib per lineal unit; bf will be double the vertical component of pressure on top board, and equals $ab - af$; also $\angle dba = \angle aef - a$.

Then $ab =$ P sec. a, and $af = ae$ sin. a, and $ae = 2ad = 2$ P tan. a.

$$\therefore bf = \text{P sec. } a - 2 \text{ P tan. } a \text{ sin. } a = \text{P} \frac{1 - 2 \sin.^2 a}{\cos. a}$$

For 0°, $bf =$ P, or the vertical component is $\frac{1}{2}$ P to be added to the nominal load.

For 45°, $bf = o$, or the pressure is that due to the weight of the top board.

For 90°, $bf = \infty$, or the ribs carry all the load.

It will thus be seen that the larger and squarer the bellows the less the effect of the ribs; but as the reverse folds are but little more trouble to make they are always given, the only disadvantage being that they waste a little cubical space as compared with inward folding ribs.

287. Now to proceed to the construction of the bellows. There are required three frames, the middle board, upon which the whole fabric is supported, with the feeders below and reservoir above ; the floating frame, which keeps the pairs of ribs together ; and the top board.

On the middle board is a shallow frame, called the trunk-band, which serves the double purpose of giving a point of attachment for the trunks, and stiffening the middle board against the heavy weight it has to carry—nearly 16 lbs. on every square foot for a 3 in. wind. About 8 ft. × 8 ft. is as large as a bellows can conveniently be made, and if more area is required, it is better to have two separate bellows.

As a matter of arrangement, it should always be possible to withdraw all the valve panels, so that each panel should be a little larger than the one below it, to admit of easy withdrawal. If the bellows can be placed high enough, the feeder valve-panels may be fastened from outside, so that they can be withdrawn without interfering with the upper ones.

An arrangement used by the writer is shown in Fig. 127, Pl. XII., whereby the whole of the top part of the bellows can be withdrawn. It consists in simply furnishing the lower ribs with a second floating frame, which sits on the trunk-band, being guided by dowels and clamped down by hooks ; the meeting faces at *a* are leathered to keep them air-tight.

288. For hot climates facility in repair should always be considered in design, as builders for temperate climates have no idea of what their work has to undergo. The writer has known the best English leather so perished in six years in India that it could be reduced to a powder by rubbing it with the fingers. Of course, in the matter of leather work, the bellows are the most vulnerable part of the organ ; they should therefore be arranged so that they can be taken out without pulling the whole organ down, which can always be arranged by a little scheming. If circumstances admit, it is far better to keep them outside the organ altogether.

For use in tropical climates also, the upper board and middle frame should be armed with 1 in. planks on their edges, so that the bellows when shut are completely boxed in.

289. The middle frame much resembles an ordinary door with movable panels, and may be of from $1\frac{1}{2}$ in. stuff for a small to 2 in. for a large bellows. Fig. 174, Pl. XV., shows the middle board of a fairly large bellows, the longitudinal planks being double tenoned into the end pieces, and the cross piece placed, not in the centre, but on the line of junction of the feeders, unless it is wide enough to reach the one furthest from the centre. Fig. 193, Pl. XVI., shows a way of framing that has been recommended, but it only seems suitable for small bellows. The ends of the pieces are mitred and tongued, the joint being made with a feather of hard wood with the grain *across* the feather, or a mitre lap-joint may be used. The trunk band can be made of $1\frac{1}{2}$ in. stuff, dovetailed at the corners, and strongly glued and screwed to the middle board. Depth should not be grudged, both for the sake of convenience in attachment of trunks and for strength, and the trunk holes should be arranged as near the supports as possible. .

The floating frame, Fig. 171, Pl. XV., can be of $\frac{3}{4}$ in. stuff up to $1\frac{1}{2}$ in. for a large bellows, and must be of the necessary width to attach the entering ribs to the outside and the salient ribs to the inside. The stiles of the top board must be at least so wide, and may require to be more for strength.

290. The top board and feeder frames should be of the substance of the middle board, see Figs. 166, 175. As wood shrinks badly in hot climates, for them, at least, all the joints should have leather glued inside them, even the junction of trunk band and middle board.

The ribs should next be prepared. They may be from 4 in. to 6 in. wide and $\frac{1}{2}$ in. to $\frac{3}{4}$ in. thick for small and for large bellows respectively, and their section is sufficiently clearly shown in Fig. 187, Pl. XVI. The longer edge is nearly the length of the piece to which the rib is attached, leaving a slight gap between the ends of adjacent ribs to prevent the gussets from being frayed, and the angle of the mitre should be cut back to 40°, so as to allow plenty of room for the gusset to fold up when closed, and all sharp edges should be avoided. The feeder ribs may be any width, as the question of disturbing the wind does not arise. The pairs lengthways of the feeder will be triangular, as shown at *a* in Fig. 199.

291. To leather the ribs, stretched sheepskin is used, so that the joints will not become slack by use, and, of course, glue is the usual cementing medium ; but here is the place to describe a cement used by the natives of India (which is much superior to glue for bellows work in that country). It is called 'ràlàm,' and is really dextrine, and the way to prepare and use it is as follows. Take a handful of flour, dip it into water, and squeeze, and work it about until no more will dissolve out, and the remnant is a very tenacious dough. Mix sulphate of copper with this to keep away insects, and store under water. When required for use, take a pinch and work it on a stone with a pinch of lime under a pestle, until it becomes fairly liquefied, when it can be laid on the leather or joint with a bit of wood or an old tooth-brush. Rub it well down, as if it were glue, and clean off with a wet sponge.

292. If glue is used, the best plan is not to trust to getting the strips of leather fixed before the glue sets, but to use hot iron bars laid over the joints to prevent any chance of the glue being left cold. For the gussets even irons shaped like a Y can be used, the ends being bevelled so that a pair can be laid on together. For the inside joint of the ribs an angle-iron heater is required. Each joint is to be well heated with these irons until the glue runs, when it is to be well rubbed and squeezed out, and the surplus wiped off with a sponge dipped into water as hot as the hand can bear, and then wrung out. A paper knife, or any such article, will do to rub down the leather with ; but the best tool for the purpose is made by taking a piece of ebony or other hard wood about $1\frac{1}{2}$ in. wide, and $\frac{5}{16}$ in. thick, and long enough to lie conveniently in the hand, to which end it is hollowed out a little in the middle. Into the two ends make a saw-cut, and let in a piece of ivory—the plate of an old key will do—and round the edges off nicely.

The neatest way to cut the leather into strips is to have

two laths 1¾ in. wide.   Lay one, called A to distinguish it, on the skin and cut the outside stroke, and before slacking hold of it, lay B alongside.   Remove A, place it behind B, and cut along the outer edge of B, thus detaching the strip which was covered by A, and repeat the operation until the skin is all used up.   With this arrangement the strips all come out with straight edges.   Before being glued, the strips must have their edges chamfered down quite fine, the most convenient tool to use for this purpose being a broad sharp chisel.

293. Supposing all the frames made, and the ribs assembled in pairs, the leathering may be undertaken.   And here a word must be said against the practice of making any bellows, however small, by simply joining up planks with ledgered ends.   Builders sometimes do this with fairly large bellows, and the writer has twice repaired organs where feeder boards, made in this way, had warped and torn the ribs away from the middle board.

The ribs should first be joined in pairs, either with double leather, or in poor work with leather outside and blind-tape in.   The old builders used to join the ribs with horse sinew before leathering, and the writer prefers to use hinges of crossed leather, as shown in Fig. 194, Pl. XVI., which effectually prevent any chance of squeaking or dislocation of the ribs.

No special arrangements are absolutely necessary for joining up the ribs, but it is worth while to fix a strip of hard wood of the section shown in Fig. 184 to a board ; this keeps the ribs steady with their edges about ⅛ in. apart. Glue them together with a strip of leather, 1½ in. or 1¾ in. wide, with bevelled edges, as described above, and when dry fold them up with a slip of wood between them, as in Fig. 182, to prevent the leather getting strained.   Then glue up the inside leather, using the heater shown in dotted lines.   Never omit to see that the edges of the ribs are as far apart as is necessary to accommodate *easily* the double thickness of the leather of the inside strip, for if the outside leather is too tightly stretched, the ribs will squeak horribly in closing.

294. The first part to assemble is the feeder.   Lay each with the ribs on into its place, mark it off on the middle

board, and at the heel glue and screw a batten for the
hinge part, a little thicker than the folded ribs, so that the
hinge shall not be strained and squeak; this is shown in
section in Fig. 181, Pl. XVI. Then bore some slanting holes
in the heel of the feeder and in the middle board for the
hinges, which are made of sash-line or other strong fine cord.
Glue a strip of leather, soft side out, on the feeder, as shown
at a, Fig. 181, to prevent squeaking, and fix up the hinges by
drawing the cord through, and then unravelling a bit of the
end, soaking it in glue and driving in a wedge which is cut
off level, while the frayed ends of the rope are trimmed round
and glued down on the boards. Leather strips are then
glued inside and outside the joint, and it must be seen that
the whole works quietly.

Next glue a strip of leather, flesh-side out, on the middle
board up to the line marked for the ribs; or perhaps this
will be most conveniently done before the feeder board is
attached. This strip must be creased down the middle, and
half the width left sticking up to form the attachment for the
ribs, which are now brought up to it and glued on, and an
outer strip placed.

295. The angle of the upper or outer folding ribs must, of
course, be cut the reverse way to that of the inward folding—
that is to say, the rib corners meet inside instead of outside.
These ribs should be laid on the middle frame, and tacked
together with a lath across the corners to keep them exactly
in position, and then turning them upside down, glue the
gussets over the upper side. When dry, secure with a lath,
turn over, take the first lath off, and finish the gussets, which
should have a tail left to come over the frames. Next, crease
some leather strips and glue half the width to the floating
frame and to the top frame, as shown in Fig. 187, and then
glue the half that was left free to the ribs, and glue down the
tails of the gussets. When dry, put a second strip over this,
and the top part will be complete.

Next prepare the lower side of floating frame and top of
trunk-band with strips as before; attach the ribs to the floating frame, and then place the lot on the trunk-band, and
make the final attachment. Put on the outside strips, and,

last of all, the gussets. It will be observed that the ribs should not be set right at the edge of the frames, but about $\frac{1}{4}$ in. to $\frac{1}{2}$ in. back.

296. The gussets are made of thick, soft leather, which should be held up to the light to detect any defects. The best way to mark off the gussets is to use a paper pattern. Fold it at the middle, and mark off the middle width plus $\frac{1}{2}$ in. or $\frac{3}{4}$ in. for slack, and $\frac{3}{4}$ in. for each margin; then mark the ends, and cut through the folded pattern, when the gusset comes out symmetrical, and can be tried in place before cutting the leather, the edges of which must be thinned off as described for the strips.

The bit of the edge which lies in the fold of the ribs must be split, and covered with a bit of leather shaped as in Fig. 183, and the ends of the gussets should be capped. For feeders and for high pressures it is well to double the gussets, and some interpose thin, tough paper; probably some fine kind of waterproof cloth would be better, as the ordinary leather is anything but impervious.

297. We have now the main part of the bellows structure completed, and it only remains to fill in the panels with their accessories. The panels may be of ordinary wood boards of a thickness suitable to the space they bridge, but to prevent warping they should be channelled and ledgered like a drawing board. Sheet iron about $\frac{1}{8}$ in. thick, japanned, is the best for hot climates, but such panels, if wide, should have a diagonal batten screwed across them to prevent noise from bucking as the wind goes in and out; but a neater way is to use buckle plates. A wooden frame for the valves can be screwed on to such panels.

Several stout ledges should be screwed to the styles of the middle board to support the weight of the top board when the wind is out. Let the top board down and mark its distance from the middle board, and make these supports a little higher, so that no weight comes on the ribs when the bellows are down, and take care that they are all exactly the same height, so as to support the top board uniformly.

298. The valve area should not be less than 3 sq. in. for every square foot of feeder area, and if any gasping or rushing

of wind is heard when the bellows are worked full speed it shows that more valve area is wanted. There are several sorts of valves—viz., holes of 1 in. to 1½ in., with a single flap of leather over them; gratings about 6 in. or 7 in. long, and 1 in. to 1½ in. wide, with little grating bars let in to prevent the leather flap from getting sucked in; a valve like an air-pump valve with a central guide, round which a loose circular flap of leather rises, as shown in Fig. 197, and a magnified pallet with guides, as shown in Fig. 188. The writer prefers this last or the simple grid, covered by a flap of the thinnest rubber insertion held by a strip lightly screwed on its tail, the front edge of which strip should be well rounded to prevent the valve bending all at one place and cracking. Double leather valves are not good, as they are very apt to curl up.

299. Safety valves are required to prevent the bellows from bursting or disturbing the wind by rising too high. A common practice is to cut a hole from 4 in. to 6 in. square in the top-board and close it by a leathered wooden valve held up by a spring, shown in Fig. 192, Pl. XVI. A string is attached to a staple in the middle board, and glued and plugged into a hole in this valve, so that when the bellows rise further than the 'full' position the valve is pulled open. But a neater arrangement is to make the valve discharge into the feeder, in which case the pallet valve, Fig. 188, may be used, the area of which then becomes available as a working valve, for it will open at every stroke of the feeders to let the air out. But when held open by the string it lets the air back again into the feeder as the latter descends, and so acts as a safety valve. The feeder valves, by the way, should be placed as near the hinge as possible, so as not to make an audible flap when the motion is suddenly reversed.

The last accessory to complete the bellows is the parallel motion to make the ribs open equally. It is generally made of sheet iron, but should not be less than $\frac{3}{16}$ in. thick, with large pins, and in the case of a large bellows at least one should be provided at each corner; but a moderately-sized bellows will do with two—one at each diagonal opposite corner.

Bellows should be well painted, both inside and out, with two coats of good oil paint, and all joints should be doubled with leather.

300. The blowing gear demands a word of notice, as it is often very flimsy, a rough $\frac{1}{2}$ in. pin through a hole in a bit of wood being considered good enough for a bellows which is otherwise well finished. The front board of the feeder should be of extra thickness, as upon it comes the whole of the pull. A scantling is bolted to this and to the back board, as shown in Figs. 199, 200, Pl. XVI., and 175, Pl. XV., and its projecting nose forms a point of attachment to the blowing gear. To hang the feeder from the lever there is nothing better than a plain round iron rod of a size sufficient to lift the weight, with a head at one end and a nut at the other, both provided with a wide, spherical-faced washer to bear against the wood, which should be charred out to fit, as shown in detail in Fig. 201, Pl. XVI., or the upper end, instead of wasting the strength of the lever by passing through a hole in it, may be formed as shown in Fig. 195, where the hanger is simply turned over, and its spherical nose rests on a brass cup on the top of the lever, or even in a depression in the wood itself.

301. The bearing for the lever is best made by a brass bush, with two feathers to keep it from turning in the wood, and a *large* smooth iron pin laid on a stout post bolted to some part of the bellows frame, with blacklead and tallow only as lubricants. A good arrangement is shown in elevation in Fig. 189, Pl. XVI., and in cross section in Fig. 190. Here a large iron pin, a, about 2 in. diam., with side collars, b, is placed on the post, and on this works the brass bearing c, screwed to the underside of the lever d. This bearing, with its large surface, will never wear, and if used in conjunction with the hanger of Fig. 195, the size of the lever can be reduced to a minimum, as there are no holes in it, and all strains are direct.

302. Having disposed of the usual type of bellows, certain variations will now be noted. The two-feeder type worked by a lever is by far the most common; but a much better effect is obtained by using three feeders, worked by a shaft with crank set at 120°, as the supply of wind is much more

uniform, and it is impossible for an unskilful or lazy blower to shake the wind by thumping the bellows, as is often done. Small bellows can do with a single feeder, and this can be fitted with a foot-blower, Fig. 289, Pl. XXX. The device used in the organ shown in section in Fig. 330, Pl. XLIII., is a good one where space is valuable, as it always is in a chamber organ. The connection here is simply a bit of hoop iron screwed to the feeder, with a loop at the top formed round a $\frac{3}{8}$ in. plate, which plays in a notch in the lever, as shown in detail in Fig. 191, Pl. XVI., where a is the lever, b the hoop-iron hanger, turned over and rivetted to the lump c, which bears on the lever. The construction is not geometrically correct, as it does not allow of swivelling in the plane of the lever ; but the amount of this movement is small, and the device works well enough.

303. When an organ is blown by hydraulic or other power, the horizontal French feeder is the type generally used, as it gives four times as much wind in a given space as the ordinary shape. This type of feeder is shown in Figs. 202, 203, and will make 16 double strokes per minute in ordinary work, the ribs being 6 in. wide and the stroke 9 in. For purposes of attaching the blowing axis, the middle board is double, held apart by blocks, and the spindle passes between these, carrying at either end the guide rollers and the connecting rod. The end boards are fast to the frame, and carry the trunks, which are wide enough to cover the delivery valves. The inlet valves can be placed in these boards or in the middle board, in which case the gap between the boards should be covered with wire gauze to prevent the entrance of dirt. For large organs a regular blowing engine may be used, with a receiver of a high pressure, where no particular pains are taken to keep the pressure uniform. From this, or from a connected trunk, each reservoir of the usual type draws its supply of wind through a valve which cuts off the supply when the reservoir is full, and admits it gradually as the reservoir falls.

304. Fig. 198 is a diagram of such an arrangement, with the reservoirs over each other, the lightest wind being on top. The reservoirs are connected by a flexible trunk, and each

trunk is covered by a valve, which can be pushed open by a stalk attached to the upper board as soon as that begins to fall. Thus, when the upper reservoir wants wind, the stalk B pushes open the valve A, and the higher pressure wind from the lower reservoir rushes in and fills it; and as the latter in its turn falls, B pushes A open, and replenishes both reservoirs from the high-pressure wind in the receiver below.

For purposes of calculating the areas of such trunks, the *difference* only of the pressure between the receiving and supplying reservoirs can be taken as the effective pressure.

In chamber organs also, where the bellows want every inch of room that can be spared, the flexible trunk is the best. Fig. 196 shows the arrangement in sufficient detail, the construction being quite simple. The trunk is made just like a concertina, and should have more play than the bellows, so as not in the least to restrict by its stiffness the movement of the latter.

305. It would be desirable in hot climates, where leather perishes so soon, to use a type of bellows independent of that material. Such a type is found in the gasometer bellows, Fig. 186; but the difficulty of using this kind to supply the pipes is, that with any convenient construction the area is much less than that of the ordinary bellows, so that to meet a given demand it has to fall so much more rapidly, and this rapid fall produces, when checked, an unevenness of wind that is very marked. If the areas were made the same, the gasometer bellows would be the best of the two, but space and money are generally against this arrangement. The weight of the moving part of the reservoir is directly proportional to its area, but the *vis viva* is proportional to the square of the velocity.

Thus, if we have a gasometer of one quarter the area of a rib bellows, it will be a quarter the weight, but move four times as fast to give the same discharge. Then, if we put W for the weight of the rib bellows and V for its velocity, the *vis viva* will be WV^2, but that of the gasometer will be $\frac{W}{4} \times (4\,V)^2 = 4\,W\,V^2$, which means that it will disturb the wind four times as much. The gasometer bellows, being absolutely air-tight, do specially well for high pressures for pneumatic purposes where perfect steadiness is not essential. The bell is made of sheet iron, and needs no description. It works in an annular space which is filled with water on which is floated a little oil, and there are four guide rollers to steady it. The object of the annular space, instead of filling all the basin with water, is to prevent the air coming into contact with a large water surface from which it might absorb moisture, which would be detrimental to the organ works.

306. It would be an improvement if, instead of putting the weights directly on the top board of the bellows, springs were interposed, because the action of the weights is not instantaneous, whereas that of a spring is. Suppose a reservoir which, with 12 in. fall, can supply the full organ for 10 seconds. A full chord struck will require the top board to descend at the rate of 1·2 ft. per second ; but it requires $\frac{1}{2 \cdot 5}$th of a second before it can fall that distance, during which time the efflux of the air is supplied by its own elasticity, and not by the weights—i.e., the pressure falls. With springs, however, the weight would follow up every movement of the top board instantaneously and keep the pressure uniform.

307. Finally, it may be noted that once the weight of wind of an organ has been settled, it is well to record the pressure for the different departments on the name-plate or some other conspicuous place, especially in organs for abroad, as the writer has known of cases where some of the bellows weights have been removed in order to diminish the loss of air from a leaky bellows, and even of one instance where the ingenious blower removed some of the weights to ease his labours.

CHAPTER VIII

ACTION : (a) MECHANICAL

308. THE action comprises all means by which the player controls the opening of the valves which define the speech of the pipes, and can be divided into two branches : the control of the *notes*, and the control of the different ranks of pipes. We will begin with the simplest cases, and gradually lead up to the accessories required in organs that are so large that the pressure required to open the pallets is more than the fingers can conveniently overcome, and therefore requires an auxiliary. We will also remind readers who have not studied mechanics that lightness is all essential for rapid action. Mere *balance* is not enough, as inertia plays a very important part in the speed of repetition, and a heavy backfall even in perfect balance cannot possibly work so well as a light one.

309. The keys form the first item in the action, and as key-making is a separate trade, the amateur will do well to buy his keys either old or new, but, as there is no insuperable difficulty in making them, we will give a description of the process. The frame must first be made, of oak, beech, or some hard wood, every piece solid, and not glued up as is sometimes done, when the rails will be certain to warp in a hot climate. Fig. 101, Pl. XI., shows the frame ; *a a* are the cheeks, not less than $1\frac{1}{4}$ in. thick, better $1\frac{1}{2}$ in., *b* the front rail, and *c* the pin rail. Sometimes a back rail and a middle rail are added, as shown by dotted lines. Where one manual is placed on the top of another, there are a couple of stout dowels in each cheek to insure the relative position being exact. The width of the keys from C_0 to g^3 is 2 ft. 7 in., making $\frac{15}{16}$ to each white key, and it will be readily understood that the width and length of the frame must depend upon the compass

and upon the design of the action. Very long keys are to be avoided, as there is more risk of warping; 2 ft. is long enough as a rule. Figs. 107, 108, 109 show the key arrangement in relation to the rails, in plan and section. There is no better wood for the keys than a good, straight-grained pine; mahogany may be used, but cases have been known of its warping in hot climates. Join up a plank of the selected wood, with the grain the long way of the key and so across the plank, but be careful to arrange the joints so that they are sawn out between two keys, and admit no wood that is not perfect, or the keys will give endless trouble by warping. Having planed the board and squared all edges, mark off the centres for the white pins, front of sharps, sharp pins, back of sharps, white centres, black centres, at the distances shown in the figure. The mean distance of the centre-pins should be about $\frac{3}{8}$ of the total length from the front. Next mark off the spaces between the keys, and observe that the black ones are not spaced equally between any two white ones, but as in Fig. 107, so as to get the tails all equal.

310. Then put the plank in the frame, with the front of the key, allowing for the ivory or beading, clear of the slip, which is screwed on afterwards to give a finish. Secure it so that it cannot shift, and bore all the pin-holes right through the keys into the frame. Modern pins are sometimes made oval—called 'cricket-bat pins'—the idea being that, when the holes are a little worn and the key rattles, the pin can be shifted slightly round, and thus, being wider, fill the hole again. Then take off the board, and, with a tool made for the purpose (Fig. 106) enlarge the holes for the heel-pins into a mortise. A small chisel can be used in default of the regular tool. Enlarge the top of the centre pin-holes in the same way, and clear them out V-shaped to meet the pin-hole in the bottom. A better style is shown in the figure, where the holes are cleared out with a clearing tool—a centre bit with a plug as thick as the pin, to within $\frac{1}{8}$ in. of the bottom—and then a slip of hard wood with the mortise in it is glued on and secured by two screws. The heel pin-holes are enlarged with the clearing tool, and on the white keys the slip is glued in by cutting the sides of the channel with a cutting gauge

and clearing it out with a router.   The object of this slip is to prevent a dark spot under the ivory.

311. Next, to plate the keys, go over them with a fine toothing plane, and glue the strip on the end grain of the front, and then coat all surfaces under the ivory with size and flake white.   Tack a straight-edge down to the line of the front ivories, and when they are all squared up and sorted, glue them down, pressing them against the rule ; cover the ivories with a cloth, and clamp down on them a wood bar about 2 in. thick, well heated.   Take it off when cooling, and clear away superfluous glue with a hot sponge.   Glue on the front ivories in a similar way.   In gluing the back ivories, drive a little tack in at their back ends, so that they have to be sprung into place to insure the joint being very tight, and take care no glue gets into it.   Clamp a hot plank over them as before. Then saw the keys apart, and just clean off the saw kerf, and drive in your pins, taking care to keep them perfectly plumb and to gauge the length, to effect both of which purposes it is not a bad plan to drive them through a hole in a bit of wood of the right thickness.   A felt washer is put around each pin to insure silent action.   When the keys are in position put on the ebonies, taking care to make them as near a fit as possible. and sloping back from the white keys.   In a hot climate it is essential that these should be secured by a screw from below, and that the ivories should be fastened by the smallest size brass screws.   Lastly, touch up the ivories with a steel scraper, finishing off with the finest glass-paper killed, then pumice stone, and lastly whiting and water, and shape the edges to taste.   The thumping-board a, Fig. 109, completes the manual.   It is often made of wood loaded with lead ; but an iron bar, about 1 in. by $\frac{3}{8}$ in., japanned and lined with green baize on the lower side, is preferable.   It works in a chase cut in the cheeks, and its office is to keep the keys on a level and prevent them rebounding.   The most sumptuous way of plating the keys is to make the ivories all in one piece, and thick ; this can well be done in celluloid.

312. The writer once had to change the centre rail of a manual sent out to India because it had been glued up in two pieces, which caused it to warp, and the way to do this will

be useful to know. A piece of the thickest paper procurable was glued, when the glue was nearly set, to the keys between the backs of the black keys and the centre pins. A batten of the proper width and length was also lined with the same paper, and then glued down on the keys with cold glue, so that they, as it were, reverted to the condition of the original panel. The defective rail was replaced by a sound one and the key-panel put back, and the pins inserted. The batten was then torn off, the cold-glue joint parting first, and the manual was thus made as good as new with very little trouble. Individual keys have also given trouble where the makers have neglected to carry out the specification to arrange the joints so that they should be sawn out. In such cases it is best not to be bothered with the defective key, but to make another at once.

313. After the manual, we may consider the pedal-board, shown in Pl. IX., where Fig. 67 is a plan, 69 an end view, and 68 a side view to 3 ft. scale. The pedals themselves should be made of hard wood a bare inch thick, and the figures give the standard dimensions, which are : length of centre natural 2 ft. 3 in., of centre sharp $5\frac{1}{2}$ in. The nose of sharp should rise 1 in. above the naturals and be slightly rounded, and the top should slant a little upwards. The fronts of the sharp noses are not in a line, but should be concave to the player on a radius of 8 ft. 6 in. The pedals are concave also to a radius of 8 ft. 6 in., and they may either be set vertically, as in the drawing, which is, perhaps, the simplest construction, or may be on the radial lines as generally preferred. Pedal-boards have been made radiating in plan ; but the College of Organists has decided in favour of the parallel arrangement. The figures also show all the leading dimensions with reference to the proper height of stool and to the key-boards, which are invariable, no matter what the size of the organ. All these points require attention, as much of the player's comfort depends upon familiar and convenient arrangements. The tops of the pedals should not be rounded off nor polished ; the corners should just be arrised, and that is all. Observe that the keys are not horizontal, but $\frac{1}{2}$ in higher at the back than they are in front. The height from

the ground is quite immaterial, and depends upon the other arrangements of the organ. There are two kinds of springs used to return the pedals; one a stout spring, like half a pallet spring, stuck into the pedal underneath and bearing against the front rail, which is the most general arrangement. The other is that preferred by the writer, and is shown in the figure, where a flat steel spring about $5\frac{1}{2}$ in. by $\frac{3}{4}$ in. by $\frac{1}{16}$ in. is screwed under the keys by two screws at one end, the other end being fastened to the heel block by one screw. The top of the heel block is not level, but slanted down so that the spring can be set up to regulate the touch to a nicety. When the spring at the fore-end of pedal is used, the heel has a mortise into which goes a pin just like the centre pin of a manual key. The board to cover the heels of the pedals may be made according to taste. There are also two ways of fixing the front of the pedals. The common plan is for the pedal nose to go through a rack or comb in the front board; but the arrangement shown in the Figs. is better, as it leaves the whole of the top of the pedals perfectly bare and accessible. A mortise is made in the key-nose, through which a stout 4 in. screw plays the part of a guide-pin. There should be a good felt washer both above and below—vulcanised rubber is too hard. The pedal nose can either work a sticker or a tracker, or both, and can easily be made removable by using stickers with a large head, which pass through registers. Where the connection is with pieces of uniform length, as a row of stickers operating squares, it pays to level up the noses of the pedals by cutting into the centre ones and adding to the side ones from below; but where the pieces are of various lengths, as a set of trackers going to rollers, it is not worth while. If the wood of which the pedals are made is very heavy, the spring can be eased by boring holes along the centre of the naturals which are the deepest, and by using a hollowed-out sharp. The fall of the pedals may be $\frac{5}{8}$ in. or $\frac{3}{4}$ in.

314. From the key generally proceeds a sticker, *a*, Fig. 169, Pl. XV. This is simply a round rod, $\frac{3}{8}$ in. diam., made by taking a $\frac{3}{8}$ in. plank of clean wood and running a bead down one side of it with a $\frac{3}{8}$ in. beading-plane, then turning it

round and running the bead on the other side till the piece
drops off. They are sometimes made rectangular, and pass
through a frame called a 'register,' on which they hang by
means of a little pin stuck through them, Figs. 102, 103,
Pl. XI., so that they are not disturbed by the removal of the
keys. The ordinary sticker has a wire stuck into the end,
which, lying in a hole in the key, retains the sticker in
position.

315. The backfall b, Fig. 169, Pl. XV., is a simple lever,
$1\frac{1}{2}$ in. wide, $\frac{5}{16}$ in. thick, and of the length required, which
should not exceed 18 in., or it will be liable to warp. The ends
have holes for the tracker or sticker to work through, and the
levers work in notches cut across a bar 3 in. wide, and about
$2\frac{1}{2}$ in. deep. When the backfalls are all at right angles to
this bar, the best way to secure them is to score a small
groove down the middle, in which lies a $\frac{1}{8}$ in. brass wire on
which the backfalls are strung. Where, however, the backfalls, as is often the case, fan out, each must have a separate
pin, held down by a little staple. In organ actions, every
moving piece must be bushed, and it is as well to describe
just here the process of bushing a hole in a piece of wood, as
there is generally a good deal to be done. Use the red cloth
made for that purpose. Cut off a little strip, and point it like
a pen, draw it into the hole, and it will curl itself up and line
the hole exactly. Note the width necessary for this, and prepare the strips accordingly. Draw them through the hole, and
put a little dab of glue near the end to secure it, and cut off
the rest. Clear the hole with the wire that has to work in it.
All wire loops should be bushed with a little tag of leather
folded over the wire and the ends glued. There is another
device shown in section in Fig. 95, Pl. XI., for making backfalls by stringing them to the bar with a loop of whipcord.
Use the best whipcord, and take the stretch out of it. A hole
is bored over each backfall; the backfall itself is notched and
the side of its channel scooped out a trifle to make room for
the cords. Fig. 96 is a longitudinal section, and 99 a view
from below. A still simpler way, only suitable to small backfalls, is shown in Fig. 98, where the top of the bar is rounded
and covered with thick leather, soft side out. The backfall

is lined in a similar way, and the two are glued together, the elasticity of the leather giving sufficient play to the back-fall. Whether these devices or the brass pivots are used, the backfall should be so arranged that the effort is towards the bar, not from it, or the strain will come on the fastenings instead of being borne by the solid bar. There is yet another way of mounting backfalls used in large organs—viz., to mount them on pins like keys, with a row of guide pins near the pull downs.

316. Trackers next claim our attention. They are gener-ally flat, about $\frac{3}{8}$ in. by $\frac{3}{10}$ in., but sometimes when horizontal are $\frac{1}{4}$ in. round, made as described for a sticker. The end has a little score made in it, and a hole bored, and a bit of brass tapped wire about No. 16 or 18, with a turned-up end, has the end stuck into it and the wire lashed on, Fig. 7, Pl. I. The tapped ends can either be bought or made with a special tool; the thread of an ordinary clock plate will not do. It makes neat work to use different colour for different depart-ments of the organs, and for hot climates all the action from keys to trackers should be well varnished, except on rubbing surfaces. Fig. 6, Pl. I., shows another form of tracker end where adjustment is not required, using soft copper wire. Here there is no lashing : the wire is twisted backwards and forwards, and the end tucked into a hole in the tracker.

317. The next detail of action is the rollers. Wooden rollers are about 1 in. wide and $\frac{3}{4}$ in. thick for moderate lengths, rounded on the edges. If very long, they must be made thicker, as there must not be the slightest yielding in a roller. Where a roller is so long as to become unsteady in the middle, it is usually run as a pair, supported by a stud between the two halves, across which the motion is conveyed by a bridle, as shown in Fig. 314, Pl. XXXVIII., in plan, where a, a are the two halves of the roller, b the stud in which they bear, and c the bridle which transmits the motion. In modern work rollers are generally made of $\frac{3}{8}$ in. pipe, with the end plugged to receive the pin, and the arms are of iron $\frac{1}{8}$ in. or a little more in thickness, rivetted into holes drilled in the iron roller. Such iron arms must be bushed with a leather eye, put in with an eyelet machine. The rollers

are carried by studs of wood or metal. The former are shown
in Fig. 18, Pl. III., and can be cut off a board with the edge
shaped as required, and the stalk then turned by a tool made
for the occasion. The pivot hole should only fit the pivot
half-way through; the other half should be enlarged. These
holes are, of course, bushed as described above. Studs are
generally about ½ in. thick. A neat form of roller-stud is
made in brass bushed with leather and screwed to the board;
they can be procured from the dealers in organ fittings. It
may here be noted that, for purposes of coupling, rollers may
have more than two arms, and sometimes a roller combines
the office of a backfall by having an arm projecting through
the roller-board.

318. A square is another article which goes to build up
an organ action, and a wooden square is shown in Fig. 132,
Pl. XII. The way to make these is to shape mahogany
scantlings across the grain to the outline of half the square,
and, having planed off the mitre dead true, glue them together. Then score off the distances at which the squares
are to be cut off, make a saw-cut in the middle of the back of
each, and insert a feather of hard wood, and after French
polishing, cut the squares off in slices, clean them, and drill
and bush the pivot holes. A cheap and nasty style of square,
which may be met with in the works of certain builders, is
shown in Fig. 133, and consists in a roller arm knocked into
a wood slip. The best squares, and those generally used
nowadays, are of steel or of phosphor bronze with bushed
eyes. Fig. 153, Pl. XIII., represents one at *f*. They are
mounted in a wooden slip, which is fastened by a screw, and
when put in exact alignment a pin is knocked into the slot.
The arms of rollers and squares are generally 2½ in. from
centre to eye; but the longer they are the better. Of minor
fittings for actions, there are the leather buttons or nuts,
which are cut out by a special centre-bit from old sole leather
or belting, and cloth washers, for which a special nipple-punch
is required.

319. The parts being now described, attention must be
given to getting them together. We will first describe the
construction of a fan-frame or set of backfalls. A line should

be taken—called, for purposes of erection, the centre of organ —and it should be scored upon all the pieces. It need not be really the centre of the organ, or of any part of it. All that is required is that this mark on the soundboards and on the manuals should be in the same vertical plane, and serve as a zero for all measurements. We had, when making the sound-boards, a rod with all the pull-downs marked on it, and we must now get another with the centres of the key-tails marked, and fix the centre of organ on both, and on the backfall bar about to be used. Pin the bar down on a table, and at the proper distances, and level with the bar, fix the two rods. Collect and number the backfalls, with one end shaped and hole made, but the other end blank, and let the hole be the keys end of the backfall. Lay the backfall with the hole over the mark on the keys rod, and bring the other end over the mark on the pull-down rod. Scribe the trace of the back-fall on the bar, and on the backfall mark the bar-centre and pull-down, and do the same with the whole set. Then, when the gaps are cut in the bar and the holes drilled in the back-falls, each will, when mounted, reach exactly from the key to the pull-down. If the backfalls lie underneath the bar, the whole will be turned upside-down in setting out. If the back-falls are parallel, they can, of course, be cut at once to the out-line dimensions of the plan, and the gaps squared off on the bar.

A similar process can be followed to set off a radiating square action, which the new style of square renders very easy to adjust. More skew can be got out of a square than out of a backfall action, and long backfalls are liable to cast.

320. For a roller action, mark off the longitudinal centres of all the rollers, and strike the vertical lines up from the key-tails and down from the pull-downs. Mark the intersec-tion of these with each roller by a circle, and with the dividers take the distance from centre of roller-arm to centre of stud, and mark the latter with a cross ; but before boring the stud-holes, see that all the upward and downward stickers are clear of each other, and that no two roller arms are over each other, unless there is ample room for the tapped ends of the trackers to clear each other.

Fig. 232, Pl. XX., shows a way of dodging action round a trunk, post, or other obstacle. The trackers *a a*, whose path is interrupted, hitch on to rollers *b b b*, which, by trackers at the side of the obstacle, move the rollers *c c*, and restore the trackers *d d* to the original line.

321. As no two organs are alike in dimensions or arrangement, it is impossible to give any standard type of action. Considerations of available depth, width, and height will rule the selection of the most suitable type; but a few diagrams may be useful. In laying out an action, facility in adjustment and repair must never be overlooked. Though often omitted, it is very desirable to furnish an adjustment for altering the depth of touch throughout without interfering with the adjustment of each note, for hygrometric changes alter the depth of touch considerably, especially if the trackers are long. The simplest plan is to make the backfall bar adjustable, as shown in Fig. 5, Pl. I. The bar is fastened to the frame by a long and stout screw, and a wedge *a* is placed under the bar to bring it hard up to the screw, so that, by tightening the screw on the wedge, a very minute adjustment can be effected. It may be as well to note here the best way of setting up an action. Begin with the lowest manual, the others being removed, and take off the thumping-board. First join up the action next the pull-downs, and set all the rollers, or backfalls, or whatever they are, just half their play above the level. The best way to do this is to set the two end ones, and judge the rest by eye. Connect backwards to the keys, and lay a little bit of wood $\frac{3}{8}$ in. square on the key next to that about to be adjusted, and screw up the key just level with the templet as it lies on a depressed key, so as to give $\frac{3}{8}$ in. stroke. Do this for all the c's, and level up between by eye. The assistant at the keys should strike them smartly two or three times, to make sure that the action is all home. Then put on the thumping-board, and run a chromatic scale up and down two or three times, and correct any keys that have gone slack. The black keys are adjusted to their neighbours. Then put on the next manual, and proceed in the same way. The pedal is adjusted by the feel. Screw up until the action is home against the pedal. When manual and pedal are in

perfect adjustment, and not before, the couplers can be done. Whether these are independent or between the keys, they are adjusted in the same way, tightening up until the coupler just gives the coupled manual its full fall.   Test by drawing all stops on the coupled manual and playing each note from the coupler, then put a finger on the coupled note and see if the sound alters.   Finally shut the coupler, and play down a chromatic scale to see that no notes sound unbidden.   Many uncouth sounds proceed from organs for want of perfect adjustment of the couplers ; but if gone through systematically nothing is easier than to put everything into perfect adjustment.   In designing the pedal, or, indeed, any couplers, the backfalls should not hang on the keys, or they may cause ciphering. The preponderance should be away from the keys. The couplers fitted between the keys are shown in Figs. 291, 293, Pl. XXXI.

322. A most useful adjunct, though never given in organs, is an adjustment between the draw-stop and backfall bar, best obtained by putting a wood screw on a trace. This, if well blackleaded, will never stick, can be turned by the fingers, and is much superior to a metal adjustment, unless the latter is made with much better finish than is usually found in organ ironwork.   A coupler should always have plenty of play to allow for lost motion, which is unavoidable, however well the action is made.

323. Fig. 291 is called the tumbler coupler, and is mentioned only to condemn it, as it is noisy and utterly bad.   It is seldom, if ever, put into modern organs.   The construction is quite simple : short stickers of wood in a wooden bar that is rotated by the draw-stop being in the dotted position when the couplers are in.   Fig. 292 shows another form where the bar, instead of rotating, slides forward. It is very little better than the other.   The ram coupler, shown in Fig. 293, is the best of the self-contained couplers, and is often used in two-manual organs.   The little sticks with leather-covered heads are strung on the bar a, which is pushed forward when the stop is drawn and engages in the inclined planes on the keys ; b is a button at the end of a tapped wire which passes through the key, and is turned by the eye at top to adjust the coupler.

But the best couplers are those which are in the action, as they work more freely, and are always capable of adjustment. No set rule can be given for these, and as they are only combinations of levers, any person who can attempt an organ will have no difficulty in arranging them. With a backfall coupler also, octave couplers are readily introduced, as shown in Fig. 295, where A is the backfall from keys, with an adjusting button, the backfall passing between the Great stickers, on which account the backfalls cannot be fanned out, and another, B, is required to bring the motion to the line of the pull-down, or a roller board may be used. C is the unison, D the super-octave, and E the sub-octave coupler, the extra sticker shown to E being a useful addition to make out the lowest 12 notes from the pedal soundboard. Extra pipes up to e or f should be provided to avoid a break where an octave coupler is used.

324. The pedal coupler may be either a slanting set of backfalls, as in Figs. 330 to 332, Pl. XLIII., or parallel backfalls, worked from rollers, the latter being the most usual arrangement. Fig. 294, Pl. XXXI., shows an action for a two-manual organ—a, the Great tracker works by an intermediate backfall, b, which allows the keys to be removed; c, the Swell tracker works from a square, the sticker to which passes through a register, to allow that manual also to be removed; e is a second backfall from the Great, which couples the Swell by pulling at the square d when the bar is raised to bring it into action. Fig. 296 gives another style, where rollers are not required. Here a, the Great backfall, is operated by a sticker, which passes between the noses of the Swell keys; b, the Swell backfalls, just rest on the rounded noses of their keys, and there is a ram coupler. The sticker of Manual to Pedal coupler is put into the backfall, and not into the key, whenever possible, so that the manual can be removed without any trouble. Otherwise it may be held by a register, as in Fig. 294; but with the lowest manual it is not quite so important. Too much attention cannot be given to accessibility for repairs and adjustment—a point too often neglected, as some organs have the Great stickers run through a hole in the Swell keys, and the writer remembers an English organ

where it is necessary to take down half the Pedal pipes to get at the blowing lever pin to grease it, a process not unfrequently required, the aforesaid pin being about half the diameter it should have been, and rough.

325. Fig. 90, Pl. X., shows an action for a three-manual organ. *a* is the double-armed square that works the Swell tracker of the same letter; *b* is the backfall of the Great, the trackers, *b*, from which lead to rollers; and *c* is the Choir backfall and tracker; *d*, the Swell to Pedal sticker, works into the square; *e*, the Great to Pedal sticker, works into the main sticker, being guided by a register *g*; and *f*, the Choir to Pedal sticker, works into backfall *c*, through the other side of the same register. The Great sticker works through a register, *h*, from which it can readily be removed by turning a button between every two, shown in detail in Fig. 89, and it will be seen that all the backfalls only rest on the rounded end of the key, so that all the Manuals can be withdrawn without disturbing the action. Next for the couplers : *k* is the backfall connecting Choir sub-octave to Great, brought into action by letting the backfall bar down; *l* is the Choir unison to Great. The adjustment for these two couplers can, of course, be made by the nuts on the tracker alone ; but an arrangement is added to enable all adjustments to be made from the front, which is better seen in Fig. 89. *a a* are two pieces, whose shape is clearly shown, pivoted on the sticker, *b* is a piece fast in the sticker, and *c* a tapped wire fast in *b* ; and by means of the nuts *d d* the levers *a* can be adjusted to a nicety while sitting at the keys ; *e e* are the keys, and it will be seen that the sticker rests on the keys by a shoulder, and the tail projects below to make connection with the Great to Pedal sticker ; *f* is the button on the register that permits a sticker to be withdrawn.

Reverting to Fig. 90, *m* is the Swell to Great coupler, brought into action by lowering. It is also adjustable in front by the button on the backfall, which engages on a lug on the sticker ; *n* is the Swell to Choir coupler, also brought on by lowering the bar which carries the squares. These squares have a forked lower arm.

326. The arrangement of the pedal action depends upon

the site. The commonest arrangement, perhaps, is to put the pedal at the back of the organ and use a radiating square arrangement to pull down the trackers. This is so simple as not to need illustration. If the pedals are arranged at the side, probably the best arrangement is a horizontal roller board, with skew-armed rollers to receive the pedal stickers, the tracker arms being above or below the rollers as the motion is required to bass or treble side. Fig. 86, Pl. X., is a plan, 87 a side view of the rollers, and 88 a cross-section of this arrangement; or a vertical square under the pedals, with a horizontal square, to carry the motion sideways, may be used. These particulars should be enough to suggest the way of treating any particular case. The parts are always the same, but their combinations are endless.

327. The draw-stop action is the next point to be noticed. This is mechanically the same as the key action, consisting of rods about 1 in. square to push and pull, called *traces*, of squares made of $\frac{1}{8}$ in. sheet-iron, or better of brass, and of rollers of wood or iron called trundles. The motion finally arrives at the levers *h h*, in Fig. 163, Pl. XIV., or the rollers *h*, in Fig. 159. Figs. 124, 125, 134, Pl. XII., show an ordinary way of leading out the stop action, the stop-jambs being slanting as they should be, so that the draws directly face the player. Fig. 134 is a horizontal section above the stops, and shows the relation of the stop-jamb to the manual. *a a* are little cleats of wood, or may be brass pins, to govern the travel of such stops as do not work sliders. For them the check must be on the slider itself, to secure the accurate opening and shutting of the holes; *b* is a metal square which sends away the trace at the correct angle to reach the stop levers; *c* is a square which takes the inner stops to the couplers. It will be understood that these arrangements must fit each particular organ. Squares *b* may be much further in the organ, and not on the same post as *c*; and, again, an outside trace may be taken off for the couplers. All these details can be readily arranged once the principles are understood. Now to describe the way in which the stops actuate the backfall bars of the couplers. The figure shows about the best way of working the pedal couplers: it is cheap,

easy running, and takes very little room. The side elevation,
Fig. 124, explains the action, which is that known as the
'toggle-joint'; d is the trace, pinned at the bottom to the
backfall bar, and passing through a guide at top, just above
the traces $e\,e$, from the draws. These traces are guided
behind, and consequently, when they are shoved forward,
the iron connecting-rod f raises the trace d and the pedal
backfall. As the pedal-stops and the couplers should always
be on the bass side, and as there are no backfalls on the
treble half of the pedal couplers, the treble end of the bar is
simply hinged. Fig. 125 is a section across the traces.
The uppermost trace represents a manual coupler trace,
which passes on into the interior of the organ, and actuates
by a roller the mechanism shown in elevation in Fig. 135,
Pl. XIII., and in plan in 137, which figures are not to scale.
Here a is the trace from the draw-stop, b one side of the
cheeks which hold all the action, c the roller, d an arm, of
which there is one each side, and e a slotted rod pinned to
the roller-arm, the end also passing through a guide f,
screwed to the lever g, which carries the backfall bar, h.
The screw k passes through the slot in e, and is screwed into
g, which pivots on a screw, m, in the cheeks. This screw
must be stout, as it has to carry the whole weight of the
action. The action is seen in the dotted lines. As the roller
revolves, the level of the pin in the arm descends, and as e
and g are constrained to move in a straight line between this
pin and the centre m, the axis of g tilts, and with it the backfall bar. The normal position of the arm of the roller a will
be d or d', according to whether it is desired to raise or lower
the bar to bring the coupler into action.

328. In connection with this, Fig. 138 shows a useful
device for attaching an arm to a bar which works in a simple
hole bored in the cheeks where a projecting arm would not
allow it to be inserted; a is the roller, b the arm, loose on the
roller, and c a stud that can be screwed into the roller. The
bar is pushed through the cheeks, threading the arms on it
as it goes, and then the studs are screwed into the roller and
the arms brought up against them and fastened with a screw.
The figure shows an iron arm, but a wooden one can

equally well be fastened, only it would be much thicker, and the stud should be long enough to take two screws. There are many other devices for actuating backfall bars in coupler. A diagram of a common arrangement is given in Fig. 123, Pl. XII., where *a* is the backfall bar sliding between guides *b* set on the cheeks; the bar has a shoulder cut to prevent endway travel, and into its end is screwed a roller *c* about 1 in. thick, of hard wood; *d* is the trace with a wide end, into which is cut an inclined slot, in which the backfall roller is an easy fit. The trace is supported on two rollers, *e e*, screwed to the cheeks. It is clear from the figure that moving the trace backwards will compel the bar to rise and fall by the travel of its roller in the inclined slot, which, by the way, is better lined with leather. Should the pull of the action be downwards, the slot can be omitted, and a simple wedge left; but if the action thrusts the bar upward, and it is at all a heavy touch, there is a tendency of the bar to lift when a full chord is played. It is, of course, understood that there is a trace on each side worked by a roller across the action at any convenient place, the roller having a third arm for the trace, much as shown in Fig. 137, Pl. XIII. Fig. 136 is a still more primitive arrangement, where the trace *a* simply ends in a wedge, and the bottom side of the backfall bar *b* is brought to an edge, a similar piece, *c*, being placed below. If the wedge is nicely made and leathered, this device works better than might be expected from its crudeness, but of all the couplers the toggle action of Fig. 124, Pl. XII., is best.

The square *g* in Fig. 124 is the connection of the double-ended composition pedal ' Great to pedal on and off,' which is a most useful attachment, and is referred to in the specifications. A trace from the other arm of the square draws the coupler trace in and out. The coupler back-fall bars can be mounted on the back of a motor, or worked by one when inflated by drawing the stop. This attachment should always be applied where the draw-stop action itself has only to open a valve, so that all the stops may run with equal ease. Where the action is all mechanical, care should be taken in the couplers to give plenty of room to make up for lost motion and to render the movement as easy as possible. Nothing is more annoying to a player than to be disturbed by an obstinate coupler, while perhaps the sliders work freely enough.

One great convenience in the ventil system is the small amount of work that has to be done by the draw-stops, the connections of which can thus be reduced to mere trackers to which combination devices can be freely applied. Even where electricity or pneumatics are used to control the stops, it is an advantage to be able to make the mechanism as light as possible, and not to have a composition liable to stick through the fault of one slider.

329. This leads to the subject of composition pedals—an important part of the action. When an organ gets at all large it would be a difficult matter for the player to shift the stops by hand as rapidly as is required, particularly in sudden changes between *piano* and *forte*. The composition pedals, by one movement of the foot, set the combination they are built for, and for a large manual there should be three—*p, mf, f.* There are single and double-acting compositions. The single only draw or reduce certain stops, while the double-action ones both draw and reduce. The old-fashioned arrangement is shown in Fig. 160, Pl. XIV., which represents the double-action kind. A trace from the pedal draws down the arm of the roller *a*, and causes it to revolve and draw the sliders connected to it ; at the same time the projection *b* engages a similar projection on the other roller *c*, and causes it to revolve the contrary way, taking in its sliders. This action may be considered obsolete, as it is noisy and cramped, and the fingers are liable to be bent. To make matters worse, the projections *b* are generally straight pieces, though their faces should be epicycloids, as they are virtually one tooth in a cogwheel. The pedals are returned by a spring, and it will be observed in the Fig. that the fingers work in slots in the sliders, otherwise drawing one slider by hand would draw all the others on that composition iron. The general arrangement now used is shown in diagram in Figs. 76 to 79, Pl. X. At any convenient point between the stop-jamb and the slider, where the traces come together, a hinged or pivoted batten of wood is placed across them, either vertically or horizontally, according as the traces lie. On each trace to be moved by a

batten is a padded stud—a block of vulcanised rubber on a
screw is a convenient form.   The batten then is connected to
the composition pedal, and, being revolved, draws the traces
which are armed with blocks with it.   The ' on ' and ' off '
fans are conveniently placed opposite each other and coupled,
or may have separate traces from the pedal.   Fig. 77 is a plan
of the compositions for one manual, where *a a* are the fans.
The F and P fans are single-acting, drawing or shutting only ;
and the M F is double-acting, drawing Nos. 1, 2, 3, and
shutting 4 and 5, *b b* are the arms which couple the two, and
c c the trace actuating them ; *d d* are the traces connecting
with the stops.   Fig. 76 is a cross-section through the traces,
and Fig. 79 a side elevation, all with the same reference
letters.   As noted above, the tier of stop-traces can be laid
vertically or horizontally, whichever suits best.   The fans can
be applied to traces in double tiers, as shown in cross-section
in Fig. 78, where *a* is an iron roller with two arms, *b b*, to
which is fastened a wooden batten, or the whole may be made
in iron.   This enables the inner tier of traces to be reached
without interfering with the outer.

330. Composition pedals lend themselves much better to
ventil than to slider organs, as one slider sticking prevents
the pedals working, and, in any case, they run much stiffer
than a simple valve ; consequently the composition action
requires to be carefully designed and substantially built.
Any rollers used in it should be of $1\frac{1}{4}$ in. iron.   The
pedals should be returned to their neutral position by a
spring, or they may make the first stop that is moved contrary to the pedal heavy by having the whole weight of the
pedal on it.   Roosevelt has introduced a very ingenious composition action, the merit of which is that the player can build
up his compositions at the moment.   The old composition
action on the slider could only be altered with a good deal of
trouble and expense.   The improved style described above
can be altered with very little trouble, since it only involves
moving one screw ; but, with Roosevelt's device, not only can
the player set a composition before a piece, but he can
actually do so while playing.   The thing is very simple, and
is shown in Figs. 72, 73, Pl. X.   The former is a section, and

the latter a front view.   Under the draw-stops, or, it may be, in a space to themselves, are arranged little levers *a a*, which if away from the draws they refer to, would bear their names. These levers pivot on the centre, and a stout wire, *b*, is screwed into each end, and passes through a bushed hole in the stop trace *c*, being flush with it when the lever is vertical; *d* is the fan of the composition, the upper one being 'on' and the lower one 'off.'   Thus it is clear that the pedal will not move any stop so long as the lever is left vertical; but if either the top or bottom be pushed in, the corresponding wire projects beyond the trace, and being moved by the fan, carries the trace with it.   The only objection to this device is, that it takes up a lot of room on the stop-jamb; but as the compositions are variable at will, so many pedals will not be required; indeed, two would be sufficient for all ordinary cases.   Fig. 72 shows the stop as engaged for the 'on' movement when the pedal is touched.

331. Another ingenious device was fitted to an organ in the Inventions Exhibition.   The draw-stops were oval, and by turning them through a quadrant they were brought on to the composition pedal, a knob or pin on the trace being all that is necessary.   The oval shape of the draws would enable the player to see at a glance what combination was set.   There would in this case be two pedals—one to draw and one to shut the stops prepared.

332. Another form of adjustable combination action is shown in Figs. 209 to 211, Pl. XVIII.   Here *a a* are stout wire trackers which work the stop action (this device can only be applied where the stops open valves, whether they are themselves ventils or the valves of a pneumatic draw-stop arrangement). Upon these trackers are strung leaf-shaped pieces of wood, *b b*, with a stout wire tail; these pieces are held between the nuts, but can revolve if pushed; *c* is the fan of the composition action, operated either direct by a pedal or by a motor worked from a piston; *d* is a comb with stout wire pins capable of lateral motion, and worked by a knob numbered to correspond with the piston to which it belongs; and *e e* are guides to the trackers.   The action of drawing a stop is supposed to raise the trackers.   Fig. 209 is a cross section, 210 a front view, and 211 a plan.   In the normal state the lugs lie aside

o

and the motion of the fan does not reach them. To build up a combination the required stops are drawn, thus raising the trackers as $a^1 a^1$. Now if the combination knob be pulled, the comb is drawn aside, and the lugs of all the trackers which have been drawn up are set square, and will be reached by the fan. The stops are then put in, and whenever the piston is touched the same stops will be drawn until, the combination knob being pushed in (while the stops are out), the lugs are restored to the slanting position. To take off, the fan would be above the lugs. The figures show two compositions, but only the upper one has been used.

333. Another species of composition arrangement is shown in Figs. 206, 207. It is called the crescendo pedal, and originated, and has been principally used, in Germany. Fig. 206 is a cross section, where a is a wheel with a roughened face on an axis b, or there may be a wheel each side of the console. This wheel, when set in motion downwards by the foot of the player, draws stops in a judiciously-selected order up to the full power of the organ, and shuts them off again when turned backwards; c is the trace from draw-stop to ventil (this arrangement cannot be used to move sliders direct), and d is a button on the trace which engages the lever e, the rising of which thus draws the stop if not already on. This lever ends in a roller, f, which rests on the stepped surface of a drum, g, of which Fig. 207 is the front view. The drum is driven by a strap from the pedal wheel. It is clear from the diagram that when the crescendo movement is entirely off, as in the figure, the rollers rest on the smaller circumference of the drum; but the moment the latter begins to revolve in the direction of the arrow, the first notch or step raises the first roller, and a further movement brings the second notch up to the second roller, and so on until the drum has all but completed a revolution, when all the stops will be on, and the drum is prevented by a catch from going any further, or all the stops would fall off again. The counter-revolution of the drum lets off the stops in the reverse order to that in which they were drawn. The lever e is pivoted at h, and Töpfer has suggested that instead of being a fixed fulcrum, it should be movable by means of a knob or second draw-stop, so that the

player can at will exclude any stops from the action of the crescendo pedal at any stage of the movement by pulling out this knob, which would drop the trace *k*, and so throw the lever *e* out of gear with *d*.

Töpfer further proposes an index, as shown in Fig. 208, where a cylinder with coloured dots is indicated. Two entries are shown in the diagram, but one only would be visible to the player at a time, through a hole in the casing, like a date rack. These dots appear in regular columns under the appropriate heading on the case, and the pointers show just where the cylinder is in its revolutions. The index would be driven by the strap *l* shown in Fig. 206. The index would not, of course, apply if the crescendo were made adjustable. The crescendo movement can also be worked by making the foot-wheel draw out a rod with steps on it, one behind the other, and finally it could be operated without a wheel at all by using a motor, with a cataract to govern the speed, which would be set by an index.

334. In ventil organs the stops draw against a spring, and must therefore act on a dead centre to prevent their springing back. Such an arrangement is shown in Fig. 231, Pl. XX., where the stop on being drawn out tilts up the levers *a a*, the levers *b b* remaining jammed. This is the ordinary harmonium action. Or the action may run in the usual way to the valve and jam that open by a wedge — a preferable arrangement where the space in the console is but limited.

Another device is shown in Fig. 226, where the trace is worked by a roller and wedge. An arrangement for selecting stops to be acted on by a composition pedal is also shown in this figure : *a* is the spindle and *b* the arm of a composition roller; and *c* a lug on the trace ; the little knob under the draw-stop thrusts forward the dog *d*, and unless this is in its place the pedal does not engage with that particular stop. Or the action can be reversed with the dog *d* normally in its place, but thrown out of gear by pulling out the knob.

335. Pneumatic pistons for combination action are a great help to the player, and are always fitted to large organs. They are little knobs in the heel rail just under the keys of each manual (see Fig. 205, Pl. XVII.), which, when pressed,

open a valve and set a motor to work, which draws the slides, or traces, which govern valves. Fig. 213, Pl. XIX., is a diagram in section of such an arrangement, and 212 a plan : *a* is the manual frame from the back (or in a console, from the side, as in Fig. 204, Pl. XVII.) of which the piston projects, ending in a button *b*; *c* is the valve of the motor *d*; it also ends in a button, and is returned by a spring. When the button is pressed the motor is inflated, and by a bell-crank other mechanism drives the fans *e e* of the usual type in composition action.

336. A curious form of pedal, which is not much used, is shown in Fig. 228, Pl. XX., the peculiarity being that when put down, the pedal shifts the stop whichever way it lies : if in, it draws it; if out, closes it. The action is as follows. The link *a* pivots on a centre *b*, and a projecting arm works the trace *c*, which leads to the coupler (the Great to Pedal, for instance) ; *d* is the trace, which is thrust upwards when the pedal is pressed. This trace ends in a roller *e*. In the figure the foot is supposed to be still on the pedal, the left end of the link having just been pushed up. On releasing the pedal the roller will drop out of the notch and roll down the link by its own weight to the other end, so that when the pedal is again pressed, the right end of the link will be thrust up, and the action is thus reversible.

337. Having finished with the action of an ordinary organ not large enough to require special appliances to lighten the touch, we have now to deal with these as applied to mechanical action. Even with a 3 in. wind a pallet soon becomes heavy in the lower notes if made of the size necessary to give a full wind-supply to the pipes. As it is only the first movement that resists, and the pressure vanishes as soon as the pallet opens the smallest distance, there have been several devices for giving a greater leverage just at first. One is shown in Fig. 162, Pl. XIV., where the first movement of the key operates the upper lever alone with considerable leverage. Directly the pallet moves, the button engages the lower system, which has no leverage at all, and opens the pallet the full run of the pull down. Another device is shown in Fig. 168, Pl. XV., where the first movement of the pull-down has a leverage

of 2 to 1 on the screw a ; but as the lever moves, it comes in contact with b, and the leverage being against the pull-down, the pallet is rapidly opened.　The lever is centred like a key upon the screw c, with a morsel of felt or soft leather both above and below.　But these devices are not much in favour nowadays, and recourse is first had to the cut pallet, Fig. 167. This is like an ordinary pallet, split as shown, with a little filling-in piece to prevent leakage into the groove at the joint on the face of the pallet.　The first movement opens the small front part only about $\frac{1}{16}$ in., and thus relieves the pressure, while the moving part engages in the screw and pulls out the body of the pallet.　Fig. 172 is another form of cut pallet, on much the same principle, but not so good.　Figs. 155, 156, and 158, Pl. XIV., show a means of relieving the pressure by a counter-pallet, a little smaller than the main pallet. This can be made movable by putting a slot in the tail and a pin at the sides under the head of a screw, the bottom board being faced with leather to make an air-tight joint. Fig. 214, Pl. XIX., shows another style of counter-pallet : a is the groove in which lies the counter-pallet b on its seat d, which is screwed to the bars.　It is prevented from opening by the lever e, which draws against the main pallet and its spring, but when the main pallet opens the counter-pallet moves to some extent.　The device has the merit of increasing the wind-supply, but has not been much used, probably from difficulty of adjustment, as if both pallets do not bed exactly together ciphering will result.　Perhaps the best arrangement would be to make the pivot of the lever e adjustable from outside, so that it could be screwed up until ciphering ceased, as it would be most difficult to tell by the eye when both pallets were just bedded.　It must be understood that all systems of cut pallets are liable to give trouble unless there is perfect adjustment, or after some wear.　That of Fig. 167, for instance, depends for its fit upon the little leather washer.　If this is not exactly right—and it will get thinner by wear—the body of the pallet will not bed tight and will cause ciphering.　So also with Fig. 172 ; if the little spring is not strong enough to return the action promptly the last $\frac{1}{16}$ in. the nose will drop.

338. These different devices of more or less efficiency are

only used for quite moderately-sized organs; directly we get
larger instruments the pneumatic lever is used. This contrivance is shown in Fig. 239, Pl. XXI., which is a longitudinal
section, 238 a cross-section, and 236 a plan of an ordinary
type. The so-called 'lever' is simply a little bellows, *a*, in
Fig. 238, which when inflated pulls the tracker of the action
at *b*. The tracker from the keys *c* has only to pull open the
small pallet *d*, of which the spring is only strong enough to
return the action. The bellows, or motors, as they should be
called, to distinguish them from wind-supplying bellows, vary
from $2\frac{3}{4}$ in. to $4\frac{1}{2}$ in. wide, according to the size of pallet they
have to open and pressure of wind available. Naturally the
heaviest pressure obtainable in the organ will be used for the
pneumatic work. As the motors are so much wider than the
spacing of the trackers and the pull-downs, it is customary to
arrange them in tiers of five, which allows the central distances to be brought down to a reasonable width. Reverting
to Fig. 239, the tracker *c* from the keys, by means of the
backfall *e*, opens the pallet *d* in the wind chamber and admits
wind to the motor. At the same time the double-action escape
valve *f* being no longer held open is closed by its spring. The
object in having this valve double is by large area and small
travel to insure very rapid action and perfect repetitions. And
the reason for allowing the valve to close itself by means of a
spring, instead of making the backfall push it to with a positive action, is that in the latter case the whole weight of the
finger would be brought upon the action and something might
carry away. Also, in the case of a coupled manual, one
escape-valve would be sure to get home before the other,
which would then be left open, as further movement would be
stopped. An arrangement could be made by having a spring
connection with the valve: but the best plan is to allow it to
close itself. It will of course be understood that, as shown
in the cross section, Fig. 238, the air-chamber *g* runs right
along, while *h* is a separate chamber or groove for each motor.
Also that the arrangement is not necessarily laid with the
backfalls horizontal. They may be vertical if the trackers
happen to be horizontal, as in the case of a swell action. Fig.
237 is an end view of the little escape valves *f*; *k* is a throttle

valve, introduced by Willis, the object of which is to regulate
the opening of the motor.　If the action happened to be slack
and the stroke of the motor rather more than was intended,
the ribs might get blown inside-out.

339. Fig. 234 shows a motor much the same in principle,
but perhaps rather simpler in construction.　The bottom part
a is a thick plank with the necessary holes bored in it, *b* being
the supply, and *e* the exhaust.　The partitions *e e* are battens
with the necessary holes bored in them, and *f* is the air-
chamber.　The escape-valve is double-beat, the upper orifice
being rather smaller than the lower so as to leave a margin
of pressure to keep the valve shut.　Fig. 235 shows a still
simpler type, where the square *a* is worked by the tracker
from the key, and pulls open the valve in the air-chamber *b*,
and the button on the end of the wire allows the escape valve
c to close.　The spring to the escape valve is a very light one,
like the hopper spring of a piano, only just sufficient to close
it ; the action spring is the spiral spring shown, or could be a
spring of the ordinary type working against the square.
There should be four guide-pins round the air-valve, to prevent its weight bending the wire.　Spiral springs should be
made of hard brass wire, and the best contrivance for making
them is to rig up, as a mandrel, a wire of the diameter of spiral
required, mounted on a board in two short uprights, one end
outside the upright being bent as a crank.　The wire to be used
is passed over a pulley, with a weight tied on, so as to secure
even coiling ; the end is stuck into a hole in the wire spindle,
which is turned round, and winds up the wire in the shape of
a spiral, which can be of any convenient length, and is cut up
afterwards into the exact lengths required for the springs.

340. Fig. 153, Pl. XIII., shows what is really a pneumatic
lever, and from the examples given it will be easy to construct
one in any style desired.　One point should be noted : there
should be a check to prevent the motors from opening too
widely, when their ribs would be liable to turn inside-out
from the internal pressure.

341. Before closing the subject of mechanical action, a
pallet of a peculiar kind invented by Hill should be described
(see Fig. 70, Pl. X.).　The pallet *a* is attached to a block

forming the seat b by four links, and c is the pull-down.
Fig. 71 shows the principle of this arrangement. If A B be
drawn representing on any scale the pressure on the back of
the pallet, and B C, A C be drawn parallel to the links and
pull-down, those lines will represent respectively the pressure
on links and pull-down to the same scales, from which it is
obvious, at a glance, how very much less resistance the pull-
down has to overcome than if it attacked the pallet direct.
The links should, of course, stand square when the pallet is
fully open, and the proper direction for the pull-down is a
perpendicular to the link at half range, and the spring should
act in the same direction. With reference to this and
similar arrangements, it may be observed that it is not possible
by any direct mechanical arrangement to alter the *amount* of
work to be done. The pull, indeed, may be reduced ; but
then it must be exerted through a correspondingly longer
distance, as in the present case. If a certain valve has to be
opened a certain distance by a key falling $\frac{3}{8}$ in., there is no
direct contrivance that gives any mechanical advantage, and
in the present case the idea that the work can be evaded by
making the links carry part of the pressure is erroneous,
as the reader will find if he will take the trouble to plot the
arrangement to a large scale. The pressure on the pull-down
is indeed diminished, but the distance through which it has to
travel is correspondingly increased. These are elementary
mechanical principles, but they are not always appreciated.
These remarks apply only to direct attachments, and not to a
compound device such as that of Fig. 162, Pl. XIV., which is
practicable because the resistance vanishes at the first movement ; but these devices have their own defects.

342. A pneumatic lever to work by collapsing, which has
the merit of taking up less room than the ordinary arrangement, has been patented by Wedlake, and is shown in Fig. 225,
Pl. XX.; h is the chest full of wind, in which the levers are
packed in as many tiers as are required, the trackers passing
through an ordinary pull-down plate. When at rest, the wind
is inside the motor, the valve a being open, and exhaust b
closed : a has an elastic seat, for which certain advantages
are claimed ; c is the tracker from the key, which, by the

lever d, reverses the valve e, closing the supply, and opening the exhaust, when the motor immediately collapses. The action is returned by the flat spring f, the other end of which holds a valve over the small hole g. Inside the motor is a stud, h, with an elastic seat. Just at the moment of closing, this stud hits and opens the valve g, admitting a puff of wind which prevents too violent a closing. The spring f keeps the valve g down after the first blow, and prevents any further wind getting into the motor until the key is let go, and a opens.

343. The tremulant is an attachment which may best be described under the head of Action. The writer considers the effect meretricious, and has good authority on his side ; but many people consider it expressive. The effect simply consists in a wavering of the tone, caused by shocks imparted to the wind, and this can be done in various ways. The old-fashioned tremulant was simply a valve placed in the wind-trunk, from the inside of which the wind flowing opened it. This valve was held down by a spring, so adjusted that after the valve had opened a certain distance the spring returned it, and again the wind repelled it, thus setting up a fluttering action. In Fig. 271, Pl. XXVI., is a longitudinal and Fig. 272 a cross section of a tremulant. The opening a which supplies the wind is covered by a pallet which the tremulant stop pulls open. The figures show the tremulant at work. b is a little bellows about 12 in. by 5 in., held down by an adjustable spring, c, in which position the pallet d, connected to the top board, is held open. A hole, e, is cut in the top board, but when it is close down the air has not a free exit. When the pallet over a is pulled open the wind enters the motor much faster than it can escape, and so lifts the motor, but in so doing the closing of d and opening of e lets the wind escape, until the spring brings the motor down again and the action is repeated, thus imparting a fluttering motion to the wind. The tremulant should be placed as near as possible to the stop—generally the Vox Humana—which it is intended to affect, and a concussion bellows left at work too near will prevent its efficient action.

344. As a reversed console is much the best arrangement

for an organ, so far as the player is concerned, a view of one
is given in Fig. 205, Pl. XVII. The three manuals are
clearly indicated in the figure, as also the attachment to the
trackers, by which the manuals can be withdrawn without
disturbing the action. The pedal couplers are shown as in
the console; but there is no occasion for this, as they can be
placed in the organ with the other couplers, and worked by a
motor; *a* is the top roller of the pedal-coupler rollers. The
draw-stops are shown in dotted lines, and they are arranged
in banks at the level of their respective manuals, which banks
should be concave to the player if there are many stops. *b* is
one of the draw-stop trackers. *c c* are the pneumatic pistons
under each manual, and Fig. 204, Pl. XVII., shows how the
motion may be taken out at the side, if there is not room
behind the manual trackers; *d d* are registers to keep the
trackers in place when the keys are removed. The proper
position and angle of the book-desk are also indicated.

If electric or pneumatic action is used, it makes very little
difference how the console is placed, as in one case wires and
in the other pipes only have to be led away under the
floor.

345. Under the head of Action also should be noted the
device for transposing the pitch a semitone up or down, which
has been applied to organs. With the console shown in the
figure, this could be done by shifting the manuals bodily the
space of one key, with a suitable modification of the pistons;
but the usual arrangement is to introduce a set of backfalls
or false keys under the keys, the heels of which are pressed
down by the keys, and the points of which raise the trackers.
These backfalls centre on a pin, and have heel-pins, like keys;
but the bars into which the pins are driven can slide laterally,
so that when drawn aside by a lever, whose centre is in the
line of trackers, each bar, connected to this lever by a link,
moves through a suitable lateral distance, leaving the tracker
end of the backfall undisturbed, but the key end under the
key adjacent to that under which it lies in the normal parallel
direction when sounding the normal pitch. The device is
more of a curiosity than practically useful.

CHAPTER VIII—*continued*

ACTION : (b) PNEUMATIC

346. PNEUMATIC—or, as it is more fully described, tubular pneumatic—action is much in favour nowadays, and nearly every builder has his own pet action, though there is a strong family likeness between them.   Pneumatic action is that in which the motion is transmitted by compressed air in pipes, instead of by levers and rods, and it can be applied either to a slider or to a ventil soundboard.

The subject can well be begun by describing an action used by the writer in several organs.   Its merits are that, as the sound-board is simply a stout plank with holes bored in it, it cannot be destroyed—the worst that can happen is that the leather puffs would have to be replaced, which, in an ordinary organ, would take a couple of days.   As all the parts are made to template and, except for the largest pipes, are all one size, they can be kept in stock and put together as required ; for they should be absolutely interchangeable, and no fitting is required.   The principal fault is the amount of room it takes up ; but this is a very good fault, as it prevents an organ being spoilt by crowding the pipes.   The limitations are that it does not do when the manuals are too far away from the sound-boards, for it seems that while the puffs will last seven or eight years in a bad climate, and give no trouble whatever when the manuals are in the organ, they are given to ciphering when the keys are far from the pipes, the reason probably being that the increased pressure necessary to obtain prompt action at a distance tells upon the puffs when a note is held down, and forces them up so hard against the tail of the valve that they get puckered, and the tail is liable to engage against this ridge, and cause a cipher by tilting the valve.   The ordinary pressure required is 8 in. to 10 in. With more than two manuals, also, the exhaust-valves of the type shown are apt to give trouble, as it is difficult to keep so many in such accurate adjustment that they all close exactly together. If any remain slack, the wind, of course, escapes with a hiss, and may so diminish the pressure that the note will not speak. In a three-manual organ with sub- and super-couplers, there may easily be six valves to be closed by one key. For such actions there should be a spring arrangement; but the action as shown does perfectly well for an ordinary two-manual organ, and is delightfully simple.

347. Fig. 62, Pl. IX., shows the key-valve. a is the key; the valve has a travel of a bare ½ in., and must, therefore, be placed at the point in the key that has this travel. The stalk of the valve is made of 15 B.W.G. wire, preferably of phosphor bronze. The valves are made of ordinary linen buttons of the best quality, of the size known as '22 lines,' faced with leather. The way to prepare them is to select a skin of best leather, not too thick, and scarify the back well; then lay it smoothly on a board, and spread the glue. At leisure place the buttons on the glued surface, and pass a flat-iron over all two or three times, and when well set, cut off and trim. The hole for the spindle should be pierced through a template to insure its being truly central, and the hole in the escape-valve should be burned, so that the valve will be loose on the spindle. b is a wad of the thickest and best felt, the elasticity of which serves as a spring, and will do wonderfully good service, though, as mentioned above, for more than a double-manual organ it is not sufficient. The hole through the felt should also be burned. The small nut c under the air-valve is made with a specially small bit, and further trimmed with a sharp knife after mounting, the object being that it should obstruct the air-passage as little as possible; d are brass guide-plates. The valves are mounted by first setting the small nut in the proper place, then, the top and bottom boards e being removed, the air valves are strung on and top board replaced. Next the escape valves are strung on and the bottom board placed, and finally the springs. The holes in the top board for the valve stalks are closed by a strip of leather along the top. The wind

supply should be furnished through a brass pipe at both ends, screwed on any convenient place. Fig. 53 is a plan of the air valves which are slightly staggered, both to give clearance between them, and to minimise the chance of the middle block splitting. Fig. 59 is a back view, showing the holes for the air pipes. These should not be ordinary gas-pipe, but a pipe made specially for pneumatic work by Mellowes & Co., Sheffield. The ordinary gas-pipe is much too thick, and therefore for a given external size of pipe causes unnecessary friction on account of smaller bore. The pipes are simply stuck into the holes, which should be bushed in the following way. Punch out washers of the softest leather, and, gluing the hair side, place a washer over the hole, and drive it in with a wooden punch, shown in Fig. 55 ; then drive a pointed iron rod, the exact diameter of the pipe, through the washer. This will make a hole right through, and spread the washer against the hole in the wood. The point of the rod should be pyramidal, not round. The ends of the pipes should be waxed to prevent the leather seizing, in case they are required to be withdrawn. Here also may be noticed a dodge to prevent the pipes closing at the bend, when it is required, as is often the case, to give them a sharp turn. Fill that part of the pipe with fine sand, and put a cork in the end; when bent, shake the sand out.

348. Fig. 54 shows the pallet, or valve, which supplies the pipes. It can be supposed applied to any of the ventil sound-boards already described. A block of wood, *a*, Fig. 56, is screwed under the pipe-hole. All the holes and blocks are one size, and the holes are marked off with a template, so that no fitting is required; only two 1½ in. round-headed screws are used, though four holes are provided in case of accidents. On this block is stamped a 'puff' of fine pneu-matic leather, with a wooden stamp shaped as required, and the holes for the gas-pipe are bushed as described above. Pieces of pipe lead from block to block, and thus there is no occasion for the blocks belonging to one note to be in a line, as the pipe can be twisted about; but where two stops are adjacent, it must be remembered that there is a limit to the bending capacity of the pipe in a very short distance. The valve *b* is a mushroom valve with a stalk of brass wire

screwed into it, and a large button on the bottom, above
which is c, a lead weight of 200 grains. This weight is not
required when the wind is in, as the pressure is then sufficient
to close the valve smartly; but in case of the wind being
cut off a stop, a valve might not close, and then the pipe
would give a yelp as the stop was drawn, and the wind,
rushing through the open valve, slammed it to. The valve
works between four guide-pins, with their heads bent over to
prevent it rising too far. The working of this device is quite
plain: the pneumatic wind, being of much heavier pressure
than that in the wind-chest, blows up the puff, and with it
the valve. The tails of the valves are all set to a gauge, so
that they are simply dropped into their places, and the guide-
pins turned over them. The top boards are made in sections,
so that it is not necessary to remove all the pipes to get at a
valve; but, as a matter of fact, they will go for years without
giving any trouble. A few valves and puffs of a larger size
are required for the bass pipes; but the bulk of the fittings
are of the size shown. Fig. 56 is a top view of the puff box;
the main hole is bored out with a centre-bit, and the elonga-
tions made with two strokes of a gouge, and then the screw-
holes bored *from both sides* through a brass template, to insure
their being perfectly plumb, and burned out with a red-hot
wire. The corresponding oval hole in the soundboard is made
in a similar way, and the holes for the screws also bored
through a template, so that no fitting is required.

349. The bellows for the high-pressure wind are best
made of the gasometer type (Fig. 186), as there is considerable
leakage through the pores of the leather gussets at high
pressures. Most of the wind consumption is due to leakage,
and the actual playing of the organ makes surprisingly little
difference. For an organ of 14 stops the blower can work
the high-pressure feeder with his foot, while blowing the big
bellows in the ordinary way. A form of feeder that has
given very good results is a cubical wooden box, about 12 in.
on the side for a small organ, with a loose wood piston, the
packing, shown in Fig. 63, being similar in action to that of
a hydraulic press. The edges of the piston are shaped as
shown, and a strip of leather, a, is held on it by the fillets b,

the smooth side of the leather being next the box, which, as well as the leather itself, is well blackleaded. This piston is quite frictionless in rising, but when raised will support the weight of a man, settling but very slowly, the escape of air is so small.

350. The draw-stop action is precisely similar to the key action, except that the valve holes are better made larger, say $\frac{3}{8}$ in. diameter. The trace has a wedge on it which moves the valve through the $\frac{1}{8}$ in. required, by a dummy lever interposed to prevent the stalk being bent. Here may be described an ingenious contrivance by Michell and Thynne for enabling a stop action to respond to the first movement of the draw while not interfering with the full travel. It can, however, only be used with a ventil or pneumatic action where the draw is very light. Fig. 60 shows the arrangement: a is the draw and b is the trace. The surfaces in contact are faced with rough leather, and pressed together by a spring sufficiently for the friction to move the trace. Thus, suppose the travel of the stop is $2\frac{1}{2}$ in., but only $\frac{3}{4}$ in. is required to actuate the ventil, the trace is moved by friction $\frac{3}{4}$ in., and then the draw slips under it for the rest of its travel. Should the friction not be sufficient by the device getting out of adjustment, the positive action at the end comes into play and draws the ventil in the usual way.

351. The ventil used by the writer is shown in Fig. 57, where it is supposed that the wind trunk is screwed down over the middle or end of the soundboards: a is the ventil itself, of sufficient diameter to give a full wind-supply to the stop—it may have to be 3 in. square or more; b is a little relief valve, 1 in. diameter, on the back of the main valve, which rises about $\frac{3}{16}$ in. and, letting the wind in, removes the pressure against the main valve, and so enables a smaller puff to be used than if it had to pull open the ventil against the wind. In rising, the small valve strikes a slip of wood, e, secured by two pins, f, screwed into the ventil, and so lifts it; c is the puff, set in a simple bit of wood, and screwed on to the top of the wind trunk; d is the pipe from the valve which admits the wind and holds the ventil open so long as the stop is drawn. Instead of a puff, a motor may

of course be used. But as leather is very pervious to high-pressure wind, the secondary valve shown in Figs. 64 to 66 has been used where there are many puffs and economy of wind is a consideration. With this, the H.P. wind only actuates a small puff and valve, and the main wind does all the work. This valve acts very well, and has the further advantage of enabling all the leather work to be inside the wind-trunk. Fig. 64 is a longitudinal section, Fig. 65 is a bottom view, and Fig. 66 a top view. The valve is easily made of a block of wood, which is then cut into three pieces, a b c : a has a large hole bored nearly through, as shown ; b has a $\frac{3}{8}$ in. hole bored nearly through, with a $\frac{3}{16}$ in. hole from the other side, and c has a large hole bored ; a and b are screwed together again with leather between, so as to be air-tight, and they, as also c, are screwed on to a hard wood bed-plate, d, by the screws e, and the exit holes are bored, of which f is the exhaust, g the pipe to puff, and h the com-munication from the valve at the draw-stop ; k k are the holes for screwing the valve up to the upper board of wind-trunk. The block c is then furnished with a puff, and a valve of the same type as the key-valve described above is fitted ; l is a brass guide to the valve-spindle, and m a guide-plate. The action of the valve will now be readily understood. In its normal state the pressure of the wind in the trunk keeps the small puff in c over, and the exhaust valve n shut, while the wind passes through the supply-valve o and pipe g, and balancing the upward pressure on puff p, the ventil remains shut by its own weight. When the stop is drawn the H.P. wind overcomes the pressure of that in the trunk, and the puff in c is blown out, closing o and opening the exhaust n. The air above the puff p immediately escapes, and the pressure of the wind in the trunk blows up the puff, and raises the ventil. The puff c is rather small for low pressures, and it would be better and quite as easy to make it double the width. Being connected by a pipe with the puff, these valves can be placed in any convenient situation in the wind trunk. The escape-aperture should be covered by a block of wood, with wire gauze on holes in the side to prevent dirt falling in. An escape-valve should be provided, both to account for any air that may leak through the main valve when shut, and to prevent the sound dying away with an unpleasant drawl when the stop is pushed in. A puff mounted in a block over a hole in the windchest, which it closes when inflated by the wind behind it, is one device, and another is to hang a valve from the ventil covering a hole in the bottom of the windchest, against which it is pulled up when the ventil rises. Both devices are so simple as not to require illustration.

352. For pneumatic action in general it will be readily understood, without further diagrams, that the key-valves may be anything larger than that described in Fig. 62, as they can be separated by splay backfalls or any other combination of ordinary action, and the valve itself may be circular, as described, or of the pallet form. The exhaust hole need never be so large as the supply hole. To insure the simultaneous bedding of all the escape-valves where many couplers are used is always a little trouble, and nothing can be better as a spring than the thickest and best felt. The introduction of a slightly more complicated detail, shown in Fig. 58, would get over any difficulty. Here a is the supply valve, b the exhaust held up by a spring, and c the tracker, while d, which connects them, is a floating lever. The first pull of c pulls b down on to its seat, and thereafter it acts as a fulcrum to raise a, the stroke of which can therefore be of unlimited length, without any reference to the seating of b.

Another arrangement is shown in Fig. 61, where the same letters refer to the same parts, only in this case a sticker is used instead of a tracker. The exhaust-valve, not having any initial pressure against it, will rise first, and become the fulcrum to open a, and as its stroke can be set to any definite length, the proportions of the parts can be adjusted as required. For instance, with c midway, $\frac{1}{8}$ in. stroke for b (which is generally sufficient) will give with a $\frac{1}{4}$ in. on c an opening of $\frac{3}{8}$ in. to a, or $\frac{1}{6}$ in. stroke will open both valves $\frac{1}{8}$ in.

353. Fig. 245, Pl. XXII., shows the application of pneumatic action to a slider soundboard. The wind-tube, fed by any type of key valve, terminates under the soundboard in a puff a, the inflation of which presses up the valve by means of a

P

wooden button, b, at the bottom of the stalk. In the normal
position the supply c is open, and the exhaust d closed, while
raising the valve reverses the conditions, and the motor e is
collapsed by the pressure of the wind in the chest, and drags
the pallet open; $f f$ are guides. The valve areas must be
ample, and the travel not more than $\frac{1}{8}$ in., to insure prompt
action. If a higher pressure of wind is supplied for the
pneumatic work, and there is not room to get in motors large
enough to work the pallets promptly, a separate chamber
filled with H.P. wind can be made for the motors, and the
pull-downs passed through an ordinary plate. The valve can
be made of two buttons faced with leather with felt between,
or of vulcanised fibre discs made for the purpose, which can
be procured from any dealer in organ fittings, and a perfectly
smooth seat can be bored into a plank by Forstner's patent
auger bits, the only drawback to which is that they are rather
expensive.

354. The draw-stop action can be made in a similar way
(see Fig. 240, where a is the button raised by the puff, b the
wind chamber, c the inlet, and d the exhaust). There are a
pair of valves to each stop, so that one of the coupled motors
$e e$ is on, while the other is off, and the trace f to the slider is
dragged backwards and forwards. These motors are mounted
on a stout plank g, in which the wind channels are formed,
Fig. 243 being a section on A A, showing the connection
between the valves and air-passage in plan. The motors
will generally require to be about 14 in. long, and their
width must depend upon the pressure of wind available, and
the pull of the slide.

As to the valve at the stop which governs the pneumatic
wind, it can either consist of a pair of valves like the key-
valves, or of a slide-valve shown in Fig. 246. Here a is the
wind supply, b the pipe to the ' on ' valve, and c that to the
' off ' valve; d is a trace connected with the draw stop, with
a hollow in it as shown, and two holes, $f f$, for exhaust passages; e is a block of wood pressed up by a spring, to keep
the valve wind-tight. The valve is shown in the ' off ' position, c being in communication with the wind, and b with the
exhaust, and drawing the stop reverses the arrangement.

Other variations of this arrangement can readily be imagined. The faces under the valve should be lined with thin leather, well blackleaded. Fig. 215, Pl. XIX., shows a similar arrangement, which hardly needs any description; the slide-valve alternately inflates and exhausts the two motors, which are coupled together. Fig. 227, Pl. XX., shows a slide-valve where the spring presses down and returns the valve.

355. An arrangement by E. Holt, of Walsall, whereby one motor will work both ways, is shown in Fig. 248, Pl. XXIII. Here the motor a is enclosed in an airtight case, b, the trace c to the stop going through a purse. The chamber c is the H.P. wind supply. In the position indicated, the stop being supposed shut, the chamber b is empty, and consequently the pressure of the wind in c holds up the exhaust-valve d by means of the puff e, while the valve f supplies wind to the motor through the passage g. On drawing the stop, the position of the other valve is altered, the exhaust h closes and supply k opens, thus filling b with wind. The pressure on e being now balanced, its valve drops by its own weight, and thus exhausts g, when the pressure in b forces the motor back. The motors can be arranged alternately, as shown in the dotted lines, the trace from the backward one passing through a space between the casing of two front ones.

356. Fig. 259, Pl. XXIV., shows the application of this style of action to a ventil soundboard, where the trunk can be placed under the soundboards, and it has the advantage of a simpler valve than that shown in Fig. 64, Pl. IX. Here a is the trunk and b the wind-chest; the ventil c is normally held up by the spring d, which need not be stronger than will just bring the valve back to its seat, where the wind-pressure will secure it. When the stop is drawn and the puff blows up the valve e, the wind is cut off and exhaust is opened from the lower side of puff (or motor) f, and it consequently collapses and drags open the ventil, closing at the same time the escape valve g. When the stop is again shut, e drops and lets the wind back into f, which being now in balance offers no resistance to d, which consequently closes the valve. The relief valve shown in Fig. 57 may be applied if desired.

It will also be seen that a precisely similar action with a

motor or a puff could be applied to any ventil soundboard. In fact, once the reader is familiar with the idea, the modes of applying pneumatic action are endless. To prevent disappointment, it is well to verify by experiment the action of any particular device at the pressure it is required for, and to remember that very short travel, certainly not more than ⅛ in., is essential to rapid action, and that 3 in. is about the lowest pressure which can conveniently be used in pneumatic work, and, of course, the higher it is the better.

357. As it is impossible to describe all the varieties of pneumatic action, we will only notice one or two, either as typical or peculiar; the rest can be imagined.

Figs. 241, 242 and 244, Pl. XXII., show in diagram a very peculiar action by Drechsler; *a a* are the wind-chests, *b* a chamber under high pressure, *c* the valve worked by a puff inflated by the pneumatic wind, *d* is a passage in the bottom board. A puff, *e*, forms in itself the valve which cuts off the wind in *a* from *f* over which the pipe stands. In the normal position, the H.P. wind from *b* fills *d* and *g*, the passage behind the puff *e*, which is tightly pressed against its seat. When *c* is raised by its puff, *d* and *g* become exhausted, and the wind in *a* blows the puff valve back, as shown in Fig. 242, and makes the pipe sound. Fig. 244 is a section through the pipe hole.

358. Fig. 249, Pl. XXIII., shows the Roosevelt soundboard. Here *a* is the chamber filled with wind of a pressure the same as, or greater than, that in the wind-chests *b b*, *c* is a false chest, left where required to make up room, *d* is the same style of valve that has been figured so often, and *e* is a hole bored through the bottom boards. With a small organ the bottom board might be in one piece, with the grain running lengthways of the chest; but for any width over 14 in. the grain must run across the soundboards, and the different planks then bear on 'fillings-in' *f f*. A further subdivision can be made by cutting the ends on the bevil, as shown at *g*, and leathering the joint, when a short length of the bottom board can be removed without the trouble of taking out all the screws; *h h* are the motors arranged in single or double file, as found convenient. Their tails carry the pipe

valves kk at the end of a stalk, and press them on the pipe
holes mm, being held open by a spring inside, like a piano
hopper spring. The action has been so often described that
it is scarcely necessary to go through the explanation again.
The same pressure of wind can be used throughout, as the
motor is returned by a spring. The motors should be
removable, as shown in plan in Fig. 247, being pushed up
under the screw a, and then hitched sideways under b, which
effectually secures them. The air-hole is, of course, sur-
rounded by a leather washer, upon which all the bearing
pressure comes and makes it air-tight. These soundboards
of Roosevelt's own make work beautifully, and complaints
against the style refer to those of the Roosevelt pattern by
other makers ; but it is a question whether the principle
would allow of a perfectly steady wind, as the play of so
many motors in a small wind-chest must tend to shake the
wind. On this point the writer, not having a personal
acquaintance with Roosevelt's organs, cannot speak with certainty. Absolute uniformity and accuracy of workmanship
are essential to success. When there are many stops the
valve should be placed in the middle of the wind-chests, or
there should be a valve at each end to secure rapid action. It
should be carefully noted that the wind consumption is perfectly awful with these soundboards, where there is un-
balanced pressure against leather, for leather is pervious,
and though the waste through one motor may not be much,
the waste through 58 × perhaps 50 or more will be.

359. There are, of course, devices for coupling peculiar to
the tubular pneumatic systems, where, to avoid the difficulty
of getting all the exhaust valves to close together, the coupling
is done in the wind, and not through the keys. If the pneumatic valve fills a miniature wind-chest with sliders, from
which different pipes take off to the wind-chests, it is clear
that, by drawing these sliders, one manual can command any
wind-chest, the only additional necessity being a back-pressure
valve on the coupling tubes, so that when the *coupled* manual
key is put down, the wind shall not run back, and escape
through the open exhaust of the other manual. There are
several patents for such devices ; but the principle is one that

cannot be expected to give satisfactory results, either as regards action or durability, unless, indeed, the pneumatic work is on the scale of a steam-engine.

In ventil actions the bulk of the pipes will get much more wind than they require; but when we come to the big pipes, care must be taken to give the pallet a lift sufficient to make the area between the valve and seat equal to that of the hole. A quarter of the diameter is the exact lift required; but the lift actually given should be a little more, because the friction under the rough surface of the pallet and eddies in going round the corner make the coefficient of friction greater than it would be for a smooth hole. A tubular action by Willis is shown in Fig. 224, Pl. XX. Here *a* is the wind-chest, *b* the pneumatic pipe from the keys, *c c* two diaphragms, the upper of which closes the exhaust *d*, and the lower opens the supply *e*; *f* is the usual throttle valve to prevent the motor being locked open. The pneumatic wind in this arrangement would have to be more than double that which works the motor, since the latter has access to the diaphragm.

360. A distinct class of pneumatic work, where the stop action works by a difference of pressure and all the pipe-valves are in one wind-chest, is cognate to the mechanical ventil action alluded to in para. 373, where the valves are arranged in the same way, and the co-operation of the draw-stop with the key is necessary to open them. Fig. 223, Pl. XX., is a section along a stop-rank, and Fig. 222 a section along a note-rank, of a German example. Here the pallets *a a* lie over little boxes, and their projecting noses are raised by stickers, propelled by puffs *b b*, when a key is put down, and the pneumatic wind through a puff (not shown) raises the key valve, closing the exhaust *f* and opening the supply *e*, thus filling the key-channel *c c*. But when the stops are in, the wind is in the stop-channels *d*, the supply *g* being open and exhaust *h* closed, so that, the pressure being equal on both sides of the puff, no action takes place. Should, however, a stop be drawn, the puff raises the valve, closes *g*, and opens *h*, and the wind in *d* escapes, allowing the puff *b* to blow up and sound the note on that particular stop. The middle valve of Fig. 222 is shown at work. *k* is the wind-chest, from which,

in the figure, the supply of pneumatic wind is drawn; but it would certainly be best to use from a special chest a much higher pressure than the pipe-wind.

361. Figs. 229, 230 give another example, in which the action depends upon wind being in the chest, as also, of course, does the speech of the pipes. Fig. 229 is a section along a note-channel, and Fig. 230 along a wind-chest. The pallets lie directly under the pipes—a great advantage for speech, but very subject to disarrangement from dirt falling down if a pipe is moved. It is, indeed, difficult to imagine how an organ with such a soundboard could ever be cleaned. With this arrangement, the wind is always in the key-channel *a*, and the pallet is held up (not pushed down) by a light spiral spring. Putting the key down lets the wind out from *a*, and then the puff is blown down in as many of the wind-chests as have their stops drawn.

CHAPTER VIII—*continued*

ACTION : (c) *ELECTRIC*

362. The application of electricity to organ action is not so very modern, as, according to Rimbault and Hopkins, more or less impracticable arrangements were patented as far back as 1852, and Barker's, the first practical arrangement, is dated 1868. His invention embraced the root idea of making the electricity operate a small valve which lets the wind into a motor, which pulls the pallet open. Bryceson Bros. took up the idea, and the arrangement used is shown in diagram in Fig. 264, Pl. XXIV., where *a* is the groove, *b* the wind-chest, *c* a collapsible pallet or motor, whose upper board forms the pallet face, and whose tail fits air-tight into the wind-bar *d* ; *e* is a chamber filled with the organ-wind, and *f* a double-beat valve which, in the normal position, leaves *e* in communication with *c*. The tail of this valve is attached to the armature of an electro-magnet *g*, which, when excited, draws up the armature and the valve, thus exhausting the interior of *c*, which collapses from the pressure of the wind in the chest, and opens the groove.

Fig. 265 is a cross-section of the pallet. A similar arrangement actuates the valves for drawstop actions, with several ingenious combinations for insuring and indicating the true position of the sliders. The direct use of a magnet to pull open the valves of a ventil soundboard has also been patented, but can hardly have been a practical arrangement from the small opening that could be obtained, and the great expense of such a large number of magnets. The numerous contacts also would be an endless source of trouble if the stops governed the magnets of each rank.

363. But even with this improvement there was a considerable consumption of battery power, as a valve large

enough to insure prompt action of the motors was heavy enough to be a tax on the magnet, and the great loss of power with increased distance of the armature from the poles caused the adjustment to be a difficulty. The latest improvement which reduced the electrical work to a minimum was introduced by Mr. Hope-Jones, an electrical engineer, who had interested himself in organ building. His ingenious device is shown in Fig. 261, and the essence of it consists in making the armature itself the primary valve, and the valve admitting wind to the motor only the secondary valve. In Fig. 261, a is the valve-box filled with wind, b is the magnet, c the disc valve or armature kept by the pressure of the wind against d, the thimble or exhaust orifice, e is a puff, and f a double-beat valve hanging from e by its stalk. Communication between a and e is made by the cap g, into which the thimble is screwed. The pressure being equal on both sides of e, the valve f remains closed by its own weight and the pressure of wind in a. When the magnet is excited, the disc c is sucked down, and opens the exhaust, closing the air-passage, with the result that the puff e is blown up and the valve f supplies the motor with wind; h is the cable wire communicating with the magnet through a brass wire with an eye stuck through the box, the magnet wire being soldered to its tail and the line wire to the eye; k is the return wire, a stout copper wire passing the whole length of the box to a binding screw outside, and the other end of each magnet wire soldered to it within; l is a wooden plug filling a hole over the puff, to enable the nut on the stalk to be adjusted.

364. Fig. 263 shows the end of the magnet full size. The poles are let into a zinc plate, which, by means of the two screws $n\,n$, fastens the magnet to the box; $o\,o$ are four fine guide-pins, between which the disc works freely; the poles and the plate are finished off dead true, and polished. The disc is merely a tiny disc of sheet iron smaller than a three-penny piece, ground dead true on both sides, and covered with thin tough paper on the side next the magnet, to prevent its sticking to the poles by the residual magnetism. The thimble shown in an enlarged view about double real size, in section in Fig. 262, and face view in Fig. 260, is of peculiar

construction. The exhaust holes are stamped up like a nutmeg-grater, each in its own nipple, and are so fine that a needle-point will hardly enter them, and the whole face is then ground off dead flat. The thimble is of brass, and screwed outside with a telescope thread, and is screwed into the wooden cap, thus admitting of the finest adjustment. The notches in the top are for the key with which it is adjusted, shown in Fig. 256. As the pull of a magnet diminishes not as the square of the distance, as is sometimes believed, but in a much higher ratio, a delicate adjustment is of the utmost importance. These valves are best adjusted by having the key struck regularly, and screwing the thimble down carefully, so as not to injure the disc, until it is so near the seat that the disc cannot lift properly, which is indicated by the pipe sounding continuously; a half, or even a quarter, turn back will then give perfect repetition, thus showing that the travel of the disc is only a quarter of the pitch of a telescope thread—say about $\frac{1}{120}$ in.—a result not attained by any other action with which the writer is acquainted.

365. The idea of the peculiar construction of the thimble is that, the holes being exceedingly small, the least possible travel completely uncovers them, while, the nipples being detached, the air has free access to each hole.

The writer, however, has had much trouble in India with the discs on this seating; with everything in perfect order the wind would blow through to such an extent that the bellows could scarcely be kept up, and trials showed that sometimes a disc would blow while at other times it would not. Substituting a plain nipple, shown in Fig. 258, completely cured this defect, and the most careful trials failed to detect any difference in the working of a disc alternately with the compound thimble and a plain nipple: they would both work with exactly the same stroke, and indeed this might be anticipated, for there does not appear to be any use in having a seat of different kind on one side of a double beat valve to what there is on the other. The makers, however, say that the amount of electricity required to operate the thimble is less than is required for a plain nipple, and that they do not have any trouble with them. It must be added, in justice to them, that in all the samples the writer has seen, even in a voicing machine which was covered with dust as usual, there was not the slightest whisper of a leak in the discs, and as the workmanship of those supplied to the writer was perfect, the reason of their not working well in this particular case must remain a mystery.

366. It should be observed that when the organ is out of use, the discs are down, and the exhaust open ; consequently, until the chests are full enough to hold up *all* the discs, the valves have a tendency to rise, and in doing so make matters worse by letting the air out.   It is, therefore, necessary to fix a snap-valve to the H.P. bellows, so that no wind at all passes into the chest until the bellows hold enough to fill them right up at once.   The liability to rust of the disc and the magnet poles in the seat is a drawback to the use of this system in tropical climates, and might give trouble after a time even in Europe ; but the danger could be avoided by putting the paper covering on the seat, and tinning or plating the discs. The makers use a varnish called 'anti-sulphuric varnish,' which is said to be a perfect preservative.

367. Consequent on the very little work the magnet has to do, but very little electricity is required, and a couple of dry cells will work a large organ ; but it should be noted that dry cells are no good in hot climates.   It remains to be noticed that the cap is simply a little block of wood turned oval, with two holes bored into it, as shown in the face view, Fig. 255, Pl. XXIV.   The large hole fits snugly round the raised magnet plate, and the small hole covers the air-hole to the puff, the face being covered with leather, to make it air-tight.   It is held in place by two stout brass pins, *m*, with crooked heads.   The exceedingly small quantity of air above the puff charged and discharged at every operation is one of the most admirable features of this device, and insures the utmost rapidity in operation.

368. The valve box, as shown, will supply a motor direct or through a length of pipe.   The writer has used it with the action shown in Fig. 54, Pl. IX.   It can also be arranged to

work by exhaust by fitting the valve as shown in Fig. 257, Pl. XXIV., where the rest of the action might resemble that shown in Fig. 245, Pl. XXII., and there are many other ways in which the valve could be arranged, the principle remaining the same.

369. The draw-stop action to supply a ventil or a slider requiring a double action is shown in Figs. 253, 254, Pl. XXIV., the former being a longitudinal and the latter a cross section. The magnet, puff and valve arrangements are just the same as described above, and are therefore not drawn in full detail. The tails of one pair of valves connect with a small wooden lever, a, bearing in its ends two stout copper wires, b b, which make and break contact between two pairs of wire ' bristles,' c c. The object of this arrangement is to prevent the consumption of electricity all the while a stop is drawn ; as it is, the act of pulling a stop in or out instantaneously throws over the valve, and when thrown over the current is off. The arrangement is this. The key wire connects direct with the magnet, as at e, but the return wire from the magnet passes through the bristles c, as shown in the cross section, so that unless the copper b is between them there is no circuit. Valve B is the one supplying wind and whose circuit is closed at the draw-stop ; but the copper having left the wires, the current is interrupted there and none passes, consequently the magnet and disc are not at work, and the pressure above and below the puff is the same. When the stop is shifted the current passes the bristles, the valve works, and the puff is forcibly blown up. This reverses the position of the valves instantaneously, and as they reach the end of their travel, A cuts its own current off and B stands ready to repeat the operation. If wind is only wanted one side, one valve remains a dummy, with the exit plugged up. As at first supplied, the bristle c was a simple wire loop ; but it proved too stiff, as either it got so loose as to fail in making a good contact, or was so tight that it gripped the copper and prevented the lever moving. After fitting the form of bristle shown, which is beautifully elastic and gives a firm contact without any friction, there was no trouble on the score of missing action, and the easiest way to make these bristles will be

described in the paragraph treating of the key action. *d* is the trough filled with wax in which the wires lie, as will be further described also under the heading of Key Action. There are also other arrangements differing a little in detail from that figured; but they all follow the principle of cutting off the current the moment the work is done, and they can, of course, be applied to any form of draw-stop action either with two motors as Fig. 240, Pl. XXII., or one inside a case, as Fig. 248, Pl. XXIII. If preferred, a small motor may be used instead of a puff to operate the secondary valve, and in the case of a slider action the valve would require to be much larger than that shown in Fig. 253, Pl. XXIV., which is designed to work the ventil action shown in Fig. 54, Pl. IX. For a large motor for a slider action the valve should be 1 in. diameter.

370. One more type is worth illustrating as a departure from the usual style of valve (see Fig. 251, Pl. XXIV., which illustrates an application to an ordinary soundboard of the style shown in Fig. 245, Pl. XXII.). The magnet and primary-valve are of the usual type, and in its normal condition the little motor *a* is neutral. The puff *b* is just large enough to hold up the valve *c*, which is of peculiar construction. Fig. 250, Pl. XXIV., is a cross-section, from which it can be seen that the valve consists of two thin strips of wood yoked together, covering a long narrow slit in the air-exit, thus giving a maximum of discharge with a minimum of lift. Being held up by the puff, the wind in the valve-box is in the passage communicating with the soundboard. When the magnet is electrified and the disc sucked down, the motor *a* is exhausted, and consequently collapses, its tail overcoming the lift of the puff, and pushing the valve down. Of course, a motor might be used instead of a puff as in Fig. 261, if preferred. .

371. Having described the way in which electricity operates the valves, it is necessary to show how the keys distribute it, as that is an important feature in the Hope-Jones patents. Hitherto mercury cups and flat springs of sorts have been principally relied on for contacts; but both are a nuisance, and the simple but effective arrangements described below are the best with which the writer is acquainted. All the electrical

contacts for keys and stops are made by the interposition of
a brass pin between two bristles of hard tinned brass wire,
which are extremely flexible, and thus insure perfect contact
without appreciable resistance.   Fig. 267, Pl. XXV., is a view
of two manuals such as would be put into a console, and the
bristles can be clearly seen, as also the L-shaped brass pins
which are merely stuck into the keys, and which, when moved,
bring the two bristles into communication, and so close the
circuit.   Figs. 268 and 269 show in elevation the relative
position of pin and bristles of the type used by Mr. Hope-
Jones ; but a little more elasticity can be gained by using the
type shown in Fig. 270, which is therefore preferred by the
writer, though it is a little more trouble to make.   All the
bristles are made of a loop and not of a single wire, an
arrangement which keeps a wire in reserve when one is worn
out, and each leg of which steadies the other.   The two first
types are simply bent to shape ; but the way to make the last
will be described, as it is not so obvious.   Take a block of hard
wood, and knock into it four wire pins projecting about $\frac{1}{16}$ in.,
so as to give the shape of the top loops, as shown in Fig. 270a,
which also illustrates the first stage of bending up the wire ;
270b shows the second stage, and the last operation is to catch
the wire between the stalks with a round-nosed pliers, and
bend the wire around to form the back loop.   Or a curl can
be given to the stalk of the spring, as shown at a, Fig. 268.
The loops can be very quickly made by doing one operation
only at a time on a whole bundle of wires, not finishing each
bristle off by itself.

372. Fig. 267 shows how the bristles are stuck into the
bristle-board, a, strengthened by two battens, b b, the hollow
space being utilised to pass the cables along.   The bristles of
alternate keys should be slightly staggered to avoid the risk
of splitting the board, through which small holes are bored,
into which the bristles are secured by a wooden plug stuck in
with shellac glue.   To the tails of wire which stick out in the
hollow under the board are soldered the ends of the cable
wires, which should be led out, half at each end, so as to keep
the cables as thin as possible. c is the notch cut in the
manual cheeks to pass the cable out, and it should be secured

in them by a strip of leather. This is necessary, as the key-boards are made to hinge up, so that one can be got at without interfering with the others. When the cables are all made and tested to be sure there is no cross-contact, the hollow under the board is run in with paraffin wax to improve the insulation and secure the wires from injury, and the board is then screwed into the cheeks.

In the figure, $d\ d$ are the pins which make contact for the manual they belong to, and e is the Swell octave coupler and f the Sw. to Gt. coupler. The keys may be quite short, and are returned by springs under them, and checked from rising on the centre pins by a wood or metal strip g. The touch is regulated by a screw, h, in each key, which falls on a strip of felt on cork. Fig. 252, Pl. XXIV., shows a device for regulating the whole of the keys at once; a is a gas-pipe mounted eccentrically on the pivot b in the key-cheeks on which it revolves, and so regulates the depth of touch all along to a nicety.

373. The draw-stop action also acts by pushing a pin between two bristles : k is the draw-stop, or, as it is called, stop-key, which rocks on its centre and is forced by the pin and spring l to the extreme positions; the wires m from the two ends connect with two narrow slips of wood, n, so that one is drawn in and one out, and consequently either the 'on' or the 'off' bristle has contact made by the pins below. These strips work between the guide-pins o, and are fitted with lugs, p, with which the arms of the composition rollers q engage. The stop-keys of the different departments are generally separated by transverse partitions in which the composition rollers revolve, and their upper arm is driven by a trace from a little motor at the back of the console connected by a $\frac{1}{4}$ in. gas pipe with a similar motor under the pedal. Putting the pedal down forces the air into the top motor, expands it, and turns the composition roller. One of the nicest forms of composition action is shown in Fig. 342, Pl. XLIV., where a little key e projects in the usual place of the pneumatic piston; f is a front view showing that the key is split; one half operates the manual stops and one half the pedals, to make a suitable bass, so that if the whole key is touched a manual

combination with suitable bass is drawn; but if, say, the right half only is depressed, the manual stops only are shifted.

374. There are several other varieties of stop keys, but that figured is the most delightful stop action it is possible to imagine. The keys are made of ivory, and the name engraved twice, once in full in the middle and again contracted in large letters on the bottom flat. The little knob just above (shown in the plate) is coloured to distinguished the different classes of stops, as red for reeds and black for couplers. In the middle of all is a black key called the Stop Switch; when this is touched it cuts the current off all the stops, so that they can be moved without producing any effect. Thus the player, while using the organ, can build up a new combination, and bring it on in an instant by touching the stop switch. The slightest touch is sufficient to work this arrangement, and any number of stops can be drawn or silenced by passing the finger along the upper or lower hollow, and being so near the keys the finger hardly leaves them for an instant even to draw all the stops of a manual. There is no need to illustrate the pedal arrangements, which are just the same as the manual, except that the pins will generally be on a separate backfall—an arrangement which, indeed, is used for the manual, as shown in Fig. 342, and which has the advantage of being more accessible than when the pins are under the keys. The contacts might also be made in the front part of the keys, and there are infinite varieties of detail which it is not necessary to note.

375. But an attachment called the 'second touch' may be referred to, as it is something sui $generis$. With this the key falls $\frac{1}{4}$ in. to the ordinary touch, but an extra pressure makes it yield another $\frac{1}{16}$ in., and causes a contact that will bring into play any stops or couplers that are drawn for this 'second touch.' Thus the melody can be made to stand out from the parts while playing with both hands on the same keyboard. One way of arranging this is shown in Fig. 342, where a is the spring like that used for harmoniums, which returns the backfall, and consequently the key: $b\,b$ are the ordinary bristles with which the key engages directly it moves; c is a bristle which is not reached until the last $\frac{1}{16}$ in. of the key's

fall; d is a second spring, the resistance of which defines the ordinary key-fall, but extra pressure allows the key to fall further and make contact at c. Another device is to put the contact for the second touch in the front rail, using a small spiral spring under the seating which the key first meets.

It does not require very much practice to acquire fair proficiency in the use of this most powerful addition to the expressiveness of the organ.

376. The most convenient way of disposing of the wires is to lead them to a 'test board' at the back of the console, where all the key-wires and couplers are led to their proper binding screw from which the cable wires start away to the organ. This board should have plenty of room and be painted white, with the different cables and numbers clearly indicated. A small round-headed screw with two or, in case of many wires, three copper washers will be all that is needed. The washers and wires must get a rub with a fine bit of emery-paper the last thing before screwing up, as bad connections give no end of trouble, and a perfect electric connection must be chemically clean. The wires that go between a pair of washers should be twisted up so that they must be forced into contact when the washers are screwed down. Fig. 266, Pl. XXV., gives a diagram of one side of a test-board for a two-manual organ, showing a convenient and symmetrical arrangement. The key cables, which, by the way, should be *quite* loose, to prevent straining connections when opening a keyboard, are brought down at the two sides from above, as are also the pedal cables from below. The main cables come up from below in the middle, and the coupler returns are led away to the coupler stop in the middle upwards. Fig. 279, Pl. XXVI., shows how the cables should be formed. A lashing of thread, or of the wire itself, is passed opposite the place where each tail of wire takes out, and the tail itself is twisted into a spiral about $\frac{1}{8}$ in. diameter, so as to afford plenty of margin for attaching and detaching. All connections should be made in this way, ending in a neat spiral. As to the exact lay-out of the test-board, that must depend upon the number of cables that have to be accommodated in each row, and anything like crowding should be carefully avoided, as it

leads to bad and false contacts, and great difficulty in getting
at the work.   The board can easily be left until the last, and
set out from a study of the actual cables.   If the key cables
come down direct from the cheeks, they can be turned to
right and left, so as to utilise the whole length of the console,
as well as the part between the cheeks only.

377. The matter of couplers here requires a special note.
In Fig. 267, Pl. XXV., there is only one shown to each
manual; but there may be any number, as they work by
electric contact only, and make no difference to the touch.
Fig. 278, Pl. XXVI., is a diagram of the circuit of the ordinary
key, where $a\,a$ are the key contacts, $b\,b$ the magnets supposed
to be at any distance, c the battery; and the wire marked by a
double line is the return wire common to all the notes, and
joined to each magnet and each key as near them as possible, to
save wire.   It can easily be seen that closing the circuit at any,
or several keys, will pass the current through the magnets concerned.   From this it might be supposed that the bristles of
the couplers could be treated in a similar way, connecting one
to the cable which goes to the test-board, and the other to a
single return-wire, with a switch on it to work the coupler.
But such is not the case, and it is worth while to explain why,
even though it requires a rather complicated diagram, since
Hope-Jones's original specification describes a manual-coupler
of this impossible type.   Fig. 275 is a diagram of the simplest
form of coupler—an octave-coupler—where $a\,a$ are the keys
(of the octaves only), $b\,b$ the contacts for the notes, and $c\,c$
those for the couplers; $d\,d$ are the connections at the test-
board, $e\,e$ the magnets, f the battery, and g the switch on the
return, which is supposed to be worked by a single wire.
Return wires are indicated by double lines.   Now, if one key
is put down, just that note sounds, and nothing particular
happens; but if an octave is put down and a current set up,
as indicated by the thick dotted lines, a cross current is derived,
as shown by the chain dotted line, and the coupler works whether
drawn or not.   But if the coupler cuts the return of *each* note,
as shown by the crosses $s\,s$, before it joins the common return;
this cross current cannot arise unless the coupler is drawn,
when, of course, it does no harm, as a direct current is also

running.   Hence the necessity for the coupler returns on the test-board shown in Fig. 266, Pl. XXV.   One side of them comes from the bristle under the key, and the other side goes away to a set of fine bristles, between which contact is made by a wire stuck into the slip n of Fig. 267, and makes contact when the stop is drawn.   There are as many bristles as notes on the coupler, and the bristles of one side connect with the wires from the test-board and on the other side with the common return.   Fig. 273, Pl. XXVI., taken in connection with Fig. 267, Pl. XXV., of which it represents a part, shows the arrangement, where n is the slip moved by the stop, p is the pin, and b the range of bristles, which are single and of very fine wire.   Of course, with these it does not matter about the consecutive numbers :   any return may pass through any bristle.

378.   Another type of coupler is used, with two sets of bristles like the key contacts and a wooden roller armed with so many pins, which when the coupler is on, make contact between the bristles of the return wire, and are taken out when the stop is put in.   This arrangement takes more room than the other, but is not likely to get out of order, whereas the first type is very delicate.   The roller device is shown in end view in Fig. 340, Pl. XLIV., and plan in Fig. 341, where coupler a is off and b is on.   The bristles shown black are connected to the direct wire to the magnet, and those shown white to the wire from the coupler.

Fig. 339 gives a general diagram of the arrangement, showing three notes only of the Swell and two successive octaves of the Great. a is the Sw. contact and b the octave-coupler contact, c is the contact for a second touch on the Great, not supposed to be at work, d is the Gt. direct contact, e the octave coupler contact, and f the Sw. to Gt. contact, both the latter being supposed at work.   The circuit is closed on c' of the Gt., and the heavy dotted lines show the wires which are charged ; $m\,m$ are the magnets, and the crosses represent where the rollers cut off the couplers.   If the rollers are placed in the console, the coupler wires will join the direct wires on the test-board, and there need only be one direct wire in the cable for every note.   But if the rollers are in the organ, the cable must have a wire for every note on each coupler. In the latter case, the rollers would be shifted by an electro-pneumatic device like that of the stops. In addition to the coupling arrangements, it is always well to provide a cut-off worked by the wind of the bellows, to prevent any accidental leakage of electricity when the organ is out of use. This can take the shape of a wire thrust between bristles, as in the key contact, except that the wire should be of a large size, and there should be several pairs to avoid any chance of a bad contact.

379. There are several devices in Hope-Jones's patents for working the swell by electricity. Fig. 274, Pl. XXVI., shows one of them; *a* is the rod that works the shutters by means of two motors *b b*, of which *c c* are the valve-boxes of the usual type. To the swell-rod is hitched a switch *d* with two quadrant-shaped arms, which play against an arc *e*. The faces of the quadrant are insulated from its arms, and connected by the wires *f f* with the valves, from which the current goes by the returns *g g* to the battery. The arc is divided into sections by insulating strips *h h*, and each segment is connected by a wire with the similar segment of another arc *k*, over which a contact *m* plays when moved by the swell pedal. To this contact is attached the return wire. As matters stand, nothing can happen, because the gap in the quadrant switch is over the segment, which is in electrical contact by means of the pedal; but if the pedal and its contact is moved to any other segment, the current will pass through the lower half of the quadrant, open the valve, and the motor will then move up the swell-rod until the turning of the quadrant brings the gap over the segment of the arc in question, when the current being cut off, the wind goes out of the motor, which simply stops as it was. Upon the next movement of the swell pedal depends whether the swell will move further up or down again.

A double-ended hydraulic piston connected with a similar one at the swell-box can also be used for a detached console; but they always work rather heavily, and as, on the whole, they are not to be recommended, no illustration of one is given.　If used, it is necessary to have a reservoir with a back-pressure valve, to insure the pipes being kept full.

380. About the nicest motor for the Swell is Roosevelt's, shown in Fig. 276, end view Fig. 277, and the device at the pedal in Fig. 280. a is a motor worked by the pedal, communicating with the motor b at the swell-box by a closed pipe, m, the joint with b being made by a bit of rubber pipe to admit of free motion ; c is the swell-rod moved by two bellows, $d\ d$, which are fed by wind from the chamber e through the valves ff, and exhausted through $g\ g$; h is the aperture through which a pipe from the windtrunk fills e, and k is a cover by which the valves can be seen and adjusted. Motor a must be larger than b to provide for waste of wind. A delicate spiral spring is placed between each pair of valves, fg, to keep them up against their nuts.　Now, as a and b are connected by a closed pipe, it is clear that any movement of a will be repeated by b ; and if, as in the figure, a is closed, it forces out b and thereby opens f and g_1, thus inflating d and collapsing d_1.　If b were mounted on a rigid base, it would, when once inflated, keep the valves open until d had received its full travel ; but as it is mounted on the back of d and moves in a contrary sense, a small movement of d tilts its arm inwards as much as the inflation had moved it outwards, and owing to the valves being closed further motion ceases unless the pedal is still further moved.　By this device b 'hunts' the valves and causes the bellows to repeat the motion of the pedal, and no more.

There are many other devices in Hope-Jones's patents connected with the electrical working of organs which would require almost a volume to themselves, so we must content ourselves with having indicated the principal features.　Other builders also have patented systems of their own, the details of which can be found in the specifications of the Patent Office, but which would demand too much space to reproduce here.

381. Although electricity cannot be treated of here, yet there are one or two hints which may not come amiss to those who wish to dabble in electric organs.　Test all connections as you go with a galvanometer, and do not pass over any that

show an unduly high resistance, or that affect the needle in the smallest degree when they should not, or they will certainly get worse. Do not put the battery into the console, or any part of the organ where the fumes may corrode connections, as nearly all batteries emit fumes of some sort. Keep down your battery power as much as possible—not so much on account of the expense, as because with too strong a current you run the risk of burning the connections; and always cut the battery off when the organ is out of use. It is best to have two groups of batteries with a switch, so that the player can use them alternately, as this prevents them running down. The question of the best arrangement of the cells, whether in series or parallel, is not generally understood. It depends upon the relative resistance of the circuit and the battery. Suppose there is very little resistance in the circuit as compared to the cell. If you couple two cells in series you double the E.M.F.; but as you also double, or nearly double, the resistance, you get no more for your money than you did with one cell. But if you couple the cells in parallel you halve the resistance by opening two paths for the current, which is consequently doubled. If, on the other hand, as in an ordinary telegraph line, the resistance of the cell forms but a small part of the total resistance, it is no use to diminish the resistance of the battery by putting two cells in parallel, because it affects the whole circuit so little; but if you couple in series you double the E.M.F., while adding only slightly to the resistance, and so get more current.

.

CHAPTER IX

FRAME AND CASE

382. THESE are items in organ-building on which it is difficult to say much that will be generally useful, as no two organs are alike, and tastes differ so much.

For all small organs it is decidedly better that the end frames, on which all the weight comes, should rest on the sills, and not on isolated legs, as the weight is much better distributed over the floor. The frame shown in Fig. 283, Pl. XXVII., would be suitable for a very small organ, such as is shown in Figs. 289, 290, Pl. XXX. Here the end frames are connected in front by a bar, upon which the cheeks of the keyboard rest, with dowels to prevent movement, and the ends of the cheeks are mortised into the middle bar of the back frame. All the frames stop off at the soundboards, except the back posts, which run up to carry the bar to which the biggest pipes are hooked. The ends of the soundboards form the case with a moulding to conceal the junction, and a board with a cornice is fitted round to the height of the rackboards, in which a set of pipes, up to 4 ft. long, can be planted. All the action can be carried on the key cheeks or brackets erected thereon. Or, instead of an apparent frame fitted with panels, the end frames can be wrought so as to appear solid, as shown in the sketches Figs. 284 and 285, Pl. XXVII.

383. The next largest size would suit the organ shown in Pls. XLII–III. Here the skeleton, Fig. 282, Pl. XXVII., is much the same, but the front posts are carried up to form a more elaborate front, and the 8 ft. pipes form the ends, being lowered to a level that will suit the available space. The cheeks of the lower manual, as before, run into the back

frame and bind the whole together, and form the foundation
for the action. This type of construction is peculiarly suitable for a chamber organ, as no room is wasted, and there is
no additional weight of a case apart from the building frame.
In this design the intermediate posts are carried partly by
the cornice and partly by the rail that carries the keyboards.
In both these types the bellows are carried by a batten
checked into the end frames, so that they can be drawn out
from the front without disturbing the rest of the instrument,
and an expanding trunk allows the bellows to occupy the full
area of the case.

384. When the organ gets too large to be accommodated
on a simple frame, one is provided built up of stout legs connected by joists of the requisite strength to carry the bellows
and soundboards, and the case is quite distinct, being only
made strong enough to carry any show-pipes that may be
placed on it. A foundation plank is used to insure the correct
relative position of the two frames, which are further connected by two stout planks, on which the keyboards and
actions are placed, as can be seen in Fig. 281, which represents the arrangement of frame for an ordinary church organ.
If of large size, intermediate supports, which can also make a
ladder, are placed, and the pedals will go at the back or sides,
as the situation may require. As floor space is often grudged,
a very common arrangement is to put the Great soundboard
in front, as shown in Fig. 281, and the Choir where the swell
is shown, while the Swell itself forms a second storey overhead,
as in Figs. 286 to 288, Pl. XXVIII. Provided ample room is
given, it does not matter much what the precise arrangement
is ; but much perverted ingenuity is displayed in attempting
to pack away organs into spaces that are too small for them.

385. Flatness is the chief thing to avoid in a front.
Almost any sober arrangement of panelling will look well if
there are bold towers of pipes, or if the impost is well corbelled out, as shown in Pl. XLI., which represents an organ
front, designed by the writer, on which no money was spent
specially on the case, but which looks well.

Here Fig. 322 is the front elevation, which alone, on
account of its flatness, does not give a good idea of the appear-

ance of the organ, which it will be seen, has to be fitted into an archway too wide and low for good proportion. Fig. 323 is a cross section at the manuals, which shows the corbelling out and the shape of the angle-towers. The corbelling not only looks well, but gains space; but it is bad for the organist, as, sitting under the organ, he cannot hear. This, however, is always to some extent the case with the keyboards in the usual place. Fig. 321 is a part plan of the pipes, showing an angle-tower, the pipes of which are bright, while the large ones in the flat are painted.

For a small organ (and occasionally extended to larger ones), and where floor-space is precious, the Mediæval style, where the organ is corbelled out all round and sometimes furnished with painted shutters like wings, is very effective.

Pl. XLV. shows another case where it was necessary to put the organist behind the screen. This front stood between columns with an architrave; the side pipes are the Pedal Violon, and the middle ones the Open, and all are painted. The middle group of pipes is carried on an elevated corbel, shown in side view in Fig. 345, and of this the central part again projects slightly. Fig. 344 is a section through the centre of the front, showing the back of the pipes which form the return. The real front of organ and organist's seat is right inside the screen.

In both these designs a way to the vestry had to be left through the organ front.

386. Discretion should be used in decorating the front pipes, and too little rather than too much should be given. The old fashion of pipes gilt all over goes well with a certain style of case, but the plainest and best of all styles is to have the front pipes of burnished tin, which is as good as silver. Even good spotted metal, with pure tin mouths, looks very well, and will keep its lustre a long time. Vellum, French-grey, or sage-green are good grounds for pipes, with a sober stencil at top, in the middle, and above the mouth, which, generally speaking, looks better gilt. Patterns on pipes should be separated from the ground by a thin black line, and it is not uncalled for to add, for the benefit of amateurs, that the colours should be flatted, as the writer has seen shiny

pipes. The way to decorate pipes is to draw out the patterns, carefully graduated as to size, on cartridge-paper, and then prick the outline through. The stencil should have a centre line marked on it, and the same should be done for the pipe, and the stencil being laid in its place, the pattern should be pounced through with any suitable dry colour. Where many pipes have to be done, cut-out stencils are used. Before painting, the pipes, especially if of zinc, should be made chemically clean, and should get a coat of turps at once : they should then get two or three coats of whitelead strained through muslin, and then the ground, putting on the lightest colours first. If there is any gilding, the mouth should be gilt. The patterns should be simple and bold, as trivial detail is not only lost, but spoils the main outlines. In an important organ, an architect should be consulted, and the style of case should bear some reference to the building; but the arch of a so-called organ chamber, fitted up with pipes, can hardly be called a case, and there is but little opportunity for displaying taste. Contrary to general ideas, a front of wooden pipes can be made to look very well, and even an archway fitted up with plain 16 ft. teak pipes, if of slender scale as the Violon, looks imposing. The ordinary English Pedal Open looks very clumsy.

387. Intimately connected with the question of the case is that of the standard dimensions of the parts where the player sits, and these have been pronounced upon by the College of Organists as follows :

1. Pedal compass to be invariably C_1 to f^0.
2. Pedals to be parallel, and not radiating.
3. To be concave, on a radius of 8 ft. 6 in., the pedal itself to lie in a radial plane, and not vertical.
4. And the noses of the sharps to be concave on plan to radius of 8 ft. 6 in., the centre sharp being $5\frac{1}{2}$ in. long.
5. The centre natural to be 27 in. long.
6. Naturals to be $2\frac{3}{8}$ in. centres.
7. Pedal C_0 under manual c^1.
8. And the centre pedal sharp to be 2 in. further from player than Great sharps.

9. Great manual to be 32 in. above centre pedal whatever the number of manuals.

10. Order of manuals from top : Solo, Swell, Great, Choir.

11. Ordinary manual compass, C_0 to g^3.

13. Manual keys $5\frac{1}{2}$ in. long and overlapping $1\frac{1}{2}$ in.

14. Height between manuals not to exceed 3 in.

15. Stops to be arranged in the following order :

Left.   Right.

Swell—Pedal—Couplers. Great—Choir—Solo.

16. And in the following vertical order :

Swell.   Solo.

Pedal.   Great.

Couplers.   Choir.

17. Swell pedal to project from front panel between upper E and F of pedals, and to be locked by a swinging-rod, released from left to right.

N.B.—This applies to the ordinary swell; but the balance pedal is a good deal in favour in modern organs.

18. Composition pedals to be placed with the p to the bass, and f to treble side, and the groups to be placed thus from the bass—Pedal—Swell—Great. If there are compositions for couplers, they should be between Swell and Great pedals. Choir or Solo composition pedals to project from treble jamb.

388. The following recommendations are also made by the same authority, viz. :

1. That the consideration of organ builders be directed to the widely expressed desire for some means of opening the Swell in addition to the ordinary Swell pedal. (The writer thinks we have a deal too much swell as it is.)

2. That there should be some contrivance to fix the Swell pedal at any point of its descent at the will of the player.

3. That some plan be devised to bring the Swell shutters into operation more gradually, so as to place the Crescendo and Diminuendo perfectly under the control of the performer.

4. That the Composition Pedals affecting the Great Organ include proportionate combinations of the Pedal Organ, but that a ventil be provided to reduce the Pedal to a soft 16 ft. tone by draw-stop and double-action pedal. (Hope-Jones's composition key, see paragraph 373, does everything that can possibly be required.)

5. That the more important couplers should be acted upon by pedals as well as draw-stops.

6. That the Great to Pedal should have a draw-stop on each side of the manuals.

7. That the stop-jambs should be oblique and vertical.

8. That no key-slip should be placed between the different manuals.

9. That the short keys of the pedal should be either lengthened or raised at the back, so as to assist in the cultivation of a more legato style of pedalling.

10. That the attention of builders be directed to the desirability of securing all centre pins in the various actions.

11. That in preparing specifications attention be given to desirability of including 16 ft., 8 ft., and 4 ft. pedal stops of characteristic qualities of tone suitable for melodic use.

389. For the average player the stool should be $22\frac{1}{2}$ in. above the centre pedals and 9 in. in front of the Great manual. It should, for comfort, be 14 in. wide, and the best covering is leather, with the rough side up. A polished top is a great mistake. There should be a rail to hitch the feet on, 4 in. above the pedal and about 5 in. from the front of the stool.

The different plates illustrate further the relative proportions of manuals and pedals, and Fig. 134, Pl. XII., shows the relative position of the stop-jambs, which are now always made so as to face the player. For a large organ the best arrangement is to have the stops in banks at the level of their own manual, and concave to the player, whose comfort in a large organ should be carefully studied. Adjustable combinations are very desirable accessories. The book-desk should be

14 in. to 15 in. high, and the angle 65° to 70°, all the better
for being adjustable ; it should be 1 in. back from the front of
the top manual and 6 in. above it, except in the case of four
manuals, when 4½ in. is enough. The ledge of the desk
should be provided with four cleats, so as to accommodate
both long and high books.

The stop knobs, if of wood, should be 1½ in. diam., with
plates 1⅛ in., which for tropical climates should be secured by
a pin or screw, or they are certain to come out. Solid ivory
(or celluloid) presents the most handsome appearance. The
lettering should be either plain block or old English, and the
tone-length of the stop should be invariably given, as well as
the name.

390. Although Schultze was of opinion that speaking pipes
should not be placed in the front, on account of the break in
tone between the pipes standing outside and those inside, yet
space will seldom allow this idea to be carried out, and as
much of the case as possible is utilised to give free speaking
room to the big pipes. In disposing of these where appearance
need not be very strictly considered, four rows can be put up
close together, two looking outwards and two inwards, the
outside rank of both faces having extra long feet, between
which, and below the bodies of the outside rank, the inside
rank speak. Where the pipes are painted, paper makes
excellent sham pipes, being both light and strong. In planning the fronts it is always best to use paper patterns, and
lay out each panel full size to prevent crowding, or the other
extreme of too few pipes, which will make it appear that the
owner could not afford to fill up his case. The organist is
generally the worst seated man in the place, so far as hearing
what he is about is concerned, and it is a curious thing that
even in many large organs with pneumatic action the key-
boards are placed under and facing the organ instead of away
from it and facing the choir. In an organ for hot climates
it will be found best to leave it absolutely open except such
parts as must be panelled for appearance' sake, since it is
impossible to so secure the case as to prevent animals
getting in, and they are much less likely to do so if the
interior is exposed than if it afforded a snug hiding place.

Any mischief that may be going on can also be seen and checked at once.

391. The construction of the swell-box belongs properly to this department, and the first and most important caution is on no account to make the swell-box too small; it *cannot* be too large, it is hardly ever large enough. Not merely must the box give the room necessary for the plantation of the pipes, but it must give them room to speak as freely as if they were not enclosed. It is on the consideration that an inefficient swell absolutely injures the tone of the pipes that the writer bases his preference for an unenclosed as second manual where money and space are not available for a box of adequate size, and those who have had to do with organs will know how seldom the condition of an adequate swell is fulfilled. Owing to the reverberations, a swell that appears amply large will still be found to injure the tone of some of the lower pipes; in particular, it is not advisable to plant them near the sides of the box. A good swell-box for a large organ should be 3 in. thick of solid wood, painted or varnished inside for the benefit of the tone. As the inside of the box is always dark, its walls and the wooden pipes are best painted white. It has been suggested that the walls should be made of thin panels, with sawdust or similar material between, to deaden the sound; but it is a question if this style of construction gives the resonance of solid wood. The shutters should be vertical, about 9 in. wide, and turning on brass cups resting in mounted pivots; the cup should be uppermost, so that dirt cannot collect. The top pivot can be a plain round one, working in a slot, in which it is confined by a cleat, by turning which the pin can be tilted out and the shutter lifted off its bearings. The edges of the shutters should be lined with felt, to make them close tight when shut, and they are sometimes made with a rebate instead of a plain face, the idea being to deaden the sound better when shut. The opening arrangement is shown in Fig. 285a, Pl. XXVII., which is a vertical section for horizontal shutters, or a plan for vertical ones, and, as in most mechanical details, there is a right and a wrong way of fitting it. There will be least strain on the pivot when in the centre of the shutter; but if

there are pipes near the front, this position will sometimes make the inside edge of the shutter project too much, so that the pivot has to be placed back of the centre. The position of the pivot should be marked on the face of the shutter, and as 45° is a sufficient angle of opening, the pin of the lug which engages in the opening trace should be $22\frac{1}{2}$° in advance of this position, and the central distance of pin and shutter centre should be as much as possible. With horizontal shutters, part of the weight should be balanced.

392. It may be useful to the beginner to describe more in detail the small organs figured in the plates. Pl. XXX. shows quite a small organ, of which Fig. 289 is a cross section, and Fig. 290 a longitudinal section, omitting the pipes, all of which appear just as they stand. There are only two stops, unison and octave, and only one draw, as of course the unison must always be out. The lowest octaves of the unison, which may be either stopped or open, stand behind, and their grooves are arranged arbitrarily among the smaller pipes, as shown in Fig. 290. The front flap of the lid over the keys folds back, and then the lid pushes back, and the single draw-stop is placed above it. Figs. 324 to 332, Pl. XLII. and XLIII., give particulars of a chamber organ built by the writer, in which Fig. 330 is a cross section, 331 a longitudinal section, and 332 a plan. Fig. 324, Pl. XLII., is an elevation, 325 an end view, and Figs. 326 to 329 plans of the feeder-board, the middle board, the floating frame, and the top board of the bellows. The organ has, on the lower manual, Open Diapason, Salicional, Principal, and Fifteenth ; and on the upper, Gedackt and Rohr Flute, the initial letters of the stops showing in the figures the parts which belong to them. The great octave of the Open Diapason is of wood, and stands at the ends of the organ, while the front pipes are selections from the 4ft. octave of Open and Principal, fed from sliders on the cheeks of the sound-board. The great octave of the Gedackt has a slider of its own, and stands at back at the ends of the organ, leaving the middle open for access for tuning. The key-cover doubles back on itself under the book-board, as shown in Fig. 330, Pl. XLIII. The manual-coupler is of the ram type, and there are two pedal-couplers, there not being any independent pedal. The section shows the

action with sufficient detail not to require further description, the only peculiarity being, as shown in the plan, that the back-falls to the rollers are on the back of the bar, and slant the reverse way to the others, in order to shorten the rollers.

The bellows occupy the whole of the frame, with an expanding trunk; *a* in the section is the top of the trunk, showing how it comes into the bottom of the wind-chests. An iron lever is used, pivoted on the hook *b*, which can be placed so that the bellows can be blown from either end of the organ, and the connection with the feeder is made by a hoop-iron strap.

The draw-stops work in panels on either side of the manuals, as shown in Fig. 324, Pl. XLII., and actuate ordinary iron trundle action. The details of the mouldings are given at the side of the figure, and though the general plan of the front is straight, the recessing of the panels removes any impression of flatness. The case is all plain teak polished, with a few incised gilt lines and gilt stars on the wood pipes; the middle part of the small square panels on either side of the book-board is dead black, with incised gilt monograms.

393. Pl. XXIX. is a sketch of the very effective organ case built by Messrs. Foster and Andrews for Holy Trinity Church, Hull, illustrated as a good example of an English organ in Töpfer's book; but the original forms the frontispiece to 'The Organ,' by W. Shepherdson, M.C.O., published by W. Reeves, 185 Fleet Street, with whose permission the sketch has been made here. It, however, hardly does justice to the carving, which is only indicated, and of which two projecting side wings have been omitted.

CHAPTER X

VOICING AND TUNING : (a) VOICING

394. WE now come to, perhaps, the most important division of the subject, for an organ may be built to an excellent design, of the best materials and workmanship, and yet fail utterly as a musical instrument, owing to poor voicing. Bad tuning can of course be put right; but bad voicing may ruin a pipe for ever. It is also the most difficult branch of the subject to impart in writing—in fact, voicing can no more be learned from a book than can the art of swimming. Exact rules can be given for the scaling of pipes to produce any required tone, and for the winding and proportions of parts of the organ ; but the most that a treatise on voicing can do is to lay down certain broad rules, and the rest must depend upon patience and natural aptitude. A musical ear and a cultivated taste are essentials, as may be learned by studying the differences between organs, which range all the way from a delightful orchestra to a bad German band. Before you start on voicing, study if possible with the deepest attention the work of a master such as Schultze or Willis, and note the different qualities of tone and the variety that can be got from pipes of the same size by different arrangements of mouth. It is a good plan to get unvoiced pipes or old ones, and experiment with them until familiar with the effect produced by different manipulations of the parts adjusted in voicing. Intelligence and patience will be rewarded ; but there is no royal road to voicing more than to any other art. Above all, do not meddle with good pipes of your own or other people's until at least you are assured that you will do no mischief, and take a look *into* a pipe before setting to work on it—or you may feel rather silly when you

R

find a shaving in a pipe you have spent half an hour in trying
to voice.

Having stocked the reader with good advice as to the
manner of learning, let us now proceed to the matter.

395. Apart from the natural division into flue and reed
pipes, the subject of voicing divides itself into two—the
coarser part of making the pipe speak its proper note without
any gross fault, and the more subtle art of making it give the
exact timbre.   A pipe may speak its note steadily and well
and yet be worthless, with a dry tone devoid of interest.
Take an Open Diapason pipe with a rich mellow tone, and
depress the languid carefully ; you will soon hear the difference
between a rich and a dry tone.

The subject of tuning is, properly speaking, interwoven
with that of voicing; and with a new organ both must proceed together.   For with such a stop as a Dulciana, if the
pipe is too long, it will speak its octave ; and if you attempt
to remedy this by cutting up the mouth, it will be too high
when the pipe is cut down to pitch.   So also it is impossible
to tune unless a pipe speaks steadily, and so the two operations must go on together, the pipes being first made to speak
sufficiently well to be roughly tuned a trifle flat, and then
carefully voiced to the exact quality, after which comes the
exact tuning, and then the picking up of any faults.

Voicing will now be taken first, and then tuning ; but it
must be remembered that in practice the two must go
together, especially in the case of reed-pipes.

396. The first step to be taken in putting the pipes into
the organ is to see that the weight of wind is exact.   This
is expressed by the height in inches of the column of water
it will balance, and Figs. 84, 85, Pl. X., show the instrument,
called a wind-gauge, or anemometer, used to measure this.
The essential part of the instrument is only a bent glass
tube, a, the legs of which are half-filled with water, which,
the wind being admitted, depresses in one leg and raises in
the other, the difference being called the *weight of wind,* or,
shortly, the *wind.*   It would be a good plan if builders
recorded the wind of the different departments of an organ
on the name-plate, as weights do sometimes get misplaced,

and the writer once doctored an organ where some of the weights had been removed 'because the bellows leaked so much.' In another case, some of the bellows-weights of an organ had been removed by the blower, he having made the marvellous discovery that it was easier to blow without them. The arrangement shown is a convenient mounting. The bent tube is bedded in felt in a block of wood provided with a lid, *b*, and foot, *c*, which may be removable. The channel behind the water part should be painted white. *d* is a slip hollowed to fit the two legs between which it is placed, with the face marked in inches and eighths. When the wind is on, the rule is drawn up till the bottom is level with the lower water surface, and the upper is read off. An ordinary wind for a medium-sized church organ is 3 in. A chamber organ should seldom receive more than $2\frac{1}{2}$ in., and the use of different pressures for different manuals or stops imparts individuality, and is always found in large organs. For instance, in the Armley organ the Pedal-Great and Swell are on a $3\frac{1}{4}$ in. wind, the Choir $2\frac{1}{2}$ in., and the Echo only $1\frac{1}{2}$ in. Reeds do well on a higher pressure, and from 6 in. to 10 in. is commonly used for them, and even as much as 20 in. The question of the wind-pressure to be used is one that enters intimately into the consideration of design and scale, as both the pitch and tone are functions of the wind-pressure. Subject to practical limits, an Open Diapason pipe might, at a certain pressure, become a Gamba.

397. The bellows weights being settled, the organ should get a good blowing-through before the pipes are put in, to clear away dust and chips. It is an excellent practice to put pipes in with the notes held down, to make sure that all is clear and they fit properly into their holes. The final voicing can never be done until the pipes are on their own sound-board; but builders use what is called a voicing-machine to voice the pipes when first made. This is nothing more than a little organ with one or two sliders and no pipes of its own, or one set tuned to the pitch intended.

398. In the consideration of the influence of different proportions upon the speech of pipes, certain broad rules can be laid down as given below, and it is upon the extent and

combination of these that timbre depends. And apart from the obvious difference between simple loud and soft, timbre passes through all variations, from the fluty tone with few harmonics of the Gedackt to the keen tone of the Gamba, as rich in harmonics as a reed. We have then—

   a. Scale. Large.—Dull, fluty tone, loudness when adequately blown.

        Small.—Keen, stringy tone. Less strength.

   b. Mouth.—Large mouth—dull tone.

        Small mouth—sharp tone.

   c. Upper lip.—Bent out—flute tone.

        Bent in—sharp tone.

   d. Languid.—High—sharp tone.

        Low—dull tone.

It will be observed that the last two propositions are particular cases of the general statement that directing the wind into the mouth gives a fluty tone, and in front of it a stringy tone.

   e. Wind supply or pressure.—Much—loud and sharp tone.

        Little—soft and dull.

Besides these important influences we have also nicking the languid and the application of ears and beards to improve the tone of certain stops, and bridges in front of the mouth to prevent the pipe breaking into harmonics.

399. The tools required in voicing and tuning are neither many nor elaborate. We require—

   (*a*) Four tuning-horns, Fig. 83, Pl. X., from ⅝ in. to 1⅝ in. diameter on the cone.

   (*b*) Three cones, Fig. 75, from 2 in. to 3¼ in. diameter, or thereabouts.

   (*c*) One or two small triangular files, ground smooth and edges sharpened, and penknife blades with wooden handle, with both edges sharp for notching.

   (*d*) The tool shown in Fig. 74, very nicely made out of an old file. One end is a notcher, and the hook at the other end, which should be quite square, smooth, and sharp, is for the purpose of pulling out the lower lip—rather a delicate operation to do without injuring the languid.

(e) A stout knife and a strong scissors for cutting pipes.

(f) Some pieces of wire from $\frac{1}{8}$ in. to $\frac{1}{4}$ in. diam., about 1 ft. to 1 ft. 6 in. long, with the ends carefully smoothed, for raising the languids of pipes by pushing them up to the foot hole. Also used for lowering the languids.

(g) Some flat pieces of sheet brass of different widths, with the ends turned up from $\frac{1}{4}$ in. to $\frac{1}{8}$ in. at right angles, for pulling out the upper lips.

(h) Mops, made of a twisted wire handle with a tuft of silk or cotton at the end, used to silence the pipes of a Mixture while one rank is being tuned. These, however, are liable to leave fluff in the pipes, and little wooden rods will do as well.

(k) Some files, for wooden pipes, and chisels, for general use. Some cubes of wood of different sizes covered with emery-paper make a very useful form of file for smoothing the windway of wood pipes.

A trough formed of two boards nailed together at right angles is useful for holding the pipes to be notched ; and a proportional compass for setting the height of the mouth is very handy, but not quite certain to give as accurate results as taking the measurements off the scale, because the width of mouth might happen to be slightly out. It may be noted here that the notching, which is popularly supposed to be the *voicing*, forms a very small part of the operation, and is by no means indispensable, as carefully-made large metal pipes will speak perfectly well without it, and the writer never uses it in wood pipes, except those with flat blocks.

400. To start upon a new stop, it is well to take half a dozen pipes from the middle and voice them roughly, finishing up until perfectly satisfied with the tone of one or two, to match which the rest will then be voiced. This is in the event of using a scale or wind-pressure, or requiring a tone for which the exact data are not to hand.

Beginning with metal pipes, cut up the mouth to the proposed height or rather less, until two or three pipes have been verified to see that it is suitable. Beginners nearly always spoil the tone by cutting too much. Knock up the foot hole with a cone, or the flat of a chisel, until with that and the windway the strength of tone is about right. When the pipe speaks as well as it can be made to, lay it down in the trough, and, holding the notcher like a pen, notch the languid just as little as will serve the purpose, remembering that too deep notching spoils any prospect of good tone. The style of notching should be studied on good examples of existing stops. The c° pipe of the Open would have a notch a bare $\frac{1}{16}$ deep, each notch following the burr of the one before it, like file-cutting. The small pipes will require very delicate handling indeed. It is seldom that a well-made pipe, with all the mouth parts adjusted visibly right, will refuse to speak; but should a pipe be dumb, hold your finger in front of the mouth to see whether the wind goes too much out or in, and deal suitably with the upper lip or languid, or both. Press the lip in with a broad chisel and draw it out with one of the brass hooks. If the edge is not straight, hold it up with the hook and press it straight with the chisel. Let the upper lip alone as much as possible after first setting it straight and truly across the pipe, also parallel with the lower one and languid. To do this, it usually requires pushing in a little in the centre. The *languid* should be *very carefully* raised or lowered to give the effect required.

401. The faults generally met with, and appropriate remedies, are these :

Slow Speech.—The note comes on with a drag, caused by wind going too far *out*; sometimes in small-scaled pipes too much wind.

Remedies.—Languid too high—depress it with a chisel or one of the long wires used like a ramrod; lower lip too far out—flat it in with a chisel; mouth too high—get a new pipe, or cut the body off and resolder it.

Overblowing or Sounding the Octave.—Generally the exact reverse of the last fault, caused by too much wind or its going too far inwards.

Remedies.—Too much wind—knock up the foot-hole;

languid too low—raise it with the wire; upper lip convex— flat it in with chisel; lower lip too concave—draw it out with the voicing tool. Mouth too low—cut it up, but be very sure that this is the real reason before you do, and remember to see that the pipe is in tune, as if too long, it may come right when cut to pitch, as shortening the pipe is equivalent to raising the mouth.

In dealing with small-scale stops also remember that if you cannot get a required strength of tone without overblowing, it may be merely a sign that the stop requires bridges or fenders. Richness of tone is much better preserved by putting a bridge than by cutting up the mouth, as cutting up the mouth destroys rich tone in nearly all cases.

Scraping or Chiffing.—Defect of windway, generally requires the notching to be carefully deepened, or perhaps the lower lip pressing closer.

Trembling or Wobbling.—Sometimes caused by too much wind. Very often by being in the swell-box or too much crowded elsewhere—the Gamba tribe are peculiarly liable to this defect. Try the pipe in another hole where it is quite clear. In the Swell the only remedy is to diminish the wind of the pipe until it ceases to wobble, by which time there will generally be no tone left. The author has *never* examined an English organ in which some of the lower pipes of the Swell were not thus affected, though, of course, there must be some free from this defect. Trembling is not unfrequently caused in large front pipes by their being loose or not perfectly round. If it stops when the pipe is firmly grasped in the hand this is the cause. An oval pipe can be put right by squeezing it carefully from the top down between two blocks of wood lined with leather, making a circular hole a little larger than the pipe. If a zinc pipe, it should be heated as hot as the hand can bear, as at the temperature of boiling water zinc becomes tolerably flexible.

The reason why a pipe squeezed oval in the middle of the body will not speak, is that the area is thereby diminished, and though an increase in section at the middle of the body does not spoil the tone of a pipe, any diminution does.

The wind not reaching the upper mouth steadily is sometimes the cause of this fault, in which case it can be cured by sticking a couple of matches in the windway : the rationale of this proceeding being that the sheet of wind probably twists like a stream poured from the mouth of a jug, and sticking the matches in seems to give it something to lay hold of and steady itself. This device is specially useful with flute and covered stops, which require to be cut high to keep down the harmonics and give a pure tone.

Windiness may be caused by something wrong with the foot-hole or a conveyance pipe. Try the pipe on another hole, and if the windiness continues it is probably caused by too deep a notch or too big a windway, or the mouth being distorted in some way. Large metal pipes may suffer from this defect if the feet are not long enough—say about 12 in. for C_o. If a pipe gives trouble, try it on the voicing-machine, or a hole where it is quite clear, as sometimes a rank of large scale or high-cut pipes will influence the speech of another rank near. In this case the best remedy is to alter the lengths of the feet. If a pipe in its place does not speak the same pitch as in the open, the tone is certain to suffer. '

402. A stopped pipe almost voices itself, and when they do not speak well, nine times out of ten the stopper is in fault; in which case do not be satisfied if the stopper merely feels tight, as it may be jammed in depth and loose in width, or vice versâ ; draw it out, and try the fit of depth and width separately by putting the stopper in edgeways.

With wood pipes we have not the resources of raising and lowering the languid, and moving the upper lip in and out; nor, indeed, are they required, as in a well-made wood pipe these parts must occupy their exact positions. The slant of the cap is, however, under our control, as well as that of the block, and the relative position of the two ; but if the pipes are carefully made with mouths of the exact shape shown in the figures, there should be no need for dodging the caps. The supply of wind at the foot is generally regulated by wooden wedges ; but a neater device is to cap the foot of small pipes for about an inch with pipe metal, and treat them like metal pipes. For larger ones, glue in a plug about ½ in. thick, and start with a hole that is known to be too small, cautiously enlarging it with a quill-bit with sharp edges, held in the hand. Very large pipes that would be troublesome to lift up and down have a throttle-valve in the foot, as shown in Figs. 80, 81, Pl. X., which is simply a turned plug the size of the bore, thinned down inside the foot for a windway, and outside for a handle, which is also an index of the position of the plug; or the wedges may be put into the foot from the throat instead of at the bottom; or, lastly, a ferrule, with a diaphragm to be bored out by the quill-bit, as shown in Fig. 82, may be inserted at the throat.

403. Having noted the more glaring faults that interfere with voicing, it remains to describe, so far as words will serve, the more artistic part of voicing relating to the different qualities of tone. To begin with the Diapason work. The notching should be full, as also the wind supply; the full tone should be taken out of the pipe, but without the least approach to screaming; the upper lip should be kept well in, so as to preserve a stringy tone with fulness, and the stop should not speak too readily, or it will lose character. If a pipe in which no other defect is apparent gives a poor, dry tone, it is almost certain to be that the languid is too low, and a mere touch with the wire will put it right. The Open of many common English organs is too loud, dull, and coarse in proportion to the other stops. It is difficult to describe tone-colour in words; but perhaps 'velvety' is that most descriptive of the quality which should be aimed at in the Open Diapason. If the lower octave, or part therof, is made in wood, the block with sharp edge of Fig. 22, Pl. IV., and a plain cap, should be used. Just a strip of leather on the sides of the pipe to make the cap fit airtight will also about give the windway required; but after some time the leather will shrink and require the introduction of a sheet of paper.

404. This appears the proper place to draw attention to the particulars of voicing wood pipes so as to get a rich or keen tone out of them—a thing which formerly English builders seemed to consider impossible, to judge by the fact of their labelling stops as 'Wooden Open,' 'Metal Open'; and a builder wrote in the 'English Mechanic' (Jan. 23, 1874), that Gambas and Salicionals could not be made in wood. The

whole secret lies in shaping the block as shown in Fig. 22, keeping the top edge quite sharp. The backward slant of the block inside the pipe also helps the tone, and seems to make it come freer. To insure a perfectly good edge, after having shaped the slope roughly, rub the edge with a pencil if light wood, or chalk if a dark wood, and finish up the slope with chisel and file, being guided by the dark or light line to guard against spoiling the edge. Then for a moderately sharp tone file the windway of cap flat; but for the sharpest possible tone make it slant up at the same angle as the slope of the block, as shown in Fig. 39, Pl. VI., taking the same precautions with the lower edge of cap as with upper edge of block. Nothing but a tubby tone can be got with the form of mouth shown in Fig. 27, Pl. IV. It is a good practice to blacklead and polish the windway of wooden pipes.

The Principal will be finished on the same lines as the Open, taking care not to let it become too prominent, and so with the Fifteenth and Mixture ranks. The greatest care should be taken to keep the upper octaves of the small pipes from getting screaming, which they are so apt to do. It is better not to notch the *lip* of the upper ranks of the Quint and Tierce sounding stops, and the wind supply should be but small with the upper lip kept well out. It is a good plan to make their mouths one-fifth only instead of quarter the circumference.

405. Next to the Diapason proper comes the Geigen, a stop rarely met with in English organs, such examples as there are under the name of Violin Diapason being quite destitute of the fire the tone of this stop should have. In fact, it is commonly spoken of as a Diapason rendered reedy by a slot in the cylinder. The slot does not render it *reedy*— it makes it *horny*, and spoils the tone as a foundation stop. The true Geigen is just a midway tone between the Open and the Gamba, combining the fulness of the former with the cutting tone of the latter, keeping the Diapason strength. The notching should be deep, the mouth lower than for the Open, and the upper lip bevelled, which should always be done for a sharp-sounding stop. The stop requires a bridge before the mouth, the best form of which is shown in Fig. 110, Pl.

XI. If a Horn Diapason is wanted, the pipes should be made
a semitone long, and at the distance of the diameter from the
top a slot begun, which should be run down till the pipe is
sharp enough. The slot may be $\frac{1}{2}$ in. wide for c°, and $\frac{3}{8}$ in.
for the smallest pipe, and the metal tongue should not be left
sticking out in a slovenly way, and pulled backwards and
forwards with the fingers, but should be neatly curled up with
round-nosed pliers, as shown in Fig. 113. If left long, and
pulled backwards and forwards, it will finally break off at the
bottom, where all the bending takes place, and it will always
shift about and put the pipe out of tune. In cutting these
slots, remember how the pipes have got to stand, and if in
zigzag in the usual way, make them in *front*, as if made at
the back they will not be readily accessible, and the pipes will
shade each other. No pipe to which it is not desired to
impart a horny tone should have these slots. For Salicional
and other small-scale stops which are not amenable to the
tuning-horn, the proper thing is to spring on a slide of stout
tin-plate with a couple of punch-marks in it to make it grip.
These do not rattle nor get loose if put on properly, and they
grip so tight that the pipes are not so liable to get out of tune
as with the slit and tongue. They can be used over slits
instead of tongues, if desired. The Geigen can be tuned with
the tuning-horn. A mouth two-sevenths of the circumference
in width is a good thing for the Geigen.

406. The Gamba should be all string, having the deepest
notching of any stop, and as much wind as the scale will allow
without getting coarse. Plain bridges over the mouth are
required, by the aid of which on a good wind pressure the
stop can be made to speak with considerable promptitude.
This class of stop requires wind of high pressure, rather than
much of it, to produce the best effect. Varieties of the Violon
Bass are met with in Germany in which the pipe has no ears
nor bridge; the mouth is low, and the windway very fine.
Consequently the speech of the pipe is very slow, and it has
a stopped 'helper' of the same width built on it, just as a
monkey carries its young clinging to it.

A C_1 pipe of this class was 6 in. by 4 in., with an inverted
mouth 1$\frac{3}{8}$ in. high; the 'helper' was the same width as the

pipe, and 3½ in. deep, with a mouth 1¼ in. high, but a length of only 2 ft. 3 in. Thus it spoke the double octave above its pipe, though the scale was suitable to C_o. There is nothing to admire in this construction; it gives far more trouble, and not as good results as that recommended by the writer. The Viol de Gamba is simply a Gamba voiced as delicately as required by keeping down the width of mouth, together with its height and wind supply.

407. With respect to the Bell Gamba, it should be noted that the stop should be cut to pitch on the *body*, not on the *bell*, except to shave the latter away, if necessary, to make it meet the line of body. The notching should be the finest, the mouth low—a bare one-fourth—and very small wind hole. The stop is generally tuned by the ears, which are made large for the purpose, but sometimes the bodies are made cylindrical, and then the bell can be made to slide. Cognate to this stop are all the delicate stringy ones, as Dulciana, Salicional, &c., and the same remarks apply. The upper lip must be kept flat, and the edge bevelled in all. They are troublesome stops to voice, and go off their speech on the slightest provocation. They can never be made to speak quickly, and more wind only makes this fault worse. If they buzz or scrape in coming on, deepen the notching, which should be very light. The whole of these stops can have the lower octave made in wood, so that the break between wood and metal is imperceptible, if the directions given above about the mouth are carefully attended to, and the wood pipe made one or two pipes smaller than the metal, because it gives a slightly thicker tone. Make the windway of the wood pipes full wide, and regulate the supply by the foot rather than by the windway.

The instructions just given should cover all cases of the Diapason work and string-toned stops, the pedals being, of course, similar to a manual stop, but an octave lower.

408. Hitherto the direction for the wind has been well outwards; but for the stopped and flute work, of which we now propose to treat, it must be kept inwards. In nothing does greater diversity of opinion exist than in voicing stopped pipes, the English plan being to give a flat block, much notched, with a hollow cap and wide windway set below the

top, with low mouth and foot nearly plugged up, the scale
being often enormous.   The German plan, on the contrary, is
to have a moderate scale, and windway full bore of foot, high
mouth and sloping block, with flat cap set exactly level. The top
of the block is also bevelled downwards.   The writer decidedly
prefers the German plan as a general rule; but the English
form of block may be used where a delicate tone is required.

For a metal Gedackt, often no leaf is provided, though it
is probably best. The mouth is simply cut up about four-fifths
of the width in the round of the pipe, and is also generally made
arched with notching like the Open.   Sometimes the Gedackt
is made with advantage with a $\frac{3}{4}$ mouth where a strong tone
is required, in which case the height would, according to
Töpfer, have to be reduced so as to keep the same area. This
point, however, is disputed.   A Lieblich would be cut up about
three-quarters, as it requires less wind and a delicate tone. If
sound and well made, there is nothing difficult in the voicing,
the only fault that is likely to occur being a cough in attack-
ing the note, caused by the mouth being too low in proportion
to the winding.   With regard to stopped wood pipes there
is nothing to be said, except as to pipes below G_0, which sometimes do not turn out satisfactory. The larger stopped pipes get,
the more difficult they are to voice; anyone can do them down
to G_0; but Schultze himself declares they cannot be voiced with
any certainty in the 32 ft. octave, because when you cut them
up high enough to stop the harmonics, which are not desirable
with this class of pipe, the wind will not reach, and even the
dodge of sticking matches in the windway fails to keep them
right.   The first thing in dealing with these pipes is to know
what to expect; a prominent or clear note cannot be got, and
what should be aimed at in a Bourdon or Sub Bass is a quiet
full deep note that is felt rather than heard, and which,
though so very unobtrusive in itself from the want of harmonics, can be heard through the loudest combination.   It is
usual to add ears and beards to the larger stopped pipes; but
if made of wood of a proper thickness it is doubtful whether
these do any real good.   It is a singular fact that, contrary to
all other pipes, the Gedackts are not injured by having others
near them or obstacles near the mouth.   Schultze not

unfrequently planted his Bourdons in the bass in such a way as to speak opposite each other's backs, and they are certainly improved by doing so, and will answer placed rather close together, allowing, say, only about 4 in. for the 16 ft. C to speak in. Small-scale Bourdons are also queer things to sound, as the note varies much in quality, according to the corner of the room in which it is heard. The Bourdon, or Sub Bass, should never be used without an 8 ft. helper.

409. The only exception to the above remarks is the Quintatön, in which the Twelfth is required as strong as the ground tone. It is often made to an ordinary Bourdon scale with a low mouth; but this gives a hard tone, and the best plan is to make it in metal to a Gamba scale, when the area of mouth may be one-third the area of pipe, and a bridge may be used if it seems necessary. The use of this stop is quite a matter of taste, and the writer does not care about it, but Töpfer recommends it as the 16 ft. stop for the second manual.

410. The characteristic stop of the flute tribe is the Harmonic Flute. It does best on a heavy wind, but can be voiced down to a $2\frac{1}{4}$ in. wind. The mouth is cut up about one-third, arched, and the lip left convex. With respect to the arched lip, a true artist in voicing has assured the writer that he does not believe it appreciably affects the tone; but it seems possible that with a high mouth, as in a Gedackt, the corners of the sheet of wind may be steadied by the sides of the mouth being lower than the middle. The harmonic portion begins at f^1, where the pipes are double length, with a small hole, or sometimes two, on opposite sides in the middle of the body. Taking the harmonic part first, the notching should be a trifle finer than the Open, and if the pipe, on being brought up to its proper strength, tries to speak the Twelfth, the mouth wants cutting up. If too loud, reducing the wind at foot will stop the pipe from breaking into the second harmonic. If the pipe speaks its fundamental note, it wants more wind, or the languid should be depressed, or the upper lip set out a little more. If the mouth has been cut too high, it is difficult to get the pipe to speak its octave steadily. There must be no hesitation with the Harmonic Flute; it

must speak its note fully and firmly. A little care is required to effect the junction between the harmonic and non-harmonic sections of this stop. The principal point is to thicken the tone of the plain pipes, which is done by reducing the wind or by cutting up. If too weak when the desired quality is obtained, cut up a little, and give more wind, repeating this operation till the desired result is attained. Below c° stopped pipes are used to complete the range of flutes, as a rule.

411. The Travers Flute, shown in Fig. 32, Pl. V., is turned solid out of wood, and is simply a Harmonic Flute. The body is pierced as with the metal stop, and the overblowing is furthered by the very small mouth. It is not a difficult stop to deal with, and when well finished exactly resembles a real flute. The best way to effect the tuning is to cut the bodies the least trifle sharp, and spring into the top a cylinder of tin-plate or cartridge brass, as was recommended for the outside of metal pipes. Below f^1 the stop should be carried down in ordinary wood pipes, with mouths gradually increasing in size up to the usual form.

412. Somewhat analogous to this last is the Flute shown in Fig. 34, and the Harmonika, Fig. 35. In voicing these, the most suitable position for the wedge and for the cap is found by actual trial, and then they are glued on, or a slot may be made permitting of a slight play from the apparently correct position, and the pieces jammed by a screw when adjusted, in which case a knife-cut should be made across the pieces, so as easily to recover their positions if disturbed. The quality of the tone depends upon the amount of mouth uncovered. The more it is covered the sharper is the tone. These stops should always have a delicate quality of tone.

413. The Clarabella, Hohl Flute, and other such flutes, whatever their name, are much of the same general character whether in metal or wood. The tone should be thick and fluty, with more or less power as required. They too often degenerate into coarseness, especially the open wood flutes. Figs. 30, Pl. IV., and 36, Pl. VI., show two flute pipes open and stopped (that they are double-mouthed makes no difference). It is usual to notch the block about ½ in. apart at c°, and English builders keep the cap a trifle below the top of the

block.   Like all flutes they are not troublesome to voice, and
require only moderate care and skill to produce a fairly good
result, though even in these the hand of the artist will be
recognised.

414. The Rohr Flute is simply a Gedackt with a perforated
stopper, and requires no special remarks, and the Clarinet
Flute is a modification with the hole about twice the diameter
of that of the Rohr Flute, and a lower mouth.

415. The Döppel Flute is simply a Gedackt with two
mouths, and there is nothing peculiar in the voicing.   The
tone is not very different to that of an ordinary Gedackt, but
in combination seems to have more body.   Fig. 30, Pl. IV., is
an open example, but this is more correctly called a Biffara,
and one mouth is often made a little higher so as to produce
a wavering in the tone.   Fig. 36, Pl. VI., is from an excellent
example by Roosevelt.

In voicing flutes it will be found easy enough to keep the
quality, except in the smallest pipes, which always have a
tendency to scream.   Schultze recommends that all open
flutes should be harmonic in the treble, and there is no difficulty in this.   The Harmonic Flute would still be distinguished by having the harmonic portion carried down as low
as possible, and by its rich fluty tone, while the other flutes
would retain their appropriate tone with perhaps the top
octave only made harmonic.   These directions should suffice
for voicing any of the flute tribe, and we will now turn to the
reeds.

416. If it is difficult to put into words the voicing of flue-
pipes, it is ten times more so to describe that of reeds.   Un-
wearied patience and good powers of observation and reasoning will enable the thing to be done somehow ; but it requires
a natural gift, or the experience of a lifetime, to produce a
really fine rich tone from reeds.   Many reed-stops in ordinary
organs are simply intolerable.

The voicing of reeds is all done on the tongue, as the
admission of wind at the foot has little or no influence on the
speech.   The only qualification to this statement is the use
of slides or shades in the Oboe, Clarinet, and other delicate
stops ; but these are rather for minute regulating when

finished than for actual voicing. Closing the shade flattens the pitch, and requires the tuning wire to be driven further down to sharpen the tongue, and this lessens the power of the pipe ; the converse, of course, takes place when the shade is raised. The good speech of the reed depends entirely upon the proper curving and perfect truth of the tongue, assuming the thickness to be about right and the reed perfectly flat. The tongue should be bent up in a curve, and when at work should make a single vibration like a pendulum, the tip not *entirely* closing, as if it does the tone becomes keen and disagreeable. A rattling is caused by the tongue not being flat, and when the pipe bubbles and squeaks and plays all sorts of extraordinary tricks it is generally caused by the tongue having a wave in its vibration, so that it beats in two halves.

417. Having, then, the pipes a little long and the tongues still flat, we have now to see how to get them to speak. It is a great point in reeds to keep the tongues as thin and the bodies as long as possible. To curve the tongues lay them on a block of hard wood and rub with any smooth metal— even the back of a knife. The best plan is to clamp them down with a screw clamp, and rub them with a steel wire about $\frac{3}{16}$ in. diam. set in two handles. The whole success of the operation depends upon the curve being perfectly square to the tongue. To try the pipe never blow into it, as the moisture of the breath will ruin it; it must be done on a voicing machine or in the organ. If the pipe will not speak at all, the tongue is too much, or too little, curved, which can be judged by the eye. If too much curved, the speech will be slow. Assuming that the tongue has been freed from the grosser faults and gives a decent note, try it with the Principal, and if it speaks late reduce the curvature of the tongue ; but if quite prompt, but poor in tone, curve the tongue more. It is scarcely necessary to remark that in replacing the reed and tongue care must be taken to get them dead square to the tuning wire, and the tongue flat on the reed. When of a suitable speech, the pipe will be below the pitch of the Principal. Drive the tuning wire down to sharpen the note, and the tone will lose brilliancy; raise it again till the pipe gives its best note, and do this for all the stop, and then start

s

cutting them to length, noting that a pipe with a bright tone will take less cutting than one with a dull tone. Cut very cautiously, and after each slice bring the tuning wire as near pitch as you can without losing quality. If by lowering the pitch with the wire the tone improves, the pipe may be cut without fear, as it shows the note of the body is below the required note. It will, of course, be understood that perfect tone is obtained when the natural notes of body and tongue coincide to a certain extent. When the pipe holds its note at the proper pitch, shade it with the hand so as to flatten it, and if it does not at once take up its note, it is still a little long, and when they are put into the organ it may happen that a pipe will require cutting a little if more shaded than it was on the voicing-machine. In trying the speech, the pipes must be left alone half a minute after striking them, or a slow pipe will not be detected, the tongue being already in vibration and ready to start off. This, by the way, applies equally to flue-pipes, and the more so the keener the tone. A faulty Violon may speak quite well if struck repeatedly.

418. The great point in reeds is to get a good bold tone, together with prompt speech and mellowness. Schultze recommends making the upper octaves harmonic, and the usual practice is to make the last two or three pipes of ordinary flue-pipes, as they are too small for effective use of reeds. He used to cone down the end of the larger trumpet bodies where they entered the boot to quite a small aperture. When all is finished, if the tuning-wire is too far down, the tongue is too thin, and if too near the block, the tongue is too thick; but the thinner the tongue, within limits, the better the tone, and the shorter the body, the more fire—this also within limits. Powerful stops do not require much thicker tongues; the strength can be obtained by increasing the opening in the reed and the scale of the body, and, of course, the pressure of wind. The lower notes of the pedal are difficult to voice. It is well to catch an exact note on another stop, and follow it note by note, driving down the wire until the reed is at pitch. If it cannot be brought down to pitch by raising the wire, it shows the tongue is too thick, and the position of the wire when the pipe is in tune and the body the right length

is an indication of the thickness of the tongue. When the pedals have once been well voiced and tuned, it is good to mark the proper position of the wire on the pipe body, so that inexperienced tuners may not mess it about. Sometimes a pipe may be made to speak by boring a hole in the boot, though it is not clear precisely what effect this operation can have. On this point see paragraph 106.

419. As regards the tone to be given the respective stops, the Trumpet in different pitches should be brilliant and bold, but still not harsh. The Oboe and Clarinet or Krumm Horn should imitate their orchestral namesakes as well as possible. To get the best results from the Clarinet, it should be inclosed in a box of yellow pine, of which the panels should not be over $\frac{3}{16}$ in. thick. In the panels should be cut a couple of sound holes, 6 in. diameter, covered with thick soft leather, and the top should be hinged, so that it could be fastened open at an angle suitable to the strength of tone required, and the bottom will require the usual panel to give access to the tuning wires.

420. The Vox Humana should not have the tubes cut. All voicing should be done with the tongue. This is quite a fancy stop, and is always used with the Tremulant, so that in voicing it should be tried with that stop drawn. As for the tone, it may be anything, from Punch's speak to the bleating of a nanny-goat. As a general indication, which is really all that can be given in a book, for soft, smooth stops the tongue should be straight, and only far enough away from the reed to speak. For a loud, full, but smooth tone, as Cornopean, the tongue may be further away, but still straight, while the peculiar clang of the Trumpet requires a tongue well curved up at the end. It is a useful study to fit tongues of different curvature to the same reed, and reeds of different aperture to the same tube, and it is only by studying the influence that different shapes and dimensions have on the tone that proficiency in the difficult art of reed-voicing will be obtained. Pedal reeds sometimes have a drop of solder run upon the ends of the tongues to assist their voicing.

421. As for voicing free reeds, they follow much the same rules as those just disposed of, but the workmanship requires to be even more perfect. The tongues are voiced, just as

s 2

those of the beating reeds, by regulating their curvature and projection from the reed, and defects are due simply to bad fitting. If the tuning wire is too far down, thinning the tongue at the tip will sharpen it, and enable the wire to be drawn back to its proper place, thus improving the tone, and the reverse can be done if the crook is too far back when the pipe is in tune, when scraping it towards the root will flatten it. These remedies must be used with caution, as tongues of unequal thickness will not give a good tone. If a free reed refuses to speak, it may be that the body, or even the boot, is not of a suitable size, on which point see the chapter on Absolute Scale.

422. Finally, it may be noted that should it be necessary to alter the length of an Oboe tube, it should be done at the bottom, sawing a piece out or putting it in just above the socket, as the piece which fits into the socket cannot, of course, be interfered with. Neither flue nor reed pipes with bells should ever be brought to pitch by cutting the top of the bell.

(b) TUNING.

423. As the voicing of a stop cannot be properly done until it is approximately in tune, so an organ cannot be well tuned until the pipes are regulated and voiced, thus the first tuning of an organ is a tedious job. Above all, it is necessary, especially with slider organs, to be sure that the pipes get their proper supply of wind, and that there is no ' running,' as with this defect it is impossible to tune properly.

We will suppose that the pipes have been cut fairly to pitch and voiced, either purchased ready done or finished on a voicing machine, and that the time has come to put them in place and tune the organ ready for use. First verify the wind-pressure, then run up and down the keys with the stop drawn to blow out dust and chips, and put the pipes into their places, and verify each to see that it speaks well, and proceed in the same way through all the stops.

424. The first operation is called ' laying the bearings,' and is the division of an octave into the different notes, and from this one octave all the rest of the organ has to be tuned. It must, therefore, be done with the greatest care, and the

beginner would be well advised to provide at least this octave
of pipes with slides, so as to avoid hacking the pipes about
with the tuning-horn. The peculiar difficulty in laying the
bearings consists in knowing just how much to falsify the
fifths ; were they tuned true, any person with a fairly musical
ear could tune easily enough.

There is also in the organ this difficulty : that as so many
pipes have to be tuned to sound together, the greatest care must
be taken in tuning the octaves to keep them dead true, and
it must be also remembered that a number of pipes, even
if tuned perfectly true together, will not remain so for any
length of time, owing to changes of temperature and other
causes.   There is also a certain margin within which the beats
are hardly perceptible, so that it will be found by experiment
that if c^1 is tuned from c^0, and c^2 again from c^1, although
both pairs may sound in tune together, yet c^1 and c^2 may not
be dead in tune, so that, by tuning from one pipe after another,
a considerable deviation from truth may arise. The best
possible result would be obtained if every pipe in the organ
could be tuned direct from one octave in which the bearings
have been laid, as then there would be no multiplication of
errors.   This is scarcely possible ; but the principle should be
steadily borne in mind.

425. The keener the sound of the stop, the more apparent
is the slightest variation from tune ; for this reason dull sounding stops as Gedackts and Flutes should never be used to tune
from, except to check a Bourdon. Note also that a strong stop
will 'draw' a weak one. Tune a Salicional note from an
Open Diapason, and the chances are that the bearings on
the Salicional will be found to be faulty. Correct them,
and the stop will still sound in tune with the Open just as
much as it did before. Tuning cannot be taught from a book
—the course only can be indicated, and the person who would
aspire to tune creditably an organ of several stops and more
than one manual will require to have practice and all his
wits about him.

426. The bearings can be laid from any note ; the writer
prefers to use the A octave, as it is nearest the middle of the
keyboard, and it is an excellent plan to put an extra band

round the top of the pitch A's and file them exactly to tune,
so that the pitch of the whole organ may never be disturbed.
The Principal is the best stop to lay the bearings on, as it is
midway between the 8 ft. and 2 ft. stops.

First, then, get the pitch A's on the Principal dead in tune,
and to do this sound them together and correct any difference,
half on each pipe, unless it is known which is out.   Then tune
two A's of the Open from one, and sound all four pipes together,
and when in perfect tune you may be sure the Principal and
Open A's are right.

There are two ways of laying the bearings : one by fifths
and octaves only, the other by fifths and fourths.   The latter is
the quickest, as you do not go outside the octave, but it is
quite a matter of taste which plan is followed.

The details of tuning are the same in both, and depend
upon the general principle that *as a series of true fifths makes
more than an octave*, the interval must be *diminished* to temper
the tuning so as to distribute the error equally throughout
the notes.   Thus, if you are tuning a downward fifth, it must
be sharpened, but if an upward fifth it must be flattened.   It
is easy to ascertain exactly whether a pipe is sharp or flat by
holding the finger or tuning horn near the top or the mouth.
Shading a pipe in that way flattens it, and will make it sound
right if too sharp; but if the beat gets worse, it is too flat
already.   It is well to instruct the player to sound the pipe *to
be tuned* first until he hears you have got it by your shading
the top.   If both were sounded together the mistake of tuning
the wrong one might be made.   In tuning, the fingers should
never touch the pipe, as that is quite enough to put a pipe out
of tune by the extra warmth; also it occasionally happens
that if the *hollow* end of a tubing cone is brought near a pipe
in order to shade it, the effect is to *sharpen* the note instead of
doing the opposite, as one might expect.   The best way for
a beginner to learn the amount of tempering is to tune an
octave with downward fifths all true, and see how much it will
be out at the end.   Then go through it again, just raising the
fifths so as to wave sharp, remembering that the wave for a
pipe at top of the octave will be more rapid than in one at the
bottom for the same *relative* amount of correction.   And so

on, until the octave closes correct and the intelligent student
has a fair appreciation of the amount of tempering necessary.
We say downward fifths, simply because it is easier to sharpen
than to flatten a pipe, though if sliders are used it will, of
course, make no difference. As regards the difference in the
beats for the same relative amount of correction, suppose a pipe
of 500 vibrations sounded with another out of tune to an
extent that will give five beats per second, the octave above,
making 1,000 vibrations, sounded with a pipe correspondingly
out of tune will give 10 beats per second.

427. To return to the tuning itself: above all things proceed
on a rigid system, and know exactly what you are doing. To
correct pipes haphazard is fatal, as you may just correct the
one that should have been left alone. Supposing the tuner of
sufficient experience to temper the fifths as he goes, the
quickest plan is to tune six notes upwards and six downwards,
keeping the tempering always within the mark, so as to mess
the pipes about as little as possible. The reason for this is
that an error is not carried through so many pipes. Suppose
an error in the third tuning; if you go right through, there will
be nine pipes to correct; but if you have tuned the last six
correctly from the other A, there will only be three to alter.
The principle of notes apparently in tune being in reality a
little out, applies to the bearings as well as the octaves, so that
to check, other landmarks are introduced, and here again we
may summarise them. *Fifths* must be less than true. *Fourths*
must be greater than true. *Major thirds* must be much
greater than true. It is better to use the expressions 'greater'
and 'less' than 'sharp' and 'flat,' because the former
express accurately the general case, while the question of sharp
or flat depends upon whether you reckon upwards or downwards. An octave can at once be marked out by the major
thirds a - $c^{\sharp}$, $c^{\sharp}$ - f, f - a, making the upper note considerably
sharp, and dividing the correction until they are all equally
out of tune. These, as they come round in the tuning, will be
a useful check on its progress, and once set should not be
altered.

428. Taking, for example, the first partition, we will trace in
detail the tuning of a few notes as a guide. The black note

is in every case the one to be tuned, and the partition is divided
into two series, the numbers in each bar showing the order of
playing, so that half are tuned upwards and half downwards,
as recommended above, if the order of the figures *above* the
stave is used.   The same notation can be used for tuning right
through, either forwards or backwards; in which case, the
black notes for the second half of the partition must be inter-
changed with the white, and the order will be that of the
figures *below* the stave.   The first half are upward fifths, and

consequently must be left flat. After tuning the *e* a trifle
flat, sound it with the upper *a* to see that the fourth is fair.
It may be that though the lower *a* and the *e* go well enough
together, yet the *e* and upper *a* do not. The *e* must be adjusted
until the fifth and fourth, and finally the three notes together,
sound well. From *e* tune *b* a fifth, leaving it a trifle flat.
Here we have no fourth to correct by; but having tuned the
lower *b*, the fourth with *e* should be tried, and not passed until
fair, when the octave *b* should be tried with it. From *b* tune
f a fifth, and check the fourth with the upper *b*, and then the

major third *f* and upper *a* can be tested. The same system should be followed right through for the final tuning; though, of course, so much detail is not necessary in laying the bearings for a rough tuning, and getting the pipes so near that none need be again lifted out of their places to cut them. Finally, when the bearings are finished and close correctly in the middle, they should be tried with all possible chords. If any fifth is left too perfect, some other must pay for it by being too rough. All the notes should, therefore, be gone over until it is quite certain that the necessary error has been equally distributed. For the tuning by fifths and fourths shown in the second partition, the first note given is a downward fifth, which must consequently be left *sharp*. The next is an upward fourth, also to be left sharp, and so on. The second series commenced with an upward fifth, which will have to be left *flat*, and the next note, a downward fourth, must also be *flat*. Thus, as all the notes, whether fifths or fourths, are tempered in the same direction, there is no fear of making a mistake. In this scheme also, every opportunity should be taken to check wherever consonant notes come in, as at first the *d* should be checked with the lower *a*, and then all three notes together. Observe that the use of the signs 'sharp' and 'flat' is purely conventional, to show whether the tuning course is upwards or downwards. *e* flat and *d* sharp are, of course, musically speaking, *not* an octave, though they have to serve for it in a keyed instrument.

429. Suppose the bearings passed, a range of two octaves may now be completed, and then another stop, say the Open, tuned note for note, and verified by the octaves, as, if the four pipes together sound all right, they are well in tune. Any error must be detected by damping one pipe of the octave, and then the other, until all waving has been eliminated. Then a trial of the bearings on the second stop will make the work absolutely secure, and the rest of the organ may be tuned with confidence. Octaves should not be taken without checking, and this can easily be done, when it is remembered that a note makes the same number of beats per second with its (imperfect) Fourth below, and with its (imperfect) Fifth above. Thus, supposing an octave finished from a^1 to a^2, and

that we want to tune the octaves up. The first note will be b^2 flat, which will be tuned from b^1 flat; but it should be checked against e^1 flat, which should beat at the same rate with the upper note as it does with the lower.

Complete the Principal in octaves; but when the second octave from the bearings is reached, check each note against the *original* note, and always the three and four notes together, when that range has been reached. Then tune the Open, either from its tuned octave, or note for note with the Principal, checking always against the middle octave, and all octaves together. After this, the stop next to be tuned depends upon its position in the organ; those most out of reach should be tuned first, so that others may not be disturbed in reaching at them. Fancy stops are best left till the last, the foundation stops on all manuals being first secured. If tuning takes more than one day, the bearings should be verified each morning, the Open and Principal, the foundation of all, being kept correct to date. It will soon be found that it is a physical impossibility to leave an organ absolutely in tune; but no harm will result if only errors are not multiplied, and everything is checked as narrowly as possible against the original octave.

430. The following notes are useful to remember. A soft stop tunes better from the Principal of another manual; but must, of course, be checked against its own, and the bearings separately tried. No accurate tuning can be got off a Gedackt or Flute as a foundation; but they may be used to check similar stops with. A stop tunes better off one that differs by an octave than off one of the same pitch.

Mixtures require particular care, as even in many organs tuned by professionals they are left very rough. In the first place, in a slider organ, verify by a wind-gauge in a pipe hole with all the stops drawn, that the Mixture gets the same pressure of wind in full organ as when used alone, for in many cases it does not. It can readily be seen that if the Mixture is tuned off the Principal alone on a pressure of 3 in., and used in the organ with all the stops drawn under a pressure of $2\frac{7}{8}$ in., the big and little pipes will no longer be in tune together. The way to avoid this is to take off as much bellows weight when tuning the Mixture as will give it the pressure it will receive in the full organ. Most particularly should this stop be tuned from the middle octave only of Principal, as small pipes never keep in accurate tune for long together, and the most convenient way of clearing off all the compound stops at once is to damp all but the middle octave of the Principal by slipping a paper in their mouths. Damp also the middle octave of the stop to be tuned. Then tune an *a* of the Mixture from the Principal *a*, then another *a*, and so on, and lastly the middle *a*.   Do all the notes in the same way, and you will have a Mixture in really good tune. If the beginner finds it difficult to recognise the very small fifth and third sounding pipes, tune them from their actual notes on the Principal—*these* fifths, of course, which represent natural harmonics are to be dead true. The style of soundboard described in paragraph 267 lends itself specially to ease and accuracy in tuning, which forms not the least recommenda-tion of the ventil system in general. With this soundboard the tuner can reach every pipe, and damp every one he does not wish to speak by putting a slip of paper in the mouth ; but the really proper way to fit up a compound stop is to put a separate slider under each rank of pipes, so that each can be dealt with alone.

431. It only remains to notice the mechanical means of tuning the different stops. Ordinary flue pipes down to about 4 ft. long are tuned by the cones and tuning-horns shown in Figs. 75 and 88, Pl. X., but care should be taken not to injure the pipes by violent use, or they may get bent at the foot or mouth. The neatest plan is to provide all pipes over 1 in. diameter with a slide, as then the pipes never need be defaced. Small scale pipes, which are peculiarly insensible to the action of the tuning-horn, should always be provided with this appendage ; but it should either rise above the rim of the pipe, which is cut a trifle sharp for the purpose, or should cover a wide shallow gap in the rim. If a small slot is made further down the pipe, it gives it a horny tone. Large pipes, when made of zinc, should be furnished with a soft metal tuning-tongue. Bell Gambas and such fancy stops are generally tuned by the ears, which are made specially

long for the purpose, as are also metal stopped pipes with fixed stoppers. Ordinary wood and metal stopped pipes are tuned by the stoppers, and here it should be noted that if a pipe has to be flattened, it is best to raise the stopper a little too high and then set it down again to insure the leather being fairly stretched. Large wood pipes are cut nearly to pitch, and then a slot is cut and provided with a slide. Small ones generally have a metal shade stuck into a saw-cut in the back of the pipe. Reed pipes are tuned by the tuning wire alone; once the pipes are voiced the shades should not be meddled with.

432. As only a small organ can be tuned in a day, the bearings will require to be verified on the Principal and Open before commencing each day's work, and when all the stops are supposed to be tuned, a final test is to play each note, drawing all the stops that are intended to be used together, and correcting any that are found to be out of tune. Weak solo stops, as the Salicional, should have their own bearings tested, as noted above. The greatest care should be taken with the very low pipes, and they cannot be tuned in a hurry. As they have a considerable margin—i.e., the tuning shade can be moved a good bit after a pipe ceases to beat sharp before it begins to beat flat—the most accurate method is to mark the two positions and set the slide in the middle. The reeds are tuned last of all because they do not stand in tune, and they should never be used to tune from except to correct each other in their octaves in tuning, and it is frequently impossible to tune the bass of an 8 ft. reed accurately except from its octaves. Care should be taken to see that all pipes are so placed that their mouths have the greatest free space possible: they should not face the opposite rank, but the mouths should be slightly skew, towards the most open space.

433. Scheibler's mechanical method of tuning merits a particular description, and learners are strongly advised to practise it, or the modification described below, until they have a tolerably accurate notion of the temperament. The efforts of the best tuners, indeed, could be improved by this mechanical check, and it may be regarded as indispensable to

persons who have but little practice or a poor appreciation of pitch. The system depends upon counting the beats given by two sounds in a measured interval of time.   Sets of forks for a whole octave are made, and in using these it is recommended to tune—not by unisons, but by raising or lowering the pitch of the instrument to give from 2 to 4 beats with the forks, the intervals being more accurately set in this way than by tuning in unison.   In the latter case there might be a dissonance, but so slight that the very slow beat would hardly be perceived, while actually counting out 2, 3, or 4 beats against each stroke of the metronome will give mathematical accuracy with the exercise of the most ordinary care.

434. Everyone knows the Maelzel's metronome, and that the divisions on it represent the number of strokes in a minute ; a metronome, therefore, set at the mark 60 beats with a seconds pendulum. It may not, however, be so generally known that a more accurate machine can be constructed with a string and a lead bullet. The length of a seconds pendulum (for the latitude of Greenwich) is 39·13926 in., and the length of a pendulum, to give any other number of vibrations per minute, is as the squares of those numbers. From 50 to 80 are all that will be required for Scheibler's method, and he gives the table below. It is best to mark the metronome

Metronome Number	Pendulum Length	Metronome Number	Pendulum Length
50	56·3	66	32·3
51	54·1	67	31·4
52	52·1	68	30·5
53	50·1	69	29·6
54	48·3	70	28·7
55	46·6	71	28
56	44·9	72	27·2
57	43·4	73	26·4
58	41·9	74	25·7
59	40·5	75	25
60	39·1	76	24·4
61	37·8	77	23·7
62	36·6	78	23·1
63	35·5	79	22·5
64	34·4	80	22·0
65	33·3		

numbers on a scale downwards from the point of suspension,

and have a pointer or mark exactly in the centre of the bullet
by which to adjust it.

The required number of beats will not always be an even
number per second, and as the whole accuracy of the method
consists in making an easily-counted number of beats, *exactly*
coincident with an easily-observed pendulum beat, the frac-
tional beats are got over by adjusting the pendulum.　The
proportion of the beats and the metronome number is an
inverse one.　Thus if the beats to be observed were 5·08 per
second, and it was desired to reduce them to four per stroke,
the proportion would be 4 : 5·08 : : 60 : x, where x will figure
out as 76·2.

435. Instead of twelve forks, a tuner can do very well with
six, which number will map out the intervals, leaving only
notes which can be tuned by comparison with their upper and
lower fifths.　As was remarked above, the great difficulty in
tuning is to know how much to vitiate the intervals ; but this
difficulty almost entirely vanishes when one only has to
equalise the error with two fifths above and below, both
known to be accurate.　The pipe under treatment is sounded
first with its fifth above, and then with its fifth below, until
the roughness on both sides appears equal.

For this operation the following forks are required—viz.,
b, c sharp, d sharp, f, g, a.　The lower octaves of d sharp, f,
g, a, are tuned, and the upper octaves of b, c sharp, d sharp,
then the remaining notes are tuned as in the subjoined table,
the best plan being to tune exact to the upper fifth, and then
sharpen till the roughness equalises.

Upper Fifth	Note	Lower Fifth
f	a ♯	d ♯
g	c	f
a	d	g
b	e	a
c ♯	f ♯	b
d ♯	g ♯	c ♯

436. The system can, however, be applied to organs to
tune exactly without forks, by the beats of the pipes themselves, as these are so well developed and can be observed at

leisure. The principle is to use two stops, one that which is to be tuned and the other an auxiliary stop, so as to divide the beats down to a recognisable number—the auxiliary stop is, of course, not in tune when all this is done. The table below is taken from Scheibler's treatise; the notes on the auxiliary stop are denoted by Roman letters, the stop to be tuned by italics, and the metronome column nearest the pitch must be used.

From	Tune	Higher or Lower	By Beats	To Pendulum Strokes	Pitch $a^2=$	840	850	860	870	880
a¹	e¹	Higher	2	1	—	80	80	80	80	80
e¹	b°	Lower	4	1	—	62	62·4	62·7	63·1	63·5
„	e°	Higher	3	1	—	66·7	66·7	66·7	66·7	66·7
e°	♯g¹	Lower	4	1	—	69·7	68·7	67·7	66·8	65·8
a¹	d¹	Higher	4	1	—	60	60	60	60	60
d¹	g¹	Lower	2	1	—	84	83·1	82·2	81·3	80·4
a¹	a°	Higher	2	1	—	80	80	80	80	80
a°	♯c¹	Higher	3	2	—	66·8	70·8	74·8	78·8	82·8
„	d¹	Lower	4	1	—	65·8	65·6	65·4	65·3	65·1
„	e¹	Lower	4	1	—	70·7	70·8	70·9	71	71·2
„	♯f	Higher	3	1	—	57·3	59·5	61·8	64	66·3
a¹	f¹	Lower	2	1	—	80	80	80	80	80
f¹	bb	Lower	4	1	—	60	60	60	60	60
b b¹	be¹	Higher	3	1	—	62·7	61·4	60·2	59	57·8
f¹	bb°	Lower	3	1	—	72·1	73·8	75·4	77	78·7
„	c¹	Lower	3	1	—	58·7	59·7	60·8	61·9	63
„	f¹	Lower	3	2	—	63·2	64·4	65·7	67	68·2

437. The weak point about this system is that in practice it is necessary to know the exact pitch of the organ, or alter it, which in the flattening direction is almost impracticable, and troublesome enough in the way of sharpening. To get over this difficulty, the late Mr. A. J. Ellis, the translator of Helmholtz, gives, in the Appendix XX. to the second (English) edition, a method of tuning by the beats of the ordinary intervals, which, though not mathematically correct, is shown by him to be within the limits of appreciable error for any pitch between $c^1=256$ and $270\cdot4$ ($a^1=430\cdot5$ and 450).

The scale he gives is as follows, where the figures between the notes give the number of beats in 10 seconds by which the intervals must be falsified, the fifths being always too small and the fourths too large, as in the ordinary tuning, which these figures reduce to a system instead of leaving the temperament to the opinion of the tuner.　The letters L and

M indicate that the interval is to be made less or more than true, and in tuning, particular care must be taken not to adjust the wrong way.

The second arrangement is really the same as the first, only the number of notes tuned either way from the pitch *a* is kept the same, for the reasons given in the first part of this chapter.　It must be clearly understood that the figures refer to the pitch *as written*.　If, for example, the bearings are laid upon those notes of the Principal, the number of beats must be doubled, or else the notes must be played an octave lower than written.　By using 10 beats which coincide with 10 beats of the pendulum, accuracy can be obtained with the most moderate care, for it is perfectly easy to recognise whether, in 10 beats, the pipe or the pendulum gain ever so little on each other.　For this method, then, nothing is required but a metronome set at the marks 60 and 90 for the 10 and 15 beat intervals respectively ; or a simple pendulum with a string 39·14 in. and 17·4 in. will do.

438.　Scheibler makes the curious suggestion that, in an organ of many stops one or two should be tuned true for one particular key, say C, to refresh the ear by contrast with the others.　Such a stop could not, of course, be used with any other, nor for any key except that in which it is tuned.　For full particulars of his system see the English translation of his work, published by Cocks & Co. (1853).

CHAPTER XI

PURCHASE AND REPAIRS

489. IT is the opinion of the writer that an organ should be treated as a work of art; but the practical result of most transactions in organ-buying is to treat it as a machine, with a very poor gauge of its efficiency at that. What would be thought of a committee who, entrusted with the purchase of a picture, should call for tenders at so much per square foot, and further indicate a size that could not possibly be properly viewed in a room the picture was intended to adorn? Yet this is no exaggeration of what is constantly done in purchasing organs, and, even where money is no object, organs that may be good in themselves are put into places for which they are much too large. It is told of Schultze that a town in the North desired him to build them an organ to a certain specification, and asked him to mention his price. He, seeing that the space allotted for the organ was insufficient, told them so, and finally, as they insisted upon the whole organ, refused to build it at any price rather than turn out an instrument which he knew would not be satisfactory. 'Just one stop more' has ruined many an organ, and even where pipes are not actually off their speech from being crowded together, the tone suffers much more than people believe, from the pipes not having sufficient room to speak in. Organ-builders, even if artists, must live by their calling, and it is the purchasers, and not the builder, who should be blamed for the miserable instruments so often seen, which have been built at the lowest possible price per stop-handle. So few people are acquainted with the details of organs, or can form any idea from a specification of how an organ will sound, that much the safest way for the intending purchaser is to put

T

himself into the hands of a builder whose tone and work are known to be good, and state either what is required, or what funds and space are available. A big factory is not the sole test of a good builder, as there are men in a small way of business who are true artists. There would be no harm in inviting proposals from two builders, so as to have a choice ; but any attempt to obtain the maximum number of stop-knobs for the minimum cost through competition will bring a just retribution. This is the beau-ideal of organ-building : You put yourself in the hands of the master, and he does his best. Unfortunately, this vision is somewhat Utopian. Given even the master, the client is not satisfied to leave matters to his judgment, but will intrude his whims, nor can the builder as a rule refuse an order because it is ridiculous. An eminent painter would certainly refuse a commission if his client insisted upon some combination of colour that would render the picture ridiculous, but scarcely any organ builder would do the same thing. The writer has in mind a church organ by one of our leading firms where the swell has only two foundation stops—and one of them a rather poor one—with a Cornopean and a *Vox Humana*. It is quite certain the builders did not approve of such a specification, and they may even have pointed out the absurdity ; but still, they built the organ as a matter of business. Let the purchaser, then, refrain from dictating to the builder unless he has a really competent adviser who has gone deeply into the matter, and let him be content with quality rather than quantity.

440. While on this subject, it would be idle to pretend to ignore the pernicious and indefensible practice of builders giving, and organists accepting, commission—or, in plain English, a bribe.

The labourer is worthy of his hire, and if those entrusted with the placing of an organ think that the organist should superintend its construction, by all means let him be paid for his trouble ; but it should be by his employers, and not by the contractor whom he is to control. It will not cost the employer any more, as he may be quite sure that the builder has to get the commission out of the price. No man who was building a house would think of employing an architect who was paid by the builder.

441. Up to a certain point, of course, an organ is a mere machine, and can be built to a specification; but while there are engineers to consult on the latter, the builder is the sole arbiter on the former. The so-called specifications of builders consist of a mere list of stops, and though it is easy to enumerate the points which should be detailed in a specification, the difficulty still remains of finding a person competent to draw it up, or to criticise it if drawn by the builder. A specification should state the scale of each stop, the proportions of tin and lead in the metal, the weight or thickness of the pipes, the size of the bellows, of the trunks, and of the principal pallet areas, and the wind pressure. When all this has been done, some idea can be arrived at of the efficiency of the organ as a machine; but no specification can cover the artistic side of the work. The only really sound advice, therefore, that can be given is to go to the best builder, and give him details of the surroundings, and leave him to do his best, with a money limit where that is necessary. The analogy of buying a picture may profitably be remembered.

To accept an organ when built, it should be tested for the grosser mechanical defects.

By playing upon the full organ, it can be seen if the bellows and trunks are large enough by using a wind-gauge on the different manuals when full chords are played, and the tuning can be tried with all the stops drawn on each manual. To test the tightness of the sliders, if a slider organ, put an arm on the keys, with the stops all shut, and note the escape of wind. Each stop should be tried through by itself, to see that all the pipes speak properly and that there is no running, and, of course, all the stops and composition pedals are expected to work freely and silently. A critical examination like this will often reveal defects that pass muster in playing upon the organ as a whole, but which, nevertheless, detract from the tone.

442. To repair an organ, the first thing is to put the action to rights, seeing that all the parts are square to their work, and renewing the bushing if any parts rattle. When the

T 2

action is in order, and the bellows and trunks proved to be
sound, the pipes can be tested. If, in playing over a single
stop, two pipes sound together, try the same notes on other
stops, and if they also jar, the defect is in the soundboards.
It then becomes a question of rebuilding the soundboard if
there are many such defects, or of the miserable expedient of
' bleeding.' This is done by boring a small hole through the
cheek, or from below into the groove, so that when a small
quantity of air leaks in from the adjacent groove it cannot
get up sufficient pressure to make the pipe sound, while still
enough wind does not escape to entirely spoil the tone of the
pipes when their own pallet is opened. The note should be
held down while the boring is going on, so as to blow out all
the dust.

If the fault is confined to one stop, it is clearly in the fit of
the slider, and may, perhaps, be rectified by screwing the
upper boards down a little ; or it may be necessary to take
out the slider and upper board to see if either has warped,
and remedy the defect. The pallets should be repaired where
necessary, and here the advantage of pin-pallets comes in, as
they can be taken out and cleaned, and, if required, releathered
without disturbing the organ. Meanwhile the pipes should be
removed and cleaned, and any obvious defects remedied. The
stopped pipes should get new leathers and be blackleaded
inside. If in an old organ the pipes have been very much
hacked about, they can all be moved up one, provided the
scale is not already too large and that there is room ; but this
should not be done with reeds, which, indeed, will not require
it, and it should be remembered that raising the pitch of a
well-voiced organ will destroy the tone, because the mouths
will become too high, unless the wind is increased to correspond. Conveyance pipes should be looked to, as they often
get trodden on, or split at the elbows, and then do not give a
proper supply of wind. The bellows, of course, will be over-
hauled, and new leather supplied where the old is perished.
Before working at the action, it is a good plan to touch the
screwed ends with a feather dipped in kerosene, as the nuts
get set fast, and are difficult to move without running the
risk of breaking the trackers.

443. But to prevent organs falling into decrepitude the best plan is to take care of them. In England there is, of course, no difficulty; but abroad, where organ-builders are not to be found, the matter is serious. For such organs it is an absolute waste of money to provide reed stops. Flue stops, well made, will keep in playable order a long time; but reeds, especially where exposed to much dust, require tuning every week to be fit to play upon, and it is quite possible to build a perfectly satisfactory organ for an ordinary church without a single reed, by making a judicious use of string-toned stops and Mixtures. A point that is needlessly neglected in organs is the upkeep of the action. This, being an ordinary combination of levers, might, it may well be supposed, be kept in order by any person with a little mechanical knowledge; yet the experience of the writer is that the adjustments are twisted about anyhow, and, as a rule, in a very short time the couplers all get out of order, and take the notes down when not drawn, or fail to pull them fully down. The barbarisms that the writer has seen practised on organs are almost incredible, and, indeed, first gave the idea of putting the principles of organ design and building into an accessible form.

444. As the writer has twice met cases where the pipes of an organ sent for repairs have been thrown loose into a deep case, a word on packing may not be out of place. First, take the quite small pipes and roll them up in packets, putting them heads and tails, with a fold of paper between each. Go on to the larger sizes, putting every pipe head down into the next largest that will hold it, and sometimes a pair thus prepared into a still larger pipe; but, as in this case there is a foot at each end, beware of its caving in the languid of the containing pipe, which should be protected by a good wad of paper, taking care also not to bulge out the mouth by cramming down too hard a wad. Pack the pipes in quite a shallow case, and if at all large, run a partition up it, and on that lay planks to form a second storey. The boots of the reeds should be done up in paper, which is then glued down to prevent dust getting in. The wooden pipes can, of course, themselves be used as packing cases. Of course, decorated

pipes must be carefully wrapped up in paper, which must
further be secured by a dab of glue at the back of the pipe
to prevent it shifting and rubbing the decorations. Hay is
the best filling, and the pipes should be well jammed together,
so as not to shake loose. Being double thickness one inside
the other is an advantage as well as a saving in room, as it
prevents their getting squeezed out of shape. The ranks of
compound stops should be carefully packed and labelled, so
as to avoid getting them mixed. The maker generally puts
marks on them thus, I, II, III, &c., to distinguish the number
of the rank. Very often in old organs, especially where base
metal has been used, it will be found that the holes in the
pipe feet have been somewhat closed in, and going over a
stop, widening the holes a little, as in regulating, has a
wonderful effect in restoring freshness of speech. As for
pipes whose feet have given way under the weight and become
wrinkled up, they are only fit for the scrap-heap.

445. Owing to the craze of many organists for more noise,
a scheme for enlarging the organ will generally crop up when
heavy repairs are decided upon. The first question should be,
Is there plenty of room?—for if there is not, the addition of
another manual or more stops may only spoil what there
already is in the organ. The room being admitted, the next
question is bellows and trunk capacity. If another manual is
in contemplation, it will generally mean a new bellows and
trunk; but if it is only a question of a new stop or two, a
careful calculation should be made to see that not only the
existing bellows and trunk, but also the pallet areas, are
adequate to the additional work, the only exception being in
the case of a fancy stop, which, being used by itself, will not
increase the volume of air demanded for the full organ.
Supposing bellows and pallet area sufficient, an easy way of
enlarging the soundboard is to build a new section of the same
groove-spacing as the old board, and sufficiently wide to take
the sliders required. The two boards are then cramped together, the adjoining cheeks being faced with leather, and
holes bored through to supply the new grooves from the old
ones. This job must be well done, or it will only furnish
another surface for ' running.'

Should the pallet area be insufficient, but in other conditions satisfactory, perhaps the new slice of soundboard can have pallets of its own which can be worked from the action, or a possible device is to take a gas-tube out of the old groove to work a small motor, which forms the primary valve for admission of wind to the new board. By the time all this is done, a new board altogether will probably be better and cheaper.

446. As to price, one might almost as well try to state the price of a horse as that of an organ, and the nearest that can be said is that 30*l*. to 40*l*. per stop may be supposed to be the average cost of an 'ordinary organ' of sound work and materials, and with no elaboration of case. Anything built at a lower rate than 35*l*. would have to be most carefully watched by a competent person, and if a builder of approved skill, on being asked to figure for an organ, should mention a price even a little above the higher limit, his offer might be accepted.

Lastly, a word may be said on the element of time. It takes time to turn out a really artistic instrument; yet the future owners of an organ, after perhaps taking several years to make up their minds that an organ is wanted, cannot afford to wait days for its construction, and press the builder for early delivery, which indeed he can effect, but at the expense of the instrument, the parts of which have to be made and thrown together at full speed. No builder who values his reputation should take an order to be executed in an impossibly short time, and committees who desire a really artistic result would do well to remember that to attain it the builder must touch and retouch the voicing, and that work done in such a way necessarily takes time.

CHAPTER XII

SPECIFICATIONS

447. A USEFUL aid to the design of organs is the study of those which have been built, criticising the tone in connection with the specification, by which document is not intended a mere list of stops, but a proper specification, giving the scale of each stop and the wind and other particulars. Rimbault and Hopkins's work contains a list of the stops of every organ of note up to the date of the book, and can be consulted on this point; but a mere name means so little that unless the actual scales are given, a list of stops conveys but a very vague idea of the quality of the organ.

The writer does not, therefore, propose to waste space in long lists of organ stops, but will note one or two organs worthy of remembrance from the excellence of the instruments, even though the detailed dimensions have not been obtained, as well as a few specifications not given in Rimbault. The first is the organ by Michell and Thynne that stood in the Inventions Exhibition at Kensington in 1885, and, it is believed, was afterwards enlarged and found its way to Tewkesbury. For beauty of tone and completeness, with the fewest possible number of slides, this organ could not be beaten, and it at once attracted attention even among the other fine organs then exhibited, and was immeasurably superior to some, so great can be the difference even between organs built for show purposes.

The specification was as follows. Compass C_0 to c^4. Six different wind-pressures, the amounts of which and the scaling of the pipes are not stated.

GREAT.

1. Violon	.	.	. 16 ft.	10. Trumpet	. . . 8 ft.
2. Large Open	.	.	8 „		
3. Small Open	.	.	8 „	ACCESSORIES.	
4. Claribel	.	.	8 „	Sub Choir to Great.	
5. Octave	.	.	4 „	Swell to Great.	
6. Harmonic Flute	.	.	4 „	Solo to Great.	
7. Quint Mixture	.	.		Prolongement Harmonique.	
8. Mixture (19, 22, 26, 29)				Two Pneumatic Pistons.	
9. Tromba	.	.	16 ft.	Three Composition Pedals.	

SWELL.

1. Travers Flute	.	.	8 ft.	8. Horn	. . . . 8 ft.
2. Open Diapason	.	.	8 „	9. Oboe	. . . . 8 „
3. Viol da Gamba	.	.	8 „	ACCESSORIES.	
4. Voix Céleste	.	.	8 „	Octave Coupler.	
5. Geigen	.	.	4 „	Tremulant.	
6. Mixture (15, 19, 22)				Two Pneumatic Pistons.	
7. Contra Posaune	.	.	16 ft.	Three Composition Pedals.	

CHOIR.

1. Spitzflute	.	.	8 ft.	7. Clarinet	. . . 8 ft.
2. Viole Sourdine	.	.	8 „	ACCESSORIES.	
3. Gedackt	.	.	8 „	Octave Coupler.	
4. Gemshorn	.	.	4 „	Swell to Choir.	
5. Zauberflöte	.	.	4 „	Tremulant.	
6. Flautina	.	.	2 „	Pneumatic Piston for No. 1.	

SOLO.

1. Harmonic Flute	.	.	8 ft.	ACCESSORIES.	
2. Violoncello	.	.	8 „	Octave Coupler.	
3. Tuba	.	.	8 „	Tremulant.	
4. Vox Humana	.	.	8 „	Two Pneumatic Pistons.	

PEDAL.

1. Harmonic Bass*	.	.	32 ft.	4. Flute Major	. . 8 ft.
2. Major Bass	.	.	16 „	5. Bombarde	. . . 16 „
3. Dolce	.	.	16 „		

All manuals couple to pedals.

The Prolongement Harmonique is a contrivance which enables the player to retain *ad libitum* any chord or notes struck. The Zauberflöte is a stopped harmonic pipe invented by Mr. Thynne, and used for the first time in this organ.

448. If mere size is a recommendation to organs, that built by Messrs. Hill for the Town Hall of Sydney should take the first place, containing, as it does, 126 speaking stops; but as the mere vulgar desire to have the largest organ in the world is equivalent to judging a picture by its size, there is nothing to be learned from the study of such specifications.

The organ for the Auditorium, Chicago, built by Roosevelt,

* This is really a Quint to draw with No. 2 and to obtain the 32 ft. resultant tone.

is a very large one, and being built for a particular purpose, and containing many peculiar devices, is worthy of description as an example of American organ-building. The specification is as follows :

GREAT.

	ft.		ft.
1. Double Open . .	16	11. Octave	4
2. Contra Gamba . .	16	*12. Gambette . . .	4
3. First Open . . .	8	*13. Harmonic Flute . .	4
4. Second Open . .	8	*14. Twelfth.	
5. Gemshorn . .	8	*15. Fifteenth.	
*6. Viol da Gamba . .	8	*16. Mixture IV. and V. ranks.	
*7. Viol d'Amour . .	8	*17. Scharff III. and IV. ranks.	
8. Principal Flute . .	8	*18. Ophicleide . . .	16
*9. Doppel Flute . .	8	*19. Trumpet . . .	8
*10. Quint . . .	5⅓	*20. Clarion . . .	4

SWELL.

	ft.		ft.
1. Double Dulciana . .	16	13. Salicet	4
2. Bourdon . .	16	14. Hohl Flute . . .	4
3. Open Diapason . .	8	15. Flauto Dolce . . .	4
4. Violin Diapason . .	8	16. Flageolet . . .	2
5. Spitz Flute . . .	8	17. Cornet IV. and V. ranks.	
6. Salicional . . .	8	18. Acuta III. ranks.	
7. Æoline . . .	8	19. Contra Fagotto . .	16
8. Vox Celestis . .	8	20. Cornopean . . .	8
9. Harmonic Flute . .	8	21. Oboe	8
10. Clarabella . . .	8	22. Vox Humana . . .	8
11. Stopped Diapason..	8	23. Clarion	4
12. Octave	4		

CHOIR (in a separate swell-box).

	ft.		ft.
1. Double Melodia . .	16	10. Flûte d'Amour . .	4
2. Open Diapason . .	8	11. Nazard	2⅔
3. Geigen	8	12. Piccolo	2
4. Dulciana . . .	8	13. Dolce Cornet V. ranks.	
5. Travers Flute . .	8	14. Euphone . . .	16
6. Lieblich Gedackt . .	8	15. Tromba . . .	8
7. Quintadena . . .	8	16. Clarinet	8
8. Octave	4	17. Carillon.	
9. Fugara	4		

SOLO.

(8 in. wind, and enclosed in separate swell-box.)

	ft.		ft.
1. Stentorphone . . .	8	9. Basset Horn . . .	16
2. Violoncello . .	8	10. Tuba Mirabilis . .	8
3. Concert Flute . .	8	11. Orchestral Oboe . .	8
4. Viola	4	12. Orchestral Clarinet .	8
5. Harmonic Flute . .	4	13. Cor Anglais . . .	8
6. Hohl Flute . . .	4	14. Tuba Clarion . . .	4
7. Harmonic Piccolo . .	2	15. Cathedral Chimes.	
8. Tuba Major . .	16		

* In a separate swell-box.

Echo (in separate swell-box).

	ft.		ft.
1. Quintatön	16	7. Travers Flute . . .	4
2. Keraulophon . . .	8	8. Armonica Ætheria IV.	
3. Dolcissimo . . .	8	ranks.	
4. Unda Maris . . .	8	9. Horn	8
5. Fern Flute . . .	8	10. Oboe	8
6. Dulcet	4	11. Vox Humana . . .	8

Stage Organ (from Solo manual).

	ft.		ft.
1. Open Diapason . .	8	3. Octave	4
2. Doppel Flute . . .	8	4. Trumpet . . .	8

Pedal.

	ft.		ft.
1. Double Open . .	32	11. Flute	8
2. Bourdon . . .	32	12. Octave Quint . . .	$5\frac{1}{3}$
3. First Open . .	16	13. Super Octave . .	4
4. Second Open . .	16	14. Mixture III. ranks.	
5. Dulciana . . .	16	15. Contra Bombarde .	32
6. Violone . . .	16	16. Trombone . .	16
7. Stopped Diapason .	16	17. Serpent (free reed) .	16
8. Quint . . .	$10\frac{2}{3}$	18. Contra Fagotto .	16
9. Octave . . .	8	19. Clarion . . .	8
10. Violoncello . .	8		

Couplers.

Swell to Great.	Solo Octaves.
Choir to Great.	Solo to Pedal.
Solo to Great.	Swell to Pedal.
Swell to Choir.	Great to Pedal.
Swell Octaves.	Choir to Pedal.

Accessories.

Swell Tremulant.
Choir Tremulant.
Solo Tremulant.
Echo Tremulant.
Echo Ventil.
Stage Ventil.
Combination release.
Crescendo & diminuendo indicator.
7 Pneumatic Pistons to Great.
8 Pneumatic Pistons to Swell.
5 Pneumatic Pistons to Choir.
5 Pneumatic Pistons to Solo.

5 Pneumatic Pistons to Pedal.
Full Organ Pedal.
Pedal Ventil.
Crescendo Pedal.
Diminuendo Pedal.
Reversible pedals for—
  Solo to Great.
  Swell Octaves.
  Solo Octaves.
  Solo to Pedal.
  Great to Pedal.
  Solo and Echo.

The compass is C_o to c^4, and the action electric. The Echo organ is placed in an attic 100 ft. away from the organ, and is operated by the Solo manual, being brought off and on by the reversible pedal; the Stage organ is on the stage for special purposes. The Carillon, a not unknown adjunct of Continental organs, is made of steel bars, and the Cathedral

chimes are described as made of drawn brass tubing, with a
'mellow and resonant tone, if anything superior to that of
real bells.' This may be so; but the writer can only say
that, with the sole exception of Burmese gongs, he has never
yet heard any of these substitutes for bells that had not an
abominable twang.

The soundboards are of Roosevelt's pattern, so that every
pipe gets a full supply of wind. The pneumatic pistons are
of Roosevelt's patent adjustable type, where the combination
is set beforehand by drawing the stops, and then pulling the
piston out about a ¼ in.; whenever it is pushed in it draws
the combination for which it is set. It throws the stop-knobs,
and they can be operated by hand without interfering with
the combination.

The Sforzando pedal brings on the full organ without
altering the draw-stops, and when unhitched the organ reverts
to the previous combinations. The Crescendo and Diminuendo pedals are a new contrivance; a single stroke on the
former brings on all the stops in regular gradation, without
altering the draws, and the speed of the effect is regulated by
the degree of speed used in pressing down the pedal. The
Diminuendo pedal in a similar way reduces the power, and
there is a dial for each pedal indicating the amount of organ
in use. The arrangement of multiple swell-boxes is also a
feature in the organ, and new and beautiful effects are obtained by closing one box while gradually opening another
controlling an opposite quality of tone. The price of the
organ is stated at 9,000l., exclusive of the supply of electricity
to the extent of 18 H.P. The resources of this instrument
are enormous; but as there are 22 composition pedals besides
three swell pedals, it would seem as if the performer, to do it
full justice, must possess some of the attributes of a cen-
tipede.

449. The Calcutta Cathedral organ, by Willis, is not only
by far the finest organ in India, but would hold its own any-
where. The foundation work is particularly fine, and if there
is a criticism to be made, it is that a little more string tone
would be desirable. The Violon is lacking in the fire that
should characterise the stop, and is rather a Double Dulciana.

So also with the Gamba, the position of which, on the Choir, indicates indeed that it is rather a Viol da Gamba. The lack of string tone is, however, made up in the full organ by the reeds, which are numerous and excellent.

The specification is as follows :

GREAT.

1. Double Open, 16 ft. c^1, $3\frac{1}{4}$ in. dia.
2. Open Diapason, 8 ft. C_0, $7\frac{1}{2}$ in. dia.
3. Open Diapason, 8 ft. C_0, 6 in. dia.
4. Harmonic Flute, 8 ft. c^0, $2\frac{11}{16}$ in. dia.
5. Harmonic Flute, 4 ft. c^0, $2\frac{7}{16}$ in. dia.
6. Principal, 4 ft., same as No. 3.
7. Fifteenth, 2 ft.
8. Piccolo, 2 ft.
9. Mixture, III. and IV. ranks.
10. Trumpet, 8 ft.

SWELL.

1. Bourdon, 16 ft. c^0, $2\frac{3}{14}$ in. dia.
2. Open Diapason, 8 ft. C_0, 6 in. dia.
3. Salicional, 8 ft. C_0, $4\frac{1}{2}$ in. dia.
4. Lieblich Gedackt, 8 ft. c^0, $2\frac{1}{8}$ in. dia.
5. Vox Angelica, 8 ft. c^0, $2\frac{13}{16}$ in. dia.
6. Principal, 4 ft. c^0, 3 in. dia.
7. Flute, 4 ft. c^0, $2\frac{1}{8}$ in. dia.
8. Twelfth.
9. Fifteenth.
10. Oboe, 8 ft.
11. Cornopean, 8 ft.
12. Vox Humana, 8 ft

CHOIR.

1. Gamba, 8 ft. c^0, $2\frac{1}{4}$ in. dia.
2. Harmonic Flute, 8 ft. c^0, $2\frac{4}{8}$ in. dia.
3. Dulciana, 8 ft. c^0, $2\frac{1}{4}$ in. dia.
4. Concert Flute, 4 ft. c^0, $2\frac{3}{8}$ in. dia.
5. Viola, 4 ft. c^0, $2\frac{1}{4}$ in. dia.
6. Gemshorn, 4 ft. c^0, $2\frac{9}{14}$ in. dia.
7. Corno di Bassetto, 8 ft.

PEDAL.

1. Open Diapason, 16 ft.
2. Violone, 16 ft. c^0, $3\frac{1}{4}$ in. dia.
3. Violoncello, 8 ft. c^1, $1\frac{1}{2}$ in. dia.
4. Ophicleide, 16 ft.

450. A very beautiful organ, by Schultze, at St. Peter's Church, Hindley, Wigan, is described below. The front pipes of this organ are the wood bass of Violon and Gamba, and any one pipe is a study in tone. This organ completely dispels the delusion that there is any necessary difference in the tone of metal and wood pipes, even with string-toned stops, for which metal is supposed to be specially suitable.

GREAT.

1. Bourdon, 16 ft. C_1, is $6\frac{3}{4}$ in. by $5\frac{7}{8}$ in., mouth $3\frac{1}{4}$ in. high.
2. Contra Gamba, 16 ft. C_1, $6\frac{1}{4}$ in. by 5 in., mouth 1 in. high ; c^0, $2\frac{3}{10}$ in. dia., mouth $\frac{5}{8}$ in. high, and $\frac{1}{4}$ circumference.
3. Major Open, 8 ft. C_0, $4\frac{3}{4}$ in. by $4\frac{1}{4}$ in., mouth 1 inch ; c^0, $3\frac{3}{8}$ in. dia., mouth $\frac{3}{4}$ in., and $\frac{2}{7}$ circumference.
4. Minor Open, 8 ft. C_0, $4\frac{5}{8}$ in. by $3\frac{1}{2}$ in., c^0, $2\frac{7}{8}$ in., mouth $\frac{11}{16}$ in. high, and $\frac{2}{7}$ circumference.
5. Hohl Flute, 8 ft. stopped bass, c^0 is triangular, $2\frac{7}{8}$ in. by $2\frac{1}{4}$ in., mouth $1\frac{1}{2}$ in. high, and arched.
6. Gedackt, 8 ft. C_0, $3\frac{7}{8}$ in. by $2\frac{7}{8}$ in., mouth 2 in.; c^1, $1\frac{1}{2}$ in. dia., mouth $\frac{9}{10}$ in., and $\frac{1}{4}$ in. circumference.

7. Quint, $5\frac{1}{3}$ ft., same scale as Bourdon, but a little wider.
8. Principal, 4 ft., same scale as Major Open.
9. Mixture III. ranks, c¹, is $1\frac{9}{16}$ in. dia., mouth $\frac{5}{16}$ in. high, and $\frac{2}{7}$ circumference.
10. Posaune, 16 ft. c⁰, is 4 in. dia. at top.
11. Posaune, 8 ft. c⁰, is $4\frac{1}{2}$ in. dia. at top.
12. Octave Coupler to 1, 2, 6, 8, 9. Pneumatic levers to this manual.
13. Octave Coupler to 3, 4, 5, 10, 11. The idea of a divided octave coupler is a good one, and gives great increase in flexibility. There is, of course, an extra octave of pipes to complete the range.

SWELL.

1. Bourdon, 16 ft. C₁, 5 in. by $3\frac{3}{8}$ in., mouth $3\frac{3}{4}$ in.
2. Open, 8 ft. C₀, $4\frac{5}{8}$ in. by $3\frac{3}{8}$ in., mouth 1 in. with bridges; c⁰, $3\frac{1}{8}$ in. dia., mouth $\frac{3}{4}$ in., and $\frac{2}{9}$ circumference.
3. Gedackt, 8 ft. C₀, 3 in. by $2\frac{1}{4}$ in., mouth $2\frac{1}{4}$ in.; c¹, $1\frac{5}{16}$ in. dia., mouth $\frac{5}{8}$ in., and $\frac{1}{4}$ circumference.
4. Salicional, 8 ft. C₀, $3\frac{1}{4}$ in. dia., mouth $\frac{1}{4}$ in. high, and $\frac{1}{7}$ circumference.
5. Principal, 4 ft. c⁰, $2\frac{7}{8}$ in. dia., mouth $\frac{5}{8}$ in., and $\frac{2}{7}$ circumference.
6. Harmonic Flute, 4 ft. c⁰, $2\frac{7}{8}$ in. dia., mouth $\frac{7}{8}$ in., and $\frac{1}{4}$ circumference.
7. Mixture III. ranks, c¹, $1\frac{5}{8}$ in. dia., mouth $\frac{7}{16}$ in., and $\frac{2}{7}$ circumference.
8. Cornopean, 8 ft. c⁰, 4 in. dia. at top.
9. Oboe, 8 ft. c⁰, $2\frac{1}{4}$ in. dia. at top.

CHOIR.

1. Viola, 8 ft. C₀, $3\frac{1}{2}$ in. by $2\frac{5}{8}$ in., mouth $\frac{7}{8}$ in. with bridge; c⁰, 2 in. dia., mouth $\frac{1}{2}$ in., and $\frac{1}{4}$ circumference.
2. Dolce, 8 ft. c⁰, diameters are $2\frac{1}{4}$ in. below, $3\frac{1}{4}$ in. above, mouth $\frac{5}{8}$ in., and $\frac{1}{4}$ circumference.
3. Flute, 8 ft. c⁰, $2\frac{5}{10}$ in. dia., mouth $\frac{1}{2}$ in., and $\frac{1}{4}$ circumference.
4. Lieblich Gedackt, 8 ft. C₀, $3\frac{1}{4}$ in. by $2\frac{1}{4}$ in., mouth $1\frac{1}{2}$ in.; c¹, $1\frac{3}{16}$ in. dia., mouth $\frac{1}{2}$ in.
5. Viol d'Amour, 4 ft. c⁰, $2\frac{3}{10}$ in. dia., mouth $\frac{1}{2}$ in.
6. Lieblich Flute, 4 ft. same as the Gedackt.

PEDAL.

1. Major Bass, 16 ft. C₁, $10\frac{3}{4}$ in. by $8\frac{3}{8}$ in., mouth $2\frac{1}{4}$ in.
2. Violon Bass, 16 ft. C₁, $5\frac{3}{8}$ in. square, mouth 1 in. bare.
3. Sub Bass, 16 ft. C₁, 8 in. by $5\frac{1}{4}$ in., mouth 4 in.
4. Posaune, 16 ft. C₀, $6\frac{5}{8}$ in. dia.
5. Quint, same scale as Sub Bass.
   Wind, Pedal $3\frac{7}{8}$ in., Great and Swell $3\frac{1}{2}$ in., Choir $1\frac{7}{8}$ in.

There is another fine organ by Schultze at Armley, near Leeds, of which the list of stops is—

GREAT.

1. Sub Principal	.	.	. 16 ft.	7. Octave	.	.	. 4 ft.
2. Bourdon	.	.	. 16 ,,	8. Hohl Flute	.	.	. 4 ,,
3. Principal	.	.	. 8 ,,	9. Quint Mixture.			
4. Gemshorn	.	.	. 8 ,,	10. Full Mixture V. ranks.			
5. Hohl Flute	.	.	. 8 ,,	11. Tuba	.	.	. 16 ft.
6. Gedackt	.	.	. 8 ,,	12. Trumpet	.	.	. 8 ,,

Swell.

. Bourdon	16 ft.		7. Octave			4 ft.
2. Geigen	8 „		8. Travers Flute			4 „
3. Gamba	8 „		9. Cymbel IV. ranks			2⅔ „
4. Salicional	8 „		10. Horn			8 „
5. Travers Flute	8 „		11. Oboe			8 „
6. Lieblich Gedackt	8 „		12. Clarion			4 „

Choir.

1. Tibia Major	16 ft.		7. Octave			4 ft.
2. Principal	8 „		8. Piccolo			4 „
3. Violoncello	8 „		9. Lieblich Flute			4 „
4. Harmonika	8 „		10. Quint Mixture.			
5. Orchestral Flute	8 „		11. Clarinet			8 ft.
6. Lieblich Gedackt	8 „					

Echo.

1. Lieblich Bourdon	16 ft.		5. Dolcissimo			4 ft.
2. Dolcan	8 „		6. Echo Flute			4 „
3. Vox Angelica	8 „		7. Nazard			2⅔ „
4. Zart Flöte	8 „		8. Flautino			2 „

Pedal.

1. Principal Bass	16 ft.		6. Violoncello			8 ft.
2. Violon Bass	16 „		7. Flute			8 „
3. Sub Bass	16 „		8. Octave			4 „
4. Quint	10⅔ „		9. Posaune			16 „
5. Octave	8 „		10. Trumpet			8 „

Wind, Pedal, Great and Swell				3¼ in.
„ Choir „				2¼ „
„ Echo „				1½ „

451. The organ in Leeds Parish Church has an effect inferior to that of no English organ, though the individual stops are not all perfect examples of voicing. The Great is not Schultze at his best, for he simply put what he could into an old organ. The Swell is brilliant and effective.

Great.

1. Double Open Diapason	16 ft.		9. Fifteenth		2 ft.
2. Bourdon	16 „		10. Sequialtera III. ranks.		
3. Large Open Diapason	8 „		11. Full Mixture V. ranks.		
4. Small Open Diapason	8 „		12. Double Trumpet		16 ft.
5. Stopped Diapason	8 „		13. Trumpet		8 „
6. Harmonic Flute	4 „		14. Trombone		8 „
7. Octave	4 „		15. Clarion		4 „
8. Twelfth	2⅔ „				

All by Schultze, except the Double Open by Greenwood.

Swell.

1. Double Open Diapason (bottom octave stopped) .	16 ft.	9. Twelfth	2⅔ ft.
2. Open Diapason . . .	8 ,,	10. Fifteenth	2 ,,
3. Keraulophon . . ,	8 ,,	11. Piccolo . . .	2 ,,
4. Cone Gamba . . .	8 ,,	12. Full Mixture V. ranks.	
5. Salicional	8 ,,	13. Contra Fagotto . . .	16 ,,
6. Stopped Diapason . .	8 ,,	14. Horn	8 ,,
7. Octave	4 ,,	15. Trumpet . . .	8 ,,
8. Wald Flute	4 ,,	16. Oboe	8 ,,
		17. Clarion	4 ,,

All by Hill.

Choir.

1. Bourdon	16 ft.	6. Gedackt	8 ft.
2. Open Diapason .	8 ,,	7. Gemshorn	4 ,,
3. Dulciana c⁰ . . .	8 ,,	8. Gedackt	4 ,,
4. Travers Flute c⁰ . .	8 ,,	9. Octave Gamba . . .	4 ,,
5. Open Bass to B₂ . .	8 ,,	10. Clarionet	8 ,,

All except the last by Schultze.

Solo (1½ in. wind).

1. Lieblich Bourdon .	16 ft.	7. Flauto Dolce . . .	4 ft.
2. Open Diapason . .	1 ,,	8. Octave	4 ,,
3. Viola di Gamba c⁰ .	8 ,,	9. Lieblich Flute . .	4 ,,
4. Dolce	8 ,,	Mixture III. ranks.	
5. Lieblich Gedackt .	8 ,,	10. Salicet 8 ft.	to be added.
6. Flauto Travers c⁰ .	8 ,,	11. Terpodion 8 ,,	

Pedal.

1. Major Bass . . .	32 ft.	6. Flute	8 ft.
2. Open Bass . . .	16 ,,	7. Contra Posaune . .	32 ,,
3. Violon Bass . . .	16 ,,	8. Posaune	16 ,,
4. Bourdon . . .	16 ,,	9. Clarion . . .	8 ,,
5. Octave	8 ,,		

The Violon by Schultze, the rest by Greenwood and Hill.

Couplers.

Solo to Great.	Swell to Pedal.
Swell to Choir.	Great to Pedal.
Swell to Great.	Choir to Pedal.

The bellows are blown by a water engine with 6¼″ cylinder and from 6½″ to 10″ stroke, making at full speed 16 double strokes per minute and delivering about 1,200 c. ft. air. There are four sets of French feeders 5′ × 3′, two at each end of the engine.

The 32′ Posaune has a percussion arrangement to ensure prompt speech.

452. The organ in the new Ton-Halle, Düsseldorf, built

by Edmond Schultze in 1866, is a beautiful instrument. It contains:

GREAT.

1. Sub Principal	16 ft.	8. Harmonic Flute	4 ft.
2. Bourdon	16 ,,	9. Rausch Quint II. ranks.	
3. Major Principal	8 ,,	10. Mixture V. ranks.	
4. Minor Principal	8 ,,	11. Cymbel III. ranks.	
5. Hohl Flute	8 ,,	12. Tuba	16 ft.
6. Gedackt	8 ,,	13. Trumpet	8 ,,
7. Octave	4 ,,	14. Clarion	4 ,,

SWELL.

1. Lieblich Bourdon	16 ft.	6. Orchestra Flute	4 ft.
2. Geigen Principal	8 ,,	7. Quinte	2⅔ ,,
3. Gemshorn	8 ,,	8. Octave	2 ,,
4. Lieblich Gedackt	8 ,,	9. Clarinet c°	8 ,,
5. Fugara	4 ,,	10. Oboe	8 ,,

CHOIR.

1. Salicional	8 ft.	4. Viol d'Amour	4 ft.
2. Harmonika	8 ,,	5. Gedackt Flute	4 ,,
3. Still Gedackt	8 ,,		

LOUD PEDAL.

1. Principal Bass	16 ft.	7. Posaune	16 ft.
2. Violone	16 ,,	8. Trumpet	8 ,,
3. Sub Bass	16 ,,		
4. Octave Bass	8 ,,	**SOFT PEDAL.**	
5. Gedackt Bass	8 ,,	9. Bourdon	16 ft.
6. Octave	4 ,,	10. Flöten Bass	8 ,,

453. The organ in the Petrikirche, Soest, Westphalia, by J. F. Schultze & Sons, is a fine example of a German organ. A grand and powerful Great on the lowest manual, a softer organ of a singing tone on the second manual, and a beautifully soft and sweet Choir on the top manual, on a 1½″ wind. Every pipe has ample room, and can be taken out without disturbing any other, a fact which contributes much towards the beauty of tone of the instrument.

I. MANUAL.

1. Sub Principal	16 ft.	7. Octave	4 ft.
2. Bourdon	16 ,,	8. Rohr Flute	4 ,,
3. Major Principal	8 ,,	9. Rausch Quint II. ranks.	
4. Minor Principal	8 ,,	10. Cornet III. and IV. ranks.	
5. Hohl Flute	8 ,,	11. Trumpet	8 ft.
6. Gedackt	8 ,,		

II. MANUAL.

1. Bourdon	16 ft.	6. Fugara	4 ft.
2. Principal	8 ,,	7. Harmonic Flute	4 ,,
3. Viol da Gamba	8 ,,	8. Quinte	2⅔ ,,
4. Gemshorn	8 ,,	9. Octave	2 ,,
5. Flauto Amabile	1 ,,	10. Oboe	8 ,,

U

III. Manual.

1. Lieblich Bourdon . . 16 ft.	5. Lieblich Gedackt . . 8 ft.
2. Geigen . . . . 8 „	6. Viol d'Amour . . . 4 „
3. Dolce . . . . 8 „	7. Gedackt Flute . . . 4 „
4. Salicional . . . 8 „	8. Flautino (1½" wind) . . 2 „

Pedal.

1. Principal Bass . . 16 ft.	6. Violoncello . . . . 8 ft.
2. Violone . . . 16 „	7. Gedackt . . . . 8 „
3. Sub Bass . . . 16 „	8. Posaune . . . . 16 „
4. Quinten Bass . . 10⅔ „	9. Trumpet . . . . 8 „
5. Octave . . . 8 „	

Couplers.

III. to II. Manual.　|　II. to I. Manual.　|　I. Manual to Pedal.

454. The following sketch of an organ for Cologne Cathedral, by Edmond Schultze, will be interesting.

Great.

1. Untersatz . . . 32 ft.	12. Octave Minor . . . 4 ft.
2. Sub Principal . . 16 „	13. Harmonic Flute . . 4 „
3. Bourdon . . . 16 „	14. Rohr Flute . . . 4 „
4. Major Principal . . 8 „	15. Rausch Quint II. ranks.
5. Minor Principal . . 8 „	16. Mixture V. ranks.
6. Hohl Flute . . 8 „	17. Scharf III., IV., and V. ranks.
Triangular and Harmonic	18. Cornet III. and IV. ranks . 16 ft.
from c².	19. Tuba Harmonic . . 16 „
7. Gedackt . . . 8 ft.	20. Trumpet . . . 8 „
8. Gamba . . . 8 „	21. Horn . . . . 8 „
9. Spitz Flute . . 8 „	22. Clarion . . . 4 „
10. Gedackt Quint . . 5⅓ „	Flue Work 3¼" wind.
11. Octave Major . . 4 „	Reeds 6" „

Swell.

1. Bourdon . . . 16 ft.	10. Viol d'Amour . . . 4 ft.
2. Principal . . . 8 „	11. Harmonic Flute , . 4 „
3. Gemshorn . . . 8 „	12. Rausch Quint II. ranks.
4. Terpodion . . . 8 „	13. Mixture IV. ranks.
5. Harmonic Flute . . 8 „	14. Contra Fagotto . . . 16 ft.
6. Viola . . . . 8 „	15. Oboe . . . . 8 „
7. Voix Céleste c⁰ . . 8 „	16. Trompete . . . 8 „
8. Gedackt . . . 8 „	17. Clarin . . . 4 „
9. Octave . . . 4 „	3¼" wind.

Composition of Mixture.

C_2	. .	.	19,	22,	26,	29	c² . . .	8,	12,	15, 19
c⁰	. .	.	15,	19,	22,	26	c³ . . .	5,	8,	12, 15
c¹	. .	.	12,	15,	19,	22				

Choir.

1. Lieblich Bourdon . . 16 ft.	7. Octave . . . . 4 ft.
2. Geigen . . . 8 „	8. Gemshorn . . . 4 „
3. Salicional . . . 8 „	9. Gedackt Flute . . 4 „
4. Lieblich Gedackt . . 8 „	10. Piccolo . . . 2 „
5. Flauto Traverso . . 8 „	11. Mixture II. to IV. ranks.
6. Harmonika . . . 8 „	12. Clarinet . . . 8 ft.

2¾" wind.

COMPOSITION OF MIXTURES.

C₀ · · 12, 15 | c° · · 8, 12, 15 | c¹ · · 5, 8, 12, 15

ECHO.

1. Lieblich Bourdon	.	. 16 ft.	6. Flauto Dolce	.	.	. 8 ft.
2. Dulciana	. .	. 8 „	7. Dolcissimo	.	.	. 4 „
3. Dolce c°	. .	. 8 „	8. Celestina .	.	.	. 4 „
4. Zart Flute .	. .	. 8 „	9. Echo Flute	.	.	. 4 „
5. Vox Angelica	. .	. 8 „	10. Rausch Quint II. ranks.			

1½″ wind.

PEDAL.

1. Sub Principal	.	. 32 ft.	13. Flöten Bass	.	.	. 8 ft.
2. Major Bass	.	. 16 „	14. Gedackt .	.	.	. 8 „
3. Minor Bass	.	. 16 „	15. Quint	.	.	. 5⅓ „
4. Violone	.	. 16 „	16. Terz Gedackt .	.	.	. 6⅖ „
5. Sub Bass	.	. 16 „	17. Octave	.	.	. 4 „
6. Viol d'Amour	.	. 16 „	18. Bass Cornet IV. ranks	.	.	8 „
7. Lieblich Gedackt	.	. 16 „	19. Contra Posaune	.	.	32 „
8. Gedackt Quint .	.	. 10⅔ „	20. Posaune	.	.	. 16 „
9. Octave Major	.	. 8 „	21. Contra Fagotto .	.	.	16 „
10. Octave Minor	.	. 8 „	22. Trumpet .	.	.	. 8 „
11. Violoncello	.	. 8 „	23. Clarin	.	.	. 4 „
12. Viol d'Amour	.	. 8 „				

Flue Work and Fagotto, 3¾″ wind. Reeds, 6″. Compass, C₀ to c⁴.

455. The organ in Armley Church, near Leeds, is a splendid instrument, by Edmond Schultze of the following specification :

GREAT.

1. Sub Principal	.	. 16 ft.	7. Octave	.	.	. 4 ft.
2. Bourdon	.	. 16 „	8. Hohl Flute	.	.	. 4 „
3. Principal	.	. 8 „	9. Rausch Quint.			
4. Gemshorn .	.	. 8 „	10. Mixture V. ranks.			
5. Hohl Flute ⎫ grooved	.	. 8 „	11. Tuba ⎫ harmonic	.	.	. 16 ft.
6. Gedackt ⎭	.	. 8 „	12. Trumpet ⎭	.	.	. 8 „

SWELL.

1. Bourdon	.	. 16 ft.	7. Octave	.	.	. 4 ft.
2. Geigen ⎫ grooved	.	. 8 „	8. Flauto Traverso	.	.	. 4 „
			9. Cymbel IV. ranks.			
3. Gamba ⎭	.	. 8 „	10. Horn ⎫	.	.	. 8 ft.
4. Salicional .	.	. 8 „	11. Oboe ⎬ harmonic	.	.	. 8 „
5. Flauto Traverso ⎫ grooved	.	. 8 „	12. Clarin ⎭	.	.	. 4 „
6. Gedackt ⎭	.	. 8 „				

ECHO.

1. Lieblich Bourdon	.	. 16 ft.	7. Dolcissimo	.	.	. 4 ft.
2. Dolce .	.	. 8 „	8. Echo Flöte	.	.	. 4 „
3. Vox Angelica ⎫ grooved	.	. 8 „	9. Nasard	.	.	. 2⅔ „
			10. Flautino	.	.	. 2 „
4. Echo Oboe ⎭	.	. 8 „				
5. Zart Flöte ⎫ grooved	.	. 8 „				
6. Still Gedackt ⎭	.	. 8 „				

CHOIR.

1. Tibia Major.	16 ft.	7. Octave	4 ft.
2. Principal	8 „	8. Piccolo	4 „
3. Violone	8 „	9. Lieblich } grooved	
4. Harmonika.	8 „	Flöte	4 „
5. Orchester-Flöte } grooved	8 „	10. Progressio } II. to V. ranks.	
		Harmonika	
6. Lieblich Gedackt	8 „	11. Clarinet	8 ft.

PEDAL.

1. Principal Bass	16 ft.	6. Violoncello	8 ft.
2. Violone	16 „	9. Flöten Bass	8 „
3. Sub Bass	16 „	10. Octave	4 „
4. Quinten Bass	10¾ „	11. Posaune	16 „
5. Octave	8 „	12. Trumpet	8 „

Great, Swell and Pedal, 3¼″ wind. Choir, 2¾″. Echo, 1½″. All the reeds are harmonic in the upper octaves.

456. The large organ in the Protestant Cathedral at Cronstadt, in Transylvania, was built by Buckholtz of Berlin in 1839, at a cost of 5,000*l*. It contains:

GREAT.

1. Sub Principal	16 ft.	9. Spitz Flute	4 ft.
2. Quintatön.	16 „	10. Wald Flute	4 „
3. Principal.	8 „	11. Quint	2⅔ „
4. Gemshorn	8 „	12. Octave	2 „
5. Gamba	8 „	13. Cornetto V. ranks.	
6. Rohr Flute	8 „	14. Scharff V. ranks.	
7. Nasat	5⅓ „	15. Cymbel III. ranks.	
8. Octave	4 „		

CHOIR.

1. Salicional	16 ft.	7. Viol d'Amour	4 ft.
2. Principal	8 „	8. Gemshorn	2⅔ „
3. Gamba	8 „	9. Octave	2 „
4. Travers Flute	8 „	10. Progressio } III.	
5. Flute	8 „	} & ranks.	
6. Octave	4 „	Harmonika } IV.	

SWELL.

1. Bourdon	16 ft.	8. Fugara	4 ft.
2. Principal	8 „	9. Rohr Flute	4 „
3. Salicional	8 „	10. Nasat	2⅔ „
4. Flute	8 „	11. Octave	2 „
5. Quintatön	8 „	12. Mixture V. ranks.	
6. Hohl Flute	8 „	13. Oboe.	8 ft.
7. Octave	4 „		

REED MANUAL.

1. Fagotto	16 ft.	5. Violino	8 ft.
2. Trumpet	8 „	6. Rohr Flute	8 „
3. Clarinet	8 „	7. Octave	4 „
4. Vox Angelica	8 „		

PEDAL.

1. Contra Principal	32 ft.	10. Gemshorn	8 ft.
2. Contra Bass	32 „	11. Quint	$5\frac{1}{3}$ „
3. Principal	16 „	12. Octave	4 „
4. Violone	16 „	13. Cornetto	4 „
5. Sub Bass	16 „	14. Mixture IV. ranks.	
6. Nasat	$10\frac{2}{3}$ „	15. Contra Posaune	32 ft.
7. Octave	8 „	16. Posaune	16 „
8. Violone	8 „	17. Trumpet	8 „
9. Bass Flute	8 „		

457. The organ in Notre-Dame, Paris, by Cavaillé-Coll in 1868, contains the following stops :

GRAND CHŒUR (1st Manual).

1. Principal	8 ft.	7. Larigot	$1\frac{1}{3}$ ft.
2. Bourdon	8 „	8. Septième	$1\frac{1}{7}$ „
3. Prestant	4 „	9. Piccolo	1 „
4. Quinte	$2\frac{2}{3}$ „	*10. Tuba Magna	16 „
5. Doublette	2 „	*11. Trompette	8 „
6. Tierce	$1\frac{3}{5}$ „	*12. Clairon	4 „

GRAND ORGUE (2nd Manual).

1. Violon Basse	16 ft.	8. Prestant	4 ft.
2. Bourdon	16 „	*9. Doublette	2 „
3. Montre	8 „	*10. Fourniture II. to V. ranks.	
4. Viol da Gamba	8 „	*11. Cymbale II. to V. ranks.	
5. Flûte Harmonique	8 „	*12. Basson	16 ft.
6. Bourdon	8 „	13. Hautbois	8 „
*7. Octave	4 „	14. Clairon	4 „

BOMBARDES (3rd Manual).

1. Principal Bass	16 ft.	*8. Quinte	$2\frac{2}{3}$ ft.
2. Sous Basse	16 „	*9. Septième	$2\frac{2}{7}$ „
3. Principal	8 „	*10. Doublette	2 „
4. Flûte Harmonique	8 „	*11. Cornet II. to V. ranks.	
5. Grosse Quinte	$5\frac{1}{3}$ „	*12. Bombarde	16 ft.
6. Octave	4 „	*13. Trompette	8 „
*7. Grosse Tierce	$3\frac{1}{5}$ „	*14. Clairon	4 „

POSITIF (4th Manual).

1. Montre	16 ft.	*8. Flûte Douce	4 ft.
2. Bourdon	16 „	*9. Doublette	2 „
3. Salicional	8 „	*10. Piccolo	1 „
4. Unda Maris	8 „	*11. Plein-jeu III. to VI. ranks.	
5. Flûte Harmonique	8 „	*12. Clarinet Basse	16 ft
6. Bourdon	8 „	*13. Cromorne	8 „
7. Prestant	4 „	*14. Clarinette aigüe	4 „

RÉCIT EXPRESSIF (5th Manual).

1. Quintatön	16 ft.	*9. Octave	2 ft.
2. Viole de Gamba	8 „	*10. Cornet III. to V. ranks.	
3. Voix Céleste	8 „	*11. Bombarde	16 ft.
*4. Flûte Harmonique	8 „	*12. Trompette	8 „
5. Quintatön	8 „	13. Hautbois	8 „
6. Dulciana	4 „	14. Clarinette	8 „
*7. Flûte Octaviante	4 „	15. Voix Humaine	8 „
*8. Quinte	$2\frac{2}{3}$ „	*16. Clairon	4 „

PEDALIER.

1. Principal Basse	.	.	32 ft.	*9. Septième	.	.	.	4⅔ ft.
2. Contre Basse	.	.	16 „	10. Octave	.	.	.	4 „
3. Sous Basse	.	.	16 „	*11. Contra Bombarde	.	.	32 „
4. Grosse Quinte	.	.	10⅔ „	*12. Bombarde	.	.	.	16 „
5. Violoncelle	.	.	8 „	*13. Basson	.	.	.	16 „
6. Flûte	.	.	8 „	*14. Trompette	.	.	.	8 „
7. Grosse Tierce	.	.	6⅖ „	*15. Basson	.	.	.	8 „
*8. Quinte	.	.	5⅓ „	*16. Clairon	.	.	.	4 „

Pédales d'accouplement et de combinaison.

Accouplements d'octaves graves.

_____

Anches et tirasses de Pédalier.
Anches Pédales.
Tirasse Grand Orgue.
Tirasse Grand Chœur.
Effets d'Orage.

_____

Récit expressif.
Positif.
Bombardes.
Grand Orgue.
Grand Chœur.

Appel des jeux de combinaison.

Accouplements sur e 1ᵉʳ clavie collectif.

The jeux de combinaison are those marked *.
Tutti collectiv.
Récit expressif.
Positif.
Bombardes.
Grand Orgue.
Grand Chœur.

_____

Expression.
Tremolo.
Récit expressif.
Positif.
Bombardes.
Grand Orgue.
Grand Chœur.

The arrangements of this organ are in a peculiar taste. There does not appear to be sufficient reason to justify the use of five manuals, and the extent to which what are really single ranks of Mixture are used as separate draw-stops is extraordinary. The sevenths in the Mixtures are a matter of taste. The pedal for 'effets d'orage' seems scarcely necessary, as, when desired, such an effect can be produced by sitting down on the keys.

458. The organ in the Protestant Church, Mulhausen, was built in 1866 by Walcker.

I. MANUAL.

1. Principal	.	.	16 ft.	12. Flûte d'Amour	.	.	4 ft.
2. Flauto Major	.	.	16 „	13. Terz	.	.	.	3⅕ „
3. Montre	.	.	8 „	14. Nasard	.	.	.	2⅔ „
4. Gemshorn	.	.	8 „	15. Doublette	.	.	2 „
5. Viole da Gamba	.	.	8 „	16. Furniture VI. ranks.
6. Hohl Flote	.	.	8 „	17. Scharff I. to III. ranks.
7. Bourdon	.	.	8 „	18. Cornet V. ranks.
8. Quintatön	.	.	8 „	19. Fagott	.	.	16 ft.
9. Nasard	.	.	5½ „	20. Trompette	.	.	8 „
10. Prestant	.	.	4 „	21. Clairon	.	.	.	4 „
11. Rohr-Flöte	.	.	4 „				

II. Manual.

1. Bourdon .	.	.	. 16 ft.	8. Spitz-Flöte	.	.	. 4 ft.
2. Montre .	.	.	. 8 „	9. Rohr-Flöte .	.	.	. 4 „
3. Salicional	.	.	. 8 „	10. Furniture V. ranks.			
4. Biffara .	.	.	. 8 „	11. Sifflöte	.	.	. 2 ft.
5. Bourdon .	.	.	. 8 „	12. Oboe .	.	.	. 8 „
6. Nasard .	.	.	. 5⅓ „	13. Corno .	.	.	. 4 „
7. Prestant .	.	.	. 4 „				

III. Manual (Swell).

1. Principal	.	.	. 8 ft.	7. Nazard	.	.	. 2⅔ ft.
2. Concert Flöte	.	.	. 8 „	8. Flageolet .	.	.	. 2 „
3. Bourdon	.	.	. 8 „	9. Basset Horn	.	.	. 8 „
4. Fugara	.	.	. 4 „	10. Æoline	.	.	. 8 „
5. Dolce .	.	.	. 4 „	11. Physharmonika	.	.	. 8 „
6. Travers Flöte	.	.	. 4 „				

Pedal.

1. Grand Bourdon	.	.	. 32 ft.	9. Bourdon .	.	.	. 8 ft.
2. Principal Bass	.	.	. 16 „	10. Terz	.	.	. 6⅖ „
3. Violon Bass	.	.	. 16 „	11. Octave	.	.	. 4 „
4. Sub Bass	.	.	. 16 „	12. Flöte	.	.	. 2 „
5. Quint Bass	.	.	. 10⅔ „	13. Bombardon	.	.	. 16 „
6. Octave Bass	.	.	. 8 „	14. Trompette	.	.	. 8 „
7. Violoncello	.	.	. 8 „	15. Clairon .	.	.	. 4 „
8. Hohl-Flöten Bass	.	.	. 8 „				

459. The organ in the Stifts- und Pfarr-Kirche, St. Leodegar, Lucerne, was built by Herr Haas in 1862.

I. Manual.

1. Principal	.	.	. 16 ft.	10. Gamba .	.	.	. 4 ft.
2. Bourdon .	.	.	. 16 „	11. Gemshorn	.	.	. 4 „
3. Principál .	.	.	. 8 „	12. Hohl-Flöte	.	.	. 4 „
4. Gemshorn	.	.	. 8 „	13. Gemster .	.	.	. 3⅓ „
5. Viol da Gamba	.	.	. 8 „	14. Quint	.	.	. 2⅔ „
6. Flöte	.	.	. 8 „	15. Wald-Flöte	.	.	. 2 „
7. Bourdon .	.	.	. 8 „	16. Mixture V. ranks.			
8. Quint Flöte	.	.	. 5⅓ „	17. Scharf V. ranks.			
9. Octave .	.	.	. 4 „	18. Octave	.	.	. 1 ft.

II. Manual.

1. Bourdon .	.	.	. 16 ft.	7. Octave	.	.	. 4 ft.
2. Principal	.	.	. 8 „	8. Flauto Traverso	.	.	. 4 „
3. Salicional	.	.	. 8 „	9. Klein Gedackt	.	.	. 4 „
4. Viol d'Amour .	.	.	. 8 „	10. Quint	.	.	. 2⅔ „
5. Bourdon .	.	.	. 8 „	11. Octave	.	.	. 2 „
6. Quintadena	.	.	. 8 „	12. Mixture V. ranks.			

III. Manual.

1. Lieblich Gedackt	.	.	. 16 ft.	7. Flûte d'Amour	.	.	. 4 ft.
2. Dolce	.	.	. 8 „	8. Quinte	.	.	. 2⅔ „
3. Salicet .	.	.	. 8 „	9. Flautino .	.	.	. 2 „
4. Harmonika	.	.	. 8 „	10. Englisch-Horn	.	.	. 8 „
5. Lieblich Gedackt	.	.	. 8 „	11. Physharmonika	.	.	. 8 „
6. Dolcissimo	.	.	. 4 „	12. Vox Angelica .	.	.	. 8 „

IV. MANUAL.

1. Quintadena . . . 16 ft.	6. Spitz-Flöte . . . 4 ft
2. Principal . . . 8 „	7. Quint . . . . 2⅔ „
3. Spitz-Flöte . . . 8 „	8. Octave . . . . 2 „
4. Bourdon . . . . 8 „	9. Trompette . . . 8 „
5. Octave . . . . 4 „	10. Vox Humana . . . 8 „

PEDAL.

1. Principal Bass . . 32 ft.	8. Flöte . . . . 8 ft.
2. Octave Bass . . . 16 „	9. Quint . . . . 5⅓ „
3. Violon Bass . . . 16 „	10. Octave . . . . 4 „
4. Sub Bass . . . 16 „	11. Tuba . . . . 16 „
5. Quint . . . 10⅔ „	12. Fagot . . . . 16 „
6. Octave . . . . 8 „	13. Trompette . . . 8 „
7. Violoncello . . . 8 „	14. Clarino . . . . 4 „

COUPLERS.

1. I. to II. Manual.	6. Collectiv Zug. I. Manual.
2. II. to III. Manual.	7. Collectiv Zug. II. Manual.
3. III. to IV. Manual.	8. Collectiv Zug. Pedal.
4. I. Manual to Pedal.	9. Tremulant to III. Manual.
5. II. Manual to Pedal.	10. Tremulant to IV. Manual.

A foot crescendo wheel to Physharmonika and to III. and IV. Manual.

460. The following specifications are taken from Töpfer. A small organ at Flensburg, by Marcussen & Sohn, Apenrade. Both manuals have a joint soundboard, and the organ is mentioned as being a very good one.

I. MANUAL.

1. Bourdon . . . . 16 ft.	3. Rohr-Flöte . . . 8 ft.
2. Gamba . . . . 8 „	4. Gambette . . . . 4 „

II. MANUAL.

1. Flute . . . . 8 ft.	4. Physharmonika (free reed
2. Fugara (grooved into 1) . 8 „	with a swell)
3. Flute . . . . 4 „	

PEDAL.

1. Sub Bass (from the Bourdon) 16 ft.	3. Gedackt (from Rohr-Flöte) 8 ft.
2. Violoncello (from Gamba) . 8 „	4. Fagotto (free reeds) . . 16 „

461. The organ in the Johanniskirche at Wernigerode was built in 1885 by Ladegast, as follows:

I. MANUAL.

1. Principal . . . 16 ft.	7. Gemshorn . . . 4 ft.
2. Bourdon . . . . 16 „	8. III. rank Cornet.
3. Principal . . . 8 „	9. Rausch Quint.
4. Doppel-Flöte . . . 8 „	10. IV. rank Mixture.
5. Bordunal-Flöte . . . 8 „	11. Trumpet . . . . 8 ft.
6. Gamba . . . . 8 „	

II. MANUAL.

1. Quintadena	. 16 ft.	6. Octave	. 4 ft.
2. Flauto	. 8 „	7. Flauto Minor	. 4 „
3. Salicional	. 8 „	8. Progressio-Harmonika II.	
4. Geigen Principal	. 8 „	to IV. ranks.	
5. Rohr-Flöte	. 8 „	9. Clarinet (free reeds).	

III. MANUAL.

1. Lieblich Gedackt	. 8 ft.	3. Flauto Traverso	. 8 ft.
2. Viol d'Amour	. 8 „	4. Octave Flöte	. 4 „

PEDAL.

1. Principal Bass	. 16 ft.	6. Octave	. 8 ft.
2. Violon	. 16 „	7. Quint	. 5⅓ „
3. Sub Bass	. 16 „	8. Octave	. 4 „
4. Bass Flöte	. 8 „	9. Posaune	. 16 „
5. Cello	. 8 „		

462. The Cathedral organ at Schwerin was built in 1871 by Ladegast.

I. MANUAL.

1st Division.

1. Principal	. 16 ft.	12. Trumpet	. 8 ft.
2. Principal	. 8 „	
3. Octave	. 4 „	*2nd Division.*
4. Third and Seventh.		13. Bourdon	. 32 ft.
5. Spitz-Flöte	. 4 ft.	14. Bourdon	. 16 „
6. Quint	. 2⅔ „	15. Gemshorn	. 8 „
7. Octave	. 2 „	16. Gamba	. 8 „
8. Mixture IV. ranks.		17. Doppel-Gedackt	. 8 „
9. Cymbel III. ranks.		18. Flauto Major	. 8 „
10.⎫ Cornet III. to IV. ranks.		19. Rohr-Quinte	. 5⅓ „
11.⎭		20. Rohr-Flöte	. 4 „
		21. Trombone	. 16 „

II. MANUAL.

1st Division.

1. Principal	. 16 ft.	9. Principal	. 4 ft.
2. Piffaro	. 8 „	10. Scharff IV. ranks.
3. Flautino	. 4 „	
4. Quintadena	. 4 „	*2nd Division.*
5. Gemshorn-Quinte	. 2⅔ „	11. Quintadena	. 16 ft.
6. Octave	. 2 „	12. Quintadena	. 8 „
7. Cornet III. ranks.		13. Bordunal Flöte	. 8 „
6. Progressio-Harmonika		14. Rohr-Flöte	. 8 „
III. to IV. ranks.		15. Fugara	. 8 „
7. Oboe	. 8 ft.	16. Flauto	. 4 „
8. Principal	. 8 „	17. Fagotto	. 16 „

III. MANUAL.

1. Lieblich Bordun	. 8 ft.	8. Gedackt	. 4 ft.
2. Geigen Principal	. 8 „	9. Quint-Flöte	. 2⅔ „
3. Doppel Flöte	. 8 „	10. Piccolo	. 2 „
4. Flauto Traversa	. 8 „	11. Progressio-Harmonika II.	
5. Salicional	. 8 „	to IV. ranks.	
6. Fugara	. 4 „	12. Clarinet	. 8 „
7. Piffaro	. 4 „		

IV. MANUAL.

1. Viola	16 ft.		7. Salicional	4 ft.
2. Zart Flöte	8 „		8. Flauto	2 „
3. Lieblich Gedackt	8 „		9. Harmonica-Ætheria II. to	
4. Viola d'Amour	8 „		IV. ranks.	
5. Unda Maris	8 „		10. Æoline	16 ft.
6. Flauto Dolce	4 „			

PEDAL.

1st Division.

1. Untersatz	32 ft.		12. Quinte	5⅓ ft.
2. Violon	32 „		13. Octave	4 „
3. Oktav Bass	16 „		14. Cornet IV. ranks.	
4. Violon	16 „		15. Trumpet	8 ft.
5. Posaune	32 „		16. Trumpet	4 „
6. Posaune	16 „			

2nd Division.

3rd Division.

			1. Salicet Bass	16 „
7. Principal	16 „		2. Sub Bass	16 „
8. Terz Gedackt	12⅖ „		3. Flöten Bass	8 „
9. Quinte	10⅔ „		4. Gamben Bass	8 „
10. Principal	8 „		5. Oktav Flöte	4 „
11. Cello	8 „		6. Dulcian	16 „

ACCESSORIES AND COUPLERS.

1 and 2. Cres. and Dim.	17 and 18. Free combinations of III.
3. Tremulant.	Manual and Pedal.
4 to 7. Manual Couplers.	19. Ventil to Parts I. and II. of Pedal.
8. Bellows Call.	20 and 21. Cres. and Dim. to Haupt-
9. Wind Indicator.	werk.
10 and 11. Ventils to Part I. and III.	22. Echowerk of IV. Manual.
Pedal.	23. Free combination of IV. Manual.
12. Pedal Coupler.	24. Ventil to IV. Manual.
13 and 14. Ventils to Parts of I.	25. Free combination of II. Manual.
Manual.	26 and 27. Ventil to both parts of
15. Free combinations.	II. Manual.
16. Ventil to III. Manual.	

463. The organ of the Peterskirche in Leipzig was built by Sauer in 1885.

I. MANUAL.

1. Principal	16 ft.		10. Rohr Flute	4 ft.
2. Bourdon	16 „		11. Gemshorn	4 „
3. Principal	8 „		12. Quint	2⅔ „
4. Flûte Harmonique	8 „		13. Octave	2 „
5. Gamba	8 „		14. Mixture III. ranks.	
6. Gedackt	8 „		15. Scharff V. ranks.	
7. Gemshorn	8 „		16. Cornet II. to V. ranks.	
8. Nasat	5⅓ „		17. Bombarde	16 ft.
9. Octave	4 „		18. Trompette	8 „

II. MANUAL.

1. Salicional	16 ft.		8. Octave	4 ft.
2. Gedackt	16 „		9. Flauto Dolce	4 „
3. Principal	8 „		10. Quint	2⅔ „
4. Rohr-Flöte	8 „		11. Octave	2 „
5. Harmonika	8 „		12. Mixture IV. ranks.	
6. Quintadena	8 „		13. Cornet III. ranks.	
7. Salicional	8 „		14. Clarinet	8 ft.

III. Manual.

1. Viol di Gamba	. . . 16 ft.	7. Travers Flöte . . .	4 ft.
2. Lieblich Gedackt	. . 16 „	8. Fugara . . .	4 „
3. Principal .	. . . 8 „	9. Quinte . . .	2⅔ „
4. Concert Flöte	. . . 8 „	10. Flautino . . .	2 „
5. Gedackt .	. . . 8 „	11. Æoline . . .	8 „
6. Voix Céleste	. . . 8 „	12. Vox Humana . . .	8 „

Pedal.

1. Major Bass	. . . 32 ft.	9. Bass Flöte . . .	8 ft.
2. Principal .	. . . 16 „	10. Dulciana . . .	8 „
3. Violon . .ᶜ . . 16 „		11. Quintadena . . .	8 „
4. Sub Bass .	. . . 16 „	12. Octave . . .	4 „
5. Gedackt Bass	. . . 16 „	13. Posaune . . .	16 „
6. Gross Nasat	. . . 10⅔ „	14. Fagott . . .	16 „
7. Principal .	. . . 8 „	15. Trompette . . .	8 „
8. Violoncello	. . . 8 „	16. Clairino . . .	4 „

464. The organ of Grace Church, New York, was built by Roosevelt in 1878, and the different organs are put in different parts of the church.

I. Manual.

Great Organ.

1. Double Open Diapason .	16 ft.	13. Trumpet . . .	8 ft.
2. Open Diapason	. . 8 „	14. Clarion . . .	4 „
3. Gemshorn	. . 8 „	In the Gallery.	
4. Principal Flute	. . 8 „	15. Open Diapason . .	8 ft.
5. Doppel Flute .	. . 8 „	16. Keraulophon . . .	8 „
6. Octave .	. . 4 „	17. Gedackt . . .	8 „
7. Wald Flute	. . 4 „	18. Principal . . .	4 „
8. Twelfth .	. . 2⅔ „	19. Twelfth . . .	2⅔ „
9. Fifteenth	. . 2 „	20. Fifteenth . . .	2 „
10. Cornet IV. to V. ranks.		21. Cornet III. ranks.	
11. Mixture IV. ranks.		22. Trumpet . . .	8 ft.
12. Ophicleide	. . . 16 ft.	23. Clarion . . .	4 „

II. Manual.

Swell.

1. Bourdon .	. . 16 ft.	12. Oboe . . .	8 ft.
2. Open Diapason	. . 8 „	In the Gallery.	
3. Salicional	. . 8 „	13. Double Diapason . .	16 ft.
4. Gedackt .	. . 8 „	14. Open Diapason . .	8 „
5. Quintadena	. . 8 „	15. Dulciana . . .	8 „
6. Octave .	. . 4 „	16. Gedackt . . .	8 „
7. Harmonic Flute	. . 4 „	17. Principal . . .	4 „
8. Flageolet .	. . 2 „	18. Cornet III. ranks.	
9. Cornet III. to IV. ranks.		19. Trumpet . . .	8 ft.
10. Contra Fagotto	. . 16 ft.	20. Oboe . . .	8 „
11. Cornopean	. . 8 „		

III. Manual.

Choir.

1. Open Diapason	8 ft.	9. Octave	4 ft.
2. Gamba	8 „	10. Flute	4 „
3. Dulciana	8 „	11. Rohr Flute	4 „
4. Concert Flute	8 „	12. Piccolo	2 „
5. Viol d'Amour	8 „	13. Fifteenth	2 „
6. Dulciana	8 „	14. Euphonium (free reed)	16 „
7. Gedackt	8 „	15. Clarinet	8 „
8. Principal	4 „	16. Cremona	8 „

Echo.

1. Quintadena	8 ft.	2. Vox Humana	8 ft.

Pedal.

1. Harmonic Bass (a 16 ft. and 10⅔ ft.)	32 ft.	6. Flute	8 ft.
2. Open Diapason	16 „	7. Superoctave	8 „
3. Gamba	16 „	8. Trombone	16 „
4. Bourdon	16 „	In the Gallery.	
5. Violoncello	8 „	9. Open Diapason	16 ft.
		10. Glocken Gamba	16 „

465. A very large organ was built for Cincinnati by Hook & Hastings, of Boston. The case is peculiar and very effective. The specification is as follows:

I. Manual.

Great.

1. Open Diapason	16 ft.	12. Harmonic Flute	4 ft.
2. Quintadena	16 „	13. Gambette	4 „
3. Bell Diapason	8 „	14. Twelfth.	
4. Open Diapason	8 „	15. Fifteenth.	
5. Gamba	8 „	16. Cornet V. ranks.	
6. Doppel Flute	8 „	17. Mixture IV. ranks.	
7. Clarabella	8 „	18. Acuta IV. ranks.	
8. Gemshorn	8 „	19. Cymbel VII. ranks.	
9. Viol d'Amour (with bells)	8 „	20. Bombarde	16 ft.
10. Quint	5⅓ „	21. Trumpet	8 „
11. Octave	4 „	22. Clarion	4 „

II. Manual.

Swell.

1. Bourdon	16 ft.	10. Violina	4 ft.
2. Open Diapason	8 „	11. Nasard	2⅔ „
3. Salicional	8 „	12. Flautino	2 „
4. Spitz Flute	8 „	13. Mixture V. ranks.	
5. Gedackt	8 „	14. Dolce Cornet VI. ranks.	
6. Quintadena	8 „	15. Contra Fagotto	16 ft.
7. Æoline (small scale flue pipes)	8 „	16. Cornopean	8 „
		17. Oboe	8 „
8. Octave	4 „	18. Vox Humana	8 „
9. Flauto Traverso	4 „	19. Clarion	4 „

III. Manual.

Choir.

1. Lieblich Gedackt	. 16 ft.	10. Violine	. 4 ft.
2. Open Diapason .	. 8 ,,	11. Harmonic Flute	. 4 ,,
8. Geigen Principal	. 8 ,,	12. Quint Flute	. 2⅔ ,,
4. Viola .	. 8 ,,	13. Piccolo	. 2 ,,
5. Rohr Flute	. 8 ,,	14. Cornet V. ranks.	
6. Melodia (wood).	. 8 ,,	15. Cor Anglais	. 16 ft.
7. Dulciana .	. 8 ,,	16. Clarinet .	. 8 ,,
8. Octave	. 4 ,,	17. Vox Angelica (free reed).	8 ,,
9. Fugara	. 4 ,,		

IV. Manual.

Solo.

1. Stentorphone (a large flute, heavily blown ; some think the tone majestic, others call it vulgar) .	8 ft.	4. Hohl Flute	. 4 ft.
		5. Harmonic Piccolo	. 2 ,,
		6. Tuba Mirabilis .	. 8 ,,
2. Keraulophon .	8 ,,	7. Clarion (steel rods, struck by hammers)	. 4 ,,
3. Philomela (a Doppel flute)	8 ,,		

Pedal.

1. Open Diapason .	. 32 ft.	10. Flute	. 8 ft.
2. Open Diapason .	. 16 ,,	11. Superoctave .	. 4 ,,
3. Violone .	. 16 ,,	12. Cornet V. ranks	
4. Dulciana .	. 16 ,,	13. Contra Bombarde .	. 32 ft.
5. Bourdon .	. 16 ,,	(free reeds, very powerful)	
6. Quinte .	. 10⅔ ,,	14. Trombone	. 16 ,,
7. Bell Gamba	. 8 ,,	15. Posaune .	. 8 ,,
8. Octave .	. 8 ,,	16. Clarion .	. 4 ,,
9. Violoncello .	. 8 ,,		

Couplers, &c.

1. Stop Valve to Great.	9. Coupler II. to Pedal.
2. Coupler II. to I.	10. Coupler III. to Pedal.
3. Coupler IV. to I.	11. Coupler IV. to Pedal.
4. Coupler III. to I.	12. Octave Coupler to IV.
5. Coupler to Lower Octave.	13. Tremolo to II.
6. Stop Valve to Pedal Combination.	14. Tremolo to III.
7. Coupler II. to III.	15. Wind.
8. Coupler I. to Pedal.	

Composition Pedals.

1. Grand Crescendo.	9. III. Manual Forte.
2. Full Organ.	10. III. Manual Piano.
3. I. Manual Forte.	11. Repeating Pedal to the Great Pedal Coupler.
4. I. Manual Mezzo.	
5. I. Manual Piano.	12. Swell Tremolo.
6. II. Manual Forte.	13. Choir Tremolo.
7. II. Manual Mezzo.	14. Swell Pedal.
8. II. Manual Piano.	

466. Töpfer gives several details for organs of various sizes, which are interesting as a sample of sound organ tone

for school or church work, but by no means for a chamber organ. The first is for the smallest organ, and has :

1. Principal, 8 ft., tone of medium strength and musical. C_o 4½ in. diameter, mouth cut up ⅔ of the diameter.
2. Gedackt, 8 ft., of full and thick tone, $C_o = 4$ in. square.
3. Octave, 4 ft., same scale as Principal.
4. Hohl Flute, 4 ft. c^o, 5 in. by 2½ in.
5. If a sharpening stop is wanted, use a Cornet of the following composition :

> C_o has c^1.
> c^o has g^1, c^2.
> c^1 has g^2, c^2, e^2.
> Or a Mixture as follows :
> C_o has c^1, g^1, c^2.
> c^2 has c^2, g^2, c^4.
> For the Pedal a sub bass of medium scale.

The leading dimensions of such an organ are given as :

Depth of grooves 3½ in., length pallets 8·3 in., width grooves $C_o - 0·95$ in., $c^o = 0·75$ in., $c^1 = 0·6$ in., $c^2 = 0·5$ in., $c^3 = 0·4$ in., and the maximum rise 0·37 in.

The soundboard is apportioned thus :

Frame	.	.	.	.	.	1·9 in.	Flute .	. . . .	1·6 in.
Principal	.	.	.	.	1·9 „	Bearer .	. . .	2·4 „
Bearer .	.	.	.	.	0·9 „	Mixture	. . .	1·9 „
Gedackt	.	.	.	.	1·9 „	Frame .	. . .	1·9 „
Bearer .	.	.	.	.	1·4 „			
Octave .	.	.	.	.	1·6 „	Total	. .	19·8 „
Bearer .	.	.	.	.	2·4 „			

And the length of soundboard to be built in two halves, each of 5·3 ft. Wind trunk 31 square inches. The foundation stops would have to be very full and the Mixture rather soft to prevent the tone getting top-heavy, and the writer would much prefer to add a Gamba instead, voiced rather soft.

467. Another specification is for an organ of the same class, but with two manuals and pedal.

I. MANUAL.

1. Bourdon, 16 ft., tone full, $C_1 = 6·3$ in. square.
2. Principal, 8 ft., tone full and strong, $C_o = 5¼$ in. diameter, mouth cut up ¼ to ⅖ of diameter, according as fulness or sweetness is most desired.
3. Gamba, 8 ft., tone medium strength and stringy, $C_o - 3·4$ in. diameter, height of mouth 0·83 in.
4. Rohr Flute, 8 ft., tone medium strength and fulness, $C_o = 4¾$ in. diameter.
5. Quint Flute, 5⅓ of wood, $G_o = 3·7$ in. square; mouth arched from ¼ to ⅓ the width.
6. Octave, 4 ft., as the Principal.
7. Rohr Flute, 4 ft., as No. 4.
8. Cornet III. ranks C_o has g^o,
> c^o has g^1, c^2.
> g^o has d^1, g^2, b^2.
9. Octave, 2 ft., same scale as No. 2.

10. Mixture IV. ranks C_0 has g^1, c^2, g^2, c^3.
 f_{0}^1 has c^2♯, f^2♯, c^3♯, f^3♯.
 f^1♯ has the same.

11. Trumpet, 8 ft.

II. Manual.

1. Quintatön, 16 ft., $C_1 = 4\frac{1}{2}$ in. diameter; mouth 1·4 in. high.
2. Geigen, 8 ft., $C_0 = 4\frac{1}{2}$ in. diameter; mouth 1 in. high.
3. Still Gedackt, 8 ft., $C_0 = 3·6$ in. square; mouth 1 in.
4. Dolce, 8 ft., C_0 has lower diameter, $3\frac{1}{2}$ in.; upper $5\frac{1}{4}$ in.
5. Flauto Amabile, 4 ft. of hard wood, $c^0 = 2$ in. square.
6. Octave, 4 ft., same scale as Geigen.
7. Clarinet, 8 ft.

Pedal.

1. Violon Bass, 16 ft., $C_1 = 6$ in. square; mouth $1\frac{1}{2}$ in. high.
2. Sub Bass, 16 ft., $C_1 = 7·9$ in. square; mouth 2·6 in. high.
3. Posaune, 16 ft.
4. Principal Bass, 8 ft. of wood, $C_1 = 7·1$ in. square.
5. Violon Bass, 8 ft., same scale as the 16 ft.
6. Gedackt Bass, 8 ft., same scale as the 16 ft.

To most tastes there would be too much mixture for the foundation on the I. manual. The leading dimensions prescribed are, 4·6″ depth of grooves and double grooves from c_0 to b^1, length of pallet 9·3″, rise 0·51″ and the following widths:

$C_0 = 0·9''$, $c^0 = 0·75''$, $c^1 = 0·55''$, all double. For $c^2 = 1''$, $c^3 = 0.87''$.

The soundboard to be in two halves, each 7′ 4″ × 2′ 6″.

The II. manual requires the following:

Length of opening 8″ widths, $C_0 = 0·9''$, $c^0 = 0·7''$, $c^1 = 0·55''$, $c^2 = 0·47''$ and pallet rise $\frac{1}{4}''$.

Each half of soundboard to be 5′ × 2′ 8″.

For the Pedal, the openings are 11″ long and breadth $C_1 = 1·6''$, $C_0 = 1·18''$, $c^0 = 0·94''$, and pallet rise $\frac{3}{4}''$. The size of each half of soundboard 7′ 10″ × 4′ 3″, but some of the pipes must have long feet, so that the others can speak through them unhindered. The size of trunks must be—I. Manual 9″ square, II. Manual $5\frac{3}{4}''$, Pedal $5\frac{1}{2}''$, and the main trunk $12\frac{1}{4}''$ square.

The total wind consumption is put at 8·88 c. ft. per second, for which Töpfer allows two feeders of $6\frac{1}{2}'$ × $3\frac{1}{4}'$, opening 1·21 at a maximum velocity of 30 strokes per minute, and a reser-

voir of 8¼' × 6½', rising 1·64', and designed to supply the full
organ 9 seconds. It will be observed, however, that he allows
much greater play, i.e., wider ribs than is usual in English
bellows, and that if these dimensions are restricted the areas
must be proportionately increased. Also 30 strokes per
minute is a very full allowance for feeder work, which the
writer would prefer to limit to 26.

As an alternative Töpfer proposes three diagonal bellows,
each of 9¼' × 4½', with a stroke of 1·8'.

468. He further gives the arrangement for a ventil soundboard, in the following way. The size of each chest is limited
by the following conditions : the area must be sufficient for the
maximum wind supply, and the width for the biggest valve
plus 0·2" clearance between valve and sides of chest. The
height of the chest is put at 8" and the necessary widths
at :

Bourdon .	.	. 16 ft.	8·0 in.	Octave .	. . 4 ft.	1·6 in.
Principal .	.	. 8 „	2·6 „	Octave .	. . 2 „	1·4 „
Gamba .	,	. 8 „	1·5 „	Cornet .	. . 2 „	1·7 „
Rohr Flöte	.	. 8 „	1·9 „	Mixture .	. . .	1·5 „
Quint Flöte	.	. 5⅓ „	1·5 „	Trumpet	. . .	2·6 „
Rohr Flöte	.	. 4 „	1·6 „			

For the widths of the partitions, the spacing of the pipes
alone has to be considered, but here the writer will remark,
that to make the chests a minimum possible and fill up the
standing room with wood or false grooves is not a desirable
arrangement ; the bigger the chests are the better, provided
they have an escape valve which opens when the stop is
closed.

469. In designing an organ the purpose for which it is
intended is a very important factor in the specification, as for
the same number of stops of a chamber, church or concert
organ, the selection and scaling would be different. The
smallest thing that can be called an organ, and used for a
chamber or school, must have two stops, as in Specification I.,
as follows :

1. Open, 8 ft. c^0, 2⅝ in. dia., Stopped Bass C_0, 3¾ in. by 3 in.
2. Octave one pipe smaller than above.

Specification II. is given by Rimbault, as having been used by Father Smith, as follows :

1. Gedackt 8 ft. C_0, $3\frac{3}{4}$ in. by 3 in.
2. Open from c^1, $1\frac{3}{8}$.
3. Octave same scale as No. 2 but $\frac{1}{4}$ mouth.

470. For a church or school organ where the building is on a larger scale than the available funds, the following Specification III. is the best :

1. Bourdon 16 ft. C_1, 6 in. by $4\frac{3}{4}$ in. c^0, $2\frac{3}{16}$ in. dia.
2. Open 8 ft. C_0, 5 in. dia., or 5 in. by 4 in. if of wood.
3. Salicional 8 ft. C_0, $3\frac{1}{4}$ in. dia., mouth $\frac{1}{4}$ circumference, or a Dolce.
4. Flute 4 ft. c^0, $2\frac{5}{8}$ in. dia.
5. Octave Coupler, the pipes being carried through to complete the range. Half measure on 17th pipe. Wind pressure, $2\frac{3}{4}$ in.

Here, by having the 16′ tone to start with, and completing the range of the octave coupler, the organ is practically equivalent to one of eight stops. The pedal can either take down the keys, or, better, use the Bourdon pipes by means of a separate pallet.

But for a chamber or chancel organ the same number of stops would be better disposed thus—Specification IV. :

1. Open 8 ft. C_0, $4\frac{1}{4}$ in. dia., mouth $\frac{1}{4}$ circumference.
2. Salicional 8 ft. C_0, $3\frac{3}{8}$ dia., mouth $\frac{1}{5}$.
3. Flute 4 ft. c^0 $2\frac{1}{4}$ in., $\frac{1}{4}$ mouth.

Pedal.—Sub Bass 16 ft. C_1, 5 in. by $3\frac{3}{8}$ in. Wind, $2\frac{1}{2}$ in.

471. But as a one-manual organ is a very poor thing, for the latter type of organ it would be better to add one more stop and thus make up Specification V. :

GREAT.	CHOIR.
1. Open 8 ft. C_0, $4\frac{1}{4}$ in. dia.	1. Geigen 8 ft. C_0, 4 in.
2. Gedackt 8 ft. C_0, $3\frac{3}{4}$ in. by 3 in.	2. Salicional 8 ft. C_0, $3\frac{3}{8}$, mouth $\frac{1}{5}$.

PEDAL.

Sub-Bass, 16 ft.
C_1, 5 in. by $3\frac{3}{8}$ in.

In a church organ, volume and solidity of tone are the first considerations, while delicacy and variety are much more wanted in a chamber organ. Thus the use of two manuals is required in the latter from the smallest sizes, while not so indispensable to the former. The financial element has also to be considered, and where the funds are not sufficient to provide an organ of adequate size, the aid of the octave coupler can very appropriately be called in, provided that a proper balance of tone is arranged for, and it is recommended that in all such cases the extra octave, or at least the most part of it, should be provided. An octave coupler would, however, be quite out of place in a chamber organ, where power is never a desideratum.

472. The following is the next step in advance for an organ for a church or school. In this and the following specifications, where the diameter of a pipe is given it is understood that a judicious economy can be effected by making the bass in wood, provided the builder has the skill to voice them up to the metal, and in that case the width of the pipe can be taken from the diagram of Fig. 9, Pl. II., also that the gedackts can either be carried through in wood or turned into metal at any pipe.

SPECIFICATION VI.

1. Open 8 ft. C_0, 5 in. dia.
2. Gedackt 8 ft. C_0, $4\frac{1}{4}$ in. by $3\frac{1}{4}$ in.
3. Salicional 8 ft. grooved to last, c^0, $2\frac{1}{8}$ in.
4. Octave 4 ft. One pipe smaller than Open.
5. Quint Mixture, the Twelfth being the same scale as Open but with $\frac{1}{4}$ mouth, and the Fifteenth one pipe smaller than Octave, both ranks being voiced quietly, the Twelfth with little wind, but the Fifteenth with as much as it will take, with a low mouth, in order to preserve the keenness and overcome the Twelfth.

Pedal.—Sub Bass 16 ft., $C_1 = 6$ in. by $4\frac{3}{4}$ in.

473. But the same number of stops for a chamber organ would be better disposed and scaled as follows:

SPECIFICATION VII.

GREAT.	CHOIR.
Open 8 ft. C_0, $4\frac{1}{4}$ in. dia.	Gamba 8 ft. C_0, $3\frac{1}{2}$ in. dia.
Gedackt 8 ft. C_0, $3\frac{3}{4}$ in. by 3 in.	Salicional 8 ft. Same scale from c^0,
Flute 4 ft. C_0, $2\frac{5}{8}$ in. dia.	but with $\frac{1}{4}$ mouth. Bass octave
	stopped, $C_0 = 3\frac{1}{4}$ in. by $2\frac{1}{8}$ in.

Pedal.—Violon Bass 16 ft. $C_1 = 6$ in. dia. $\frac{1}{4}$ mouth, or Sub Bass, 5 in. by $3\frac{3}{4}$ in.

For all the above small organs, the wind-pressure should not exceed $2\frac{1}{4}$ in.

474. The next step is to a two-manual church organ, and the smallest that can reasonably be built is

SPECIFICATION VIII.

GREAT.

1. Open 8 ft. C$_0$, 5¼ in. dia.
2. Gedackt 8 ft. C$_0$, 4 in. by 3 in.
3. Salicional 8 ft. C$_0$, 3½ in. dia., mouth ⅕.
4. Principal 4 ft., one pipe smaller than Open.

CHOIR OR SWELL.

1. Geigen 8 ft. C$_0$, 4½ in. dia., ⅔ mouth.
2. Harmonic Flute 8 ft. C$_0$, 3¾ in. by 2¼ in. stopped bass; c^0, 3 in. dia.
3. Gemshorn 4 ft. c^0, 3 in. dia. at bottom, 1½ in. at top, mouth ¼.
4. Quint Mixture, as in Specification VI.

Pedal.—Violon Bass 16 ft. C$_1$ = 6 in. dia., mouth ¼, or Sub Bass 6 in. by 6 in.   Wind 2½ in. to 3 in. according to the size of building.

In the matter of the second manual the writer is in accord with Mr. Dickson, in a preference for omitting the swell-box where money is at all a consideration, it being much better spent on pipes than on a box to put them in.   Certainly a full range of pipes is the first consideration, and when these have been provided a box may be put over them, but to cut out the finest octave of the foundation stops is a mistake.   So also grooving should not be carried to excess.   A stopped bass is a very poor substitute for a good Salicional which retains its character to the lowest notes.   In the pedal the invariable rule in English organs is to put a sub-bass, but a softly-voiced Violone is a far preferable stop if height and funds admit.

It will be observed that for the string-toned stops, much variation of scale is not required.   A Salicional can be made the same scale as a Gamba, the difference in tone being obtained by varying the width of the mouth and the voicing, and the delicate pipes if made of moderate scale with a small mouth do not give so much trouble as those of a very narrow scale.   A judicious use of string-toned stops also gives quite a satisfactory tone-colour without the aid of reeds for a small organ, and in places where they cannot be looked after and tuned every week, these latter are better omitted.

475. A corresponding organ to the last for chamber use would be :

x 2

SPECIFICATION IX.

GREAT.

1. Open Diapason 8 ft. C₀, 4⅝ in. dia.
2. Gedackt 8 ft. C₀, 3 in. by 2½ in.
3. Salicional 8 ft. C₀, 3¼ in. dia., mouth ⅕.
4. Principal 4 ft., one pipe smaller than Open.

SWELL.

1. Viol da Gamba 8 ft. C₀, 3½ in.
2. Harmonic Flute 8 ft. C₀, stopped ; bass 3¼ in. by 2¼ in. c⁰, 3 in. dia.
3. Gemshorn 4 ft. c⁰, 3 in. and 1½ in. dia., ⅛ mouth.
4. Quint Mixture. Dulciana scale.

Pedal.—Sub Bass 16 ft. C₁, 5½ in. by 4¼ in. or a soft Violon. Wind 2½ in. The usual couplers are understood.

With the two last specifications the addition of a pedal octave coupler, with extra pipes to complete the range, would be an improvement.

476. A larger would be as follows :

SPECIFICATION X.

GREAT.

1. Open Diapason 8 ft. C₀, 5½ in. dia.
2. Gamba 8 ft. C₀, 3⅓ in. dia.
3. Harmonic Flute 8 ft. C₀, stopped bass 3¾ in. by 3 in. c⁰, 3 in. dia.
4. Salicional 8 ft. C₀, 3½ in. dia., ⅓ mouth.
5. Principal 4 ft. One pipe smaller than Open.
6. Harmonic Flute 4 ft. One pipe smaller than No. 3.
7. Quint Mixture.

SWELL.

1. Geigen 8 ft. C₀, 4½ in. dia., mouth ⅔.
2. Gedackt 8 ft. C₀, 4 in. by 3 in. mouth ⅔ when in metal.
3. Hohl Flute 8 ft., grooved with above c⁰, 3¼ in. dia.
4. Viol da Gamba 8 ft. C₀, 3½ in. dia.
5. Principal 4 ft. Same scale as Open.
6. Quint Mixture. Small scale.
7. Oboe.

PEDAL.

1. Violon Bass 16 ft. C₁, 5½ in. square.
2. Sub Bass 16 ft. C₁, 6½ in. square.
3. Octave Couplers.

Wind 3 in.
Three Composition Pedals to Great.
  I. Draw and reduce to 3:
 II. Draw and reduce to 3, 4, 6.
III. Full.
Two to Swell.
  I. Draw and reduce to 2, 4.
 II. Full.

And the usual couplers.

477. Specification XI. will be for a chamber organ, and was given to the writer by Mr. Audsley. The scale of the pipes is not stated, but from the other specifications the reader will have no difficulty in suiting himself. The effect of more than one swell box enclosing contrasting tones is here introduced, and the peculiarity of a V. rank Dulciana Mixture is one that has been approved by experience. The compass is to be to a³ and the wind 2½ in.

First Manual.

1. Open Diapason	.	.	. 8 ft.	†6. Viol d'Amour . . . 4 ft.
*2. Doppel-Flöte	.	.	. 8 „	†7. Dulciana Cornet V. ranks.
*3. Concert Flute	.	.	. 4 „	†8. Trumpet . . . . 8 ft.
*4. Piccolo	.	.	. 2 „	†9. Clarinet . . . . 8 „
†5. Violoncello	.	.	. 8 „	

Second Manual.

*1. Viol da Gamba	.	.	. 8 ft.	*4. Flauto d'Amore . . 4 ft.
*2. Dulciana	.	.	. 8 „	*5. Orchestral Oboe . . 8 „
*3. Lieblich Gedackt	.	.	. 8 „	

Pedal.

1. Sub Bass	.	.	. 16 ft.	3. Violoncello . . . . 8 ft.
2. Flute (by octave coupler)	.	8 „	4. Bassoon . . . . 16 „

* In swell box No. 1.   † In swell box No. 2.

This organ is about as large as any chamber organ in the proper sense of the word need be ; beyond this size an instrument would need a regular hall to do it justice.

478. Mr. Audsley had a very beautiful chamber organ of his own building, the specification of which was as follows :

Lower Manual.

1. Open Diapason	.	.	. 8 ft.	6. Flauto Primo . . . 8 ft.
	In front swell box.			7. Flauto Secondo . . . 8 „
2. Flauto Tedesca	.	.	. 8 ft.	8. Viol d'Amore . . . 8 „
3. Flauto Traverso	.	.	4 „	9. Octave . . . . 4 „
4. Piccolo	.	.	. 2 „	10. Dulciana Mixture V. ranks.
5. Oboe	.	.	. 8 „	11. Tromba . . . . 8 ft.
	In back swell box and governed			12. Clarinet . . . 8 „
	by ventil.			13. Vox Humana . . 8 „

Upper Manual (in front box).

1. Principale Dolce	.	.	. 8 ft.	3. Flauto d'Amore . . . 4 ft.
2. Corno di Caccia	.	.	. 8 „	

Pedal.

1. Open Diapason	.	.	. 16 ft.	3. Saxophone . . . . 16 ft.
2. Bourdon	.	.	. 16 „	

Wind $2\frac{3}{8}$. The scale of the Open Diap. is $5\frac{1}{4}''$ dia. A V. rank mixture in an organ of that size would, in the ordinary acceptation of the word, be a monstrosity, but to Dulciana scale, and with every pipe regulated and voiced with the utmost care, it has a beautiful effect. The composition is :

C_0, 19, 22, 24, 26, 29.	c^1, 8, 12, 17, 19, 22.
c^0, 12, 15, 17, 19, 22.	c^2, 1, 8, 10, 12, 15.

and for a III. rank the following is recommended :

C_0, 15, 19, 22.	c^1, 12, 15, 17.
c^0, 12, 17, 22.	c^2, 8, 12, 15.

The pedal reed on this organ is a free reed, and has a most beautiful smooth tone, without the slightest suspicion of harshness. The C_o of the trumpet is $3\frac{1}{2}''$ dia. Mr. Audsley is a strong advocate for free reeds for chamber organs, and certainly his own may be said to give that example which is better than precept. He recommends the following as good chamber organ scales, but with a $2\frac{3}{8}''$ wind they are rather large:

Pedal Open C_1, 11 in. by 9 in. to 10 in. by 8 in.
Open Diapason C_0, $5\frac{1}{4}$ dia.
Geigen C_0, $4\frac{1}{2}$ in. dia.
Gamba C_0, 4 in.
Lieblich Gedackt $3\frac{1}{4}$ in. by $1\frac{3}{4}$ in.

Dulciana $3\frac{1}{4}$ in. dia.
Harmonic Flute c^0, $2\frac{1}{8}$ in. dia.
Wald Flute c^0, $2\frac{1}{2}$ in. by 3 in.
Doppel Flute c^0, $1\frac{3}{4}$ in. by $2\frac{15}{16}$ in.
Oboe C_0, $2\frac{3}{4}$ in. dia.
Clarinet C_0, $1\frac{1}{2}$ in. dia.

While on the subject of chamber organs, it may be as well to note that the ordinary Harmonic Flutes are too powerful for chamber work, and unless of fairly large scale, and copiously winded, the true harmonic tone is not obtained.

479. Fig. 316, Pl. XXXVIII., shows an ingenious arrangement for economising space in chamber organs by getting two semitones out of one pipe, which is worth applying to the lower six pedal pipes, as they take up so much room. Here a is the top of the pipe, tuned in the usual manner to, say, C_1, b is a slide containing an aperture, which is so fixed that when it is opened the pipe sounds $C\sharp$, the sides are faced with leather c, d is the face of a motor normally held back by a weight e, but closing the aperture when inflated through the conveyance pipe f. Both the C and the $C\sharp$ pallets feed the pipe, but C feeds the little motor in addition, so that when C is touched, the motor shuts and covers the hole, which makes the pipe give the deeper note.

480. But to go back a step. Specification XII. is for a chamber organ, midway between IX. and XI., as follows:

GREAT.

1. Open Diapason 8 ft. C_0, $4\frac{5}{8}$ in. dia.
2. Gamba 8 ft. C_0, $3\frac{1}{2}$ in. dia.
*3. Harmonic Flute 8 ft. C_0, stopped bass $3\frac{1}{4}$ in. by $2\frac{1}{4}$ in., c^0, 3 in. dia.
4. Principal 4 ft., one pipe less than Open.

*5. Travers Flute 4 ft. c^0, $2\frac{1}{2}$ in. by 2 in, o^2, $1\frac{1}{2}$ in. dia.
*6. Rausch Quint 2 ft.

SWELL.

1. Geigen 8 ft. C₉, 4 in. dia. ⅞ mouth.
2. Doppel Flute 8 ft. c¹, 3 in. by 1¾ in.
3. Salicional 8 ft. C₉, 3¼ dia., ¼ mouth.
4. Gemshorn 4 ft. c⁹, 3 in. and 1¼ in. dia., ⅓ mouth.

5. Dulciana Mixture III. ranks.
6. Orchestral Oboe.

PEDAL.

1. Violon Bass 16 ft. C₁, 5¼ in. square.
2. Sub Bass 16 ft. C₁, 6 in. by 4¾ in.

3. Octave Coupler.

The stops marked * on the Great might if desired be put in a separate swell box. If ordinary composition pedals or pistons are used, the following might be placed on the

Great I. draw and reduce to 3 and 5.
II. draw and reduce to 1-2-4.
III. Full.
And on the Swell I. reduce to 3.
II. draw and reduce to 1-2-4.
III. Full.

481. Specification XIII. is for a church organ where power is required but money is not abundant. It will be the same as X., only with the addition of an Octave Coupler (with the extra pipes) to the swell, and this will require a Bourdon 6″ × 4¾″ to keep the balance of tone. The whole if carefully voiced would make a powerful and full-toned organ, especially if a Trumpet were added to the Great.

It is indispensable to have an adequate pedal tone before embellishing the manuals with reeds. Most ordinary English church organs sin greatly in this respect; they have only one dull Bourdon or thumping Open to be used as bass for all the manual changes, while the money that should have provided another stop has been spent on two reeds, which, for want of tuning, are never in a state fit to be used. *When* the needful in foundation and pedal work has been provided, let reeds be added by all means, as they will upset nothing. A reed can be added if desired to any of the above specifications.

At and over 20 stops is just about the border line between two and three manuals. For a large church where volume of sound is required, two manuals should be used, but for a small church or chamber organ three manuals would be more suitable. It will be understood that the mere number of stops or manuals has nothing whatever to do with the noise, and the fatal error of putting up organs too big for their place is treated of elsewhere.

482. Specification XIV. is for an organ after the German style for a large church, giving a good solid tone with sufficient variety.

GREAT.

1. Bourdon 16 ft. C_1, $6\frac{1}{2}$ in. by 5 in. Full tone.
2. Principal 8 ft. C_0, $5\frac{1}{8}$ in. dia.
3. Hohl Flute 8 ft. C_0, stopped bass 4 in. by 3 in., c^0, $3\frac{1}{8}$ in. by $2\frac{1}{2}$ in.
4. Viol da Gamba 8 ft., 4 in. dia.
5. Octave 4 ft. As No. 2.
6. Hohl Flute 4 ft. As No. 3.
7. Quint $2\frac{2}{3}$ g^0, $2\frac{3}{4}$ in. dia.
8. Octave 2 ft. As No. 2.
9. Mixture IV. ranks as No. 2, viz.:
   C_0 note has g^1, c^2, g^2, c^3.
   $F_0\sharp$ „ „ $f\sharp^1$, $c\sharp^2$, $f\sharp^2$, $c\sharp^3$.
   $f^0\sharp$ „ „ $c^2\sharp$, $f^2\sharp$, $c^3\sharp$, $f^3\sharp$.
   $f^1\sharp$ „ „ $f^2\sharp$, $c^3\sharp$, $f^3\sharp$, $c^4\sharp$.
   $f^2\sharp$ „ „ $c^3\sharp$, $f^3\sharp$, $c^4\sharp$, $f^4\sharp$.

CHOIR.

1. Gedackt 8 ft. C_0, 4 in. by 3 in.
2. Flauto Amabile 8 ft. C_0, $3\frac{3}{8}$ in. by $2\frac{3}{4}$ in.
3. Flauto Traverso 8 ft. from c^1, $1\frac{1}{4}$ in. dia., lower octaves grooved with No. 2.
4. Flauto Amabile 4 ft. As No. 2.
5. Gemshorn 4 ft. c^0, $2\frac{1}{4}$ in. dia. at mouth.
6. Oboe 8 ft.

PEDAL.

1. Principal 16 ft. C_1, $7\frac{3}{4}$ in. by 6 in.
2. Sub Bass 16 ft. C_1, $7\frac{3}{4}$ in. by 6 in.
3. Principal 8 ft. C_0, 6 in. by $4\frac{3}{4}$ in.
4. Gedackt 8 ft. As No. 2.
5. Posaune 16 ft.

483. Specification XV. is that of the organ built for Allahabad Cathedral by the writer, and the tone is quite satisfactory. The organ is built on the ventil principle described in paragraph 346, and stands on both sides of the chancel, over the ambulatory, the architect having as usual neglected to provide a place where an organ built in the ordinary way could be squeezed in. The console stands with the choir in the transept, and the electric action enables a number of couplers to be used. The Violon Bass is made to rather a large scale to compensate the want of a Major Bass.

GREAT.

1. Bourdon 16 ft. C_1, $5\frac{1}{2}$ in. by $4\frac{1}{4}$ in.
2. Open Diapason 8 ft. C_0 $5\frac{1}{2}$ in. dia.
3. Gamba 8 ft. C_0, $3\frac{1}{8}$ dia.
4. Gedackt 8 ft. C_0, $3\frac{3}{4}$ in. by 3 ft.; c^0, $2\frac{1}{4}$ in. dia., $\frac{2}{7}$ mouth.
5. Principal 4 ft. One pipe smaller than Open.
6. Harmonic Flute 4 ft. c^1, $1\frac{3}{4}$ in. dia.
7. Quint Mixture, in which the Twelfth has a $\frac{1}{5}$ mouth.
8. Blank. Intended for Trumpet.

SWELL.

1. Geigen 8 ft. C_0, 4 in. by $3\frac{3}{4}$ in.; B_0, $3\frac{1}{4}$ in. dia., mouth $\frac{2}{7}$.
2. Hohl Flute 8 ft. C_0, $3\frac{3}{4}$ in. by $2\frac{3}{4}$ in. stopped; c^0, 3 in. dia.
3. Viol da Gamba 8 ft. C_0, $3\frac{1}{8}$, mouth $\frac{1}{5}$.
4. Principal 4 ft., same as Open.
5. Quint Mixture, bright.
6. Oboe 8 ft.

CHOIR.

1. Lieblich Gedackt 8 ft. C$_0$, 3$\frac{1}{4}$ in. by 2$\frac{1}{2}$ in.; c^0, 1$\frac{7}{8}$ in. dia.
2. Salicional 8 ft., C$_0$, 3$\frac{1}{4}$ in. by 2$\frac{3}{4}$ in.; B^{0}b, 2$\frac{3}{8}$ in. dia.
3. Travers Flute (bored) 4 ft. c^0, 2$\frac{1}{4}$ in. by 2 in.: c^2, 1$\frac{1}{8}$ in. dia.
4. Clarinet, 8 ft.

PEDAL.

1. Violon Bass 16 ft. C$_1$, 5$\frac{3}{4}$ in. square.
2. Sub Bass 16 ft. C$_1$ 6$\frac{1}{2}$ in. square.
3. Posaune 16 ft.
4. Octave Coupler with extra pipes.

Wind on Great and Choir 3$\frac{1}{8}$ in. Swell and Pedal 3$\frac{1}{4}$ in.

COUPLERS.

Swell Sub Octave.
Swell Octave.
Swell to Choir.
Swell Sub to Great.
Swell Unison to Great.

Swell Super to Great.
Choir Sub to Great.
Choir to Pedal.
Great to Pedal.
Swell to Pedal.

COMPOSITIONS.

GREAT.

I. Draw and reduce to 4–6.
II. Draw and reduce to 1–2–3–4.
III. Full.

SWELL.

I. Draw and reduce to 2–3.
II. Draw and reduce to 1–2–6.
III. Full.

CHOIR.

I. Draw and reduce 1–2.
II. Full.

It should be observed that the electric action with the wealth of couplers was added after the organ was built, for with such an arrangement it would have been better to have put the Bourdon on the Swell, since the Great has the Choir sub-oct. coupler to supply a 16′ tone.

484. This organ would be much too full for a small church, so Specification XVI. is given for the same number of stops, but delicate tone.

GREAT.

1. Bourdon 16 ft. C$_1$, 5 in. by 3$\frac{1}{2}$ in.
2. Open 8 ft. C$_0$, 5 in. dia.
3. Keraulophon 8 ft. C$_0$, 3$\frac{1}{4}$ in. dia.
4. Gedackt 8 ft. C$_0$, 3$\frac{1}{4}$ in. by 2$\frac{3}{4}$ in.
5. Gemshorn 4 ft. c^0, 3 in. dia. at mouth.
6. Harmonic Flute c^1, 1$\frac{3}{4}$ in. dia.
7. Fifteenth. As No. 2, but mouth $\frac{1}{5}$.

SWELL.

1. Geigen 8 ft. C$_0$, 4$\frac{1}{4}$ in. dia.
2. Hohl Flute 8 ft. C$_0$, stopped 3$\frac{3}{4}$ in. by 2$\frac{3}{4}$ in.; c^0, 2$\frac{1}{4}$ in. dia.
3. Viol da Gamba 8 ft. C$_0$, 3$\frac{1}{4}$ in. dia. mouth $\frac{1}{5}$.
4. Principal 4 ft. as Open.
5. Quint Mixture same scale as last, but mouth $\frac{1}{5}$.
6. Oboe.

CHOIR.

1. Lieblich Gedackt 8 ft. C$_0$, 3$\frac{1}{4}$ in. by 2$\frac{1}{8}$ in.
2. Salicional 8 ft. C$_0$, 3$\frac{1}{2}$ in. dia. mouth $\frac{1}{4}$.
3. Travers Flute 4 ft. c^2, 1$\frac{1}{2}$ in. dia.
4. Clarinet 8 ft. In wooden box. Wind 2$\frac{1}{4}$ in.

PEDAL.

1. Violon Bass 16 ft. C$_1$, 5$\frac{1}{2}$ in. square.
2. Sub Bass 16 ft. C$_1$, 6$\frac{1}{2}$ in. by 5 in.
3. Contra Fagotto 16 ft.
4. Octave Coupler with extra pipes.

COMPOSITION PEDALS.
COUPLERS.

Swell to Great.
Choir Sub to Great.

Swell to Choir.
Manuals to Pedal.

GREAT.

I. Draw and reduce to 3-6.
II. Draw and reduce to 1-2-3-4.

III. Full.

SWELL.

I. Draw and reduce to 3.
II. Draw and reduce to 1-2.

III. Full.

The octave coupler to the Pedal is not for the sake of noise, but to give the 8-foot tone when it is not desired to couple the manuals.

485. As a further contrast of tone and purpose with the same number of stops, the following study for a chamber organ is given as Specification XVII.

GREAT.

1. Open Diapason 8 ft. C$_0$, 4$\frac{1}{4}$ in. dia., mouth $\frac{2}{3}$.
*2. Doppel Flute 8 ft. c^1, 3 in. by 1$\frac{3}{4}$ in.
*3. Salicional 8 ft. C$_0$, 3$\frac{1}{4}$ in. dia.
*4. Harmonic Flute 4 ft. c^0, 2$\frac{3}{4}$ in. dia.
*5. Salicet 4 ft. As No. 3.
*6. Fifteenth 2 ft. As No. 1.
*7. Clarinet.

SWELL.

†1. Geigen 8 ft. C$_0$, 4$\frac{1}{4}$ in. dia.
†2. Viol da Gamba 8 ft. C$_0$, 3$\frac{1}{4}$ in., mouth $\frac{1}{4}$.
†3. Gedackt 8 ft. C$_0$, 3$\frac{1}{4}$ in. square.
†4. Gemshorn 4 ft. c^0, 2$\frac{3}{4}$ in. at mouth.
†5. Dulciana Mixture IV. and V. ranks.
†6. Orchestral Oboe.

CHOIR.

1. Lieblich Gedackt 8 ft. C$_0$, 3$\frac{1}{8}$ in. by 2$\frac{1}{8}$ in.
2. Harmonika 8 ft. C$_0$, 3 in. by 2$\frac{3}{8}$ in.
3. Travers Flute 4 ft. c^2, 1$\frac{1}{4}$ in. dia.
4. Echo Oboe 8 ft. This stop is not a

reed but is made of hard wood, the c^1 being 1$\frac{1}{8}$ in. by $\frac{3}{4}$ in., mouth cut up $\frac{3}{16}$ in. and provided with bridge, voiced as reedy as possible.

PEDAL.

1. Contra Bass 16 ft. C$_1$, 5 in. dia., mouth $\frac{1}{4}$.
2. Sub Bass 16 ft. C$_1$, 6 in. by 4$\frac{3}{4}$ in.
3. Contra Fagotto 16 ft.
4. Octave Coupler. Wind 2$\frac{1}{4}$ in., but only 1$\frac{3}{4}$ in. on choir.

If the effects of various swell boxes are desired, the stops marked * might be put in one and those marked † in another.

For such an organ it is infinitely better to have adjustable composition pedals or pistons.

486. For the next advance in size, say to about 30 stops, it would be impossible to improve on the Hindley organ given in detail above, or on Michell & Thynne's specification, which contains 35. The scales of this organ are not given in the description of it, but an equivalent specification for a large church or hall is given below as Specification XVIII., and the accessories can be selected at will from the description of the organ. The wind is supposed to be $2\frac{1}{2}''$ for Choir, $3''$ for Great, $4''$ for Swell and Pedal, and $8''$ for the strong reeds. The style is perhaps more suited to the concert hall than the church, and the fourth manual is introduced for the first time.

GREAT.

1. Contra Gamba 16 ft. C_1, $5\frac{3}{4}$ in. dia.
2. Open Diapason 8 ft. C_0, $5\frac{3}{4}$ in. dia.
3. Gamba 8 ft. C_0, $3\frac{7}{8}$ dia., mouth $\frac{2}{7}$.
4. Claribel 8 ft. C_0, $5\frac{3}{4}$ in. dia.
5. Principal 4 ft. As No. 2.
6. Harmonic Flute 4 ft. As No. 4.
7. Quint Mixture. As No. 2.
8. Great Mixture IV. ranks.
9. Posaune 16 ft.
10. Trumpet 8 ft.

SOLO.

1. Harmonic Flute 8 ft. C_0, 6 in. dia.
2. Violoncello 8 ft. C_0, $3\frac{3}{4}$ in. dia.
3. Tuba 8 ft.
4. Vox Humana, 8 ft.

SWELL.

1. Geigen, 8 ft. C_0, $4\frac{1}{2}$ in. dia., mouth $\frac{2}{7}$.
2. Harmonic Flute 8 ft. c_0, $3\frac{1}{2}$ dia.
3. Viol da Gamba 8 ft. C_0, $3\frac{1}{2}$ in. dia. mouth $\frac{1}{4\cdot5}$.
4. Saliciona $3\frac{1}{2}$ dia., mouth $\frac{1}{5}$.
5. Geigen 4 ft. As No. 1.
6. Mixture III. ranks.
7. Posaune 16 ft.
8. Horn 8 ft.
9. Oboe 8 ft.

CHOIR.

1. Spitzflöte 8 ft. C_0, $4\frac{1}{2}$ in. at bottom, $1\frac{1}{2}$ in. top.
2. Dolce 8 ft. C_0, $2\frac{1}{2}$ in. at mouth, $3\frac{1}{4}$ in. at top, mouth $\frac{1}{5}$.
3. Gedackt 8 ft. C_0, 3 in. by $2\frac{1}{4}$ in.
4. Gemshorn 4 ft. c^0, $2\frac{1}{2}$ in. and $1\frac{1}{4}$ in.
5. Zauberflöte 4 ft. As No. 3.
6. Piccolo 2 ft. c^2, $1\frac{1}{8}$ in.
7. Clarinet.

PEDAL.

1. Major Bass 16 ft. C_1, $10\frac{3}{4}$ in. by $8\frac{3}{4}$ in.
2. Violon Bass 16 ft. C_1, $5\frac{1}{4}$ in. square.
3. Quint (stopped) G_1, $6\frac{1}{4}$ in. by 5 in.
4. Flute 8 ft. C_0, 7 in. by $5\frac{1}{4}$ in.
5. Posaune 16 ft.

487. Beyond this we get into quite large organs, and the next Specification No. XIX. would do for a church or hall, and for the former purpose it would not do much harm to omit the Solo manual. For an organ of this size there must be a 16′ manual backed up by a 32′ pedal to obtain proper dignity of tone, and the 16′ tone is introduced by a Bourdon into the Choir to the extent that by the Choir sub. to Great Coupler the Great will acquire a soft 32′ tone, which is very effective.

Great.

1. Principal 16 ft. C_1, 10 in. dia.
2. Quintatön 16 ft. C_1, 6 in. dia.
3. Principal 8 ft. C_0, 5¾ in. dia.
4. Gamba 8 ft. C_0, 3⅞ in. dia., mouth 2/7.
5. Harmonic Flute 8 ft. c^0, 3 in. dia.
6. Quint 5⅓ G_0, 3⅝ square.
7. Octave 4 ft. As No. 3.
8. Rohr Flute 4 ft. c^0, 2½ in. square.
9. Quint Mixture. As No. 3.
10. Full Mixture. As No. 3.
11. Trumpet 8 ft.
12. Clarion 4 ft.

Wind 3¼ in.

Swell.

1. Bourdon 16 ft. C_0, 6½ in. by 5 in.
2. Geigen 8 ft. C_0, 4½ in. dia., mouth 2/7.
3. Gedackt 8 ft. C_0, 4 in. by 3 in.
4. Hohl Flute 8 ft. c^0, 3¼ in. dia.
5. Viol da Gamba 8 ft. C_0, 3½ in. dia.
6. Octave 4 ft. c^0, 3 in. dia.
7. Harmonic Flute 4 ft. c^0, 3¼ dia.
8. Octave 2 ft. As No. 6.
9. Scharff V ranks.
10. Oboe 8 ft.
11. Horn 8 ft.

Wind 4 in.

Solo.

1. Harmonic Flute 8 ft. c^0, 3⅝ in. dia.
2. Violoncello 8 ft. C_0, 4 in. dia.
3. Viola 4 ft. As No. 2.
4. Concert Flute 4 ft. As No. 1.
5. Tuba 8 ft.
6. Vox Humana 8 ft.

Wind 5 in.

Choir.

1. Double Dulciana or Bourdon 16 ft. C_1, 5 in. by 3⅝ in.
2. Spitz-Flöte 8 ft. C_0, 4½ in. and 1½ dia.
3. Salicional 8 ft. C_0, 3½ in. dia., mouth ⅕.
4. Lieblich Gedackt 8 ft. C_0, 3¼ in. by 2½ in.
5. Gemshorn 4 ft. c^0, 2¾ in. and 1⅝ in. dia.
6. Travers Flute 4 ft. c^2, 1⅛ in. dia. bored.
7. Piccolo 2 ft. As No. 6.
8. Clarinet 8 ft.

Wind 2¾ in.

Pedal.

1. Untersatz 32 ft. C_2, 18¼ in. by 14 in.
2. Major Bass 16 ft. C_1, 10¾ in. by 8 in.
3. Violon Bass 16 ft. C_1, 5¾ in. square.
4. Sub Bass 16 ft. C_1, 7¼ in. square.
5. Octave 8 ft. As No. 2.
6. Violoncello 8 ft. C_0, 3½ in. square.
7. Posaune 16 ft.
8. Contra Fagotto 16 ft.
9. Trumpet 8 ft.

Wind 4 in.

All the heavy reeds are 8 in. wind.

COUPLERS.

Swell to Great.
Swell to Choir.
Choir Sub to Great.
Solo to Great.

All Manuals to Pedal.
Pneumatic Pistons to each Manual,
adjustable preferred.

It is quite a matter of taste whether any stops of the Solo, Great and Choir should be put into separate swell boxes.

488. A final Specification, No. XX., may be given for a first-class organ which would meet all reasonable requirements. The Vox Humana will of course have a swell box and tremulant of its own. In this as well as in any of the foregoing specifications fancy stops may be added *ad lib.* once a good foundation is secured.

GREAT.

1. Principal 16 ft. C_1, 10 in. dia.
2. Violon 16 ft. C_1, $6\frac{1}{4}$ in. dia.
3. Principal 8 ft. C_0, 6 in. dia.
4. Gamba 8 ft. C_0, $3\frac{7}{8}$ in. dia., $\frac{2}{7}$ mouth.
5. Spitz Flute 8 ft. C_0, $4\frac{1}{2}$ in. dia. at mouth, 2 in. at top.
6. Harmonic Flute 8 ft. c^0, $3\frac{5}{8}$ in. dia.
7. Doppel Flute (stopped) 8 ft. C_0, $4\frac{3}{4}$ in. by $2\frac{3}{4}$ in.
8. Quint $5\frac{1}{3}$ ft. G_0, $4\frac{1}{4}$ in. by $3\frac{1}{4}$ in.
9. Octave 4 ft. One pipe less than Principal.
10. Harmonic Flute 4 in. One pipe less than 8 ft. Flute.
11. Spitz Flute 4 ft. As the 8 ft. Flute.
12. Quint Mixture II. The Twelfth to have a $\frac{1}{4}$ mouth.
13. Full Mixture V. ranks.
14. Posaune 16 ft.
15. Trumpet 8 ft.
16. Clarion 4 ft.
Wind $3\frac{1}{4}$ in.

SWELL.

1. Contra Gamba 16 ft. C_1, $5\frac{1}{2}$ in. square.
2. Bourdon 16 ft. C_1, 6 in. by 5 in.
3. Geigen 8ft. C_0, $4\frac{1}{2}$ in., $\frac{2}{7}$ mouth.
4. Principal 8 ft. C_0, $5\frac{3}{4}$ in. dia.
5. Gedackt 8 ft. C_0, 4 in. by 3 in.
6. Hohl Flute 8 ft. c^0, $3\frac{1}{4}$ in. dia.
7. Viol da Gamba 8 ft. C_0, $3\frac{1}{4}$ in. dia.
8. Quint Flute $5\frac{1}{3}$ G_0, $3\frac{5}{8}$ in. square.
9. Octave 4 ft. As Principal.
10. Hohl Flute 4 ft. As 8 ft. Flute.
11. Gemshorn 4 ft. c^0, $3\frac{1}{4}$ in. dia. at mouth, 1 in. at top.
12. Quint Mixture II.
13. Scharff V.
14. Ophicleide 16 ft.
15. Horn 8 ft.
16. Oboe 8 ft.
17. Clarion 4 ft.
Wind 4 in.
Reeds 8 in.

Choir.

1. Contra Basso 16 ft. C_1, $5\frac{3}{4}$ in. dia., $\frac{1}{4}$ mouth.
2. Gemshorn 8 ft. C_0, $5\frac{1}{4}$ in. dia. at bottom.
3. Salicional 8 ft. C_0, $3\frac{1}{2}$ in. dia., $\frac{1}{4}$ mouth.
4. Dolce 8 ft. C_0, $2\frac{1}{2}$ in. dia. at mouth, $3\frac{1}{4}$ in. at top, mouth $\frac{1}{6}$.
5. Travers Flute 8 ft. C_0, $4\frac{1}{4}$ in. by $3\frac{1}{2}$ in. c^1, $1\frac{1}{8}$ in. dia. Solid wood bored.
6. Lieblich Gedackt 8 ft. C_0, $3\frac{1}{4}$ in. by $2\frac{1}{6}$ in.
7. Quint Flute $5\frac{1}{3}$ ft. Two pipes larger than Lieblich.
8. Octave 4 ft. c^0, 3 in. dia.
9. Travers Flute 4 ft. As the 8 ft. Flute.
10. Dolce 4 ft. Same scale as No. 4.
11. Piccolo 2 ft. As Travers Flute.
12. Dulciana Cornet V.
13. Euphone 16 ft.
14. Clarionet 8 ft.
    Wind $2\frac{3}{4}$ in.

Solo.

1. Harmonic Flute 8 ft. c^0, $3\frac{3}{4}$ in. dia.
2. Violoncello 8 ft. C_0, $3\frac{1}{2}$ in. dia.
3. Harmonika 8 ft. C_0, $3\frac{3}{4}$ in. by $3\frac{1}{4}$ in.
4. Terpodion 8 ft. C_0, $3\frac{3}{4}$ in., mouth full $\frac{3}{4}$ in., on 8 in. wind. (This is a stop invented by Schultze.)
5. Concert Flute 4 ft. As the 8 ft. Flute.
6. Viola 4 ft. As Violoncello, but slightly taper.
7. Tuba 16 ft.
8. Contra Fagotto 16 ft.
9. Tuba 8 ft.
10. Orchestral Oboe 8 ft.
11. Tuba Clarion 4 ft.
    Wind 5 in.

Pedal.

1. Untersatz 32 ft. C_0, 19 in. by 13 in.
2. Major Bass 16 ft. C_1, 10 in. square.
3. Minor Bass 16 ft. C_1, $10\frac{1}{2}$ in. dia.
4. Violon Bass 16 ft. C_1, $5\frac{3}{4}$ in. square.
5. Double Dulciana 16 ft. C_1, $5\frac{3}{4}$ in. dia., $\frac{1}{4}$ mouth.
6. Sub Bass 16 ft. C_1, $7\frac{1}{4}$ in. square.
7. Quint $10\frac{3}{4}$ ft. As Sub Bass.
8. Octave 8 ft. As Minor Bass.
9. Violoncello 8 ft. As Violon Bass.
10. Gedackt 8 ft. As Sub Bass.
11. Quint Mixture II. Same scale as Great Principal.
12. Mixture III. ranks.
13. Posaune 32 ft.
14. Posaune 16 ft.
15. Contra Fagotto 8·6 ft.
16. Serpent 16 ft.
17. Clarion 8 ft.
18. Bassoon 8 ft.
    Wind 4 in.

All heavy reeds on 8″ wind, and the usual couplers and combination actions.

489. There are 76 stops in this organ and nothing much would be gained by increasing the number. The different qualities of tone are all represented, and to repeat, for instance, soft stops on the Great would add nothing to the organ, nor would the duplication of fancy stops under different names.

So far as mere noise is concerned it is difficult to think that more is required for musical enjoyment than this organ would make, provided only that the pipes are adequately voiced, as the solidity and freshness of tone of an organ depend more on the judicious selection and voicing of stops than on their mere number. For this reason the mere duplication of the

Diapason work either on the same manual, or on another with the sole difference of being enclosed in a box, as is too often the case with the average church organ, is but a poor way of using up money and space. The writer has in mind a pretentious (and costly) so-called 'grand organ' of 41 stops, in which there is not a single string-toned stop, the whole being made up of woolly diapasons and flutes, with so little character that, except for mere loudness, one stop might just as well be drawn as another. It is not too much to say that a better full organ tone could be obtained with ten less stops properly selected and voiced. Schultze was of opinion that nothing was to be really gained by going much beyond 60 to 70 stops, and that sufficient variety and volume could be obtained from that number for all except very extraordinary purposes.

CHAPTER XIII

SUMMARY AND BIBLIOGRAPHY

490. THE reader who has gone thus far will probably find himself tolerably familiar with the general construction of an organ, and may even have formed ideas of how he would design an organ for any particular case, but it will not be waste of space to insist again upon what the writer feels to be the artistic side of organ-building. Due allowance being made for difference in taste, a good perception of ' tone colour ' is absolutely essential to a satisfactory result, and to those whose ears or tastes are critical in this respect there is just as much difference between organs as there is between a tawdry chromo-lithograph and the work of a master in painting. But there are plenty of people who do not appreciate these differences, and are satisfied with an organ so long as it makes plenty of noise.

Quality and not quantity should, however, be the motto, which cannot be too often repeated, and the quality should extend to every stop in the organ. Just as an orchestra is built up of instruments each of which is pleasing in itself, but suitable for combination, so should the selection of organ stops be arranged. One pipe of a master like Schultze is a musical treat, and all the stops are in balance and support each other. The story of how he commenced his career in England is worth repeating—both as illustrating what has been said above on the appreciation of tone, and as showing that the supposed improvement of organs by age is not due to that circumstance, but to the original good voicing and often to the excellent site. The first organ sent by Schultze to England was a small one in the Exhibition of 1851, and the late Jeremiah Rogers, of Doncaster, as keen a judge of tone as ever lived, sat down to try the organ. A friend of his, passing by, saw him standing on the stool and peering into the organ, and when he caught sight of his friend he called out excitedly, 'Come here, come here!' 'What is the matter?' replied his friend. 'They are not old pipes,' replied Rogers; 'there are no old pipes in the organ, and I never heard such a tone from new pipes. Just hear it,' and with that he began playing again. This led to Schultze building the Doncaster organ and many others, and the influence he has had on English building is very marked. Thus, for the second time, England has been indebted to Germany for an advance in the art of organ-building, in which so far as the flue work is concerned our neighbours were until recently superior to us. But in reeds the English work of the best class has always been preferable to either the German or the French. To this day, however, there is in the work of even good builders a deficiency of string tone in the flue work as a rule, and the employment of Horn Diapasons and the wide-spread idea that slotting is desirable, shows that the true feeling for that tone has yet to be cultivated. An excellent test is to build an organ without any reed work, which can be done to a most satisfactory extent by the judicious combination of foundation tone. Many small organs where the reeds are always out of order would be much better without them, especially as the quality of such reeds is often brazen to a degree.

491. The organ of one stop as the smallest unit can be made melodious by having that one stop of fresh, even though it may be soft, intonation. After the foundation tone has been provided for, if space and funds admit, the string and flute tones claim admittance, and upon which of these two is chosen depends the precise character the foundation tone should assume. Should flute tone be first introduced, the diapason work will need to be much keener than if string tone is selected, and when in the third stage of size both are admitted, the diapason must retain its peculiar character. To the writer's taste the average English Open Diapason is far too much like a big flute. It is wanting in freshness and tubby in the bass, 'firm,' as it is called. As the size of the

organ increases, each family of tone is more fully represented, and each manual should have quite a distinct character, not merely a difference in loudness; and an appropriate pedal should accompany every addition to the manual. This is a point where the Germans have never been at fault, but English builders until lately most remiss, one thumping Bourdon being expected to do duty for an appropriate bass to perhaps twenty stops. Or even, it is said, if you make the stopped pipe big enough it is almost as good as an open. Fatal mistake; you can no more replace an open pipe, even a small one, by a stopped pipe, than you can replace the 'cello and contra basso in an orchestra by adding a drum. The only explanation of such an opinion is that those who hold it have never heard any really good string work such as Schultze's, and as can now be found in the organs of some few builders. Not that a stopped pipe is not a most excellent thing in its proper place, which is to thicken the tone in balance to the brightening of it by reeds and mixtures. The reeds as generally applied fulfil the purpose of the brass and not of the reeds in an orchestra, being put in simply to make a noise—witness the Trumpets and Cornopeans on manuals much too weak in flue work to support them, and so voiced as to show that noise was the only idea. Even a good reed is out of place if it overpowers instead of blending with the foundation work. A conductor who wishes to enlarge his orchestra does not as a rule engage a man with a big brass instrument and make him blow his loudest. There appears to be in a majority of people an inability to appreciate the distinctions of tone; they will call anything shut up in a box till it can hardly be heard, 'sweet,' although the pipe on its own merits may have no tone at all in the proper sense of the word. So also even with voicers; there is a want of appreciation of keenness, as contrasted with flutiness in tone, which has nothing to do with the absolute loudness. A pipe may be as *keen* as you please, but still soft. Now the fault with screaming Mixtures is that they are loud and fluty, whereas they should be soft but yet bright or keen.

492. A complete family of string tone stops on a separate manual, or section of one, would have a most charming effect

and would be most appropriate for a chamber or concert hall organ, but the writer does not know of any organ where this idea has been carried out.

To Mr. Audsley (in the columns of the 'English Mechanic') is due the credit of having been the first to propose a more rational use of the swell, by enclosing stops of different character of tone in different boxes, so as to obtain what he calls a dissolving view effect, melting the flute tone into the string tone gradually, and producing much finer effects than can be obtained by the mere duplication of a manual, by putting similar stops in a box. But even adopting this principle the organ can never from its construction be strictly an expressive instrument, and legitimate organ music must depend upon judicious phrasing and the use of the stops with a solidity of the 'ensemble' rather than upon individual effects.

The writer, however, is not favourable to the use, which generally means the abuse, of the swell box, since he has found that in nine cases out of ten it simply means ruin to the tone and even to the speech of the enclosed pipes. *If,* indeed, a swell box can be made large enough not to hurt the pipes, well and good, but in how many cases can this be done? Just as an organ crammed into a chamber loses all delicacy and freshness of tone, so do pipes in a box, and even to a greater extent. It would be better to put only the reeds, a Principal, a Quint or other Mixture, and perhaps the Gedackt into the box, and let the rest of the flue work of that manual have a chance in the open air. A good player can with the combination appliances of a modern organ produce all the (desirable) effects of a swell without the actual shutters; the crescendo pedal, for example, by itself does what the swell is supposed to do, but far more effectively.

493. Even a small room ruins the tone of an organ. The great drawback to the chamber organ is that few people possess rooms sufficiently large to put it in; an organ that fills up half a room is an absurdity.

No special notice has been taken in this work of the many devices for borrowing, each more complicated than the other. The writer does not know of any that he can fully recommend, and the ingenuity of the reader will doubtless enable him to devise as good a plan for himself as any extant. Except to complete a pedal by borrowing by the aid of pneumatic action, the idea that one stop is to do duty on a number of manuals is not one that has much to commend it. As for such contrivances as Voix Celestes, Vox Humanas and Tremulants, the writer frankly avows that he never could find any pleasure in their bleating and quivering effects, and considers that they form no part of legitimate organ work. Many people indeed who rave about a Vox Humana have not the least idea of what it is like, and are prepared to accept any stop or combination that takes their fancy, as the stop they have heard so much about.

494. The mechanism of the modern organ has advanced mightily, and the player has now many advantages of easy touch and combinations which were out of the reach of the preceding generation, but in point of tone the old organs can still hold their own. Nor has the writer been able to discover that the theory has been much advanced, and here is a splendid field for research. It is not of course to be expected that the production of delightful tone can be reduced to a mathematical formula, any more than a person devoid of colour sense will be enabled to rival Rubens because he understands the reasons why certain colours harmonise. But an analysis of the effects of different proportions upon the sound waves caused by pipes would be a most profitable and interesting study, and if this book should induce anyone to take up the task, or publish any researches already made, it will not have been written in vain.

495. The following list of works connected with organ-building may be interesting. Most of them are in the collection bequeathed by the late Col. Conway-Gordon to the British Museum. Those which are merely descriptions of particular organs are classified separately under the name of the place to which they refer, and when the author's name is not known, the work is classified by the title.

1. 'A Short Account of Organs in England from the Reign of Charles II to the Present Time.' London : J. Masters, 1847.

2. Adlung, Jakob: 'Anleitung zu der Musicalischen Gelehrtheit,' &c. Erfurt: J. D. Jungnickol, 1758.

3. Adlung, J.: 'Musica Mechanica Organædi,' &c. 2 vols. Berlin: W. Birnstiel, 1767.

4. Allihn, Max: 'Die Theorie und Praxis des Orgelbaues' (an enlarged and revised edition of Töpfer's great work. The best book on organ-building extant.) Weimar: B. F. Voight, 1888.

5. Anding, J. M.: 'Handbuch für Orgelspieler.' Hildburghausen: Kesselring, 1872.

6. Antony, Joseph: 'Geschichtliche Darstellung der Entstehung, &c., der Orgel.' Munster: Coppenrath, 1832.

7. Baake, F.: 'Neuer Beitrag zur Beleuchtung und Würdigung der Parteilichkeit, Inkonsequenz und Ignoranz des Musikdirector Wilke,' &c. Halberstadt, 1847. (This work, as may be imagined from the title, is rather amusing than instructive, and shows that music does not always soothe the savage breast.)

8. Baron, Rev. J.: 'Scudamore Organs,' &c. London: Bell & Daldy, 1862.

9. Becker, C. F.: 'Rathgeber für Organisten,' &c. Leipzig: Schwichert, 1828.

10. Bedos de Celles, Dom J. F.: 'L'Art du Facteur d'Orgues.' Paris, 1766-78. (A grand old folio. Hamel's work, q.v., is a smaller edition of this.)

11. Bendeler, J. P.: 'Organopoia,' &c. Frankfurt, 1739.

12. Bertrand, Ed.: 'Histoire Ecclesiastique de l'Orgue.' Paris, 1859.

13. Biermann, J. H.: 'Organographia Hildesiensis,' &c. Hildesheim, 1738.

14. Biovia, Giambattista: 'Pel nuovo Organo, Opera di S. Serassi Santuario del Conciliso.' Lettera ed incrizione di Como, per C. A. Ostinelli, 1808.

15. Bishop, C. K.: 'Notes on Church Organs,' &c. London: Rivingtons.

16. Blanchinus, F.: 'De Tribus Queribus Instrumentorum Musicæ,' &c. Rome, 1742.

17. Bony, Louis: 'Une Excursion dans l'Orgue.' Paris: Fischbacher, 1892.

18. Braun, B.: 'Praktische Orgelschule,' &c. Gmünd: Schmid, 1849.

19. Buck, Dudley: 'The Influence of the Organ in History' (a lecture at Boston University). London: W. Reeves, 1882.

20. Bühler, F.: 'Etwas über die Musik, die Orgel,' &c. Augsburg: Guber, 1811.

21. Bühler, Franz: 'Etwas über,' &c. Freiburg: Werder, 1815.

22. Büttner, J.: 'Anweisung, wie jeder Organist verschiedene,' &c. Glogau: Günther, 1827.

23. Buliovsky de Dulioz, M: 'De Emendatione Organorum,' &c. Strasburg, 1680.

24. Calla: 'Bulletin de la Société d'Encouragement pour l'Industrie Nationale Rapport sur la Construction . . . de M. Cavaillé-Coll.' Paris.

25. Carustius, C. E.: 'Examen Organi,' &c. Küstrin, 1683.

26. Casson, H. T.: 'Reform in Organ-Building.' London: W. Reeves, 1888.

27. Casson, T.: 'The Modern Organ.' Denbigh: T. Gee & Son, 1883.

28. Cauna, Baron de: 'Orgues des Basses Pyrénées,' &c. Bordeaux, 1874.

29. Cavaillé-Coll, A.: 'Etudes Experimentales sur les Tuyaux d'Orgues.'

30. Cavaillé-Coll, A. : ' De l'Orgue et de son Architecture.' Paris : Ducher et Cie, 1872.

31. Cavaillé-Coll, A. : ' Projet de l'Orgue pour la Basilique de St. Pierre de Rome.' Bruxelles : Rossel, 1875.

32. Christ F. : ' Die Einrichtung der Kirchenorgel Nördlingen.' Beck, 1882.

33. Chrysander : ' Historische Nachrichten von Kirchen Orgeln.' Rinteln, 1755.

34. Clark, W. H. : ' An Outline of the Structure of the Pipe Organ,' &c. Indianapolis, U.S.A., 1877.

35. Clerk, A. le : ' Recueil de Procès-Verbal de Reception, &c. . . . et Notice des Travaux de l'Etablissement Merklin-Schütze. Paris, 1863.

36. Couwenburg : ' L'Orgue Ancien et Moderne.' Lierre et Paris, 1888.

37. Danjou, F. : ' Sur l'Origine de l'Orgue.' Nuremberg, 1771.

38. Deimling, E. L. : ' Beschreibung des Orgelbaues,' &c. Offenbach : Weiss und Brede, 1792–94.

39. Delezenne : ' Memoires de la Société Imperiale des Sciences de Lille. 2e series, I vol. Note sur le Ton des Orchestres et des Orgues.' Paris, 1855.

40. Dickson, W. E. : ' Practical Organ-Building.' London : Lockwood, 1882.

41. Dionel, O. : ' Die Moderne Orgel,' &c. Berlin, 1891.

42 Edwards, C. A. : ' Organs and Organ-Building.' London : Gill, 1881.

43. Eichler, C. : ' Die Orgel,' &c. Stuttgart : J. B. Metzler, 1858.

44. Engel, D. H. : ' Beitrag zur Geschichte des Orgelbauwesens,' &c. Erfurt : Körner, 1855.

45. Fabricius, Werner : ' Unterricht wie man ein neues Orgelwerk . . . probieren soll.' Frankfurt und Leipzig, 1756.

46. Fage, Adrien de la : ' Bericht an die Gesellschaft der freien Künste. Paris, 1845.

47. Faulkner, T. : ' Designs for Organs.' London, 1838.

48. Ferroni, Pietro : ' Memoria sull'uso della Logistica nella Construzione degli Organi,' &c. Modena, 1804.

49. Fêtis : ' Extraits des Rapports du Jury, Exposition 1867 à Paris.' Paris : Plon, 1868.

50. Fischer, E. G. : ' Die Pflege der Orgel,' &c. Glogau : Holstein, 1859.

51. Flottwell, Christian : ' Ein wohlgerühmtes Orgelwerk,' &c. Königsburg, 1721.

52. Förner, Christian : ' Vollkommener Bericht, wie eine Orgel . . . probiert und gebraucht werden,' &c. 1684.

53. Forckel, J. N. : ' Allgemeine Geschichte der Musik.' 2 vols. Leipzig, 1790.

54. Fourmeaux, N. : ' Traité, Theorique et Pratique de l'Accord,' &c. Paris : E. Repos, no date.

55. Fritzen : ' Anweisung, wie man Klaviere . . . und Orgeln nach einer mechanischen Art in allen 12 Tönen gleich rein stimmen Könne,' &c. Leipzig : Breitkopf, 1756–80.

56. Furstman, M. : ' Zur Geschichte der Orgelbaukunst in Sachsen.' 1861.

57. Gartner, J. : ' Kurze Belehrung über die innere Einrichtung der Orgeln,' &c. Prague : Wittere, 1855.

58. Gerhardt, Dr. R. : ' Die Rohrflöte,' &c. Dresden : Blockmann u. Sohn, 1884.

59. Girod, le Père L.: 'Connaissance Pratique de la Facture des Grandes Orgues.' Paris: Haton Libraire.

60. Grässner, A.: 'Hilfsbuch . . . über Bau und Pflege der Orgel.' Leipzig: C. Merseburger, 1877.

61. Gregoir, E. G. J.: 'Histoire de l'Orgue,' &c. Antwerp, 1865.

62. Gregori, J.: 'De more canendi symbolum Nicæum.' Publiée à Londres, 1650-63.

63. Haas, F.: 'Anlectung über Scheiblers . . . Tonmessung.' Erfurt: E. Werngart, 1886.

64. Halle, J. S.: 'Werstatte der Künste. Der Orgelbauer.' 1764.

65. Halle, J. S.: 'Die Kunst des Orgelbaues,' &c. Brandenburg, 1779.

66. Hamel: 'Nouveau Manuel Complet du Facteur d'Orgues' (mostly an abstract of Dom Bedos, with some more modern matter). Paris: Roret, 1849.

67. Hamilton: 'Catechism of the Organ.' London: R. Cocks & Co., 1865.

68. Havinga, Gerhardus: 'Vorsprong en Foortgang der Orgelen,' &c. Alkmaar: J. van Bayern, 1727.

69. Haynes, L. G.: 'Hints on the Purchase of an Organ.' London: Novello, 1878.

70. Heinrich, J. G.: 'Orgellehre,' &c. Glogau: C. Hemming, 1861.

71. Heinrich, J. G.: 'Orgelbaudenkschrift,' &c. Weimar: B. F. Voight, 1877.

72. Heiss, J. R.: 'Auch ein Votum in der Zürcherischen Orgelfrage.' Zürich: Höhr, 1847.

73. Hemstock: 'On Tuning the Organ.' London: Weekes & Co., 1876.

74. Herstell, C.: 'Kurze Anleitung zur Kenntniss der Orgelstimmen,' &c. Cassel, 1824.

75. Hess, Johann: 'Dispositien der merkwaardigste Kerk-Orgeln,' &c. (of Holland). Gouda: J. van der Klos, 1774.

76. Heurn, Jan van: 'De Orgelmaaker.' 2 vols., 1804.

77. Hiles, J.: 'Catechism of the Organ,' &c. London: Brewer & Co., 1878.

78. Hill, Arthur G.: 'The Organ Cases, &c., of the Middle Ages.' London: Bogue, 1886.

79. Hinton, J. W.: 'Guide to the Purchase of an Organ.' London: W. Reeves, 1882.

80. Hopkins and Rimbault: 'The Organ.' London: Cocks & Co., 1877.

81. Hoppius, Rector von: 'Ruppinische Marckwürdigkeiten.' Neu-Ruppin, 1641.

82. Kircheri, Athanasius: 'Musurgia Universalis,' &c. Rome: Corbelletti, 1650.

83. Kircheri, Athanasius: 'Phonurgia Nova,' &c. Campidonce per R. Dreherr, 1673.

84. Kirmberger: 'Construction d'un Tempérament égal.' 1760.

85. Klipstein, G. G.: 'Rat- und Hilfsbuch für Organisten,' &c. Breslau: Max & Co., 1826.

86. Knecht, J. H.: 'Vollständige Orgelschule,' &c. 1795.

87. Knock, N. A.: 'Dispositien der merkwardigste Kerk-Orgeln.'

88. Köckert, A.: 'Die Orgel, ihre Struktur und Pflege,' &c. 1875.

89. Kothe, B.: 'Kleine Orgelbaulehre,' &c. Leobschütz: K. Kothe, 1880-83.

90. Kothe, B.: ' Führer durch die Orgel,' &c. Leipzig : F. E. C. Leuchart, 1890.

91. Kützing, Karl: ' Theoretisch-praktisches Handbuch der Orgelbaukunst.' Leipzig : Dalp, 1836.

92. Lehmann, G. : ' Kleine Orgelbaukunde.' Liebenwerda : R. Conrad, 1868.

93. Lehmann, J. T. : ' Anleitung die Orgel rein und richtig zu stimmen, &c. Leipzig : Breitkopf, 1831.

94. Lewis : ' Organ-Building.' London : John B. Day, 1871.

95. Locker, Karl . ' Erklärung der Orgelregister,' &c. Bern : Nydegger u. Baumgart, 1887.

An English translation. London : Kegan Paul, Trench, & Co., 1888.

Also a French one. Paris, 1889.

96. Löhr, J. J. : ' Ueber die Scheibler'sche Erfindung,' &c. Krefeld : Schüller, 1836.

97. Ludwig, J. A. : ' Essai d'une méthode sur la disposition des tuyaux d'orgues.' Wulderburg, 1778.

98. Ludwig, J. : ' Gedanken über die grossen Orgeln,' &c. Leipzig : Breitkopf, 1762.

99. Ludwig, J. : ' Traktat von den universchämten Entehrern der Orgel.' Erlangen, 1763.

100. Maine, J. T. : ' Organs in India and America. Madras, 1860.

101. Marpurg, F. W. : ' Versuch über die musikalische Temperatur,' &c. Breslau : Korn, 1776.

102. Massmann, J. : ' Die Orgelbauten des Grossherzogtums Mecklenburg-Swerin,' &c. Wismar : Hinsdorf, 1875.

103. Mattheson : ' Der volkommene Kapellmeister,' &c. Hamburg : Herold, 1739.

104. Meijer, S. : ' De Forte-piano en het Orgel,' &c. Groningen: J. B. Huber, 1881.

105. Mettenleiter, B. : ' Die Behandlung der Orgel.' Regensburg : Pustet, 1870–86.

106. Meyer, Carl Gottfried (Editor) : ' Sammlung einiger Nachrichten von berühmten Orgeln,' &c. Breslau, 1757.

107. Michaelis, C. F. : ' Zur Geschichte der Orgel,' &c.

108. Mittag, J. G. : ' Historische Abhandlung von der Erfindung . . . der Orgeln.' Lüneberg, 1756.

109. Moser, L. : ' Gottfried Silberman, der Orgelbauer,' &c. Langensalza : Schulbuchhandlung, 1857.

110. Moser, L. : ' Das Brüderpaar, die Orgelbaumeister A. u. G. Silbermann.' Freiburg : Frotscher, 1861.

111. Müller e Rinck : ' Breve Metodo per l' Organo,' &c.

112. Müller, Donat : ' Kurze Beschreibung der einzelnen Teile der Kirchorgeln.' Augsburg : B. Schmid, 1848.

113. Müller, G. : ' Kurze und fassliche Anweisung für Lehrer, Organisten,' &c. Wittenberg : Herrosé, 1866.

114. Müller, G. F. : ' Historisch-philogisches Sendschreiben von Orgeln,' &c. Dresden, 1748.

115. Müller, W. A.: 'Die Orgel, ihre Einrichtung,' &c. Meissen: W. Gödsche, 1830.

116. Müller, W. A.: 'Orgellexicon,' &c. Schneeburg: Gödsche, 1860.

117. Müller: 'Manière d'accorder l'orgue par tempérament égal.' 1830.

118. Nichols, W. G.: 'The Cincinnati Organ,' &c. Cincinnati: R. Clarke & Co., 1878.

119. Niedt-Metthesen, F. E. N.: 'Musikalische Handleitung. Anderer Teil von der Variation des General-Basses,' &c. Hamburg: Kissner, 1721.

120. Norbury, J.: 'The Box of Whistles: a Book on Organ Cases.' London: Bradbury, 1877.

121. Oehme, Fritz: 'Handbuch über ältere und neuere berühmte Orgelwerke im Königreich Sachsen.' Dresden: Hoffman.

122. 'Organ Voicing and Tuning.' London: Brabner, 1879.

123. Pallisov, C. E.: 'Berichtigung eines Fundamentalsatzes der Akustic,' &c. Halle: Anton, 1833.

124. Pescard, A.: 'Application de l'électricité aux grandes orgues.' Caen: F. Le Blanc-Hardel, 1865.

125. Petri, J. S.: 'Anleitung zur praktischen Musik.' Lauban: J. C. Wirthgen, 1767.

126. Petri, J. S.: The same. Leipzig: Breitkopf, 1782.

127. Philbert, C. M.: 'L'Orgue du Palais d'Industrie d'Amsterdam,' &c. Amsterdam: Binger, 1876

128. Philbert, C. M.: 'Etudes sur les tuyaux d'Orgues' ('Comptes Rendus'). Paris, 1877.

129. Pillant, Léon: 'Instruments et Musiciens.' Paris: Charpentier, 1880.

130. Ponticoulant, Le Comte Ad. de: 'Organographie,' &c. Paris: Castel, 1861. 2 vols.

131. Poole, H. W.: 'Essay on Perfect Intonation, &c.' 1850.

132. Postel, E.: 'Orgel, Violone,' &c. Langensalza: Schulbuchhandlung, 1873.

133. Prætorius: 'Syntagma Musicum,' &c., Vol. I. Wittenburg: J. Richter, 1615. Vol. II. At Wolfenbüttel, by Elias Holwein, 1619 (a facsimile has been published).

134. Preuss, G.: 'Grundregeln von der Struktur und den Requisiten einer untadelhaften Orgel,' &c. Hamburg, 1722.

135. Ran, L.: 'Der Orgel-Erfindung,' &c. Giessen: B. C. Ferber, 1832.

136. Rachersberg, J. H. E.: 'Stimmbuch,' &c. Breslau and Leipzig: Gehr, 1804.

137. 'Recueil de quelques relations sur les orgues les plus célèbres de l'Allemagne, par un amateur de musique.' 1757.

138. Régnier, J.: 'L'Orgue, sa connaissance et son jeu.' Nancy: Vagner, 1850.

139. Rehm, Dr. H. F: 'Der Orgel hoher Zweck,' &c. Marburg: Christian Gar he, 1826.

140. Reichmeister, J. C.: 'Unentbehrliches Hilfsbuch beim Orgelbau,' &c. Leipzig: A. Fest, 1832.

141. Reichmeister, J. C.: 'Die Orgel in einem guten Zustande . . . zu erhalten,' &c. Leipzig: Fest, 1828.

142. Reiter, Dr. M.: 'Die Orgel unserer Zeit,' &c.   Berlin: Peiser, 1880. (This promised well, but the first number only came out.)

143. Remondini, P. C.: Intorno agli organi italiani,' &c.   Genova, 1879.

144. Richter, C. F.: 'Katechismus der Orgel.'   Leipzig: J. J. Weber, 1885.

145. Riegger: 'Sur les orgues de la Bohème.'

146. Riemann, Dr. H.: 'Katechismus der Orgel.'   Leipzig, 1888.

147. Rimbault, Dr.: 'The Early English Organ-builders,' &c.   London: Cocks & Co., 1864 (?).

148. Ritter, A. G.: ' Die Kunst des Orgelspiels,' &c.   Leipzig: Körner, 1877.

149. Ritter, A. G.: 'Die Erhaltung und Stimmung der Orgel.'   Leipzig: Körner, 1861.

150. Ritter, A. G.: ' Zur Geschichte des Orgelspiels.'   Leipzig: Max Hesse, 1884.

151. Rolle, Carl: 'Neue Wahrnehmungen zur Aufnahme . . . der Musik.' Berlin: Weber, 1784.

152. Saalschütz: ' Geschichte der Musik bei den Hebräen,' &c.   Berlin: Kampfmeyer, 1829.

153. Samber: 'Manuductio ad Organum,' &c.   Salzburg: J. B. Mayrs, 1704.

154. Samber: 'Conductio ad Manuductionem,' &c.   Salzburg: J. B. Mayrs, 1707.

155. Sattler, H.: 'Die Orgel nach den Grundsätzen der neuesten Orgel-baukunst.'   Langensalza: F. G. L. Gresler, 1868.

156. Sauveur: ' Mémoires de l'Académie Royale des Sciences, Application des sons harmoniques à la composition des jeux d'orgues.'   P. 308.   1702.

157. Scheiber, J. G. F.: ' Zeichnung und Beschreibung der Orgelpedal-Hilfs-Claviatur,' &c.   Görlitz: Heyn, 1846.

158. Scheibler, H.: ' Der physikalische und musikalische Tonmesser,' &c.   Essen: Bädeker, 1834.

An English translation, 'An Essay on the Theory and Practice of Tuning.'   London: Cocks & Co., 1853.

159. Scheibler, H.: 'Anleitung die Orgel vermittelst der Stösse . . . zu stimmen.'   Crefeld: Schüller, 1834.

160. Scheibler, H.: ' Ueber mathematische Stimmung,' &c.   Crefeld: Schüller, 1836.

161. Scheibler, H.: ' Mitteilungen über das Wesentliche des musikalischen und physikalischen Tonmessers.'   Crefeld: Schüller, 1836.

162. Scheider, W.: 'Lehrbuch des Orgelwerk,' &c.   Merseburg: F. Kobitzsch, 1823.

163. Schlich, A.: 'Spiegel der Orgelmacher und Organisten.'   Heidelberg, 1511 (?).   Berlin, 1870.

164. Schlimbach, G. C.: ' Ueber die Struktur . . . der Orgel,' &c.   Leipzig: Breitkopf, 1801-1843.

165. Schmahl, H.: 'Die pneumatische Kastenlade,' &c.   Hamburg, 1887.

166. Schmerbach, G. H.: ' Prolusio de Organis,' &c.   1770.

167. Schmitt, G. M.: 'Organiste praticien,' &c.   Paris.

168. Schneider, W.: ' Die Orgelregister,' &c.   Leipzig: Friese.

169. Schotto, Gaspare: ' Mechanic Hydraulic-Pneumatica.'   Frankfurt: 1657.

170. Schröter, J. G.: ' Orgelmacher in Erfurt,' &c.   Erfurt, 1720.

171. Schubert, F. L.: 'Die Orgel: ihr Bau,' &c. Leipzig: Merseburger, 1867.

172. Schubert, F. L.: (Dutch translation) 'Het Orgel,' &c. Haarlem: Bohn, 1868.

173. Schubiger, A.: 'Musikalische Spicilegien über . . . Orgelbau,' &c. Berlin, 1876.

174. Schütze, Dr. F. W.: 'Handbuch zu der praktischen Orgelschule. Leipzig: Arnold, 1868.

175. Schyven, P.: 'Notice sur le nouveau système d'orgues inventé par P. Schyven et Cie.' Bruxelles: Hayez, 1884.

176. Seidel, J. J.: 'Die Orgel und ihr Bau,' &c. Breslau: Leuckart, 1844–75. Leipzig: Kothe, 1887.
    An English translation. London, 1852.
    A Dutch translation. Groningen, 1845.

177. Shepherdson, W.: 'The Organ: Hints,' &c. London: Reeves & Turner, 1873.

178. Sorge, G. A.: 'Zuverlässige Anweisung Klaviere und Orgeln gehörig zu tempieren,' &c. Leipzig and Lobenstein, 1758.

179. Sorge, G. A.: 'Der in Rechen . . . und Messkunst wohl erfahrene Orgelbaumeister,' &c. Lobenstein, 1773.

180. Spark, Dr.: 'Choirs and Organs,' &c. 1852.

181. Sponsel, J. U.: 'Orgelhistorie.' Nürnberg: P. Monath, 1771.

182. Spengel, P. R.: 'Handwerke und Kunst der Orgelbau.' Berlin, 9th series, 1795.

183. Statz, V.: 'Orgeln, &c., im Gothischen Styl.' Berlin: C. Claesen & Cie.

184. Stehlin, S.: 'Anleitung zur Behandlung und Beurteilung einer Orgel,' &c. Wien: F. Klemm, 1855.

185. Stein, A.: 'Praktischer Ratgeber zur gründlichen Anweisung Orgeln, &c., rein stimmen zu lernen.' Leipzig: Franke, 1830.

186. Storius, 'De Organis.' Leipzig, 1698.

187. Sutton, Rev. F. H.: 'Some Account of the Mediæval Organ Case at Old Radnor,' &c. London: Hatchard, 1868.

188. Sutton, Rev. F. H.: 'Church Organs: their Position,' &c. London: Rivingtons, 1884.

189. Tauscher, J. G.: 'Versuch einer Anleitung zur Disposition der Orgelstimmen.' 1778.

190. Tempelhoff, G. F.: 'Von . . . Gedanken über die Temperatur,' &c. Berlin and Leipzig, 1775.

191. Töpfer, J. G.: 'Die Orgelbaukunst,' &c. Weimar: Hoffman, 1833.

192. Töpfer, J. G.: 'Erster Nachtrag zur Orgelbaukunst,' &c. Weimar: Hoffman, 1834.

193. Töpfer, J. G.: 'Anleitung zur Erhaltung und Stimmung der Orgel. Jena, 1840.

194. Töpfer, J. G.: 'Die Scheibler'sche Stimmethode,' &c. Erfurt: Körner, 1842.

195. Töpfer, J. G.: 'Die Orgel,' &c. Erfurt: Körner, 1843 (see Allihn supra).

196. Töpfer, J. G.: 'Lehrbuch der Orgelbaukunst,' &c. Wiemar: Voight, 1855.

197. Töpfer, J. G.: 'Anleitung zur Erhaltung und Stimmung der Orgel,' &c. Jena: F. Mauke, 1865.

198. Türk, D. G.: 'Von den wichtigsten Pflichten eines Organisten.' Leipzig: Schwickert, 1787.

199. Vigreux, L.: 'Notions élémentaires de la théorie des Vibrations,' &c. ('Annales du Génie Civil,' 6e anneé, No. 11, November 1867). Paris.

200. Vincent, A. J. H.: 'Mémoire sur la théorie des battements,' &c. Paris, 1849.

201. Vogler, G. J.: 'Erklärung der Buchstaben die im Grundrisse der nach dem Vogler'schen Simplifications-System neu zu erbauenden St. Peters-Orgel in München vorkommen.' München, 1806.

202. Vogler, G. J.: 'Vergleichungsplan der nach seinem Simplifications-System ungeschaffenen Neu Münster Orgel.' Würtzburg: Stahl, 1812.

203. Vollbeding, J. C.: 'Kurzgefasste Geschichte der Orgel,' &c. Berlin: Felisch, 1793.

204. Volckmar, Dr. W.: 'Der Organist,' &c. Langensalza, 1881.

205. Walther, J. G.: 'Musikalisches Lexicon,' &c. Leipzig: W. Deer, 1732.

206. Wangemann, Otto: 'Geschichte der Orgel,' &c. Demmin: A. Frantz, 1880-81-87.

207. Warman, J. W.: 'The Organ; its Compass,' &c. London: Reeves, 1884.

208. Weber, E.: 'Ueber Orgel-Dispositionen,' &c. Regensburg, 1890.

209. Weippner, J.: 'Die Orgel,' &c. Regensburg: Mauz, 1885.

210. Weissbeck, J. M.: 'Etwas über D. G. Türks wichtige Organisten-Pflichten.' Nürnberg, 1798.

211. Welker von Guntershausen, H.: 'Verfertiger musikalischer Instrumente.' Frankfurt a. M., 1855.

212. Werkmeister, A.: 'Muskalische Temperatur,' &c. Frankfurt and Leipzig, 1691.

213. Werkmeister, A.: 'Orgelprobe,' &c. Frankfurt and Leipzig, 1681-89, 1716-54.

A Dutch translation. Amsterdam: A. Olofsen, 1755.

214. Werkmeister, A.: 'Erweiterte und verbesserte Orgelprobe,' &c. Quedlinburg: Calvisici, 1698.

215. 'Organum Gruningense redivivum,' &c. Quedlinburg and Aschersleben, 1704.

216. Werner, J. G.: 'Orgelschule,' &c. Meissen: C. E. Klinkicht, 1807.

217. Werner, J. G.: 'Lehrbuch das Orgelwerk . . . zu kennen,' &c. Merseburg, 1823.

218. Wicks, Mark: 'Organ-Building for Amateurs' (a very good little book). London: Ward, Lock, & Co., 1887.

219. Wilke, F.: 'Ueber die Wichtigkeit und Unentbehrlichkeit der Orgel mixturen,' &c. Berlin: Trautwein & Co., 1839.

220. Wilke, F.; 'Offenes Sendschreiben an die Herrn Musikdirector W. Bach,' &c. &c. (see Baake). Hamburg: Schuberth & Co., 1845.

221. Wilke, F.: 'Beiträge zur Geschichte der neueren Orgelbaukunst,' &c. (another quarrel.) Berlin: Trautwein and Co., 1848.

222. Wolfram, J. C.: 'Anleitung zur Kenntniss, &c., der Orgeln,' &c. Gotha, 1815.

223. Zang, J. H.: 'Kunst- und Handwerksbuch.' 2. Teil. 'Orgelmacher.'
Nürnberg, 1804.

224. Zang, J. H.: 'Der vollkommene Orgelmacher,' &c. Nürnberg, 1829.

225. Zimmer, F.: 'Die Orgel,' &c. Quedlinburg: Vieweg, 1884.

Many of the titles of the above works, especially the older and the conten-
tious ones, are so intolerably tedious that they have been abbreviated. The
following periodicals also contain much valuable information on organ matters,
viz.: 'English Mechanic;' 'Zeitschrift für Instrumentenbau,' Leipzig, Paul
de Wit; 'Urania,' Erfurt, Gottschalk; 'Orgelbau-Zeitung,' Berlin, Reiter.

Many devices are also described in the Patent Office records of England and
Germany.

List of Works referring to Particular Organs.

226. Aix: 'Organ im Kurhaussaale,' by G. Stahlhut, of Burtscheid, builder
Author is H. Böekeler. Aachen: Jacobi & Co., 1876.

227. Altona: 'Hauptkirche,' H. Schmahl. Hamburg: H. Grüning, 1867.

228. Altona: 'St. Johanniskirche.' H. Schmahl. Hamburg: G. E. Nolte,
1873.

229. Alt-Rahlstedt: 'Organ,' by Marcussen und Sohn. H. Schmahl. Hamburg: G. E. Nolte, 1880.

230. Angoulême: 'Cathedral.' P. de Fleury. Angoulême: G. Chasseignac,
1890.

231. Augustenburg (zu Weissenfels). J. C. Trost. Nürnberg, 1677.

232. Autun: 'Cathedral.' M. J. Merklin. Lyons: Perrin et Marinet, 1876.

233. Avallon: 'Notice sur l'Orgue d'Avallon construit par M. Paul Chay-
elle pour l'église Saint-Pierre, Saint-Lazare,' &c. Par M. l'Abbé Thiesson.
Plancy: Société de St. Victor, 1854.

234. Bar sur Aube: 'Notizen über die Orgel zu St. Peter. Lété, Orgelbauer zu Mirecourt. Mirecourt,' 1845.

235. Billwärder (an der Bille): 'Der Umbau, die Renovation, &c., durch den
Orgelbauer C. H. Wolfsteller aus Hamburg,' &c. H. Schmahl. Hamburg:
Grüning, 1870.

236. Bolton: 'Memorials of the Parish Church Organs.' J. C. Scholes,
1882.

237. Breslau: 'Geschichte, &c., der grossen Orgel in der Hauptkirche zu
St. Maria Magdalena in . . .,' &c. J. W. Fischer: Breslau, 1821.

238. Brooklyn: 'The New Organ for the Brooklyn Tabernacle.' New York,
1890.

239. Brussels (?): 'Rapport adressé à M. le Ministre de l'Intérieur sur le
grand Orgue construit pour le Conservatoire de Musique dans le Palais de la
rue Ducale.' Bruxelles: Delavigne, 1867.

240. Caen: 'Le grand Orgue de l'église Saint-Pierre de . . . Cavaillé-Coll.'
Par J. Carlez. Paris, 1881.

241. Catwyk: 'Het nieuw Orgel in de orge Herrlykheid van Catwyk aan
den Phyn.' By F. Burmannus. Utrecht, 1765.

242. Chambéry: 'Du nouvel Orgue construit par M. Zeiger,' &c. M. G.
Pigeon. Lyons, 1847.

243. Cincinnati: 'The Cincinnati Organ.' G. W. Nichols. Cincinnati.
1878.

244. Clermont Ferrand: 'La Cathédrale de . . . et ses Orgues,' &c. M. J. Merklin. Lyons: Perrin et Marinet, 1878.

245. St. Dizier: 'Notice sur le Grand Orgue de Notre Dame de.' Cavaillé-Coll. M. A. Boudon. Bar le Duc: Numa Rolin, 1863.

246. Doncaster: 'A Description of the Great Organ built by Herr Schultze for the Parish Church.' W. Shepherdson. London: Reeves & Turner, 1873.

247. Einige zur Musik gehörige Poetische Gedanken bei Gelegenheit der schönen neuen in der Frauen Kirche in Dresden Perfertigten Orgel von Teodoro Christ lieb Reinholdt. Dresden, 1736 (?)

248. Exhibition: 'Description of the Organ in the French Department of the . . . 1851,' &c. M. Ducrocquet. London, 1857.

249. Erlangen: 'Den unverschämten Entehrern der Orgeln . . . zu Erlangen,' &c. J. A. Ludwig. Erlangen: W. Walther, 1763.

250. Fribourg (Swiss): 'L'Orgue d'Aloyse Mooser,' &c. J. Schmid. Fribourg, 1840.

251. Fribourg (Swiss). 'Étude sur le Grand Orgue de.' Abbé R. de Liechty. Lyon: Perrin et Marinet, 1874.

252. Geneva: 'Notice sur le Grand Orgue de la Cathédrale de, construit par Merklin-Schütze.' Paris: H. Plon, 1867.

253. Görlitz: 'Ausführliche Beschreibung der grossen neuen Orgel in der Kirche zu St. Petri u Pauli zu . . . .' C. L. Boxburg. Görlitz, 1704.

254. Görlitz: 'Historische Nachricht von den Orgeln der,' &c. C. D. Brückner. Görlitz, 1766.

255. Hamburg: 'Die neue Orgel in der St. Petrikirche zu, erbaut von Walker & Komp.' C. F. Armbrust. Hamburg: Nolte, 1885.

256. Hamburg: 'Die Orgel in der Kirchhofskapelle der St. Jakobikirche zu.' H. Schmahl. Hamburg: G. E. Nolte, 1869.

257. Hamburg: 'Nachrichten über die . . . der Orgel der St. Catherinenkirche in.' H. Schmahl. Hamburg: H. Grüning, 1869.

258. Hamburg: 'Die von C. H. Wolfsteller neu aufgebaute Orgel in der St. Thomaskirche zu,' &c. H. Schmahl. Hamburg: Nolte, 1885.

259. Kempen am Niederrhin: 'Die neue Orgel in, &c. Erbaut von Fr. W. Sonreck.' A. Jepkens. Köln: M. du Mont Schauberg, 1876.

260. Leeds: 'A Description of the Grand Organ in the Town Hall.' Gray and Davison. London: W. Brettel.

261. Lichtenburg: 'Versuch von den Eigenschaften eines rechtschaffenen Orgelbauers bei Gelegenheit des von Herrn J. J. Graichen und Herrn J. Ritter, &c., erbauten neuen Orgelwerks zu,' &c. J. A. J. Ludwig. Hof: Hetschel, 1759.

262. Lübeck: 'Beschreibung der grosser Orgel in der St. Marienkirche zu, &c., von J. F. u. E. Schultze.' H. Jimmerthal. Erfurt und Leipzig: Körner, 1859.

263. Lucerne: 'Die Altäre und die grosse Orgel in der Stifts und Pfarrkirche zu,' &c. H. Schmit-Maréchal. 1862.

264. Lyons: 'La Facture Moderne étudiée à l' Orgue de St. Eustache.' L'Abbé J. Ply. Lyon: Perrin et Marinet, 1880.

265. Manchester: 'Description of the Grand Organ, St. Peter's Church.' B. St. J. B. Joule. London, 1872.

266. Manchester: 'Organs in.' B. St. J. B. Joule. 1872 (reprint from *Manchester Courier*, Ap. 1872).

267. Merseburg: 'Ausführliche Beschreibung der Grossen Dom-Orgel zu,' &c. W. Schneider. Halle: A. Kummel, 1829.

268. Montpelier: 'Le Nouvelle Orgue du Collège à.' M. J. Merklin. Paris, 1878.

269. Murcia: 'Inauguration Solennelle des Grandes Orgues placées dans la Cathédrale de.' Don Hilarion Esclava. Bruxelles, 1859.

270. Murcia: 'Inauguration, &c., par Merklin-Schutze et Cie.' A. de la Fage. Bruxelles: Guzot, 1859.

271. Nancy: 'Notice sur le Grand Orgue de la Nouvelle Église St. Epore de, construit par Merklin-Schütze et Cie. Paris: H. Plon, 1867.

272. Oliva: 'Die Grosse Orgel in, &c. Orgelbaumeister Kaltschmidt zu Stettin.' Dr. F. Doneker. Dantzig: C. G. Hoffmann, 1865.

273. Paris, Notre Dame: 'Grand Orgue de l'Église Métropolitaine, par A. Cavaillé-Coll,' &c. Paris: H. Plon, 1868.

274. Paris, St. Denis: 'Procés-Verbal de Reception du Grand Orgue de.' Paris, 1841.

275. Paris, St. Denis: 'Orgue de l'Église Royale de.' A. de la Fage. Paris: S. Richault, 1846.

276. Paris, St. Eustache: 'Rapport sur l' Orgue de.' Paris, 1844.

277. Paris, St. Eustache: 'Le Grand Orgue de.' M. J. Merklin. Lyon: Perrin, 1879.

278. Paris, Madeleine: 'Rapport sur les travaux du Grand Orgue de.' Paris, 1846.

279. Paris, St. Sulpice: 'Étude sur l'Orgue Monumental de.' Abbé Lamazou. Paris.

280. Paris, St. Sulpice: 'Rapport sur le Grand Orgue de.' M. Lissajous. Paris: Bouchard-Huzard, 1865.

281. Perleberg: 'Beschreibung einer in der Kirche zu, neuen Orgel.' F. Wilke. Neu-Ruppin: Oemigke, 1832.

282. Philadelphia: 'Rapport de la Délégation, à l'Exposition de, 1876.' Paris: Sandoz, 1878.

283. Pötewitz: 'Die Einweihung der neuen Orgel zu.' G. Lange. Zeitz, 1821.

284. Rendsburg: 'Der Um- und Neubau der Orgel in der Christ- und Garnisonskirche zu, von den Orgebauern Marcusson und Sohn.' H. Schmahl. Hamburg, 1879.

285. Revel: 'Kurze Beschreibung der neuen Orgel in der Ritter- und Dom-kirche zu.' F. Ladegast. Weissenfels, 1879

286. Rotha: 'Etwas zu Feier des erstens Jubiläums der beiden Silberman-nischen Orgeln in.' J. L. Ritter. Leipzig, 1821.

287. Rouen: 'Causerie sur le Grand Orgue de la Maison C. Coll. à St. Ouen.' C. M. Philbert. Avranches: H. Gibert, 1890.

288. Salzburg: 'Die neue Orgel im Dom zu.' J. Peregrinus. Salzburg: H. Kerber, 1883.

289. Salzwedel: 'Beschreibung der St. Katharinen-Kirchen-Orgel in.' F. Wilke. Berlin: Trautwein und Ko, 1839.

290. Schleswig-Holstein: 'Orgel Dispositionen in.' L. J. Corsovius. Kiel: A. Jensen, 1872.

291. Senlis: 'Le Nouvel Orgue de la Tribune de la Cathédrale de.' M. J. Merklin. Lyon: Perrin, 1876.

292. Sheffield: 'Le Grand Orgue de la Nouvelle Salle de.' Cavaillé-Coll. Paris: Plon, 1874.

293. Temple Organ: 'A few Notes on.' E. Macrory. London: Reeves, 1855.

294. Versailles: 'Notice sur le Grand Orgue de la Cathédrale de.' H. Schmit-Marechal. Versailles: Beaujeune, 1864.

295. Vienna: 'Die neue Orgel zu Maria Treu in, von K. F. F. Buckow.' J. F. Kloss. Wien: Staats-druckerei, 1858.

296. Wandsbeck: 'Die Orgel in der Kirche zu.' H. Schmahl. Hamburg: H. Grüning, 1869.

297. Wismar: 'Beschreibung der grossen Orgel der Marienkirche zu,' &c. F. Baake. Halberstadt: Franz, 1846. (This is part of the dispute between Baake and Wilke.)

298. Wismar: 'Einige nöthige Worte über die Broschüre Beschreibung,' &c. (as above), by F. Turley. Hamburg: Schuberth, 1847.

299. Wolfenbüttel: 'Geschichte der alten Orgel in der Hauptkirche B. V. Mariæ in.' S. Müller. Braunschweig: M. Bruhn, 1877.

APPENDIX I

$$\frac{m}{n}\ \sqrt{\ }\ \text{of}\ 2$$

m	n=31 No.	n=31 Log	n=24 No.	n=24 Log	n=18 No.	n=18 Log	n=17 No.	n=17 Log	n=16 No.	n=16 Log	n=12 No.	n=12 Log	m
1	1·032611	·0097106	1·029303	·0125499	1·039259	·0167239	1·041616	·0177076	1·044273	·0188144	1·069443	·0250858	1
2	1·064734	·0194213	1·059463	·0250858	1·070034	·0334478	1·084963	·0354153	1·090507	·0376287	1·122462	·0501716	2
3	1·069879	·0291318	1·090507	·0376287	1·122462	·0501716	1·130116	·0531229	1·138788	·0564431	1·189207	·0752574	3
4	1·093559	·0388424	1·122462	·0501716	1·165528	·0668955	1·177146	·0708306	1·189207	·0752575	1·259920	·1003432	4
5	1·118987	·0486530	1·155353	·0627145	1·212326	·0836194	1·226135	·0885382	1·241857	·0940718	1·334839	·1254290	5
6	1·143872	·0582636	1·189207	·0752574	1·259920	·1003433	1·277161	·1062458	1·296839	·1128862	1·414212	·1505148	6
7	1·169430	·0679742	1·224059	·0878033	1·309384	·1170672	1·330311	·1239535	1·354256	·1317005	1·498306	·1756006	7
8	1·195872	·0776848	1·259920	·1003432	1·360790	·1337910	1·385674	·1416611	1·414213	·1505150	1·587400	·2006864	8
9	1·222913	·0873954	1·296839	·1128861	1·414218	·1506149	1·443339	·1593688	1·476826	·1693293	1·681791	·2257722	9
10	1·250565	·0971064	1·334839	·1254290	1·469733	·1673388	1·503405	·1770764	1·542211	·1881437	1·781796	·2508580	10
11	1·278940	·1068170	1·373953	·1379719	1·527434	·1839627	1·565973	·1947840	1·610489	·2069681	1·887747	·2759438	11
12	1·307758	·1165276	1·414213	·1505148	1·587400	·2006866	1·631141	·2124917	1·681799	·2257724	2·0		12
13	1·337339	·1262382	1·455652	·1630577	1·649720	·2174104	1·699028	·2301993	1·756351	·2445868			13
14	1·367647	·1359488	1·498306	·1756006	1·714487	·2341343	1·769799	·2479070	1·834008	·2634012			14
15	1·398489	·1456594	1·542210	·1881435	1·781797	·2508583	1·843378	·2656146	1·915206	·2822155			15
16	1·430112	·1553700	1·587400	·2006864	1·851748	·2675820	1·920092	·2833222	2·0				16
17	1·462449	·1650806	1·633918	·2132293	1·924446	·2843069	2·0						17
18	1·495516	·1747912	1·681791	·2257722	2·0								18
19	1·529332	·1845018	1·731072	·2383151									19
20	1·563913	·1942124	1·781796	·2508580									20
21	1·599274	·2039230	1·834007	·2634009									21
22	1·635436	·2136336	1·887747	·2759438									22
23	1·672415	·2233442	1·943061	·2884867									23
24	1·710231	·2330548	2·000000	·3010296									24
25	1·748896	·2427654											25
26	1·788444	·2524760											26
27	1·828880	·2621866											27
28	1·870034	·2718972											28
29	1·912528	·2816078											29
30	1·956087	·2913184											30
31	2·000000	·3010290											31

APPENDIX II.—*Table of the Vibration Numbers in Three Pitches, viz.: $a' = 430\cdot4$, 435 and 440 per Second.*

	C_2 32'	C_1 16'	C_0 8'	c^o 4'	c' 2'	c^2 1'	c^3 6"	c^4 3"	c^5 1½"
c	15·9	31·9	63·9	127·9	255·9	511·8	1023·6	2047·2	4094·4
	16·1	32·3	64·6	129·3	258·6	517·2	1034·4	2068·8	4137·6
	16·3	32·7	65·4	130·8	261·6	532·2	1064·4	2128·8	4257·6
c♯	16·9	33·8	67·7	135·5	271·1	542·2	1084·4	2168·8	4337·6
	17·1	34·2	68·5	137·0	274·0	548·0	1096·0	2192·0	4384·0
	17·3	34·6	69·3	138·6	277·2	554·4	1108·8	2217·6	4435·2
d	17·9	35·9	71·8	143·6	287·3	574·6	1149·2	2298·4	4596·8
	18·1	36·2	72·5	145·1	290·3	580·6	1161·2	2322·4	4644·8
	18·3	36·7	73·4	146·8	293·7	587·4	1174·8	2349·6	4699·2
d♯	19·0	38·0	76·0	152·1	304·3	608·6	1217·2	2434·4	4868·8
	19·2	38·4	76·9	153·8	307·6	615·2	1230·4	2460·8	4921·6
	19·4	38·8	77·7	155·5	311·1	622·2	1244·4	2488·8	4977·6
e	20·1	40·3	80·6	161·2	322·4	644·8	1289·6	2579·2	5158·4
	20·3	40·7	81·4	162·9	325·9	651·8	1303·6	2607·2	5214·4
	20·6	41·2	82·4	164·8	329·6	659·2	1318·4	2636·8	5273·6
f	21·3	42·7	85·4	170·8	341·6	683·2	1366·4	2732·8	5465·6
	21·5	43·1	86·3	172·6	345·3	690·6	1381·2	2762·4	5524·8
	21·8	43·6	87·3	174·6	349·2	698·4	1396·8	2793·6	5587·2
f♯	22·6	45·2	90·4	180·9	361·9	723·8	1447·6	2895·2	5790·4
	22·8	45·7	91·4	182·9	365·8	731·6	1463·2	2926·4	5852·8
	23·1	46·2	92·5	185·0	370·0	740·0	1480·0	2960·0	5920·0
g	23·9	47·9	95·8	191·7	383·4	766·8	1533·6	3067·2	6134·4
	24·2	48·4	96·9	193·8	387·6	775·2	1550·4	3100·8	6201·6
	24·5	49·0	98·0	196·0	392·0	784·0	1568·0	3136·0	6272·0
g♯	25·3	50·7	101·5	203·1	406·2	812·4	1624·8	3249·6	6499·2
	25·6	51·3	102·6	205·3	410·6	821·2	1642·4	3284·8	6569·6
	25·9	51·8	103·6	207·6	415·3	830·6	1661·2	3322·4	6644·8
a	26·9	53·8	107·6	215·2	430·4	860·8	1721·6	3443·2	6886·4
	27·1	54·3	108·7	217·5	435·0	870·0	1740·0	3480·0	6960·0
	27·5	55·0	110·0	220·0	440·0	880·0	1760·0	3520·0	7040·0
a♯	28·5	57·0	114·0	228·0	456·0	912·0	1824·0	3648·0	7296·0
	28·7	57·5	115·2	230·4	460·9	921·8	1843·6	3687·2	7374·4
	29·1	58·2	116·5	233·1	466·2	932·4	1864·8	3729·6	7459·2
b	30·1	60·3	120·7	241·5	483·1	966·2	1932·4	3864·8	7729·6
	30·5	61·0	122·0	244·1	488·3	976·6	1953·2	3906·4	7812·8
	30·8	61·7	123·4	246·9	493·9	987·8	1975·6	3951·2	7902·4

APPENDIX IIA.—*Theoretical Wave Length of Notes to correspond with the Pitches given above. Velocity of Sound = 1120' per Second.*

	C_2 32'	C_1 16'	C_0 8'	c^0 4'	c^1 2'	c^2 1'	c^3 6"	c^4 3"	c^5 1¼"
c	69·92	34·96	17·48	8·74	4·37	2·19	1·09	0·55	0·27
	69·28	34·64	17·32	8·66	4·33	2·16	1·08	0·54	0·27
	68·48	34·24	17·12	8·56	4·28	2·14	1·07	0·53	0·26
c♯	66·04	33·04	16·52	8·26	4·13	2·06	1·03	0·51	0·26
	65·28	32·64	16·32	8·16	4·08	2·04	1·02	0·51	0·25
	64·64	32·32	16·16	8·08	4·04	2·02	1·01	0·50	0·25
d	62·24	31·12	15·56	7·78	3·89	1·94	0·97	0·49	0·24
	61·60	30·80	15·40	7·70	3·85	1·92	0·96	0·48	0·24
	60·96	30·48	15·24	7·62	3·81	1·90	0·95	0·47	0·23
d♯	58·88	29·44	14·72	7·36	3·68	1·84	0·92	0·46	0·23
	58·24	29·12	14·56	7·28	3·64	1·82	0·91	0·45	0·22
	57·60	28·80	14·40	7·20	3·60	1·80	0·90	0·45	0·22
e	55·52	27·76	13·88	6·94	3·47	1·73	0·86	0·43	0·22
	54·88	27·44	13·72	6·86	3·43	1·71	0·85	0·42	0·21
	54·24	27·12	13·56	6·78	3·39	1·69	0·84	0·42	0·21
f	52·32	26·16	13·08	6·54	3·27	1·63	0·82	0·41	0·21
	51·84	25·92	12·96	6·48	3·24	1·62	0·81	0·40	0·20
	51·20	25·60	12·80	6·40	3·20	1·60	0·80	0·40	0·20
f♯	49·44	24·72	12·36	6·18	3·09	1·54	0·77	0·39	0·19
	48·96	24·48	12·24	6·12	3·06	1·53	0·76	0·38	0·19
	48·36	24·16	12·08	6·04	3·02	1·51	0·75	0·37	0·18
g	46·72	23·36	11·68	5·84	2·92	1·46	0·73	0·36	0·18
	46·08	23·04	11·52	5·76	2·88	1·44	0·72	0·36	0·18
	45·60	22·80	11·40	5·70	2·85	1·42	0·71	0·35	0·17
g♯	44·00	22·00	11·00	5·50	2·75	1·37	0·69	0·35	0·17
	43·52	21·76	10·88	5·44	2·72	1·36	0·68	0·34	0·17
	43·04	21·52	10·76	5·38	2·69	1·34	0·67	0·33	0·16
a	41·60	20·80	10·40	5·20	2·60	1·30	0·65	0·32	0·16
	41·12	20·56	10·28	5·14	2·57	1·28	0·64	0·32	0·16
	40·64	20·32	10·16	5·08	2·54	1·27	0·63	0·31	0·15
a♯	39·20	19·60	9·80	4·90	2·45	1·23	0·62	0·31	0·15
	38·88	19·44	9·72	4·86	2·43	1·21	0·61	0·30	0·15
	38·40	19·20	9·60	4·80	2·40	1·20	0·60	0·30	0·15
b	36·96	18·48	9·24	4·62	2·31	1·15	0·58	0·29	0·14
	36·64	18·32	9·16	4·58	2·29	1·14	0·57	0·28	0·14
	36·16	18·08	9·04	4·52	2·26	1·13	0·56	0·28	0·14

APPENDIX III.—*Length in Inches of Bodies of Free Reed Pipes after Weber. See para. 126.*

—	I.	II.	III.	IV.	V.	VI.	VII.
C_1	89·0	92·5	95·6	97·8	100·5	102·5	104·1
$C\sharp_1$	84·4	87·3	90·6	92·7	95·5	97·0	98·5
D_1	80·1	83·3	85·9	87·8	90·0	91·8	93·1
$D\sharp_1$	76·1	78·9	81·7	83·2	85·3	86·8	88·0
E_1	72·3	74·9	77·1	78·8	80·8	82·2	83·3
F_1	68·7	71·0	73·1	74·7	76·8	77·7	78·8
$F\sharp_1$	65·2	67·3	69·3	70·9	72·3	73·9	75·5
G_1	61·9	64·1	65·7	67·1	68·4	69·5	70·5
$G\sharp_1$	58·8	60·7	62·3	63·6	64·3	65·8	66·6
A_1	55·8	57·6	59·0	60·2	61·4	62·3	63·0
$A\sharp_1$	53·0	54·6	55·9	57·0	58·0	58·9	59·6
B_1	50·3	51·8	53·0	54·1	54·9	55·8	56·4
C_0	47·8	49·1	50·3	51·2	52·0	52·7	53·3
$C\sharp_0$	45·3	46·6	47·5	48·5	49·1	49·9	50·4
D_0	42·9	44·1	45·0	45·5	46·6	47·2	47·6
$D\sharp_0$	40·7	41·8	42·6	43·4	44·0	44·6	45·0
E_0	38·6	39·6	40·4	41·1	41·6	42·2	42·6
F_0	36·6	37·5	38·2	38·8	39·4	39·8	40·2
$F\sharp_0$	34·7	35·5	36·1	36·7	37·2	37·7	38·0
G_0	32·9	33·5	34·2	34·8	35·2	35·5	36·0
$G\sharp_0$	30·3	31·8	32·8	33·3	33·3	33·6	34·0
A_0	29·5	30·0	30·6	31·1	31·5	31·9	32·1
$A\sharp_0$	27·9	28·4	29·9	29·4	29·9	30·1	30·3
B_0	26·0	27·0	29·0	28·0	28·1	28·4	28·6
c_0	25·1	25·5	27·5	26·3	26·6	26·9	27·1
$c\sharp_0$	23·8	24·2	26·0	24·9	25·1	25·4	25·5
d_0	22·5	22·9	24·5	23·9	23·9	24·0	24·1
$d\sharp_0$	21·4	21·6	23·3	22·2	22·5	22·8	22·9
e^0	20·1	20·5	22·0	21·0	21·2	21·4	21·5

APPENDIX III.—*continued.*

—	I.	II.	III.	IV.	V.	VI.	VII.
f⁰	18·0	19·3	20·9	20·0	20·1	20·2	20·4
f♯ ⁰	18·1	18·4	19·8	19·0	19·0	19·1	19·3
g⁰	17·1	17·3	17·6	17·8	18·0	18·1	18·1
g♯ ⁰	16·1	16·4	16·6	16·9	17·0	17·1	17·1
a⁰	15·3	15·5	15·7	15·9	16·0	16·1	16·2
a♯ ⁰	14·4	14·7	14·9	15·0	15·1	15·2	15·3
b⁰	13·6	13·8	14·0	14·0	14·3	14·4	14·4
c¹	13·4	13·5	13·3	13·4	13·5	13·6	13·6
c♯ ¹	12·3	12·4	12·5	12·6	12·8	12·9	13·0
d¹	11·6	11·7	11·9	12·0	12·0	12·1	12·2
d♯ ¹	11·0	11·1	11·2	11·2	11·4	11·4	11·5
e¹	10·3	10·5	10·6	10·7	10·8	10·9	11·0
f¹	9·9	10·0	10·0	10·0	10·1	10·2	10·3
f♯ ¹	9·3	9·4	9·4	9·5	9·6	9·8	9·8
g¹	8·8	9·0	9·0	9·0	9·0	9·2	9·2
g♯ ¹	8·2	8·3	8·4	8·4	8·5	8·6	8·6
a¹	7·9	7·9	8·0	8·0	8·0	8·1	8·1
a♯ ¹	7·4	7·5	7·6	7·6	7·6	7·7	7·7
b¹	7·0	7·0	7·1	7·1	7·2	7·2	7·3
c²	6·6	6·6	6·7	6·7	6·9	6·9	7·0
c♯ ²	6·2	6·2	6·3	6·3	6·4	6·4	6·4
d²	5·9	6·0	6·0	6·0	6·0	6·1	6·1
d♯ ²	5·6	5·6	5·6	5·6	5·8	5·8	5·8
e²	5·3	5·3	5·3	5·3	5·4	5·4	5·4
f²	·4·9	5·0	5·0	5·0	5·0	5·0	5·0
f♯ ²	4·7	4·7	4·9	4·9	4·9	4·9	4·9
g²	4·4	4·5	4·5	4·5	4·5	4·5	4·5
g♯ ²	4·2	4·2	4·2	4·2	4·3	4·3	4·3
a²	4·0	4·0	4·0	4·0	4·0	4·1	4·1
a♯ ²	3·7	3·7	3·9	3·9	3·9	3·9	3·9
b²	3·5	3·5	3·6	3·6	3·6	3·6	3·6
c²	3·3	3·3	3·3	3·4	3·4	3·4	3·4

APPENDIX IV.—*Weight of Stops* 3 *tin* 2 *lead.* *Compass* 58 *pipes.*

		lb.
Principal	16′	992
,, ...	8′	286
Octave	4′	62
Gemahorn.	8′	165
Viol da Gamba	8′	119
Quintadena	8′	88
Fugara	8′	143
Rohr flute.	8′	88
Geigen	8′	220
Salicional	8′	110
Viola d' Amore	8′	110
Lieblich Gedackt . . .	8′	83
Spitz flute	4′	50
Rohr flute.	4′	31
Fugara	4′	39
Piffero	4′	72
Salicional.	4′	35
Twelfth	2⅔′	24
Fifteenth	2′	20
Mixture III. rank . . .	—	28
,, IV. ,, ...	—	44
Cornet V. c°	—	55
Trumpet	16′	330
,, ...	8′	88
Oboe	8′	94
Fagotto	16′	75
Pedal open	16′ (30 notes)	1,265
,, ...	8′	232
Violoncello	—	108
Quint	5⅓′	50
Octave	4′	53
Trumpet	8′	88

Thickness of Pipe Walls

	32′	16′	8′	4′	2′	1′	6″	3″
	″							
c	0·135	0·103	0·078	0·058	0·045	0·033	0·026	0·020
d	0·129	0·098	0·074	0·051	0·043	0·032	0·025	0·019
e	0·123	0·094	0·071	0·054	0·042	0·031	0·024	0·019
f♯	0·118	0·089	0·068	0·051	0·039	0·030	0·022	0·018
g♯	0·112	0·085	0·065	0·049	0·037	0·029	0·021	—
a♯	0·107	0·083	0·062	0·047	0·035	0·028	0·021	—

Appendix V.—*Wind* 8¼″.

—		Diameter	Height of Mouth	Wind Consumption. Cubic in. per sec.	Windway	Bore
Ratio 1 : √8						
Medium 1st open . .	C_o	5″·57	1·25″–1·4	274	0″·058	1″·04
Large open . .	C_o	6·67	1·48	340	0·077	1·2
Geigen . .	C_o	4·72	1·18	220	0·055	0·95
Fugara and violon .	C_1	6·67	1·5	278	0·048	1·12
Gamba . .	C_o	3·48	0·87	128	0·041	0·75
Ratio 1 : 2·6						
Large open .	C_o	6·22	1·7	276	0·051	1·1
Wide principal bass .	C_2	18·7	3·7	1,250	0·077	2·2
Medium open .	C_o	5·27	1·17	225	0·048	1·0
Geigen .	C_o	4·5	1·08	215	0·049	0·95
Fugara . .	C_1	6·3	1·5	242	0·045	1·04
Gamba . .	C_o	3·38	0·85	124	0·035	0·72
Viol d' Amore . .	C_o	2·9	0·7	73	0·028	0·6
Salicional, arched mouth .	C_o	3·1	0·82	74	0·026	0·6
Dolce ¼″ mouth, arched .	C_o	5·27 } 3·44 }	0·75–1·1	65	0·027	0·57
Violon (large scale) .	C_1	6·25	1·4	270	0·045	1·1
Quint flute, square (arched)	G_o	3·66	0·92–1·22	130	0·035	0·75
Doppel flute (arched) .	C_o	8·35 × 4·15	1·04–1·38	265	0·028	1·04
Holh flute, square (arched)	c^o	3·82	2·0	165	0·038	0·86
Small do., an octave smaller	—	—	—	—	—	—
Flauto amabile (arched) .	C_o	3·24	0·64–0·85	81	0·022	0·62
Wald flute (¾ width at top)	c^o	3·98	0·85	177	0·05	0·86
Gemshorn, lower diameter .	C_o	5·26	1·25	187	0·042	0·91
Spitz flute (½ diameter at top)	C_o	4·5	1·13	185	0·034	0·8
Untersatz open, square .		19·7	3·68	1,670	0·085	3″·2
Ratio 1 : 2·519						
Large open . .	C_o	5·21	1·16–1·3	248	0·054	1·1
Pedal . . .	C_1	10·4	2·3	730	0·079	1·84
Small open .	C_1	4·5	1·04	196	0·052	0·95
Bourdon, square .	C_1	6·33	2·11	313	0·045	1·2
Rohr flute, dia. .	C_o	7·68	1·78	238	0·051	1·04
Sub bass, square .	C_1	8·0	2·65	500	0·065	2·1
Lieblich Gedackt, square .	C_1	5·62	1·88	240	0·039	1·1
Large Quintatön .	C_1	5·23	—	220	0·044	1·04
Small „ .	C_1	4·5	1·42	160	0·041	0·87
Quint . . .	G_o	5·05	1·0	200	0·039	1″·0

APPENDIX VI.—*Scale in the Ratio* $1 : \sqrt{8}$ (*half on 16th pipe*).

No.	Note	Diameter	Circum-ference	Equal square	Width	Mouth Height	Wind-way	Cubic in. Wind per sec.	Bore
1	C₂	16·40	52·08	14·64	13·02	4·10	·0881	1,213	1·91
2	C₂♯	15·72	49·88	14·04	12·47	3·93	—	—	—
3	D²	15·04	47·76	13·44	11·94	3·76	·085	1,085	1·83
4	D₂♯	14·40	45·72	12·84	11·43	3·60	—	—	—
5	E₂	13·80	43·80	12·32	10·95	3·45	·0825	970	1·74
6	F₂	13·20	41·92	11·80	10·48	3·30	—	—	—
7	F₂♯	12·64	40·12	11·28	10·03	3·16	·0803	860	1·67
8	G₂	12·12	38·44	10·80	9·61	3·03	—	—	—
9	G₂♯	11·60	36·84	10·36	9·21	2·90	·0790	770	1·59
10	A₂	11·12	35·28	9·92	8·82	2·78	—	—	—
11	A₂♯	10·64	33·76	9·48	8·44	2·66	·0755	690	1·52
12	B₂	10·20	32·32	9·08	8·08	2·55	—	—	—
13	C₁	9·76	30·96	8·72	7·74	2·44	·0730	610	1·46
14	C₁♯	9·32	29·64	8·32	7·41	2·33	—	—	—
15	D₁	8·96	28·40	8·00	7·10	2·24	·0702	550	1·39
16	D₁♯	8·56	27·20	7·64	6·80	2·14	—	—	—
17	E₁	8·20	26·04	7·32	6·51	2·05	·0693	490	1·33
18	F₁	7·86	24·74	7·02	6·19	1·96	—	—	—
19	F₁♯	7·52	23·88	6·72	5·97	1·88	·0673	430	1·26
20	G₁	7·20	22·86	6·42	5·71	1·80	—	—	—
21	G₁♯	6·90	21·90	6·16	5·47	1·72	·065	390	1·20
22	A₁	6·60	20·96	5·90	5·24	1·65	—	—	—
23	A₁♯	6·32	20·06	5·64	5·01	1·58	·0634	345	1·15
24	B₁	6·06	19·22	5·40	4·81	1·51	—	—	—
25	C₀	5·80	18·42	5·18	4·61	1·45	·0628	310	1·10
26	C₀♯	5·56	17·64	4·96	4·41	1·39	—	—	—
27	D₀	5·32	16·88	4·74	4·22	1·33	·0602	275	1·05
28	D₀♯	5·10	16·16	4·54	4·04	1·27	—	—	—
29	E₀	4·88	15·48	4·36	3·87	1·22	·0586	245	0·99
30	F₀	4·66	14·82	4·16	3·70	1·17	—	—	—
31	F₀♯	4·48	14·20	4·00	3·55	1·12	·0571	220	0·95
32	G₀	4·28	13·60	3·82	3·40	1·07	—	—	—
33	G₀♯	4·10	13·02	3·66	3·25	1·02	·055	195	0·91
34	A₀	3·93	12·47	3·51	3·12	0·97	—	—	—
35	A₀♯	3·76	11·94	3·36	2·99	0·94	·0532	175	0·87
36	B₀	3·60	11·43	3·21	2·86	0·89	—	—	—
37	c⁰	3·45	10·95	3·08	2·74	0·85	·0525	155	0·83
38	c⁰♯	3·30	10·48	2·95	2·62	0·82	—	—	—
39	d⁰	3·16	10·03	2·82	2·51	0·77	·050	140	0·79
40	d⁰♯	3·03	9·61	2·70	2·41	0·75	—	—	—
41	e⁰	2·90	9·21	2·59	2·30	0·72	·0492	125	0·76
42	f⁰	2·78	8·82	2·48	2·21	0·69	—	—	—
43	f♯	2·66	8·44	2·37	2·11	0·66	·048	110	0·73
44	g⁰	2·55	8·08	2·27	2·02	0·63	—	—	—
45	g⁰♯	2·44	7·74	2·18	1·94	0·61	·0468	95	0·69
46	a⁰	2·33	7·41	2·08	1·86	0·58	—	—	—
47	a⁰♯	2·24	7·10	2·00	1·78	0·56	·0452	85	0·65
48	b⁰	2·14	6·80	1·91	1·70	0·53	—	—	—
49	c¹	2·05	6·51	1·83	1·63	0·51	·0441	78	0·63
50	c¹ ♯	1·96	6·23	1·75	1·56	0·49	—	—	—

APPENDIX VI.—*continued.* (All dimensions in inches.)

No.	Note	Diameter	Circum-ference	Equal square	Width	Mouth Height	Wind-way	Cubicin. Wind per sec.	Bore
51	d¹	1·88	5·97	1·68	1·49	0·47	·0425	70	0·60
52	d¹♯	1·80	5·71	1·60	1·48	0·45	—	—	—
53	e¹	1·72	5·47	1·54	1·37	0·43	·0414	62	0·57
54	f¹	1·65	5·24	1·47	1·31	0·41	—	—	—
55	f¹♯	1·58	5·01	1·41	1·25	0·39	·0401	55	0·55
56	g¹	1·51	4·81	1·35	1·20	0·37	—	—	—
57	g¹♯	1·45	4·61	1·29	1·15	0·36	·039	49	0·53
58	a¹	1·39	4·41	1·24	1·10	0·35	—	—	—
59	a¹♯	1·33	4·22	1·18	1·05	0·34	·0384	44	0·50
60	b¹	1·27	4·04	1·13	1·01	0·32	—	—	—
61	c²	1·22	3·87	1·09	0·97	0·31	·037	40	0·48
62	c²♯	1·16	3·70	1·04	0·92	0·29	—	—	—
63	d²	1·12	3·55	1·00	0·89	0·28	·0365	36	0·46
64	d²♯	1·07	3·40	0·95	0·85	0·27	—	—	—
65	e²	1·02	3·25	0·91	0·81	0·26	·035	32	0·43
66	f²	0·98	3·12	0·88	0·78	0·25	—	—	—
67	f²♯	0·94	2·98	0·84	0·74	0·24	·0338	28	0·42
68	g²	0·90	2·86	0·80	0·71	0·23	—·	—	—
69	g²♯	0·86	2·69	0·77	0·67	0·22	·0336	25	0·39
70	a²	0·82	2·62	0·74	0·65	0·21	—	—	—
71	a²♯	0·79	2·51	0·71	0·63	0·20	·0318	23	0·38
72	b²	0·76	2·40	0·67	0·60	0·19	—	—	—
73	c³	0·72	2·30	0·65	0·57	0·18	·0311	20	0·36
74	c³♯	0·69	2·21	0·62	0.55	0·17	—	—	—
75	d³	0·66	2·11	0·59	0·53	0·16	·0301	18	0·34
76	d³♯	0·64	2·02	0·57	0·51	0·16	—	—	—
77	e³	0·61	1·93	0·54	0·48	0·15	·0295	16	0·32
78	f³	0·58	1·85	0·52	0·46	0·14	—	—	—
79	f³♯	0·56	1·77	0·50	0·44	0·14	·0286	14	0·31
80	g³	0·53	1·70	0·48	0·42	0·13	—	—	—
81	g³♯	0·51	1·63	0·46	0·41	0·13	·0280	13	0·30
82	a³	0·49	1·56	0·44	0·39	0·12	—	—	—
83	a³♯	0·47	1·49	0·42	0·37	0·12	·0275	11	0·29
84	b³	0·45	1·43	0·40	0·36	0·11	—	—	—
85	c⁴	0·43	1·37	0·39	0·34	0·11	·0268	10	0·27
86	c⁴♯	0·41	1·31	0·37	0·33	0·10	—	—	—
87	d⁴	0·39	1·25	0·35	0·31	0·10	·0256	9	0.26
88	d⁴♯	0·38	1·20	0·34	0·30	0·09	—	—	—
89	e⁴	0·36	1·15	0·32	0·29	0·09	·0248	8	0·25
90	f⁴	0·35	1·10	0·31	0·27	0·09	—	—	—
91	f⁴♯	0·33	1·05	0·29	0·26	0·08	·024	7	0·24
92	g⁴	0·32	1·01	0·28	0·25	0·08	—	—	—
93	g⁴♯	0·31	0·97	0·27	0·24	0·08	·0235	6	0·23
94	a⁴	0·29	0·93	0·26	0·23	0·07	—	—	—
95	a⁴♯	0·28	0·89	0·25	0·22	0·07	·0224	6	0·22
96	b⁴	0·27	0·85	0·24	0·21	0·07	—	—	—
97	c⁵	0·26	0·82	0·23	0·20	0·06	·0216	5	0·21
98	c⁵♯	0·25	0·81	0·23	0·20	0·06	—	—	—
99	d⁵	0·24	0·78	0·22	0·19	0·06	·0208	5	0·20
100	d⁵♯	0·23	0·75	0·21	0·19	0·06	—	—	—

APP. **VI.** *continued—Scale in the Ratio* 1 : 2·6 *(half on* 17*th pipe)*.

No.	Note	Diameter	Circum-ference	Equal square	Width	Mouth Height	Wind-way	Cubicin. Wind per sec.	Bore
1	C₂	14·52	46·08	12·96	11·52	4·10	·0744	950	1″·91
2	C₂♯	13·92	44·24	12·44	11·06	3·93	—	—	—
3	D₂	13·36	42·48	11·92	10·62	8·76	·0780	855	1·83
4	D₂♯	12·84	40·76	11·48	10·12	3·60	—	—	—
5	E₂	12·32	39·16	11·00	9·79	3·45	·0712	775	1·74
6	F₂	11·80	37·52	10·56	9·38	3·30	—	—	—
7	F₂♯	11·36	38·08	10·16	9·02	3·16	·0697	690	1·67
8	G₂	10·92	34·64	9·72	8·66	3·03	—	—	—
9	G₂♯	10·48	33·24	9·36	8·31	2·90	·0685	625	1·59
10	A₂	10·04	31·92	8·96	7·98	2·78	—	—	—
11	A₂♯	9·64	30·64	8·60	7·66	2·66	·067	565	1·52
12	B₂	9·28	29·44	8·28	7·36	2·55	—	—	—
13	C₁	8·88	28·24	7·92	7·06	2·44	·0654	511	1·46
14	C₁♯	8·52	27·12	7·60	6·78	2·33	—	—	—
15	D₁	8·20	26·04	7·32	6·51	2·24	·636	460	1·39
16	D₁♯	7·88	25·00	7·02	6·25	2·14	—	—	—
17	E₁	7·56	24·00	6·74	6·00	2·05	·0623	410	1·33
18	F₁	7·26	23·04	6·48	5·75	1·96	—	—	—
19	F₁♯	6·96	22·12	6·22	5·53	1·88	·0606	370	1·26
20	G₁	6·68	21·24	5·96	5·31	1·80	—	—	—
21	G₁♯	6·42	20·88	5·74	5·09	1·72	·0594	335	1·20
22	A₁	6·16	19·58	5·50	4·89	1·65	—	—	—
23	A₁♯	5·90	18·76	5·28	4·69	1·58	·0575	300	1·15
24	B₁	5·68	18·04	5·08	4·51	1·51	—	—	—
25	C₀	5·46	17·32	4·86	4·33	1·45	·0566	275	1·10
26	C₀♯	5·24	16·62	4·68	4·15	1·39	—	—	—
27	D₀	5·02	15·96	4·48	3·99	1·33	·0556	245	1·05
28	D₀♯	4·82	15·32	4·30	3·83	1·27	—	—	—
29	E₀	4.64	14·72	4·14	3·68	1·22	·0543	220	0·99
30	F₀	4.44	14·12	3·96	3·53	1·17	—	—	—
31	F₀♯	4·26	13·56	3·80	3·39	1·12	·0531	200	0·95
32	G₀	4·10	13·02	3·66	3·26	1·07	—	—	—
33	G₀♯	3·94	12·50	3·51	3·13	1·02	·0523	180	0·91
34	A₀	3·78	12·00	3·37	3·00	0·97	—	—	—
35	A₀♯	3·63	11·52	3·24	2·88	0·94	·0508	160	0·87
36	B₀	3·48	11·06	3·11	2·77	0·89	—	—	—
37	c⁰	3·34	10·62	2·98	2·66	0·85	·050	149	0·83
38	c⁰♯	3·21	10·19	2·87	2·55	0·82	—	—	—
39	d⁰	3·08	9·79	2·75	2·45	0·77	·0485	134	0·76
40	d⁰♯	2·95	9·38	2·64	2·35	0·75	—	—	—
41	e⁰	2·84	9·02	2·54	2·26	0·72	·0476	120	0·79
42	f⁰	2·73	8·66	2·43	2·17	0·69	—	—	—
43	f⁰♯	2·62	8·31	2·34	2·08	0·66	·0465	108	0·73
44	g⁰	2·51	7·98	2·24	2·00	0·63	—	—	—
45	g⁰♯	2·41	7·66	2·15	1·92	0·61	·0452	98	0·69
46	a⁰	2·32	7·36	2·07	1·84	0·58	—	—	—
47	a⁰♯	2·22	7·06	1·98	1·77	0·56	·0445	89	0·65
48	b⁰	2·13	6·78	1·90	1·70	0·53	—	—	—
49	c¹	2·05	6·51	1·83	1·63	0·51	·0434	80	0·63
50	c¹♯	1·97	6·25	1·75	1·56	0·49	—	—	—

APPENDIX VI.—*continued.* (All dimensions in inches.)

No.	Note	Diameter	Circum-ference	Equal square	Width	Mouth Height	Wind-way	Cubicin. Wind per sec.	Bore
51	d¹	1·89	6·00	1·68	1·50	0·47	·0425	72	0·60
52	d¹♯	1.81	5·76	1·62	1·44	0·45	—	—	—
53	e¹	1·74	5·53	1·55	1·38	0·43	·0414	65	0·57
54	f¹	1·67	5·31	1·49	1·35	0·41	—	—	—
55	f¹♯	1·60	5·09	1·43	1·27	0·39	·0405	59	0·55
56	g¹	1·54	4·89	1·37	1·22	0·37	—	—	—
57	g¹♯	1·44	4·69	1·32	1·17	0·36	·0399	53	0·53
58	a¹	1·41	4·51	1.27	1·18	0·35	—	—	—
59	a¹♯	1·36	4·33	1·21	1·08	0·34	·0388	47	0·50
60	b¹	1·31	4·15	1·17	1·04	0·32	—	—	—
61	c²	1·25	3·99	1·12	1·00	0·31	·0378	43	0·48
62	c²♯	1·20	3·88	1·07	0·96	0·29	—	—	—
63	d²	1·16	3·68	1·03	0·92	0·28	·037	39	0·46
64	d²♯	1·11	3·53	0·99	0·88	0·27	—	—	—
65	e²	1·06	3·39	0·95	0·85	0·26	·0362	35	0·43
66	f²	1·02	3·25	0·91	0·81	0·25	—	—	—
67	f²♯	0·99	3·12	0·88	0·78	0·24	·0354	32	0·42
68	g²	0·94	3·00	0·84	0·75	0·23	—	—	—
69	g²♯	0·91	2·88	0·81	0·71	0·22	·0346	28	0·39
70	a²	0·87	2·76	0·78	0·69	0·21	—	—	—
71	a²♯	0·83	2·65	0·74	0·66	0·20	·0338	26	0·38
72	b²	0·80	2·55	0·72	0·64	0·19	—	—	—
73	c³	0·77	2·45	0·69	0·61	0·18	·033	23	0·36
74	c³♯	0·74	2·34	0·66	0·59	0·17	—	—	—
75	d³	0·71	2·25	0·63	0·56	0·16	·0321	21	0·34
76	d²♯	0·68	2·16	0·61	0·54	0·16	—	—	—
77	e³	0·65	2·07	0·59	0·52	0·15	·0315	18	0·32
78	f³	0·63	1·99	0·56	0·50	0·14	—	—	—
79	f³♯	0·60	1·91	0·54	0·48	0·14	·0311	16	0·31
80	g³	0·58	1·84	0·52	0·46	0·13	—	—	—
81	g⁴♯	0·55	1·76	0·49	0·44	0·13	·0307	15	0·30
82	a³	0·53	1·69	0·47	0·42	0·12	—	—	—
83	a³♯	0·51	1·63	0·46	0·41	0·12	·0299	13	0·29
84	b³	0·49	1·56	0·44	0·39	0·11	—	—	—
85	c⁴	0·47	1·50	0·42	0·37	0.11	·0291	12	0·27
86	c⁴♯	0·45	1·44	0·41	0·36	0·10	—	—	—
87	d⁴	0·43	1·38	0·39	0·34	0·10	·0283	11	0·26
88	d⁴♯	0·42	1·33	0·37	0·33	0·09	-·-	—	—
89	e⁴	0·40	1·27	0·36	0·32	0·09	·0279	10	0·25
90	f⁴	0·39	1·22	0·34	0·31	0·09	—	—	—
91	f⁴♯	0·37	1·17	0·33	0·29	0·08	·0272	9	0·24
92	g⁴	0·35	1·13	0·32	0·28	0·08	—	—	—
93	g⁴♯	0·34	1·08	0·30	0·27	0·08	·0264	8	0·23
94	a⁴	0·33	1·04	0·29	0·26	0·07	—	—	—
95	a⁴♯	0·31	1·00	0·28	0·25	0·07	·0260	7	0·22
96	b¹	0·30	0·96	0.27	0·24	0·07	—	—	—
97	c⁵	0·29	0·92	0·26	0·23	0·06	·0252	6	0·21
98	c⁵♯	0·28	0·88	0·25	0·22	0·06	—	—	—
99	d⁵	0·27	0·85	0·24	0·21	0·06	·0248	5	0·20
100	d¹♯	0·26	0·81	0·23	0·20	0·06	—	—	—

APP. VI.—*cont.*—*Scale in the ratio* 1 : 2·5 (*half on* 18*th pipe*).

No.	Note	Diameter	Circumference	Equal square	Width	Mouth Height	Windway	Cubic in. Wind per sec.	Bore
1	C₂	13·00	41·32	11·64	10·33	4·10	·0693	760	1·91
2	C₂♯	12·52	39·76	11·20	9·94	3·93	—	—	—
3	D₂	12·04	38·04	10·76	9·51	3·76	·068	690	1·83
4	D₂♯	11·60	36·84	10·36	9·21	3·60	—	—	—
5	E₂	11·16	35·44	9·96	8·86	3·45	·0669	620	1·74
6	F₂	10·72	34·08	9·60	8·52	3·30	—	—	—
7	F₂♯	10·32	32·80	9·24	8·20	3·16	·0656	570	1·67
8	G₂	9·92	31·56	8·88	7·89	3·03	—	—	—
9	G₂♯	9·56	30·36	8·52	7·59	2·90	·0642	520	1·59
10	A₂	9·20	29·24	8·20	6·81	2·78	—	—	—
11	A₂♯	8·84	28·12	7·92	7·03	2·66	·0635	470	1·52
12	B₂	8·52	27·04	7·60	6·76	2·55	—	—	—
13	C₁	82·0	26·04	7·32	6·51	2·44	·0621	435	1·46
14	C₁♯	7·88	25·06	7·04	6·26	2·33	—	—	—
15	D₁	7·60	24·12	6·78	6·03	2·24	·0611	390	1·39
16	D₁♯	7·30	23·20	6·52	5·80	2·14	—	—	—
17	E₁	7·02	22·32	6·28	5·58	2·05	·0602	350	1·33
18	F₁	6·76	21·48	6·04	5·37	1·96	—	—	—
19	F₁♯	6·50	20·66	5·82	5·16	1·88	·0591	325	1·26
20	G₁	6·26	19·88	5·60	4·97	1·80	—	—	—
21	G₁♯	6·02	19·02	5·38	4·75	1·72	·0582	290	1·20
22	A₁	5·80	18·42	5·18	4·61	1·65	—	—	—
23	A₁♯	5·58	17·72	4·98	4·43	1·58	·057	260	1·15
24	B₁	5·36	17·04	4·80	4·26	1·51	—	—	—
25	C₀	5·16	16·40	4·62	4·10	1·45	·0561	247	1·10
26	C₀♯	4·96	15·78	4·44	3·94	1·39	—	—	—
27	D₀	4·98	15·18	4·26	3·79	1·33	·055	225	1·05
28	D₀♯	4·60	14·62	4·10	3·65	1·27	—	—	—
29	E₀	4·42	14·06	3·96	3·51	1·22	·0541	205	0·99
30	F₀	4·26	13·52	3·80	3·38	1·17	—	—	—
31	F₀♯	4·10	13·02	3·66	3·26	1·12	·0533	185	0·95
32	G₀	3·94	12·53	3·52	3·13	1·07	—	—	—
33	G₀♯	3·80	12·06	3·39	3·02	1·02	·052	170	0·91
34	A₀	3·65	11·60	3·26	2·90	0·97	—	—	—
35	A₀♯	3·51	11·16	3·14	2·79	0·94	·0512	155	0·87
36	B₀	3·38	10·74	3·02	2·69	0·89	—	—	—
37	c⁰	3·25	10·33	2·91	2·58	0·85	·0504	141	0·83
38	c⁰♯	3·13	9·94	2·80	2·49	0·86	—	—	—
39	d⁰	3·01	9·57	2·69	2·39	0·77	·0496	130	0·79
40	d⁰♯	2·90	9·21	2·59	2·30	0·75	—	—	—
41	e⁰	2·79	8·86	2·49	2·22	0·72	·0488	117	0·76
42	f⁰	2·68	8·52	2·40	2·13	0·69	—	—	—
43	f⁰♯	2·58	8·20	2·31	2·05	0·66	·0484	105	0·73
44	g⁰	2·48	7·89	2·22	1·97	0·63	—	—	—
45	g⁰♯	2·39	7·59	2·13	1·80	0·61	·0472	96	0·69
46	a⁰	2·30	7·31	2·05	1·88	0·58	—	—	—
47	a⁰♯	2·21	7·03	1·98	1·76	0·56	·0464	87	0·65
48	b⁰	2·13	6·76	1·90	1·69	0·53	—	—	—
49	c¹	2·05	6·51	1·83	1·63	0·51	·0455	80	0·63
50	c¹♯	1·97	6·26	1·76	1·56	0·49	—	—	—

APPENDIX VI.—*continued.* (All dimensions in inches.)

No.	Note	Diameter	Circumference	Equal square	Width	Mouth Height	Windway	Cubic in. Wind per sec.	Bore
51	d¹	1·90	6·03	1·69	1·51	0·47	·0447	72	0·60
52	d¹♯	1·87	5·80	1·63	1·45	0·45	—	—	—
53	e¹	1·75	5·58	1·57	1·39	0·43	·0439	65	0·57
54	f¹	1·69	5·37	1·51	1·34	0·41	—	—	—
55	f¹♯	1·62	5·16	1·45	1·29	0·39	·0431	59	0·55
56	g¹	1·56	4·97	1·40	1·24	0·37	—	—	—
57	g¹♯	1·50	4·78	1·34	1·19	0·36	·0427	53	0·53
58	a¹	1·45	4·60	1·29	1·15	0·35	—	—	—
59	a¹♯	1·39	4·43	1·24	1·11	0·34	·0418	48	0·50
60	b¹	1·34	4·26	1·20	1·06	0·32	—	—	—
61	c²	1·29	4·10	1·15	1·02	0·31	·041	45	0·48
62	c²♯	1·24	3·94	1·11	0·98	0·29	—	—	—
63	d²	1·19	3·79	1·06	0·95	0·28	·0386	40	0·46
64	d²♯	1·15	3·65	1·02	0·91	0·27	—	—	—
65	e²	1·10	3·51	0·99	0·88	0·26	·0382	37	0·43
66	f²	1·06	3·38	0·95	0·85	0·25	—	—	—
67	f²♯	1·02	3·25	0·92	0·81	0·24	·0374	33	0·42
68	g²	0·99	3·13	0·88	0·78	0·23	—	—	—
69	g²♯	0·95	3·02	0·85	0·75	0·27	·0366	30	0·39
70	a²	0·91	2·90	0·82	0·72	0·21	—	—	—
71	a²♯	0·88	2·79	0·79	0·70	0·20	·0358	27	0·38
72	b	0·84	2·69	0·76	0·67	0·19	—	—	—
73	c³	0·81	2·58	0·68	0·64	0·18	·0354	26	0·36
74	c³♯	0·78	2·49	0·70	0·62	0·17	—	—	—
75	d³	0·75	2·39	0·67	0·60	0·16	·0346	24	0·34
76	d³♯	0·72	2·30	0·65	0·57	0·16	—	—	—
77	e³	0·70	2·22	0·62	0·55	0·15	·0351	21	0·32
78	f³	0·67	2·13	0·60	0·53	0·14	—	—	—
79	f³♯	0·65	2·05	0·58	0·51	0·14	·0337	19	0·31
80	g³	0·62	1·97	0·56	0·49	0·13	—	—	—
81	g³♯	0·60	1·90	0·53	0·47	0·13	·0326	18	0·30
82	a³	0·58	1·83	0·51	0·46	0·12	—	—	—
83	a³♯	0·55	1·76	0·49	0·44	0·12	·0322	16	0·29
84	b³	0·53	1·69	0·48	0·42	0·11	—	—	—
85	c⁴	0·51	1·63	0·46	0·41	0·11	·0319	15	0·27
86	c⁴♯	0·49	1·57	0·44	0·39	0·10	—	—	—
87	d⁴	0·48	1·53	0·42	0·38	0·10	·0311	14	0·26
88	d⁴♯	0·46	1·45	0·41	0·36	0·09	—	—	—
89	e⁴	0·44	1·40	0·39	0·35	0·09	·0307	13	0·25
90	f⁴	0·42	1·34	0·38	0·33	0·09	—	—	—
91	f⁴♯	0·41	1·29	0·36	0·32	0·08	·0303	11	0·24
92	g⁴	0·39	1·24	0·35	0·31	0·08	—	—	—
93	g⁴♯	0·38	1·20	0·34	0·30	0·08	·0295	10	0·23
94	a⁴	0·36	1·15	0·32	0·29	0·07	—	—	—
95	a⁴♯	0·35	1·11	0·31	0·28	0·07	·0291	9	0·22
96	b⁴	0·33	1·07	0·30	0·27	0·07	—	—	—
97	c⁵	0·32	1·03	0·29	0·26	0·06	—	8	0·21
98	c⁵♯	0·31	0·99	0·28	0·25	0·06	—	—	—
99	d⁵	0·30	0·95	0·27	0·24	0·06	—	8	0·20
100	d⁵♯	0·29	0·91	0·26	0·23	0·06	—	—	—

APPENDIX VII.—*Theoretical Speed of Air flowing under Pressure.*

Height of water gauge	Speed inches per sec.	Height of water gauge	Speed inches per sec.
0·009	″76·7	1·85	″1090
0·049	174	1·94	1110
0·092	243	2·03	1140
0·185	344	2·12	1162
0·295	422	2·22	1190
0·370	487	2·31	1215
0·463	545	2·40	1240
0·555	602	2·50	1260
0·647	642	2·59	1280
0·740	690	2·68	1305
0·832	730	2·78	1330
0·925	770	2·86	1350
1·03	805	2·96	1375
1·11	845	3·05	1394
1·20	885	3·14	1415
1·295	910	3·24	·1435
1·38	940	3·33	1455
1·48	970	3·42	1475
1·57	1010	3·51	1495
1·66	1030	3·61	1515
1·75	1058	3·70	1535

NOTE.—The above figures are according to Töpfer's calculation, and are independent of the shape of the orifice, for which an allowance must be made. The coefficient for a thin plate is 0·6, and for a short pipe 0·8.

To find the speed for other heights of water gauge than are given the formula 15,974 $\sqrt{\dfrac{H}{H+406·7}}$ may be used, where H = height of water gauge in inches.

APPENDIX VIII.—*The reader of old books on organ-building will frequently be perplexed by the various outlandish measures used, to convert which the following table will be useful. A ' line ' is the twelfth of an inch.*

English	Saxony Weimar	Baden	Bavaria	Paris	Austria	Prussia Denmark	Mètre
1	1·076	1·016	1·044	0·938	0·964	0·971	0·305
0·929	1	0·944	0·970	0·872	0·986	0·902	0·283
0·984	1·059	1	1·028	0·924	0·949	0·956	0·300
0·958	1·031	0·973	1	0·898	0·923	0·930	0·292
1·066	1·147	1·083	1·113	1	1·028	1·035	0·325
1·037	1·116	1·054	1·083	0·973	1	1·007	0·316
1·030	1·108	1·046	1·075	0·966	0·993	1	0·314
3·281	3·531	3·333	3·426	3·078	3·164	3·186	1
0·940	1·012	0·955	0·982	0·882	0·906	0·913	0·286

NOTE.—The last line is an early Würtemberg foot, showing its relation to Töpfer's (the Weimar) foot, and the measures of other countries.

APPENDIX IX.—Töpfer's Table of size of bore in inches for consecutive pipes and octaves. Whatever size of bore is started from, the size for all the other pipes, up and down, can be taken from the Table.

Whole Tones	1st Octave	2nd Octave	3rd Octave 32'	4th Octave 16'	5th Octave 8'	6th Octave 4'	7th Octave 2'	8th Octave 1'	9th Octave 6"	10th Octave 3"	11th Octave 1½"	12th Octave	13th Octave
1	3·38	2·54	1·92	1·45	1·10	0·83	0·62	0·47	0·36	0·26	0·20	0·15	0·11
2	3·20	2·42	1·83	1·38	1·05	0·79	0·60	0·45	0·33	0·25	0·19	0·14	0·11
3	3·03	2·32	1·75	1·32	0·99	0·75	0·57	0·43	0·32	0·24	0·18	0·14	0·10
4	2·93	2·22	1·67	1·26	0·95	0·72	0·54	0·41	0·31	0·23	0·17	0·13	0·10
5	2·80	2·10	1·59	1·20	0·91	0·68	0·52	0·39	0·30	0·22	0·16	0·12	0·09
6	2·66	2·0	1·53	1·14	0·86	0·65	0·50	0·37	0·28	0·21	0·15	0·11	0·09

INDEX OF FIGURES TO TEXT

A A

INDEX

(The numbers refer to the paragraphs.)

AUTHOR'S NOTE.

Corrections and suggestions addressed to the care of the Publishers will be thankfully received by the Author.

PRINTED BY
SPOTTISWOODE AND CO., NEW-STREET SQUARE
LONDON

Outstanding Books on the Organ available from The Organ Literature Foundation. . . .

Milne, H. F.
How to Build a Small Two-Manual Chamber Pipe Organ. (1925 reprint) $10.00

Milne, H. F.
The Reed Organ: Its Design and Construction. (1930 reprint) $5.00

Wicks, Mark
Organ Building for Amateurs. A practical guide for Home-Workers. (1887 reprint) $10.00

Williams, Peter
The European Organ 1450–1850. (1966) $20.00

Robertson, F. E.
A Practical Treatise on Organ-Building. (1897 reprint) Text and Atlas. $35.00

Send for our catalogue listing over 400 items on the subject.

The Organ Literature Foundation
Braintree, Mass. 02184 (U. S. A.)

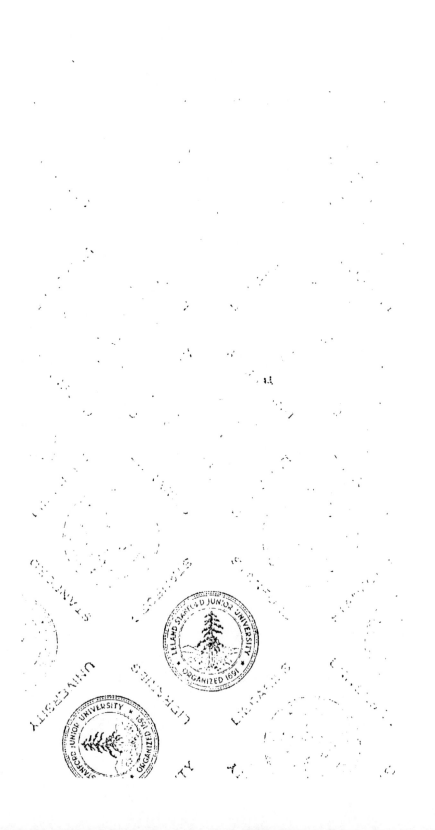

Lightning Source UK Ltd.
Milton Keynes UK
UKHW022302080223
416651UK00001B/383